"Yellowed newspapers tell the story"

GARY NUMAN
An Annotated Scrapbook
1977-1981

by Paul Sutton

In celebrating the four Gary Numan albums that comprise The Machine Quartet I have produced an annotated scrapbook. This gives the clearest view of the era. It brings into permanent storage a selection of the contemporary articles written about Gary Numan, all of which have been out of print for more than thirty years, and which have been declining rapidly into yellow dust. Some of the articles do deserve to be lost because they are no good at all, such were the standards of critical thought and writing of the day. The gap between the achievements of an artist and his critics was never greater in my lifetime. Inadvertently, therefore, the book provides a look at the curious spectacle of children's scrapbooks of the time reluctantly filled with cuttings that were seething with all the low emotions, from nonsense to hate. That was the strange fate that befell the young Gary Numan and his fans in the last decades of the twentieth century. Fans had to weigh up whether or not to include in their scrapbooks articles in which their favourite star was derided in every paragraph.

So why dig them up and preserve them? The simple reason is that they happened. And I'm an historian. I don't seek to whitewash the truth. Reprinting a selection of these articles gives me leave to comment on them, because to publish without comment historical documents that are, in part, calculatedly false, is wrong, as time (and common sense) has proved.

That said, it's not all doom and gloom and nonsense. There are more good pieces here than bad, and there is a very splendid collection of illustrations, as befits one of the very first pop artists to place equal emphasis on image and sound. This book collects together, and republishes for preservation and study, several characteristic interviews with Mr. Numan; some of the advertising and sales imagery of the Machine Music albums and singles; articles from England, America, Japan, Spain, Italy and Germany (mostly for the collector, and partly 'translated' by Google). I include too an advertisement for the Touring Principle concert in Paris, and a whole host of things relating to the first glory years of the modest young Englishman, a true Warholian artist who advanced on Andy's light and sound experiments with The Velvet Underground by bringing a real grandeur to live performances, and by changing the music of the world with a single finger.

Paul Sutton, Cambridge, 2016

Contents

The Overture

Twenty Confirmed Gigs, a Demo
and Two Singles

In two weeks and two days in June 1977, Mean Street (formerly a band with Numan as guitarist and vocalist) went from sharing the bill with The Police and Adam and the Ants, to being blown off the stage by Numan's own band, Tubeway Army. In his autobiography, Numan wrote: "I told this man (Kevin St. John) the whole story about Mean Street (dropping me) and he thought it would be fun to put us on the same bill and not tell them. It was fun actually… and I watched them slide quickly into oblivion from thereon."

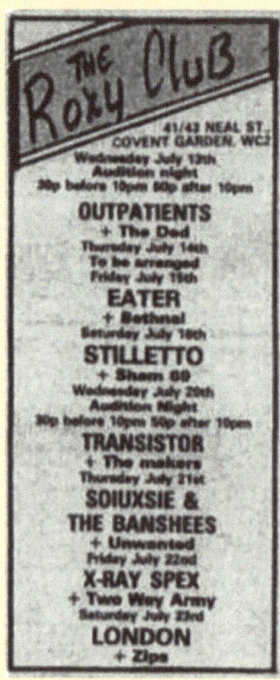

Friday 10.6.77: the Lurkers, Mean Street, the Police

Saturday 11.6.77: Wire, Adam & the Ants, Mean Street

Sunday 12.6.77: Johnny Moped, Mean Street

Thursday 16.6.77: Johnny Moped, Mean Street

Friday 17.6.77: Police, the Mutants

Saturday 18.6.77: the Boys, Mean Street

Wednesday 22.6.77: Ed Banger & the Nosebleeds, Shoplifters, Gloria Mundi

Thursday 23.6.77: the Electric Chairs, Alternative TV, Ed Banger & the Nosebleeds

Friday 24.6.77: the Saints, Neo, Bethnal

Saturday 25.6.77: the Saints, Mean Street, Tubeway Army

The listing above is from Paul Marko's book, *The Roxy London WC2: A Punk History.* Numan's biographer, Ray Coleman, wrote that the first Tubeway Army gig was on a bill with Mean Street, and that Numan's band called themselves The Lasers for that one gig. The *Sounds* advert (above left and, like everything on this page, poor quality because I pulled it off the internet) is for the first named Tubeway Army concert. If I were a pop psychologist, I would say that the very deliberate typo ('Two Way' i.e. bisexual) was an added spur to Numan writing the gig-ending song, *Kill St.Joy* ('Oh, what the hell are you!') first heard on the bootleg *Live at the Roxy* and included on *Living Ornaments 1978 CD.* Adolescents are particularly sensitive to what they perceive as slights on their sexuality. Kevin St. John was a gay gangster who managed The Roxy. Numan had rejected John's crude advances, hence St. John gleefully calling out Numan in print, whilst ruining the pleasure the 19-year-old would have had on first seeing his band's name in a national newspaper.

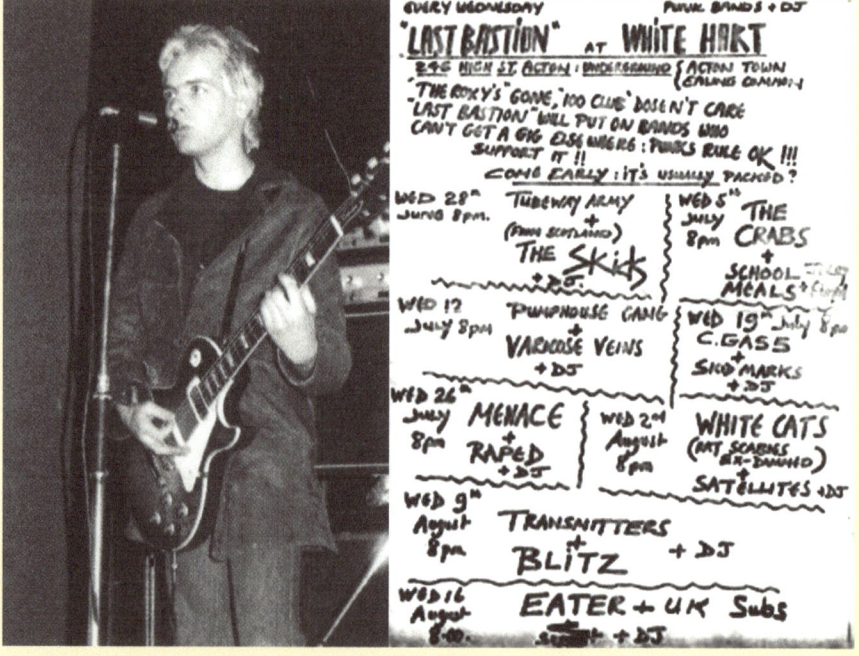

The Tubeway Army Gigs

Adequate documentation hasn't yet been found to provide a satisfactorily accurate listing.
This is a working document:

June 25th 1977 - The Roxy (Numan, Paul Gardiner, Jess Lidyard as The Lasers)
July 22nd 1977 - The Roxy
September 10th 1977 - The Roxy (morning gig)
September 15th 1977 - The Roxy
October 1st 1977 - The Roxy
December 6th 1977 - The Vortex, supporting The Doll. The first with Bob Simmonds. The gig was arranged by Beggar's Banquet to see Numan and Tubeway Army play live. Having heard them play in the rehearsal room at the Beggar's shop in Fulham, they wanted to see them play in front of an audience. Impressed, they signed them afterwards. Martin Mills (Beggars): "When they played at the Vortex in Wardour Street, Gary was just incredible up there on that stage. He seemed incredibly nervous beforehand but the way he looked at the audience, the confidence, the way he held the microphone, just everything about him was magnetic. He had blond hair, his look really had something, and he handled the audience brilliantly." (*Coleman*, p45)
December 12th 1977 - Oriel Youth Centre, Northolt
January 28th 1978 - The Rochester Castle (Stoke Newington)
February 4th 1978 - Dingwalls
February 5th 1978 - The Marquee (supporting The Lurkers)
February 9th 1978 - Ashford Grammar School (from which Numan had been expelled)
February 19th 1978 - The Marquee
February 21st 1978 - Rock Garden
February 24th 1978 - Cambridge Corn Exchange (supporting The Adverts)
March 7th - The Vortex
March 10th 1978 - Dingwalls
March 18th 1978 - Battle of Britain Hall (RAF Uxbridge)
April 3rd 1978 - The Vortex. The last ever gig before the club closed.
April 17th 1978 - Upstairs at Ronnie Scotts, London
April 20th 1978 - The Marquee
May 1st 1978 - The Bones Club (Reading)
June 28th 1978 - White Hart (Acton)
The Brook House, Hayes (advertised for May 1978, but cancelled)

Unconfirmed/undated gigs:

Wraysbury Scout Hut (my sister runs the nursery there)
Stanwell Village Hall / The Pegasus (Stoke Newington)
YMCA Galaxy Club (Harlow) / Greenford Hall (Ealing) / The Last Bastion, March 1978
Bell & Dolphin (Bridge St, London); Royal Hotel (Luton) / The Royal Holloway College
The Hope and Anchor (Islington, the first headline gig).

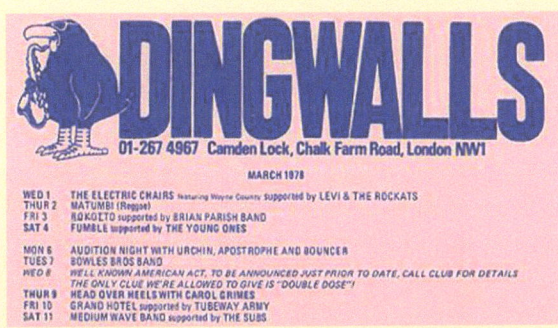

Vintage 1977 pin badge

MOTHERLESS FACES	THAT'S TOO BAD
BOYS	BASIC JOE
BLUE EYES	DO YOUR BEST
YOU DON'T KNOW ME	DIDN'T I SAY
MY SHADOW IN VAIN	I'M A POSER
ME MY HEAD	PURE ST. JOY

GARY NUMAN

TUBEWAY ARMY

LIVE AT THE ROXY - 1977

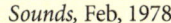

Sounds, Feb, 1978

Tubeway Army
Dingwalls   *MICK WALL*

TUBEWAY ARMY (Beggars Banquet's very own child prodigé) began the festivities and at once succeeded in making a favourable impression. They're a threesome from the London vicinity all aged just 17 and they play some pretty damn good rock and roll . . . this being one of their first gigs, it's the potential you have to look for rather than the finished article. Kudos everywhere to them for turning in such a promising debut. In Valeriun (vocals, guitar) they have going for them what undoubtedly is their strongest visual asset. Blond-haired, blue-eyed visage that promises to dampen the knickers of many a sweet young thing once given the right kind of exposure (*Flashy, eh? — Ed*).

Probably the first mainstream review of a Numan gig. It is interesting to note that the writer focuses on the visual aspect of the performer, and that there is a more open and understanding approach to teenage sexuality than would be allowed now, an attitude that is reflected in Gary Numan's lyrics.

SUBWAY SECT Ambition (pic)	*Sounds 23.9.78*	75
SWELL MAPS Dresden Style (pic)		75
TEARDROP EXPLODES Sleeping Gas EP (pic)		65
TELEVISION PERSONALITIES Bill Grundy EP (pic)		75
THROBBING GRISTLE United (pic)		75
JOHNNY THUNDERS Arms round memory (pic)		80
TOM ROBINSON Bully for you (pic)		80
TUBEWAY ARMY Too Bad (pic)		80
TUBEWAY ARMY Bombers (pic)		80
UK SUBS C I D (yellow) (pic)		80

Before Tubeway Army, there was a London punk band called Subway Sect. A direct influence on the name? Probably. Subconsciously? Possibly. Here's Paul Morley in *NME* 15/7/78:

Compared to the likes of The Prefects, Subway Sect have to some extent had things 'easy'. They've had comfortable access to gigs, and have also made a record — "Nobody's Scared", a sub-standard recording from a vague period in their existence.

The band have passed through many distinct periods; early basic minimal aggressive punk, through blank, flatly improvised rock, then, as their control of instruments became sturdier, into tough, strong, coherent rock songs.

Now, fully technically able, they have arrived at a music that is unpredictable only in the surprising orthodoxy of its components. The cool, very American style is probably obvious when Goddard's lyrical and musical pretensions are taken into account. He fancies himself as some sort of modern balladeer — a role to which he could do justice.

The Subways' set now relies on drive and exhilaration; they play compact, accessible, emphatic songs, short and self conscious, with just a dash of discordancy and some absurd tinges of country rock.

THAT'S TOO BAD

BY TUBEWAY ARMY
ON BEGGARS BANQUET
RECORDS

Looked up and the camera eye is searching my room
The TV screen is calling me but for what or whom?
Please Mister, do be careful — I'm so fragile
Maybe they'll let me down to Speedy's place for a while

Chorus
Oh, oh well, that's too bad
Oh, oh well, that's too bad
Oh, oh well, that's too bad
Oh, oh well, that's too bad

Talk a lot, a sign of fear, I thought you should know
I can see pictures of me — well, they're so-so
I'll come on to the leader like I'm some hero
He'll laugh and raise his dying eyes and then tell me to go

Repeat chorus

1920 flashbacks for an hour or more
Of crazy actors hiding in the doorways top floor
Machines scream in anger from a thousand dead ends
I turn my face, I crawl away, I look for a friend

Repeat chorus to fade

Words and music by Valerian
Reproduced by permission Beggars Banquet/Andrew Heath Music Ltd.

Requested by Leigh Griffiths, Swansea.

The song was recorded on 16th October 1977 at Spaceward in Cambridge and remixed at the Manor Studio, Oxfordshire. The single was released on 10 February 1978. The original recording was released in 1983, and re-issued on yellow vinyl in 1985. Both mixes are on the CD of *The Plan*. The above spread is from the Christmas 1980 edition of *Smash Hits*.

GARY NUMAN: "The Plan" (Beggar's Banquet BEGA 55); "1978/1979 Volumes 2 & 3" (BEG 123E/124E)

THE PLAN

These songs were recorded in the early part of 1978. The intention was not to release them in this form, if at all, but to give the record company a rough idea of the songs we had at the time. I wrote the "punky" songs with the sole intention of obtaining a record contract. It seemed at the time that contracts flowed like water for this kind of music. I soon found out that it wasn't quite that easy, but did, eventually, manage to sign a deal with Beggar's Banquet. My thanks and gratitude to them forever. It was interesting to me to see how some of these songs, or parts of them, had developed in to others that today are quite well known, and how the transition from guitar to synthesizer began. I'd forgotten that I'd ever written half of these.

Gary Numan

Over recent months, the Beggar's Banquet label have embarked on a major retrospective review of Gary Numan's career with the label, which has led to the unearthing of many archive tapes, originally recorded as demos or left over as out-takes from later album sessions.

The final three releases of the series are now in the shops. "The Plan", a twelve-track picture disc album recorded in March 1978, is best explained by Numan's own sleeve-notes: "The intention was not to release them in this form, if at all, but to give the record company a rough idea of the songs we had at the time. I wrote the 'punky' songs with the sole intention of obtaining a record contract. It seemed at the time that contracts flowed like water for this kind of music. I soon found out that it wasn't quite that easy, but did, eventually, manage to sign a deal with Beggar's Banquet. . . . It was interesting to me to see how some of these songs, or parts of them, had developed into others that today are quite well-known, and how the transition from guitar to synthesiser began." Most of these songs are in the heavy punk style of Numan's earliest recordings: they include familiar titles such as "Bombers", "Something's In The House" and "My Shadow In Vain", alongside the likes of "Basic J", "Thoughts No. 2" and "Critics".

Three tracks recorded at the same sessions, but with a completely different sound, make

"There is more real Numan here than silicone slap. He offers a little of himself before the shell of total imagery is slammed shut around him." *Melody Maker*, 1984

up Side One of "1978/1979 Volume Three", one of two 12" mini-albums also issued this month. "The Monday Troop" and "Crime Of Passion" are both acoustic, while "The Life Machine" has only minimal instrumentation, and they offer a fascinating and refreshing contrast to the harder material — besides bringing back that old spectre of how much Numan could sound like David Bowie when he tried. On the flip of this 12" are three other out-takes, two instrumentals ("Random" and "Ocean"), recorded during the sessions for "The Pleasure Principle", and the rocky "A Game Called Echo", dating from the "Telekon" sessions.

Completing this batch of releases (in red vinyl, while "Volume Three" is in blue) is "1978/1979 Volume Two", a four-track collection. One side features the experimental "Fadeout 1930" (from the sessions for the first Tubeway Army LP), "The Crazies" and "Only A Downstat" (the latter two from the "Replicas" sessions), while on the flip is the long and interesting "We Have A Technical" — another "Replicas" out-take. All three releases can only help add to the interest which Numan's early career is now attracting.

Record Collector
December 1994

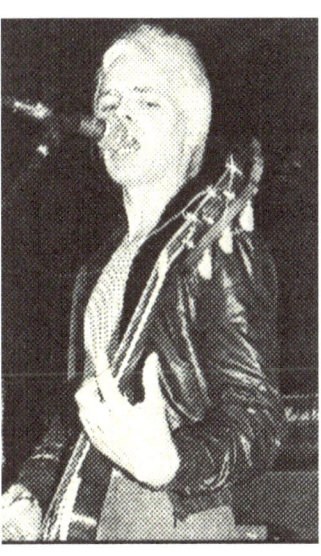

"This is my life. Welcome to me tonight. I don't feel too glad to be here for sure... I don't really think I wanna stay", sings Numan on the first song on the demo album. All through to the farewell concerts at Wembley, his were songs of leaving. He arrived by saying 'goodbye'. In the context of the album, this could be read as a farewell to Punk, especially since *The Plan* ends with a song about escaping to a new life with a trusty mechanical friend (the newly discovered Minimoog?). In between are songs about being sacked by Mean Street (a very formative experience) and his first song about Jo The Waiter, whom we learn had just started working at 'zero cafe number 9' and who introduced himself by "spilling wine over some ex-friends of mine", i.e. Mean Street.

BOMBERS

By Tubeway Army on
Beggars Banquet Records

Look up I hear the scream
Of sirens on the wall
I see a policeman crying
In the back seat of a dying Ford
Hotel waiters leave the bedrooms
Of stars who are far too old
And no one ever told me
That I could be so cold

Chorus
Bombers fight at zero
Feet
Bombers fight at zero

I see an old man
Knocked to the ground
And beaten by the vicar's wife
No one stops to help they're far
To busy trying to save their own lives
A tiny girl screams for mother
And wanders out into the street
I saw her go down underneath
A thousand peoples running feet

Repeat chorus

All the junkies pulling needles
From their arms
And hope it lasts the night
All the soldiers curse the day they
Joined the army and prepare to fight
In silent bars, in silent rooms
In silent cars you hide where you can
And me, I know just where you are
You see, I'm a bomber man

Repeat chorus to fade

*Words and music by Gary Numan.
Reproduced by permission Beggars
Banquet/Andrew Heath Music.*

Requested by: *Andrew Dollard,
Grangemouth, Scotland; Craig Sutton,
Sarah Phythian, Anna Thacker, William
Crippin, Jayne Saunders, Tracey V. Nood,
Christopher Lant, Carol Lynn, Philip
Rockliffe, S. Blakemore, Susan Jenkins,
Jennifer Forbes, Michele, Gina Iddles, Tracey
Davies, June Wilson, Barrie Harding, Maria
Skinner, Samantha Smith, Jill Glindon,
Karen Tattershall, Russell Pallett, Sandra
Dodds, G. L. Cooksey, Elaine Thorpe, Lesley,
Brian Furnell, Julie Dobson, Tony Bird,
Steven Kingham, Annette Smith, Robert*

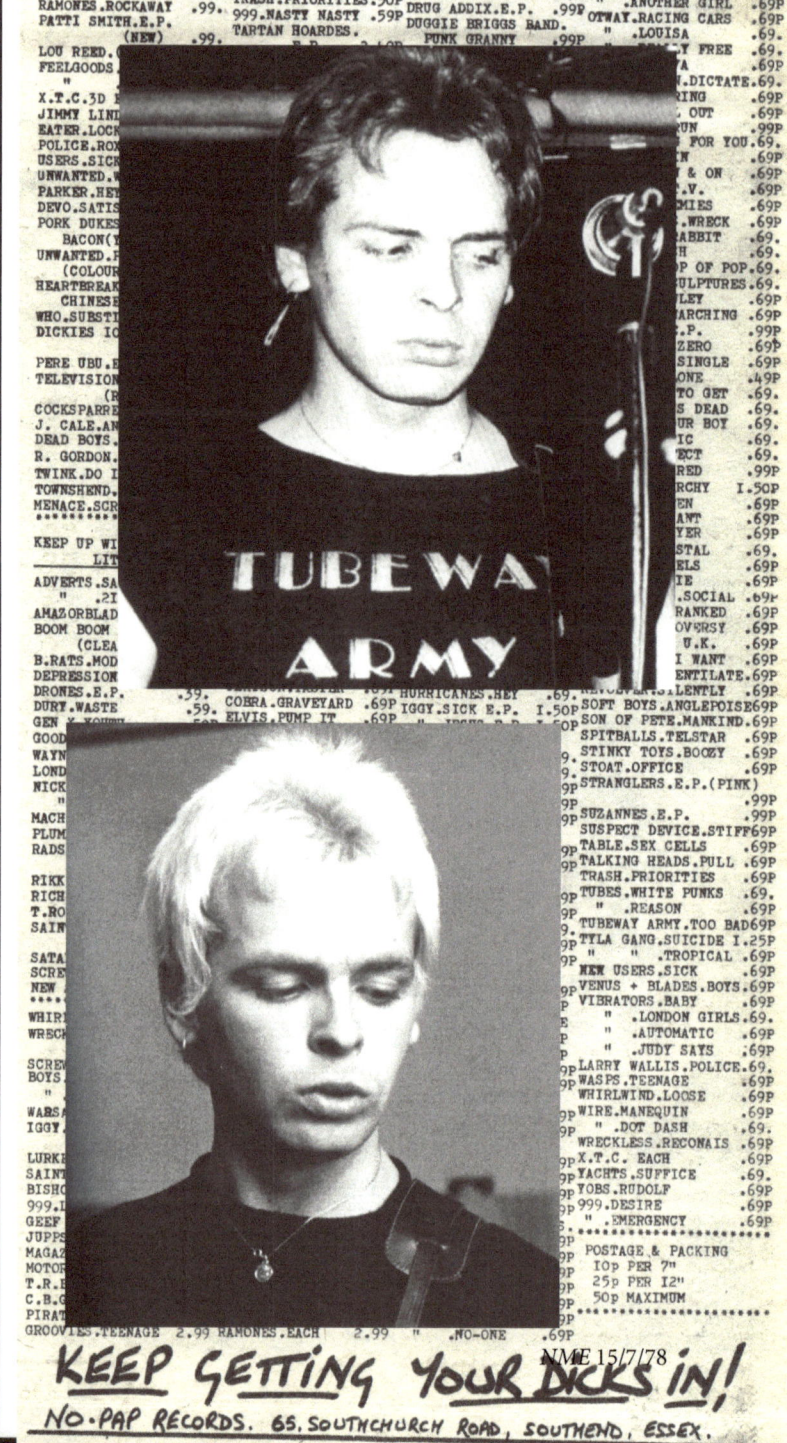

NME 15/7/78

**TUBEWAY ARMY: 'Bombers'
(Beggars Banquet)** Would you
believe a Billy Idol lookalike
already? A peculiarly '78 style
of thin, nasal vocals, whose
chicness derives from the snot-
tiness level you can convey per
syllable. More use of repetition,
unintentional this time. The
drummer makes a valiant effort
to sound like a drum machine
Sounds like a rough demo half-
mixed of a potentially good
single.

SOUNDS 12/8/78

**TUBEWAY ARMY:
'Bombers' (Beggars
Banquet BEG 8).** Please
give up gracefully. Look
here, old chums, the
market for this sort of
heavyweight monotony
has died. Never mind,
you can sit and tell your
grandchildren how you
nearly made it.

ROBIN SMITH

RM Oct 21

**TUBEWAY ARMY: "Bomb-
ers" (Beggars Banquet).**
Interesting if flawed. The
song is hardly great but the
treatment shows they're beginning to scour the studio for
possibilities. The progression
is well-paced and atmospheric,
bolstered by some good old
siren effects and undercut by
some strident rhythm chops. A
nifty blueprint.

M.M. 19/8/78

16

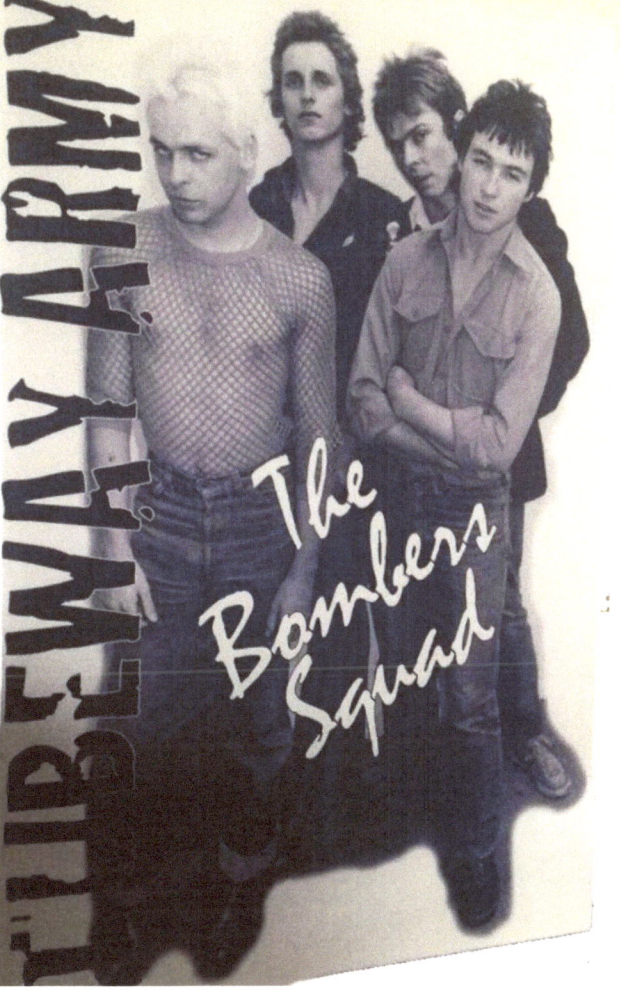

Upper left, a wondrously rare flyer. Bottom right, a spectacularly valuable advertising poster.

17

BEGGARS BANQUET are deleting the first six singles on their catalogue, including the first two Lurkers singles, and efforts from the Doll, Johnny G and Tubeway Army. *Sounds 23/9/78*

Meanwhile, in the same issue of *Sounds*, a bit of light-hearted fun as Sandy Robertson went Back to the Future and sort-of accused the first Numan collaborator-to-be of having inspired the album sleeve and the title of the next but one Numan LP:

ROBERT PALMER: 'Best Of Both Worlds' (Island 12")
Three tracks from three albums by Mr Palmer. Glossy sleeve is a rip-off of Magritte painting, glossy music is a rip-off of other, more talented, white men ripping off American negro music.

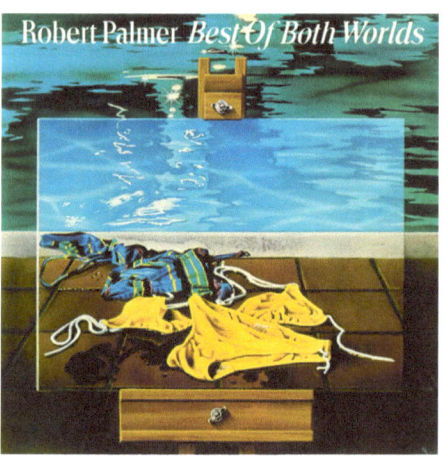

Alternative Chart

1. BANANA SPLITS, Dickies, A&M
2. GREAT NEW SOLDIERS, The Pack, SS
3. HEARTS IN EXILE, Homosexuals, Lorelei
4. CHARLES EP, Skids, No Bad
5. PSYCHOANALYSIS, They Must Be Russians, Gemme
6. PSEUDO EXISTORS EP, Dead Good
7. NO PICTURES, The Sods, Stortbeat
8. FEEDING OF THE 5,000, Crass, Small Wonder
9. FATAL MICROBES/POISON GIRLS 12" EP, Small Wonder
10. ELECTRIC HEAT, Visitors, Deep Cuts
11. RED BOX, I Jog, Tyger
12. OUT IN THE DARK, Lurkers, Beggars Banquet
13. PICTURES, Echo and the Bunnymen, Zoo
14. NO DRY ICE, Leyton Buzzards, Chrysalis
15. HARDWARE EP, Narc
16. WRONG TREATMENT, The Four Plugs, Disposable
17. BOMBERS, Tubeway Army, Beggars Banquet
18. SID VICIOUS IMPORT 12", Barclay
19. CARRIE, Another Pretty Face, New Pleasures
20. MANCUNIAN WAY, The Tunes, Rhesus
21. FAIRY TALE, Raincoats, Rough Trade
22. FACADE, Alter Nomen Unlimited, Spherical Object
23. DECISIONS, The Bears, Good Vibrations
24. GANGSTERS, The Special AKA, 2-Tone
25. CUPS AND SAUCERS EP, Tea Set, Waldos
26. KOJAK, Minny Pops, Plurex
27. JOHNNY WON'T, Killjoys, Raw
28. JILLY, The Piranhas, Attrix
29. THE WALL EP, Small Wonder
30. BIG IN JAPAN, Big In Japan, Eric's

Sounds 2.6.79

Compiled by Small Wonder Records, 162 Hoe Street, Walthamstow, London E17. Tel: 01-520 5036.

JET TO WEA RECORDS (MARCH 1979) ON COMPLETION (APRIL 1979, ARE FRIENDS ELECTRIC RELEASED

261425 WEAREC G
ATTN DAVE JARRETT
MARCH 28
RE. TUBEWAY ARMY

TUBEWAY ARMY? IT PRESENTS A CONFUSING PARADOX, BECAUSE TUBEWAY ARMY DISBANDED IN JULY 1978 YET HERE IS THE NEW TUBEWAY ARMY ALBUM. BUT DIDN'T THE FIRST ALBUM OPEN WITH AN EPITHAPH TO TUBEWAY ARMY ON 'LISTEN TO THE SIRENS'? AND AREN'T THE MUSICIANS THE A SAME AS ON THE VERY FIRST SINGLE? WELL YES, BUT TUBEWAY ARMY IS REALLY GARY NUMAN WHO CURRENTLY WRITES, PRODUCES, SINGS AND PLAYS ALL THE INSTRUMENTS EXCEPT BASS (PAUL GARDINER) AND DRUMS (GARY'S UNCLE - JESS LIDYARD). WHEN THE GROUP STOPPED LIVE APPEARANCES AND 2 MEMBERS LEFT, THE TUBEWAY ARMY NUCLEUS SPENT THREE DAYS RECORDING DEMOS WHICH HAD SUCH BRILLIANT UNPOLISHED ACCESSIBILITY THAT BEGGARS BANQUET RELEASED THEM AS THE FIRST ALBUM IN A 5,000 LIMITED EDITION WITH NO BACK UP PUBLICITY OR MAJOR DISTRIBUTION. REVIEWERS EITHER IGNORED OR WERE FAVOURABLY CONFUSED BY THE STRANGELEY ATTRACTIVE AND COMPELLING MUSIC BUT, WITH THE SUPPORT OF SPECIALIST RECORD SHOPS AND FANZINES (HERE AND ABROAD) AND A GRADUAL GROWING AWARENESS OF THE MUSIC, A CULT FOLLOWING HAS BUILT UP AROUND TUBEWAY ARMY AND GARY NUMAN.

THE NEW ALBUM 'REPLICAS' USING THE SAME MUSICIANS, PRESENTS THE PROOF THAT GARY NUMAN IS ONE OF THE MOST POWERFUL NEW TALENTS TO MATURE OVER THE LAST 18 MONTHS. MORE MELODIC AND STRUCTURED THAN THE LAST LP, THE MUSIC RETAINS ITS CHILLING STARKNESS BUT HAS A NEW DEPTH AND STRENGTH IN ITS DECEPTIVE SIMPLICITY AND ACCESSIBILITY.

GARY IS CURRENTLY WORKING WITH AN EXPANDED GROUP ON A THIRD ALBUM ('THE PLEASURE PRINCPAL') AND PREPARING TO PLAY LIVE AGAIN, THIS TIME NOT AS TUBEWAY ARMY BUT AS HIMSELF - GARY NUMAN........ SO ENDING THE PARADOX OF TUBEWAY ARMY.

DISCOGRAPHY
AS TUBEWAY ARMY
SINGLES: THAT'S TOO BAD / OH DIDN'T I SAY (DELETED)
         BOMBERS / O.D. RECEIVER / BLUE EYES (DELETED)

ALBUMS: DOWN IN THE PARK DO YOU NEED THE SERVICE? BEG17
         TUBEWAY ARMY BEGA 4 (UNAVAILABLE)
         REPLICAS BEGA 7

BEG 17T A 10 INCH VERSION ALSO FEATURING A GARY NUMAN SOLO TRACK
'I NEARLY MARRIED A HUMAN'

Army defeated

TUBEWAY ARMY, whose debut single 'Bombers' was released recently by Beggars Banquet, have split due to "different musical directions". Blond frontman Valerium remains under contract to pursue a solo career with an album planned for release later this year.

SOUNDS Sept 9

TUBEWAY ARMY, who only recently released their first single, "Bombers", have disbanded. Beggar's Banquet still intend to release a group LP comprising demos, and lead singer-guitarist Valerium is now recording solo for the label.

NME Sept 2

Tubeway Army

Listen to the Sirens

My Shadow in Vain

The Life Machine

Friends

Something's in the House

Everyday I Die

Steel and You

My Love is a Liquid

Are You Real?

The Dream Police

Jo The Waiter

Zero Bars (Mr. Smith)

TUBEWAY ARMY: Tubeway Army (Every Day I Die)' (Beggars Banquet BEGA 4).

TUBEWAY Army is not the kind of album one surprises one's impressionable friends with for Christmas.

Nor is it the kind of album which can be found nestling within the Easy Listening racks at the local record shop.

In fact Tubeway Army is an album which 98 per cent of the population would take an instant and furious dislike to. Being a perverse creature, I have taken quite a fancy to it.

Tubeway Army (the band) basically revolves around one Mr. Gary Numan. The lad looks like Sting of the Police, attempts to sing like Bowie and writes ostentatiously pretentious lyrics. In

spite of this however, he does come up with some very infectious rhythms, which open into what I find to be highly enjoyable tunes.

Much of the album features the chilling calculated music structures currently so a la mode - but fortunately the more one listens, the more these individual sounds grow.

Keyboards and synthesizers are the main key to the tunes (and I use the word hesitatingly) on this LP, but on certain tracks, notably the consecutive numbers 'Friends' and 'Something's In The House', guitar (once again played by Numan) plays a surprisingly dominant role — often bearing what seem to be strong heavy metal tendencies.

I still find the lyrics a little too overbearing to take - but the music on this strange, cold album I find interesting, if somewhat out of character, enjoyable listening, + + + ½
KELLY PIKE

The Wall 2

AT LAST someone has decided to review the Tubeway Army LP, but why does it have to be by the sort of person who likes the Bee Gees (aagh) and listens to Tony Blackburn (puke).

So Mr. Wall, you only see fit to compare this album to the 'recent Clash abortion'? Jeez, is it that bad? Strange how some people seem to like — even buy — Clash records. And the lyrics on the album mean bugger all do they? Well you tell the readers of

TUBEWAY ARMY

'TUBEWAY ARMY — *Jo the Waiter* (2.40)
Commencing in exactly the same acoustically-driven manner as my own *Unisex Cathedral*, Gazza's homoerotic tale of being groped in the gents displays a melancholic Subway Sectarianism that might not be accidental: hell, even the name of Gazza's band is just a far more terraced-up versh of Subway Sect. Located in the boneyard of Tubeway Army's first LP for Beggar's Banquet, there's a charming & disarming Desperate Bicycles-plays-BEARD OF STARS D.I.Y. element to *Jo the Waiter* that stood in fair opposition to the rest of Gazza's clattery Chrome-informed Thin White Muse.
Anyhow, regarding this particular song, the absence of an 'e' at the end of Joe turned out to be a cunning clue: Jo was Gazza's waitress girlfriend of the time. Ah, sweet.'
Julian Cope, *Postpunksampler 2,/* January 2010

TUBEWAY ARMY: Tubeway Army (Beggars Banquet BEGA 4) Prod: Gary Numan
Interesting exponents of the 'I am a machine' syndrome currently popular in what used to be called the new wave Tubeway Army proves to be an inventive threesome specialising in doomy words intoned over quirky, interesting riffs of the clockwork variety with occasional sorties into guitar or synthesiser solo territory which prove the band has the ability to take its ideas a step further. Gary Numan, lead vocals, guitars and keyboards also produced the LP and sounds quite a talent. Initial copies are in blue vinyl.

RECORD BUSINESS Dec 4

Numan at Spacewood studios in Cambridge with the very synth that changed rock music.

gary numan vocals, guitars, keyboards

"Strong heavy metal tendencies? You won't see me in the *Kerrang* charts..."

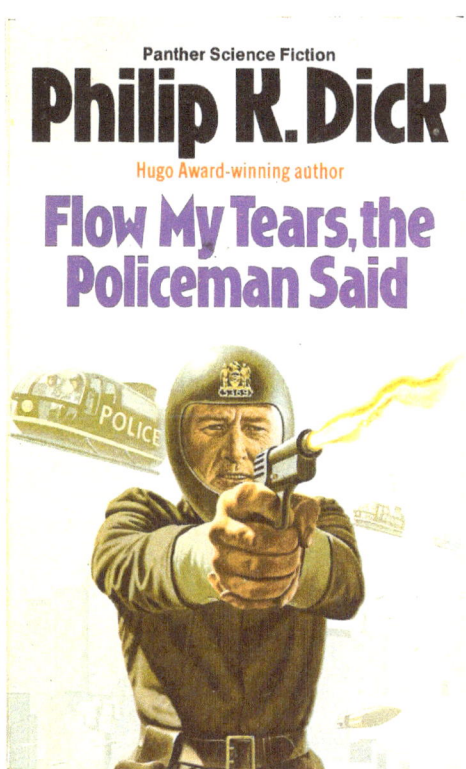

Panther Science Fiction
Philip K. Dick
Hugo Award-winning author
Flow My Tears, the Policeman Said

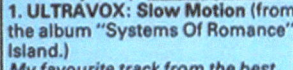

"Flow   My   Tears"   The   new

23

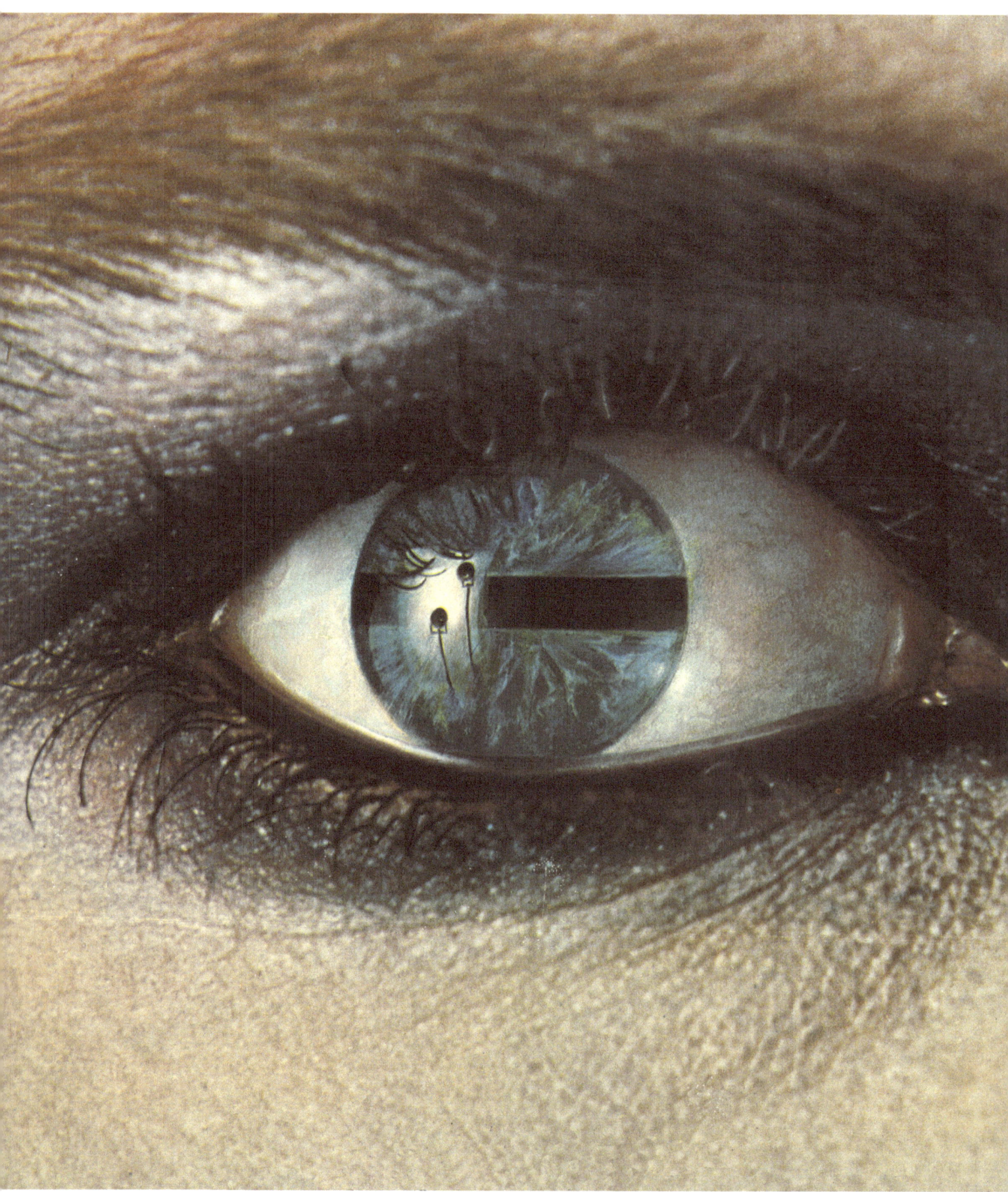

Replicas

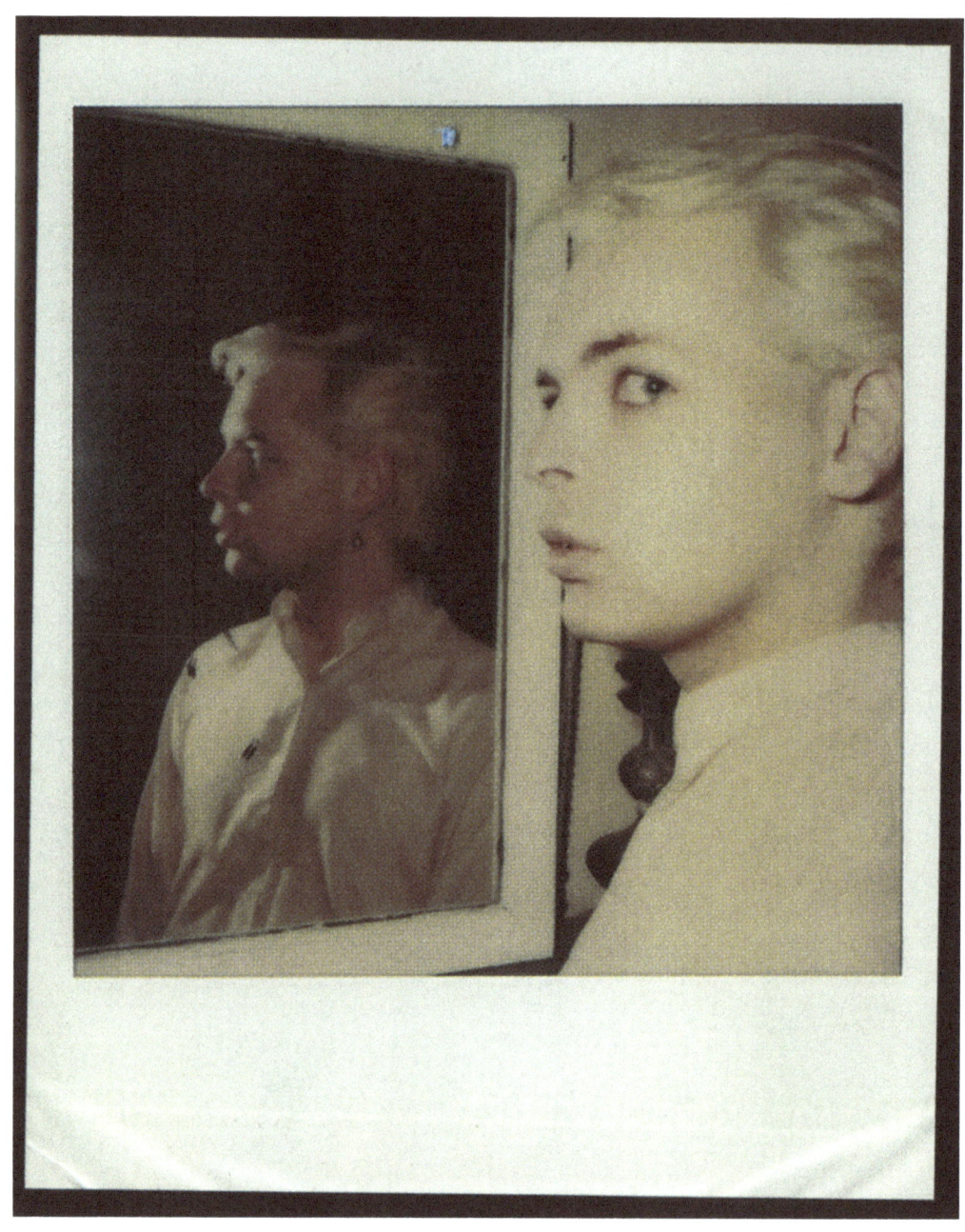

Polaroid test for the *Replicas* cover art.
First published on the CD of *The Complete John Peel Sessions.*

Mary Vango, makeup artist: "When I was commissioned to do Gary's makeup. I started off by listening to the music. Gary had caught the zeitgeist, the new mood for electronic sounds, but was doing his own thing with it. I worked with a lot of musicians in the 1970s and 80s, but Gary always stood out: he seemed the most unreachable. Where David Bowie was theatrical, Gary was more otherworldly – remote, but not aloof or arrogant. He was terribly shy and couldn't make eye contact. We spent an entire day in the dressing room, and I don't remember a single bit of conversation. I imagined him as someone who never saw the sun – not because of lots of partying, but because he seemed so disconnected from nature. I wanted his skin to look pallid, so used a very light base. To make him look weary, I put on lots of dark, heavy kohl. He had to seem like a very complicated character: dark and remote, but not sinister, just cut off from his emotions. At the back of my mind was a Stanley Kubrick film I'd been really taken with, *Barry Lyndon*, which was set in the 18th century and shot in candlelight. I'd been wanting to use that look on someone for ages – then Gary came along." *Guardian*, 18 /2/14

Murray Melvin and Marisa Berenson in Stanley Kubrick's *Barry Lyndon* (1975)

A press ad with a Warhol-style screen print of replicas of Numan. It recalls Warhol's life-size silver and black screen prints of Elvis Presley. The replicated images fuse nicely with the carefully shadowed realism of the one-and-fixed image in the reflection, which opens up a whole world of metaphor and interpretation, e.g. it's a figurative interpretation of the prism as seen on Pink Floyd's *The Dark Side of the Moon* album cover. This work of art by Malti Kidia further improves on Warhol's *Silver Elvis* by reducing the 'action' image to a pose, an iconography-style representation of Numan himself as the future in the present, the man-machine of his forthcoming stage persona.

The subsequent ad (*Melody Maker* 14/4/79) added another replica and moved the Beggars Banquet logo to the far right so it didn't look like a codpiece.

Don't Be a Dummy

Gary Numan sang the vocal for the *Don't be a Dummy* advert for Lee Cooper jeans, which played in heavy rotation on television and in cinemas, and was the hit of the playground early in 1979. Two balletic *West Side Story*-style fifties kids in white T-shirts and Lee Cooper jeans dance around a crowd of bleached haired punk zombies with dead eyes that glow green, imagery which sparked a better idea that Spring when it came to designing a picture disc. It's not easy unearthing barely known material from the early part of Numan's career, but I think I've managed a scoop here, courtesy of a popular English film star:

From *The Confessions of Robin Askwith*: "Monday March 20th 1978, 10.30 a.m. Prince of Wales Theatre. Rehearsals for *I Love My Wife*. My dressing room after the show was always full of champagne and friends. It was a chance to meet other performers as well. Liz Robertson was being hotly pursued, in the professional sense, by up and coming producer Cameron Mackintosh. He wanted her to play Eliza Doolittle in his forthcoming production of *My Fair Lady*. The cast was to include Dame Anne Neagle. Dame Anna came to see our show one Saturday matinée. That afternoon my jingle writing friend, Ronnie Bond, left his King Charles Spaniel in my dressing room while he popped round the corner to record *Don't be a Dummy* for Lee Cooper Jeans. The singer was a seventeen-year-old, later to rename himself Gary Numan. Poor Sammy the spaniel shat himself, probably as a result of listening to my singing over the tannoy. Knock-knock on the dressing room door after the show. 'I'd like to introduce you to Dame Anna Neagle.' 'Do come in, nice to meet you, mind you don't tread in the...' Too late. A nine-inch doggy poo embraced her delicate left foot. 'What a charming performance, you did so well. Come on Liz, I have to get going. I'm dining with the Queen in an hour.' "

BRIGHT EYES WILL GERTCHA

IF YOU'RE a TV-watcher then the face above will be familiar. The punk with the flashing eyes (they're green in case you have a black and white set) is one of the stars of "Dummy", the 30 second TV commercial for Lee Cooper jeans. Along with Foster Grants sunglasses, it's one of the best TV ads currently on the screen.

The kids themselves were "pulled in off the street" according to the people who made the ad, and the song is sung by Gary Numan of punk outfit Tubeway Army, backed up by session musicians.

Tubeway Army have their own minor hit right now — a song called "Are 'Friends' Electric" on the Beggars Banquet label — though there is talk of Gary Numan recording the "Dummy" song for a future single.

For those of you who've written in asking, here are the lyrics: "Don't be a dummy/Move like honey/Don't be a dummy/Use your money/Come out proud/Don't hide in the crowd/Find the gear that's worth the grind/Find the jeans that'll do your mind/They'll suit ya/Lee Cooper." Lyrics copyright Ronnie Bond/John Wilkinson.

Singles from ads are nothing new. A few years back David Dundas made the charts with "Jeans On" and before that the New Seekers sang the pleasures of Coca Cola.

Another distinctive current commercial is the pub ad for Courage Breweries, seen in the south of England only. The music for this, "Gertcha", is sung by Chas and Dave who have re-recorded the song for their new single. *Smash Hits* has a feeling we are going to be hearing an awful lot of "Gertcha" this summer.

Gary Numan: singer of "Dummy"

GARY NUMAN besingt Jeans

Um etwas Geld zu verdienen, sang Gary Numan in einem Werbespot über die Qualitäten einer bestimmten Jeans-Marke. Das war vor einem Jahr. Jetzt erhofft sich die Firma einen ähnlichen, kostenlosen Werbe-Effekt wie bei dem Hit „Jeans on" von David Dundas. Doch Gary möchte die Reklame im Fernsehen verbieten lassen. „Sonst ist es mit meiner Karriere ebenso schnell zu Ende wie bei David", meint der Sänger von Tubeway Army. *GARY NUMAN Sings Jeans—*

'To earn some money, Gary Numan sang in a commercial about the qualities of a particular brand of jeans. That was a year ago. Now, the company expects a similar free advertising effect as the hit *Jeans On* by David Dundas. But Gary wants the advert to be banned from television, "Otherwise my career will end as quickly as David's", says the singer of Tubeway Army.'

A fascinating ad, not because the copyist got Numan's wrong but because it references the Lee Cooper ad that made Numan's voice famous before his face and name became widely known.

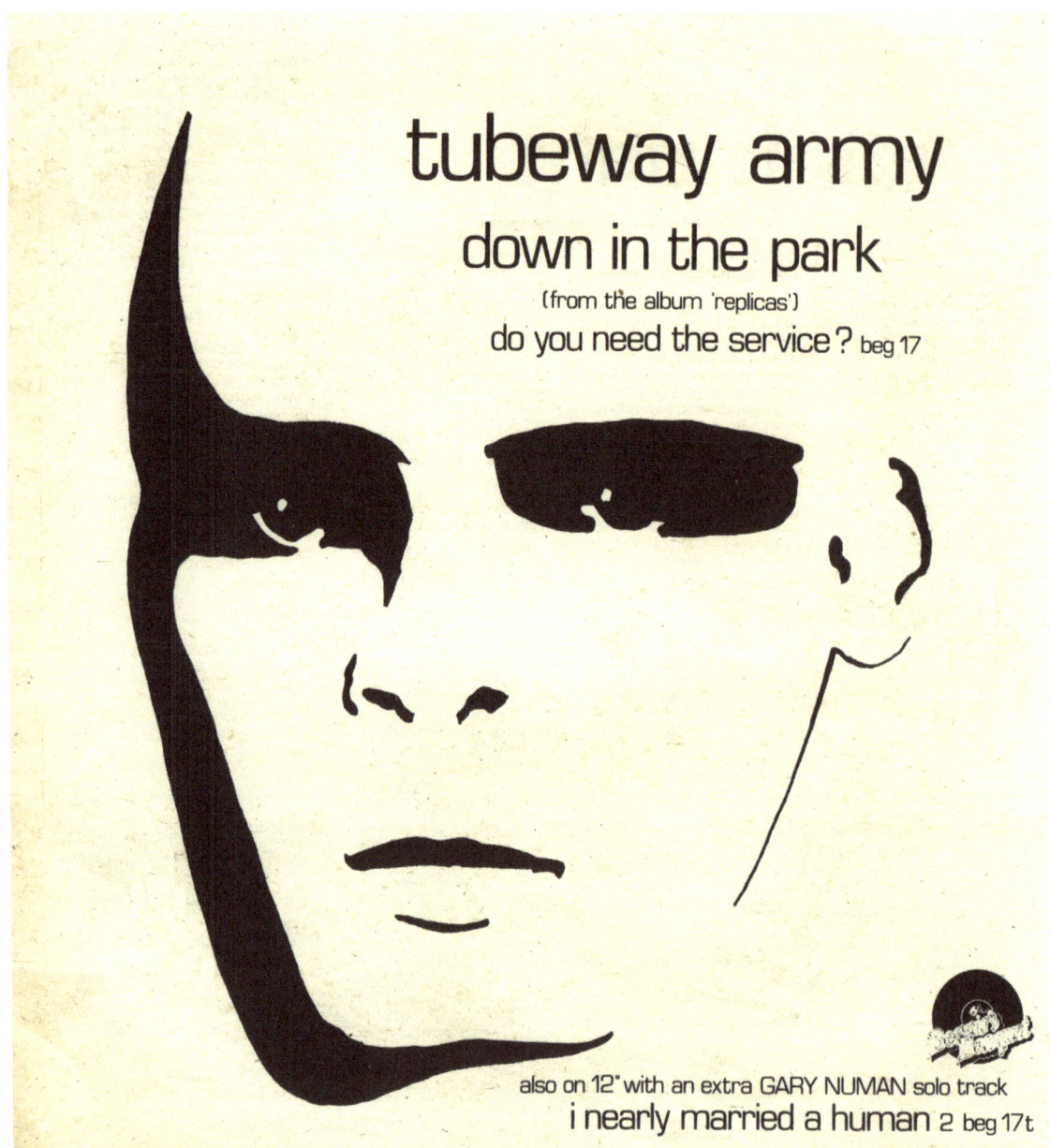

March 3rd 1979 marked the first public appearance of the famous logo drawn by Numan's schoolfriend, Garry Robson. Robson traced Numan's face from on the cover of *Bombers* single to provide this visual link between the two singles. The image was tidied up (the shadow round the cheek bone and jaw line was thinned) and it became Numan's band and business logo. Several months later, in August 1979, in the long wake of the success of the subsequent single, *Are 'Friends' Electric?*, the revised version was used as the cover of the reissued *Tubeway Army* album.

This advert is also important because it marks the official start of Gary Numan's solo career. It announces the first track credited solely to 'Gary Numan' and offered for sale to the public: *i nearly married a human 2*. The '2' differs from the unnumbered instrumental track that closes *Replicas*, in that Gary Numan sings on it (in a quiet voice, modestly low in the mix). He sings "I nearly married a human" over and over and over. All songs recorded from this point onwards were credited not to Tubeway Army but to Gary Numan. That '2' in the title is quite possibly the inspiration for the pre-text-speak titles of Prince songs. *Replicas* was a formative influence on Prince (see page 87).

Down in the park
Where the machmen
Meet the machines
And play 'kill-by-numbers'
Down in the park
With a friend called 'five'

I was in a car crash
Or was it the war
But I've never been
Quite the same
Little white lies
Like 'I was there'

Come to 'zom zoms'
A place to eat
Like it was built
In one day
You can watch the humans
Trying to run

Oh look
There's a rape machine
I'd go outside
If he'd look the other way
You wouldn't believe
The things they do

Down in the park
Where the chant is
'Death, death, death'
Until the sun cries morning
Down in the park
With friends of mine

'We are not lovers
We are not
Romantics
We are here to serve you'
A different face
But the words never change

Words and music by Gary Numan
Produced by permission
Beggars Banquet/Andrew Heath Music Ltd

Request Spot

ARTIST TUBEWAY ARMY

SONG DOWN IN THE PARK

LABEL BEGGARS BANQUET

YEAR 1979

REQUESTED BY SARAH DONADEL,

KNOWLE, BRISTOL

TUBEWAY ARMY: 'Down In The Park' (Beggars Banquet BEG 17). A (space) oddity, blending early-Bowie vocals with late-Bowie instrumentation, all sepulchral synth and gloomy atmospherics. Gary Numan (the one-man band who masquerades as Tubeway Army) even looks like a Bowie clone; very Berlin, very 1930s, very Boots makeup counter. And despite all that, (or because) of all that, it's a very compelling record.

Five Bowie references in one paragraph? Mr. Lewis (the editor himself) is obsessed, or else grasping to describe music that is beyond his understanding. Thinking that criticism means contextualisation, Lewis tries and fails, then fails again, and five-times fails. How can you over-contexualise, or *mono*-contexualise, music that is this original? And why drag Bowie into it? He had as much to do with the writing and performing of *Down in the Park* as I did, and I was only a kid at the time. Did Bowie ever write a song of such grandeur? *Five Years*? It's a good song but it is hardly *Down in the Park.*

Bowie advanced the art of modern music by fusing Brecht-Weill cabaret with politics-free rock (in the long step to realising his life's ambition to write a West End musical). With *Down in the Park*, Numan restored politics to a cabaret-rock fusion and then used an electronic orchestra the likes of which had never been heard before on a rock song. And by *song* I don't mean shapeless doodles of noise by Eno. *Down in the Park* is a metaphorical song about extreme Neo-Conservatism. The rich gather on high to watch the raping of the poor. At the time of *Down in the Park,* Bowie was going through a Teddy Boy phase and aping Tommy Steele (*Boys Keep Swinging*), and making the front page of the papers for getting slapped in a London restaurant by Lou Reed. Two-years-later, inspired by Numan's art and professionalism, though he never could match Numan's talent for lyrics, Bowie wrote a two-thirds good (but one-third filler) album, *Scary Monsters,* before falling back to Quincy Jones disco dross and a cover version of *Dancing in the Street* ("and Iggy can I use that old *China Girl* thing of ours, I'm struggling to fill up the album?"). The disco dross was copied from Lou Reed who had two disco filler songs on his nine-minute *Ringing Anita* LP, AKA *The Bells. The Bells* was released the same month as *Replicas* and eclipsed completely by *Replicas.* Reed is a mighty talent but he followed *The Bells* with a decade long decline (eventually pulled back by Poe, again, and by Hegarty's voice). Numan followed *Replicas* with *The Pleasure Principle, Telekon* and *Dance* (for starters).

In the week of *Down in the Park,* Alan Lewis gave The Single of the Week to *Silly Thing,* the post-Lydon, Ramones-cloned, Cook-and-Jones version of the Sex Pistols, and wrote: "I'm a sucker for this sort of boozy-shouty stuff." And there you have it. Asking a boozy-shouty fan to write intelligently about *Down in the Park* is like asking (insert your own most despised celebrity) to write about (insert your favourite innovatory work of art).

TUBEWAY ARMY: Down In The Park (Beggar's Banquet). Not to be confused with The Clovers' 'Down In The Alley' but just as spooky. Gary Numan's Tubeway Army may be besotted with the eerie subterranean wastelands of Burgess and Bowie but they can keep a spectre alive. If this don't make you look over your shoulder in horrified disbelief then you're a better man than I am gunga din. Waaugh . . .

When the reviewer starts by referencing a Blues song that has the kind of totally naff lyric she understands: "Janie, Janie, Janie, Janie, Jane Jane / Janie, Janie, Janie, Janie, Jane Jane / Down in the alley, just you and me / We're going bowlin' till half past three," you know she's going to struggle when asked to review something that isn't grown from howlin' in the bayou. Like an errant child trying to hide her blushes, she fills her one paragraph with reference to *four* other works/artists and fails to write anything about the song itself except for one word, *spooky.* And that's not good enough.

ALBUMS

+++++   Unbeatable
++++   Buy it
+++   Give it a spin
++   Give it a miss
+   Unbearable

A ONE MAN ARMY

TUBEWAY ARMY: 'Replicas'
(Beggar's Banquet Bega 7)

ARTICULATE, ultimate wallpaper; thought-locked, formulated output from the recluse and (purported) maestro, Gary Numan. Personal, but to the casual onlooker, readily accessible, stimulating, immediate modern electronic pop music.

Gary Numan effectively is Tubeway Army, Paul Gardiner's bass configurations mixed almost out on occasions, Jess Lidyard's drums preserving no identity, guiding the music along like a programmed, machine pulse; literally electronic in mood and assertion. Songwriting credits go almost exclusively to Numan: this is a one-man show.

And it's his lyrics which habitually marr this record, though they're not (quite) noxious enough to see a musical downfall. Generally, the man is concentrating on human emotions, and their place in a modern, liberated, industrialised context. At least what he's **striving** for is apparent, but the songs mostly cascade onto symmetrical platforms of art-for-art's-sake.

On the LP sleeve, he fixes an icy gaze upon his own distorted reflection in a window; he looks like one of them Bowie - clone mannequins that hang out in Chelsea fashion boutiques . . . bleached out. face, black - varnished finger nails . . . yeah, **arty** type.

So if the outward trained visage prompts a pre-cynical-conception of the actual music on the album, then that's understandable. But when that album, obviously flawed though

it is, proves to be such a surprisingly pleasurable — if one-dimensional — record, then the Artist can be forgiven.

Simplistic, synthetic beat music, relying heavily on structure and melody, Tubeway Army's approach puts them, inevitably, in a clique. But they are sufficiently adept and individual to secure their own corner within it.

'Me, I Disconnect From You' opens and establishes the band's sound before giving way to 'Are ''Friends'' Electric?, the album's most extreme highlight, whose time, pace and gripping keyboard patterns are sufficient to almost totally overshadow the lyrics.

Like the Mancunian, Numan's vocals (he also plays all keyboards and guitars here) suffer when he overplays his own characteristics; then his technique starts to appear trite and adopted.

'Down In The Park' and the instrumental, 'I Nearly Married A Human', provide the record with two further zeniths, while the remainder of the tracks hold the fort admirably.

How seriously Numan really takes all this humanoid/robotic mouthwash remains to be seen, but then, who am I to complain? I like his record.

'Replicas' can be listened to, or used as subliminal musical backdrop: it is visual, evocative, occasionally wringing with excellence but also damaged by intermittent lapses into pretentiousness.

When the machines rock . . . they will sound like **this**. **++++** CHRIS WESTWOOD

GARY NUMAN: personal songs

TUBEWAY ARMY:
Replicas (Beggars Banquet)

Gary Numan (human?) has restored my faith in the future. He plays modern music which does not leave me fold. Every song is a real melody, with controlled keyboards and android vocals.

Numans' Tubeway Army stay well clear of the pitfalls surrounding these kind of futuristic sounds. All the tracks are dominated by the computerised keyboard rhyrhms, which are controlled and never become self indulgent. The titles tell you what to expect—*I Nearly Married A Human, Praying To The Aliens* and *The Machman*—all are lyrically strange with mechanically infectious hook lines.

I even found singing myself along withe the forceful *You Are In My Vision* while reading my brothers sci-sci-fi comics. The low key vocals are reminiscent of Bowie, though Numan always remains original. Check out the atmospheric single *Down In The Park* and experience this technically emotional music. This is a 2000AD chart album.
Joe Philips

N.M.E. 20.1.79

'** (out of five) Tubeway Army, and this much has *certainly* been said before, are basically Gary Newman (sic), his sympathies, songs and (mercy) vision. Young Gary has his hair dyed blonde, his eyes made up, his picture taken under a bare light bulb after the manner of a showroom dummy. He writes songs about machines and disorientation and then wonders why people aren't interested in him. The basic scam is the *Low* Bowie stuff, the vocals following the old 'play the limp London boy and make a million bucks' method, the rhythm section playing as if they were actually a rhythm machine, all of it given two coats of Munchen polish from the ubiquitous keyboard gadgets. On odd occasions it can almost work; he garnishes *Are 'Friends' Electric?* with a pleasant buzzing structure and only rarely indulges himself in anything showy. But it's all a long way from the concentrated pop of Bowie and barely even Ultravox! Problem is, and here is a plain prejudice, people who talk about how 'weird' the world is and would like to live out their lives in an obscure sci-fi movie are, to my mind, the 1979 edition of the folks who lost themselves in Tarot and spray-on mysticism back in '67. They neither comfort nor amuse but they would have us feel that we are missing something.'
David Hepworth, *Sounds* 28/4/79

"There's a man outside in a long coat, grey hat..."

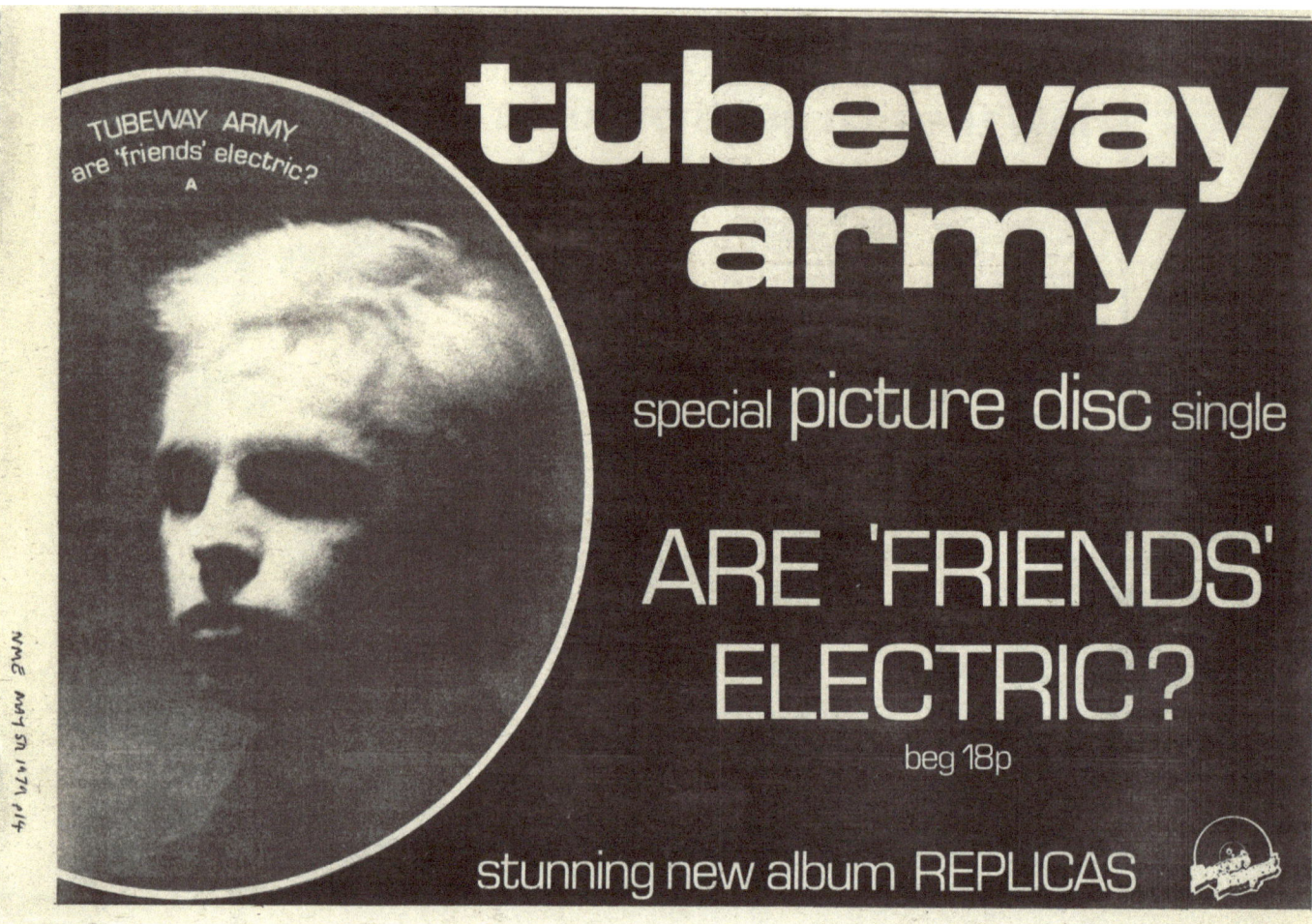

tubeway army

special picture disc *single*

ARE 'FRIENDS' ELECTRIC?

beg 18p

stunning new album REPLICAS

TUBEWAY ARMY
are 'friends' electric?
A

● Out this weekend on Beggar's Banquet is the Tubeway Army single 'Our Friends Electric' from their second album 'Replicas'. The first 20,000 copies are in picture disc form.

**TUBEWAY ARMY
'Are Friends' Electric?'
Beggars Banquet**

More electronic / computer whizzardry. So fashionable these days. Hypnotic and highly recommended. Slow and surely a hit?

TUBEWAY ARMY 'Are 'Friends' Electric?' (Beggars Banquet) You talkin' ta me? YOU TALKIN' TUH MEEE?! How should I know the answer to your meaningless question, you bums.... Whyn't you go and ask Ultravox, since you obviously listen to their albums so much. I confess, Army: your record is despicably listenable, for all your identity problems and jumped up notions. Just take it easy on the acid drops.

SOUNDS MARCH 12, 1979

Are 'Friends' Electric

ARTIST Gary Numan And The Tubeway Army RELEASE DATE May 1979 WRITER Gary Numan PRODUCER – LABEL Beggars Banquet UK CHART PEAK/WEEKS 1/16 US CHART PEAK/WEEKS –

Gary Numan joined the Lasers as a guitarist and rapidly took over the helm of the punk band, who, with a name change to Tubeway Army, were signed to Beggar's Banquet in 1978 and released some suitably aggressive singles. But by the time they started work on an album, the synth had entered Numan's life, and he ditched the guitar completely. The rest of the band quit in disgust and Numan completed *Are 'Friends' Electric* with his uncle on drums.

Tubeway Army sound like Bill Nelson before he learnt to tie his judoka. **Ian Penman, NME, May 1979**

Gary Numan: "All my early songs were about being alone or misunderstood. As a teenager, I'd been sent to a child psychiatrist and put on medication. I had Asperger's and saw the world differently. I immersed myself in sci-fi writers: Philip K. Dick, J. G. Ballard. The lyrics came from short stories I'd written about what London would be like in 30 years. These machines – "friends" – come to the door. They supply services of various kinds, but your neighbours never know what they really are since they look human. The one in the song is a prostitute, hence the inverted commas." *The Guardian*, 18 February 2014

The painting is by Tony Escott

Gary Numan

IT'S COLD OUTSIDE
AND THE PAINT'S PEELING
OFF MY WALLS
THERE'S A MAN OUTSIDE
IN A LONG GREY COAT
SMOKING A CIGARETTE
OH OH OH OH OH OH OH OH
OH OH OH OH OH OH OH OH

CHORUS
NOW THE LIGHT FADES OUT
AND I WONDER WHAT I'M DOING
IN A ROOM LIKE THIS
THERE'S A KNOCK ON THE DOOR
AND JUST FOR A SECOND
I THOUGHT I REMEMBERED YOU

OH OH OH OH OH OH OH OH
OH OH OH OH OH OH OH OH

SO NOW I'M ALONE
NOW I CAN THINK FOR MYSELF
ABOUT LITTLE DEALS AND S.U.'S
AND THINGS THAT I JUST
DON'T UNDERSTAND
LIKE A WHITE LIE THAT NIGHT
OR A SLY TOUCH AT TIMES
AND I DON'T THINK IT MEANT
ANYTHING TO YOU

OH OH OOOH OH OH OOOH
OH OH OOOH OH

REPEAT CHORUS

OH OH OH OH OH OH OH OH
OH OH OH OH OH OH OH OH

YOU KNOW I HATE TO ASK
(BUT ARE FRIENDS ELECTRIC)
ARE THEY
MINE'S BROKE DOWN
AND NOW I'VE NO ONE TO LOVE

OH OH OH OH OH OH OH OH
OH OH OH OH OH OH OH OH

SO I FIND OUT THE REASON
FOR THE 'PHONE CALLS
AND THE SMILES
AND IT HURTS AND I'M LONELY
AND I SHOULD NEVER HAVE TRIED
AND I MISS YOU TONIGHT
SO IT'S TIME TO LEAVE
YOU SEE THIS MEANS
EVERYTHING TO ME

OH OH OOOH OH OH OOOH
OH OH OH OH

WORDS AND MUSIC GARY NUMAN
REPRODUCED BY PERMISSION NUMA
MUSIC
ON NUMA RECORDS

Are friends Electric

This is the hat-less version of the lyrics,
to point out only one error.

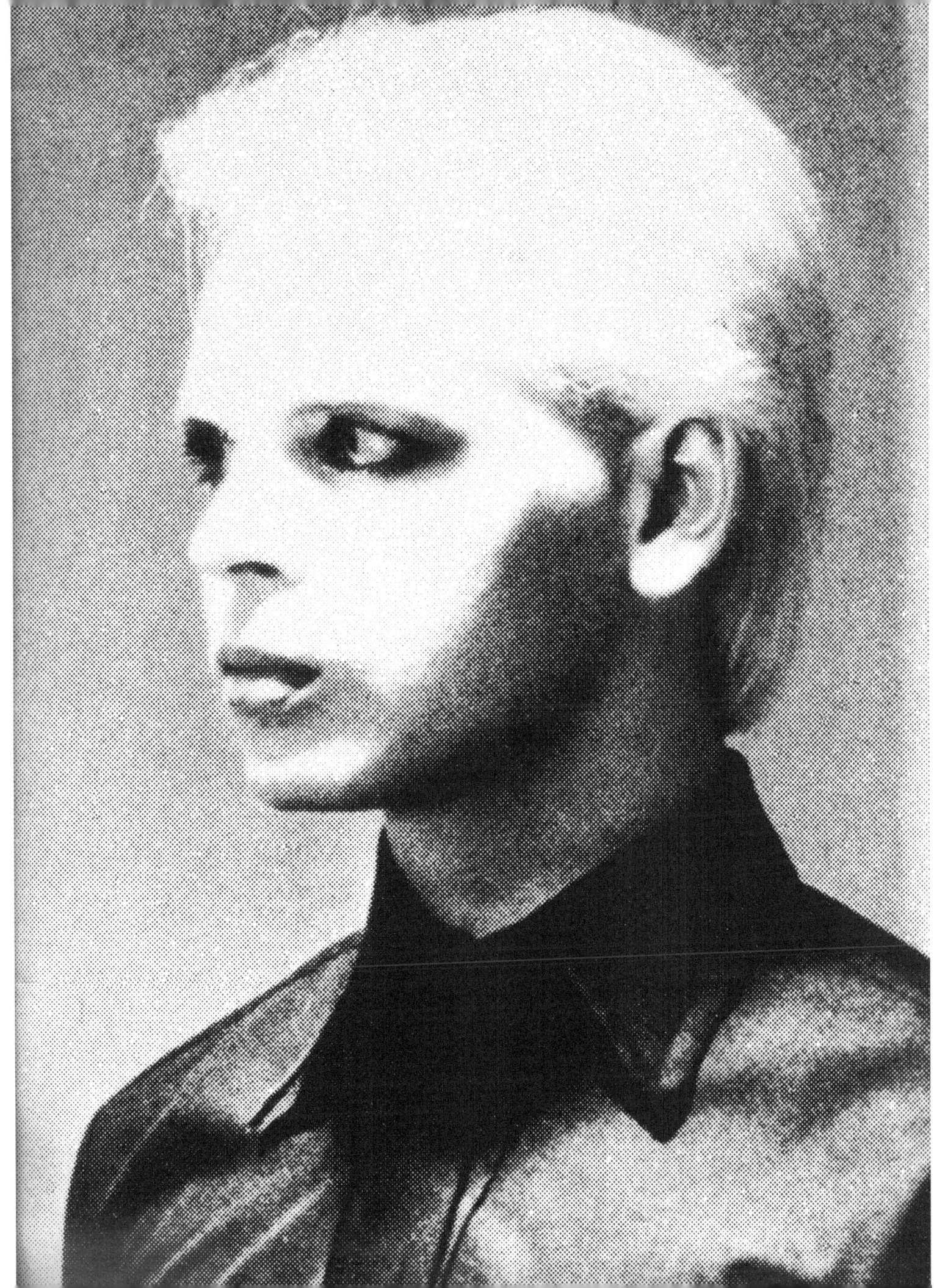

On 19th May 1989, *Are Friends Electric?* entered the Top 75 at number 71. Four days later, Gary Numan made his television debut on *The Old Grey Whistle Test* on BBC 2. He performed *Are 'Friends' Electric?* and *Down in the Park*.

Numan enters from the lower left of the screen. He walks from the back of the stage to the front. He starts to sing.

 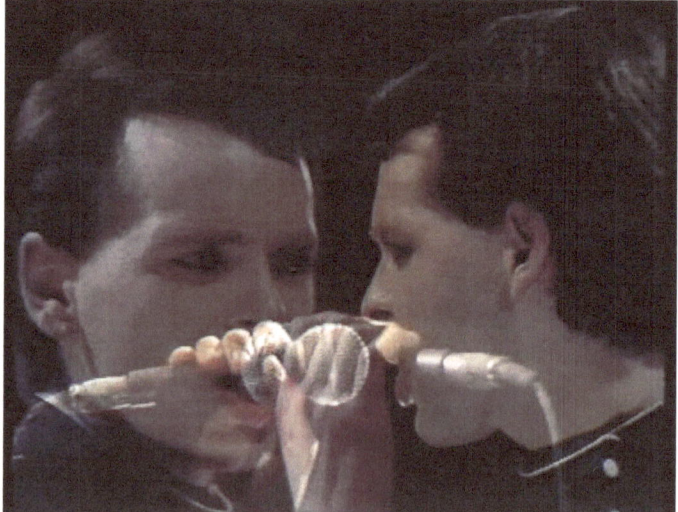

He and the band perform in white light and black clothes. There are no coloured lights at all. Numan's jacket has a white trim The director uses two-camera split-screen mirror images of Numan. This, and the cheaper equivalent, one-camera mirror images, became a hallmark of Numan's videos. The technique is referencing a sequence in Led Zeppelin's *The Song Remains the Same* (1976), the feature film that provided the blueprint for quality concert filming in the UK, particularly on the BBC.

At the end of the song, after an intense, whole-heartedly serious performance, as befits a song about loneliness, Numan has his back turned to the television audience to underline his calculated disconnection. The stage set was designed by Numan and was the foundation stone for the *Touring Principle* set - keyboard players (Chris Payne and Billie Currie) in towers left and right; the drummer (Cedric Sharpley) on a rise at the back, bass (Paul Gardner) and lead guitar (Trevor Grant here, but soon to be replaced by Rrussell Bell) flanking him at the back left and back right.

A fascinating sad photograph of the young musician on the day of his television debut. Uncontrived moroseness. How could anyone not see how damaged he was?

NUMANOID

THE CREATIVE PROCESS BEHIND TUBEWAY ARMY (SERIOUS THING). BY JOHN GILL

"A Machman is a human being who has had intercourse with a machine. I am a Machman . . ."
Garth Murphy. 'Twilight Of The Machman.' Oz 43, July 1972.

GARY NUMAN sits in a half-lit wine bar in Ealing, sipping a coke (he's teetotal) and relaxing after rehearsing Tubeway Army for an OGWT session. He blinks large, moonish eyes and talks in a friendly, broad London 'working class' accent — the antithesis to the 'Machman' image he portrays on the front cover of Tubeway Army's latest album, 'Replicas'.

He's somewhat nervous of public exposure — especially at the hands of the press. This is only the second interview he's ever given (the first was published in the fanzine, In The City). When the press has cared to review Tubeway Army either live or on record, the criticism has ranged between, at best, outrageous hatchet-jobs and, at worst, what Numan sees as very "personal" criticism.

Yet, despite all that, Numan seems open and honest, at times perhaps unwisely so. He's no art-school wordsmith and tends towards inarticulacy when dealing with the cerebral aspects of his music, unwittingly laying himself open to vicious criticism at the hands of the opportunist interviewer.

Numan started his career three years ago: "Someone said to me I'd been sitting on my arse and talking about being a star for a long time, and that I hadn't done anything about it. So I persuaded a friend to learn to play drums and it started like that."

His main influences (in chronological order from the age of 4) are the Dave Clark Five, The Monkees, T. Rex, Bowie and, more recently, Ultravox. The Bowie influence led him to write his own version of Ziggy Stardust about five years ago: "I did a counter-song with a different title for each song on the album. It was terrible! But that's where it started."

After a couple of unsuccessful liaisons in the pre-punk and punk days, Numan joined a band called The Lasers just over two years ago. Within a week, Numan's song-writing abilities and personality led to a powershift within the band and he became frontman. A couple of line-up changes later, Tubeway Army was born in Spring '77.

The band was playing "Very punky stuff. Short, three-minute catchy stuff" and managed to play about 30 gigs before splitting. Numan was moving in a direction the other members didn't care to follow. He'd also become disenchanted with live gigging. "I just don't like it," he says. "I don't like the uncertainty of the crowds."

Madness? Not exactly. Numan signed to Beggar's Banquet (a 'subsidiary' of the enormous WEA conglomerate) who, highly impressed with his work, put him on a retainer. He has concentrated on studio work since mid-'78, recording 'Tubeway Army' in August 1978 and following it up almost immediately with 'Replicas' in January of this year.

cont...

UMAN sits
-lit wine bar
g, sipping a
tal) and
hearsing
for an
He blinks
eyes and
ly, broad
g class'
nthesis to
image he
front cover
my's latest
s'.
t nervous
ure —
hands of
s only the
he's ever
was
fanzine, In
the press
iew
either live
e criticism
een, at best,
het-jobs
hat Numan
rsonal''

ll that,
en and
perhaps
's no art-
h and tends
lacy when
cerebral
usic,
g himself
criticism at
opportunist

his career
''Someone
en sitting
talking
ar for a
t I hadn't
out it. So
nd to learn
d it started

uences (in
der from
the Dave
Monkees,
nd, more
x. The
led him to
sion of
bout five
d a counter-
erent title
the album.
But that's
''

of
ns in the
nk days,
band called
ver two
n a week,
riting
onality led
within the
ame
ple of line-
Tubeway
n Spring

playing
ff. Short,
by stuff''

GARY NUMAN: pic by Mike Stone

doin
pull
night
up a

Stu
Num
synth
Army
over
punk
music

Nu
synth
music
finge
piano
onto
synth
grow
the n
plans
guita

O
publi
In it'
'Mac
mank
to up
meta
Num
origi
name
preda
appea
album

It'
Num
proce
vehem
plagi
that
artist
his w
of ''s
Burro
and U
some
point
speci
album
Finge
Lunc
Repli

''I
every
every
a ban
out o
learn
take
using

''N
Numa
Bowi
just
influe
(inclu
want

''I
singi
are ha
don't
listen
about
living

He
'prete
to off
''whic
rathe
prose
at ho
''in te
nihilis
wanto

Numan doesn't think he was cheating his audience by 'hiding away' in the studio. "There wasn't an audience until we started doing albums. We didn't pull more than five people a night. Now we're building up a following."

Studio work introduced Numan to the use of synthesisers, and Tubeway Army changed virtually overnight from a bunch of punky wavers to a neu musick ensemble.

Numan uses the synthesiser as a non-musician, picking out one-finger tunes on a battered piano and transferring them onto a Mini-Moog. Yet the synthesiser content has grown with each album, and the next album (which he plans to record soon) has no guitars on it at all.

OH YES, *that* quote. It comes from an ecology manifesto published in *Oz* way back In it's original context, 'Machman' refers to mankind's use of machines to upset the ecological metabolism of the Earth. Numan had read the original article and used the name to describe the predatory humanoids appearing in his 'theme album', 'Replicas'.

It's an example of Numan's, er, 'creative process'. Although vehemently denying plagiarism, Numan does say that he relies on other artists to act as a catalyst on his work. His main sources of "stimulus" are William Burroughs, Philip K. Dick and Ultravox. This sometimes extends to the point where he can relate specific books to specific albums. F'rinstance, *"Dead Fingers Talk* and *The Naked Lunch,"* he says, "are Replicas."

"I'm a 'parasite' on everyone, I take things from everyone. I don't go and see a band unless I get anything out of it. If I enjoy a band I learn from them. Then I take it all away and start using it for myself.

"Nothing's original," Numan says, "not even Bowie". Perhaps Numan's just more honest about his influences than others (including Bowie) might want to be.

"I don't see the point in singing about things which are happening every day. I don't want to go out and listen to a bloke prattling on about how terrible it is living on the dole."

He also rejects the 'pretentious' tag, preferring to offer his audience lyrics "which make them think" rather than 'safe' bland prose. 'Replicas' is his guess at how London might be "in ten years time," where nihilism, depersonalisation, wanton violence and rape are norms. "It's the way all things might go," he says, adding, "I'm not worried about it."

'Replicas' seems pretty ambisexual, a blur of genders where gay, straight or human/android sex alternates between the frigid and the callous.

"Everything's getting pretty ambisexual, or asexual, isn't it? Everyone's suddenly bisexual in interviews. All the boys are looking like girls, and all the girls are looking like boys. Not everyone, but in little sects. And that'll spread, I'm sure it will. And one day, everyone will be like worms."

Is he playing games with futureshock images or really envisaging how you'll be at the age of 30?

Think about it.

This, the first interview with Gary Numan in a mainstream newspaper, fed all the others that followed in its immediate wake (and the wake was immediate and full) and, alas, the negativity starts right away with the headline, *Numanoid*, used here in print for the first time, and intended to point a laughing finger. But the insult had a catchy futuristic ring to it and was soon taken up by Numan's fans as a compliment because it happened to chime with the character, or the persona, that Numan was portraying in his songs. The fans' appropriation of the term is rather like taking away a bully's power by laughing in his face. As Gill himself concedes in his follow-up piece, *Superman or Victim?* (published in *Sounds* on October 18th 1980 and reproduced in this book on page 244), Gary Numan's success robbed the music press of their power. He rendered them redundant, literally. In the ensuing decades, the presses would fall and fold in exact proportion to the rise of Numan's critical standing.

The second calculated insult is the tag-line in parenthesis "(serious thing)". In addition to telling us that the writer (and his publisher) had no knowledge that resolute seriousness is a personality trait associated with Aspergers Syndrome (for which they can be forgiven because the article was written in 1979 when the condition wasn't widely understood), that *serious thing* insult tells us that the ethos of the writer and the paper is amateurism. The denigration of Numan's professionalism sets out their stall as defenders of amateurism and sewed the seeds of their own destruction. Lampooning professionalism is a very English characteristic, and a reason why Numan got such bad press in the first years of his fame. Professionalism went against everything that Gill and his ilk adored in music, e.g. the shambolic 'happening' concerts of, say, Joy Division and Fad Gadget, which is not a slight on the abilities or recorded output of the artists - I'm just stating a fact that their gigs, and gigs of the era in general (outside the superstar arena shows) were rarely of a professional standard, i.e. they are characterised as being under-rehearsed, with little if any attention paid to the sound and lighting systems, and often performed whilst under the influence of alcohol. Numan's über professionalism stood out against all that and has always been a defining characteristic that separated him from his peers and which contributed hugely to his success. Gill is the author of several books about Bob Dylan, an artist whose music was so backward looking it was dropped into Sam Peckinpah's great film about Billy The Kid , set in 1881, and it didn't seem out of place. Dylan's live performances have often been touch and go at best, 'which Bob is going to turn up tonight?'.

The professionalism that John Gill witnessed, and which shocked him to the core, and made him a lifelong hater of Gary Numan, isn't mentioned here, but he brings it up in his *Superman or Victim* 'think piece'. He wrote that he saw Gary Numan "bullying his band into line for the rehearsal" for their appearance on *The Old Grey Whistle Test*. He doesn't say what the behaviour consisted of. If it had been outrageous he would have mentioned it in this the first article, but he does concede that it was performance related. Numan had been driven into action to make sure the band achieved the professional standard he had set for the performance.

Additionally, by mentioning that Numan is teetotal in the very first sentence of his *Numanoid* article (start with a shocking fact to grab the readers' attention) tells us that Gill was a heavy drinker, i.e. teetotalism *was* A Shocking Fact to Gill. And it tells us that Gill would doubtless have been more sympathetic towards Numan if, at that rehearsal, Numan had been drunk and shambolic. Lacking a proper professional standard, Gill neglects to mention the importance of the performance that Numan was rehearsing, so I'll do it for him:

It was the very first time that Gary Numan had appeared on television. It was his very first live performance as an electronic musician; the first time he had ever performed without a guitar; and it was his very first live performance for more than a year. And he was twenty-one-years old, i.e. he wasn't a seasoned musician or an established star. This was the biggest night of his whole young life. It was a break or make moment. He didn't want the band to fuck it up. Gill concedes that Numan was nervous (On *The Old Grey Whistle Test* DVD, the producer, Annie Nightingale says Numan never forgave her for laughing at him when he was being sick from stage fright and nerves). So, you have a nervous kid about to make his television debut playing a completely new type of music, with notoriously difficult and unreliable instruments, and showing a steely professionalism to make it go as well as he can possibly can. Oh, and Numan writes in his biography that, when the cameras were about to roll, the fire department decided to throw their weight around and cause some trouble by trying to set fire to Numan's specially built stage set, thus further elevating his difficulties and his stress (another point that Gill forgets to mention). That Gill doesn't openly admire Numan's professional attitude, and in fact calls him a 'bully' is not only crass, and frankly idiotic, but it shows that Gill has no understanding of the requirements of art, nor of the needs of artists performing at the highest level. How would Beethoven have responded to an orchestral player not performing at the very highest standard at a rehearsal? If you were working for Ken Russell and you did not do your job to the very best of your ability you would be sacked immediately (Rick Wakeman told me that on the very first day he worked with Ken Russell, Russell sacked the entire sound crew). Top professionals maintain top professional standards at all times when-they-are-on-the-job. Numan was twenty-one years old, making his first ever TV appearance, and he was acting like a top professional. That is not to be confused with acting like a prima donna. Professionals lose their temper when the behaviour of other people has a negative impact on the work they are doing, particularly if that neglect could reflect negatively on the artist. Prima donna's lose their temper for reasons not connected to the work itself. Gill shot himself in the foot by criticising Numan's professionalism.

I've laboured the point because it is an important one in understanding the culture clash between Gary Numan and the music press in this period.

Getting back to the article, with three insults in less than the first three sentences (including the headline and the subtitle), Gill, in his infamous first sentence, puts 'working class' in commas to describe Numan's accent. If Gill is middle class then that is intended as an insult. In any case, the inverted commas are there to denote that Gill, as a person and as a writer, is hamstrung by a provincial obsession about class, and the commas are used to suggest that Numan is pretentious, i.e. he is not authentically working class. I'm sure that *authentically working class* has never been a requirement for Art and Artistry but it seems to have been a Gill/*Sounds* requirement for praise. In the second article, Gill will call Numan 'an aggressive spoilt kid', which is an even sillier way of saying that he is not authentically working class.

The fourth and fifth sentences of Gill's rant-along are about the negative personal criticism Numan has received so far (Gill is nothing if not hypocritical). He points out Numan's candour and nervousness, states that this is the first interview Numan has given to a professional writer, and then, talking in the third person, and of course leaving us in no doubt that he, Gill, is talking about Gill, Gill says that Numan's candour and inarticulacy *"Lay himself open to vicious criticism at the hands of the opportunist interviewer"* i.e. himself. The problem for Gill is that he thinks he is being clever by taking opportunist and vicious pleasure at Numan's candour and inarticulate re-sponses to questions about "the cerebral aspects of the music", but he's only confirming to us that he has asked the wrong questions.

The candour here that opened Numan up to the vicious opportunism of a crooked opportunist like Gill, is giving Gill the Rosetta Stone of his influences. Gill held the stone aloft and used it to batter him. Drawing ideas from books and music and films and magazines is called living and is a part of being a human being. Every thinking person does it. Every creative person does it, has done it, and will continue to do it (in interviews, Keith Richards is a walking-talking encyclopedia of his right-back-to-the-mud influences). Gill knows that but, because he doesn't like or understand Numan, he decides to trump this 'confession' into a slanderous and calculatingly damaging lie. The damage was immediate. One week later, the other music papers published their interviews with Gary Numan. They quoted Gill and they parroted his false charges. Numan (backed by his record company) should have sued Gill into poverty. Instead he wrote *I Die You Die*, a prophecy that came half true. Numan grew to live and prosper in a castle in Los Angeles, but the weaseling critics and their papers died in their holes.

UK SINGLES

1	1	ARE FRIENDS ELECTRIC, Tubeway Army	Beggars Banquets
2	2	SILLY GAMES, Janet Kay	Scope
3	3	C'MON EVERYBODY, Sex Pistols	Virgin
4	21	GIRLS TALK, Dave Edmunds	Swan Song
5	12	GOOD TIMES, Chic	Atlantic
6	8	LADY LYNDA, Beach Boys	Caribou
7	6	NIGHT OWL, Gerry Rafferty	Electric
8	5	LIGHT MY FIRE/137 DISCO HEAVEN, Amii Stewart	Atlantic
9	4	UP THE JUNCTION, Squeeze	A&M
10	13	WANTED, Dooleys	GTO
11	7	BABYLON BURNING, Ruts	Virgin
12	26	BREAKFAST IN AMERICA, Supertramp	A&M
13	25	BORN TO BE ALIVE, Patrick Hernandez	Gem/Aquarius
14	17	MAYBE, Thom Pace	RSO
15	—	DON'T LIKE MONDAYS, Boomtown Rats	(Ensign ENY 30)
16	14	DO ANYTHING YOU WANT TO, Thin Lizzy	Vertigo
17	15	GO WEST, Village People	Casablanca
18	11	LIVING ON THE FRONT LINE, Eddy Grant	Ensign
19	38	CAN'T STAND LOSING YOU, Police	A&M
20	32	DEATH DISCO, Public Image Ltd	Virgin
21	16	SPACE BASS, Slick	Fantasy
22	22	BAD GIRLS, Donna Summer	Casablanca
23	48	ANGEL EYES/VOULEZ VOUS, Abba	Epic
24	24	MY SHARONA, Knack	Capital
25	34	IF I HAD YOU, Korgis	Rialto

UK ALBUMS

1	2	REPLICAS, Tubeway Army	Beggars Banquet
2	—	THE BEST DISCO ALBUM IN THE WORLD,	Warner Brothers
3	1	DISCOVERY, Electric Light Orchestra	Jet
4	3	LIVE KILLERS, Queen	EMI
5	4	PARALLEL LINES, Blondie	Chrysalis
6	5	BRIDGES, John Williams	Lotus
7	6	I AM, Earth Wind and Fire	CBS
8	7	BREAKFAST IN AMERICA, Supertramp	A&M
9	10	BACK TO THE EGG, Wings	Parlophone
10	13	NIGHT OWL, Gerry Rafferty	United Artists
11	11	COMMUNIQUE, Dire Straits	Vertigo
12	8	VOULEZ VOUS, Abba	Epic
13	9	LAST THE WHOLE NIGHT LONG, James Last	Polydor
14	17	MANILOW MAGIC, Barry Manilow	Arista
15	15	DO IT YOURSELF, Ian Dury	Stiff
16	22	RUST NEVER SLEEPS, Neil Young and Crazy Horse	Reprise
17	16	LODGER, David Bowie	RCA
18	14	THE BEST OF THE DOOLEYS, The Dooleys	GTO
19	—	MADE IT THROUGH THE RAIN, Gerard Kenny	Victor
20	18	RICKIE LEE JONES,	Warner Brothers
21	20	MANIFESTO, Roxy Music	Polydor
22	21	DIRE STRAITS, Dire Straits	Vertigo
23	12	SKY, Sky	Ariola
24	23	OUTLANDOS D'AMOUR, Police	A&M
25	28	THE WORLD IS FULL OF MARRIED MEN,	

NEW NUMAN

IN THE wake of the enormous success of "Are Friends Electric?" and "Replicas", Beggars Banquet Records are re-releasing the first Tubeway Army album, known as "The Blue Album", on August 4. At the same time, they will be making available Gary's first two singles, "That's Too Bad" and "Bombers", as a double-pack retailing at £1.60. All three discs were initially released as limited editions and have not been available for quite some time.

Meanwhile Gary's *new* single, "Cars", should be released about the middle of this month, also on Beggars Banquet. Still no news of a fan club, however.

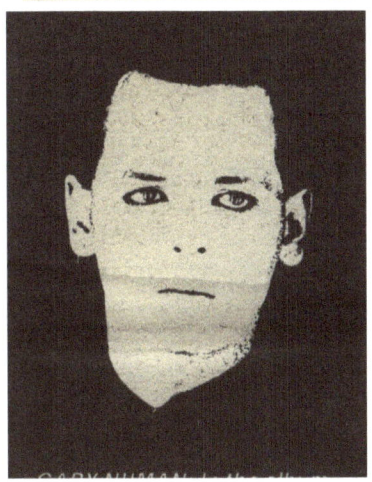

Atco Records presents the spectrum of rock 'n' roll.

Chuck Berry
His new album, "Rock It." SD 38-118
Includes single, "Oh What A Thrill."
Produced by Chuck Berry   Atco 7203

Gary Numan & Tubeway Army
Their new album, "Replicas." SD 38-117
Produced by Gary Numan

On Atco Records and Tapes

25/8/79 Billboard

It seems that *You Are in My Vision* was prepped for a single in France or in Canada. It didn't make it past the production of a couple of very valuable acetates and the mysterious poster on the left. One of the acetates is backed with *When Machines Rock*. The other B-side is the mighty *Replicas* itself. The song was the B-side to *Are 'Friends' Electric?* on the USA release.

55

Confessions of an honest poseur

TIM LOTT takes a liking to Gary Numan – he of Tubeway Army

Readout: Gary Numan is basically Nick Lowe with a printed circuit for creative spark ie he is an electronic thief. He steals his music from Ultravox, his image from David Bowie his ideas from William Burroughs and Philip K Dick, his hairstyle from Rolf Hutter, his eyes from Biba, his concepts from the past, his vision from the future.

And to all this he confesses, which makes him the first honest poseur ever.

GARY NUMAN is not a stupid man, but he **is** innocent. Gary Numan has not learnt how to lie, and this may damage him.

Gary is 21 years old and in command of Tubeway Army, whose 'Are Friends Electric?' is very successful. It sounds just like Ultravox, no bad thing in both our opinions.

Gary wants an image and has been adroit, if obvious, in manufacturing one for himself. He wears — owns — only black clothes. On posters, he looks bleached out and rather starkly romantic, like a dead man who got his mortician mixed up with his beautician.

He tends not to smile for his audience, and generally tries to give the impression of being someone who is aloof, intellectual, perverse, mysterious and completely inhuman.

What Gary doesn't understand yet — and what makes him terribly likeable and outrageously vulnerable — is that image is not only pictures but words. Image encompasses personal information. Learn to lie, boy. Your manager will tell you, if ever you get one.

Can you believe in an android who lives with his parents, loves dogs, hates the city and confesses to once having a residency in a pub singing 'Tie A Yellow Ribbon Round An Old Oak Tree'? Of course not.

The fact is that Gary Numan is really very talented. But knowing the current journalistic idiocy for image, I fear he might be crucified. I don't intend to be first in the queue. 'Are Friends Electric?' is all it takes to win my respect.

Gary is a fidgety person with a genuine streak of shyness which is occasionally discarded when a subject strikes him particularly interesting.

Then he will lean forward with what looks like a giant twitch, speak fast for a few seconds, before settling back again into a sort of defensive crouch.

Of course, he wears black. His hair is not the bleached straw of the album cover but has reverted to its natural dark brown. There are traces of mascara around his eyes.

Mascara.

Gary is not in a hurry to foist his opinions on others, probably because he doesn't seem too sure about them.

This whole thing isn't easy for him.

Gary looks like a technocrat, but is in fact very cautious about machines and the future they bring.

"The Replicas album represents my ideas about the future" he says. "And I suppose it's a bit bleak.

"Violence seems to go hand in hand with technological advance. Over the last 30 years, things have become more and more unpleasant.

"Everyone is getting more leisure time, because of machines. And with all this time on their hands, people are beginning to revert to their primal instincts — that is, being violent."

Gary is drinking a Coke. He got out of the habit of drinking alcohol after he was on tranquillisers for a year as a teenager. I wonder if perhaps he didn't stay on them long enough.

"What do people do for fun now? They go to a disco, have a fight and try to pick someone up.

"Ultimately, because of machines, people are going to wipe each other out. Without work — which all the machines will be doing — there isn't going to be any combined interests any more. People are going to be ultimately controlled by machines.

"People are dominated by them. No way are people going to take over again. Once machines are in, that will be it."

So far, so unlikely.

Gary Numan has probably been reading too much science fiction — Philip K Dick is one of his favourite authors — but of course, that's no reason to hold him in contempt.

In fact, 'Replicas' itself originally started out as a science fiction book called, tentatively, 'Praying To The Aliens'. Gary Numan never wrote it.

But he did formulate a few ideas. The book was to be based around certain society types — Machmen, Crazies and UDs.

Crazies and UDs were elements of society that failed the 'Quota Test' set by Greymen. They were hunted down and disposed of by Machmen, a term stolen from OZ.

Gary, on the cover of 'Replicas' is a Machman, as he is onstage.

"If you're going to sing about something, you've got to look like it so that the audience know what's in your mind.

"The Machman thing is all tied in with the lyrics, the perfect skin and the strange eyes. I wear make up because its no good trying to be a Machman with a spotty face. It's not a question of me just trying to be glamorous.

"People seem to be against anything showy or contrived. I've never understood that anti hero thing. If you get the slightest bit showy then you're labelled pretentious.

"This is showbiz, after all."

Showbiz.

The Tubeway Army started two and one half years ago as a straightforward punk band. Gary's father, who's a driver at British Airways, put up six thousand pounds to help the band with PA and instruments.

He also helps out roadying with the band and lets them rehearse in the house, in Wraysbury, near Slough.

"My dad's fantastic. He gets more excited about the band than I do. When we were on the Old Grey Whistle Test, he was incredibly nervous. If ever I get successful enough I'm going to do everything I can to pay him back. He sank his savings into the band. He loves everything we do.

"I still live at home with my parents. I don't like London. I like my dogs and the peace and quiet."

Dogs.

"All this has happened very suddenly. I can hardly even believe that I've been on television. It just hasn't sunk in.

"In a sense, I've finished now, already. I've done what I've wanted to do. The ambition I have now is to make music that provokes people into thinking things they wouldn't have otherwise."

Tubeway Army was once a nepotistic affair. Apart from Dad putting up the cabbage, Gary's uncle played drums for a while. He has been dropped now. Everybody has been dropped now, from a studio point of view. Gary Numan is now a solo artist, though the name Tubeway Army will remain. The next album will be Army will remain. The next album will be All His Own Work. Of course he is the puppet of his synthesiser ("People are dominated by machines")

Gary is full of admiration for his masters. "Synthesiser" he says," no limitations. They can sound like a rock band or orchestra or Kraftwerk. I really have no idea what can be done with them.

"It does tend to be like operating a machine. You spend more time turning filters up and down than actually playing notes.

"They have far more feeling than guitars. They are probably the most human of all machines. Synthesisers are as variable as humans — different every time you play them. There are an incredible amount of sounds you can get out of them."

Here are some more components to his word circuit.

Past: Gary Numan started his musical career at the age of 16 doing rewrites of Ziggy Stardust songs. To quote him from 'In The City' (a fanzine) "Everyone was a rip off from the tracks on Ziggy Stardust. All the names were changed but apart from that they were the same. I still do that, but I disguise them more."

The first Tubeway Army gig was at The Roxy supporting Mean Street and The Saints.

Now that's what I call a prestige gig.

The first Tubeway Army single was 'Thats Too Bad'. It was.

Present: Gary Numan is sitting in an armchair playing with a paper clip.

Future: Although Gary Numan will work in solitary in the studio, he intends to tour in the Autumn with a band, among which will be the electronics man in Ultravox, who Gary admires almost to the point of indecency.

Gary has some interesting ideas about presenting Tubeway Army onstage (Electronic music is traditionally sterile in live framework)

"We're going to have two 30 foot high pyramid towers for the keyboards, encased in perspex. White light will come from the floor.

"No leads will show. The PA will be white. It's going to be completely monochrome, which is very effective, very powerful.

"And there will be props which I'm going to bring on from time to time. I want to have a plain black perspex cube, lit by a strobe from behind.

"Ideally there would be several of these cubes, radio controlled so that I can do dance routines with them."

Dance routines.

Get this for a set of contradictions: this man has an abnormal, fearful distrust of people, yet wants to entertain them; loathes large crowds, yet wants to play for them; and now has a hit single where his mentors cum heroes Ultravox failed.

The man around which these contradictions revolve is Gary Numan, leader and occasional embodiment of Tubeway Army, the entity which has inspired in critics a surprisingly virulent loathing.

Not often seen or heard, because of his professed reluctance to play live, Numan seemed to attract flak prompted by the glam pose he adopted on the current "Replicas" album sleeve.

Suddenly, though, with a surprising chart entry in "Are 'Friends' Electric," at number 27 and rising (predicted a Beggars Banquet man happily), the aforementioned writers — or their patrons, at least — had to take notice of him, if only to dig out an explanation for its success.

Thus this meeting has been arranged, in a backroom of Beggars Banquet Earl's Court record store — above, it would seem, the tube line, so conversation is punctured by the persistent passing of trains.

TWENTY-ONE and nervous, Numan is strikingly different in appearance from the blond black-clad mannequin of the album sleeve. His hair now dyed black to replenish its health after all that bleaching, he's just returned from a photosession. Far removed from the studied poses of the album picture and his TV appearances, he slips easily into conversation, cracking little jokes, beginning by offering probable reasons for the rise of "Are 'Friends' Electric."

"It was a picture disc, to start with, and I'm sure that got it off the ground. It had already got to 48 by the time we got to do the Old Grey Whistle Test. Maybe we were just lucky with the timing but the press coverage, or the ads at least, did help and the picture disc helped it sell enough to get us on Top Of The Pops — we thought we might get onto Old Grey Whistle Test, but we never thought we'd get onto Top Of The Pops . . ."

Released on May 4, the single's rise has been phenomenally fast. If its success surprises Gary, that's only because, in his master-scheme, the next one ("Cars") was scheduled to be The Hit. Obviously he's not deterred by his upset plans.

Why he's made it, while he acknowledged foremost influence Ultravox failed, he puts down to the efficiency of their respective record companies. Coming under the umbrella of WEA, Beggars Banquet have at their disposal the machinery to make it. The company has a proven record of breaking acts through picture discs. But after its initial flurry of sales, when all the pretty pictures are gone, its success is ultimately down to whether people like the record or not.

ALL YOU ENGLISH SO CALLED PUNX ARE JUST POSEURS!

JILL FURMANOVSKY

Ultravox's failure saddens and mystifies Numan, who displays what is bordering on reverence for the band. He makes no bones, either, about how much he actually got from them, once admitting that most of "Replicas" is based on their music. "Are 'Friends' Electric," though, owes less than other tracks.

"I prefer to listen to 'Slow Motion' (an Ultravox single) to my single, but whether it's better or not I don't know. I'm obviously too close to my own music to make any value judgements about it."

WHAT sets him apart from most other plagiarists is that he admits and acknowledges his sources, pre-empting criticism. Whether that makes you want to listen to his music, rather than to its source, of course depends on you.

Because of Ultravox's perennial unpopularity, Numan claims that nobody even noticed his debt to them until he pointed it out. Writers previously related his music to David Bowie's, although the latter's influence is minimal — or so he says, despite an earlier assertion that when he was 16 he did his own private version of "Ziggy Stardust," basing each of his songs on those from the album.

His regard for Bowie doesn't rise above fan status — David is, he says, up there with Ultravox and Human League in the short list of people he would swallow his fear of gatherings to go see. His music and Bowie's is probably more genuinely linked by common sources, insofar as he was led to writers such as William Burroughs by Bowie's constant references.

Burroughs and science fiction writers like Philip K. Dick provide the acknowledged basis of many of his songs. The Gary Numan writing technique goes something like this: "I don't listen to stuff as a fan, I listen to stuff to get ideas from. I listen to what other people are doing with tones with synthesizers, and . . . who's that other guy's name . . . oh, Vonnegut, but I didn't get a lot out of him, though it was a good book. Breakfast Of Champions. It was funny.

"It was Bowie who got me into Burroughs. There was so much talk about him that I read him to see what all the fuss was about. And it was good. I could see why Bowie relies on him quite a lot . . . well, I don't know, maybe he doesn't. I think Bowie relies on him for actual technique, whereas I rely on him more for words and structures.

"But I don't do anything like cut-ups. I take a line out of a book, and I'd have a lot of lines written down in a notebook. So when I write a song I go through all the lines I have got, I've got pages and pages of them written down, until I find one which is what the song is about and then I cross it out, so I don't use the same line twice. I use those lines to spark off lines of my own."

HIS reliance on others for material obviously gives his work a distracting second-hand feel. But he

Alone in a crowd

Has Gary Numan's acute paranoia touched the national subconscious, or is he just the latest beneficiary of the picture-disc marketing method? CHRIS BOHN talked to the misanthrope who masquerades as Tubeway Army.

hopes his doomladen observations will provoke thoughts in others, as did his sources with him. His third album, set for autumn release, will have a lighter feel, he says, related more to himself than the previous two, with their sci-fi connotations.

"The next one is more statements about things now. Well, not things, but me now. There's a song called 'Observers,' which is about when I go out. I don't go up to people and chat away, I'll just stand in corners and observe people. Basically it's about the fact that I just don't talk to people."

You don't like talking to people?

"Well, yeah, I don't mind talking to people — it's just really weighing people up, deciding whether they are worth me getting to know or not. It's a position I've maintained more in the past few years than when I was younger . . .

"When I was at school, they sent me to a psychologist, because they thought I was a bit random. One day I'd be talking happily, then another I'd be dead quiet, then another I'd fight. I didn't think there was anything wrong with me.

"The psychologists were stupid. The first one was obviously convinced that it was me Mom and Dad, that there was friction at home, and it was affecting me at school and everything. It was a load of cock . . .

"Me Mom and Dad are great. They're so into it. Me Dad sometimes roadies for us. He roadied for us on the Whistle Test, humped away the gear. He's put thousands of pounds, all his life-savings, into us. He drives us to gigs and if there's any trouble at them, he sorts it out. It's fantastic the way he gets behind us. And me Mom . . . she cuts me hair and things like that.

"Before that, they wanted me to have an education, but when I kept getting kicked out of schools and that, they went behind me in this. I was expelled from Grammar school, asked to leave secondary school and college because I didn't have enough hours. Well I did go but never got past the common room . . . table-football, whoo!

. . . table football, whoo!

"I used to read books, but they were the wrong ones, the teachers said. My teacher caught me reading Mickey Spillane, and she hit the roof. I thought it was great, but she went really over the top. She said it was disgusting. She said I must have been raised in the gutter.

"But I've always read books, especially big books; Lord Of The Rings, stuff like that. I've just read The Magus and that was *baaad*. I've always been distrustful of people and that book just about finished me off. I'm not that bad, really, but I don't trust people at all. It's 'Why do they want that? Why do they want to talk to me? What is it about me that makes them want to get friendly with?'

"It's completely the opposite of them thinking that I'm important. It's very hard to explain. They must be after something, not that it's important, but . . . now that I've been on the telly . . . it's not easy, I'm not easy to get on with.

"I don't like crowds at all. I'd rather not walk down the high street or go into restaurants when there's a lot of people about. I don't like being in crowds where you're so close to people that, if anything happens, you can't get away. I don't like being in situations where you're restricted, just in case something happens. I like to see who's near me, so I can look at them and decide whether they're going to do anything or not."

HE begins to talk about how disgusting he thinks people are.

"I don't think much of people, do you? They have two pints and they're looking for someone to hit. They don't get drunk and want to do something nice." (Numan doesn't drink.)

Then why did he choose to start his career in a new wave band? A quick backtrack:

Numan's first band was a more conventional punk affair in which he played guitar and sang, taking an increasingly dominant role. Eventually it evolved into Tubeway Army.

"I did that because it was the only way to get a contract at the

time. Anyway, punk and new wave wasn't violent until the press started to write about trouble. That's when it got violent, when people who weren't punks started going just for trouble."

He handled occasional outbursts of fights by playing right through them, hoping that most people would carry on watching them and not notice the trouble.

About getting his contract: "If I'd started by playing the stuff I'm doing now, I'd never have got anywhere. So I started by playing the stuff they were doing then. Get signed, and then you're in and can do what you like. I enjoyed what I was doing at the time. It served its purpose, and it was good fun, but what I really wanted to do was always in the back of my mind."

With his general contempt "for the race as a whole," why does he bother to try reaching people through music?

"It's very hard to explain. You read all these things, and see the fighting, and you really hate it. But then you see something like a little old man and an old woman driving in their Morris Minor, and they've been in love for 60 years, and you think it's really nice. Then you think, 'Ahhh, it's not so bad,' but as a whole it's pretty shitty."

Yet he's now preparing to put himself back in front of people whatever he thinks of them, with a new band. He wants to go straight to larger halls, colleges, and universities, for which he's preparing a lavish stage set — providing, of course, he can get the finances or know-how together in time for a projected 12 dates in September.

"Well, it is show business. You go onstage so that people can see you. If they just want to listen to you, they can stay at home and listen to records. I'd rather go and see somebody onstage with big lights, towers and little robots moving about than somebody in jeans and an old mac in the back of a pub.

"I think I'll be giving people what they haven't had in a long time by putting on a good show. People seem to have been brainwashed into thinking that putting on a show is very . . . just isn't on, you know. So, I'll put on a show and see how it goes. If they don't like it, I'll stop doing live work again."

New Musical Express   June 9th, 1979

ARMY'S OVER ARNHEM...

Looking through Gary Numan's eyes

THE LIST went something like: 2.00pm — *Jackie*, 2.30pm — *My Guy*, 3.15pm — *Patches*, 4.00pm — *Record Mirror*, 4.45pm — *Smash Hits*, 5.30pm — Paul Morley.

I am part of someone else's blur. For Gary Numan — who is Tubeway Army — the last few days have been a blur of brand new excitement and confusion. His song 'Are Friends Electric' has surprisingly sneaked into the Top 30.

The success went something like this:

The first few singles are pressed as an attractive picture disc, which pushes the single into the lower part of the chart. The single then receives some airplay and, not being especially repulsive, slides a little deeper into the charts. There then comes the invitation to appear on *TOTP*, which coincides with an appearance on *The Old Grey Whistle Test*. The single then strolls into the Top 30. For Gary Numan all this has happened within a month.

Three weeks ago no one wanted to talk to him. Except me. Now there's a queue. And I'm at the end of it.

"I'm enjoying it," Numan admits limply, coughing from the strain of the day's interviews, "and I'm making the most of it in case the single bombs next week. Two weeks ago I was nothing. For two years it's been like that, exactly the same, and then bang! I've been on the telly twice and done half a dozen interviews in a day. It's like being blinded by your own dream really . . ."

We talk in a noisy pub just off Wardour Street in the centre of London. In such surroundings Numan flinches a lot and looks a little worried. Numan dislikes pubs. He's teetotal, and the smoke that wafts all around us doesn't help his cough. He also confesses a dislike for crowds of people.

"I'm over the top paranoid," he explains. Wary, weary eyes set deep into a forlorn face seem to confirm this. His hair is black and threatens to recede. Clothes are black and tight, his boots are button up high heels. He's 21.

GARY NUMAN has been Tubeway Army for two years. His backing personnel has constantly switched and changed: "I'm very intolerant and I get fed up with people easily."

Prior to conceiving Tubeway he spent time with groups on the British Legion circuit, and four or five months in Meanstreet, who appeared on the lamentable 'Live At The Vortex' album — by which time Numan had been thrown out. It's a period he looks back on with distaste.

"Some of the songs from that period I used on my first album. I was attracted to them like old photographs and I just wanted those songs out to show *them*, if nothing else. There's a lot of that in it, a lot of revenge motives all over the place. There's a lot of people who I haven't forgotten who were unkind to me. Now when I'm in the charts and on the telly I sort of smile inside, that they're watching. I'm waiting for them to ring up — 'Oh do you remember me, I used to go around with you'."

I ask Numan what his ambitions were during those Meanstreet days, expecting him to say "I wanted to make my own music". Instead his answer comes quick and wistful: "I want to start my own airplane business. I'm going to buy two Dakotas, paint them up in war colours and do, er, nostalgia trips to Arnhem — you know, where the old paratroppers used to go — and charge them about twenty quid a time. I'd go on the same route as they used during the war. I'm more interested in this than keeping the music going. I don't want to stay in music for too many years.

"I got involved in music because I love everything about it, but now I'm in it you see the other side and it isn't much fun. Not as glamorous and enjoyable as you imagine . . . All this chart and TV thing, it's only fun while it's new and then it won't be long before it's a job and a strain, and when the whole thing becomes too much business then I'd stop."

Wouldn't there be anything seductive in prolonged success?

"No, I'd find it easy to stop because I'm so interested in flying, I'd have another complete love to go into. It's like giving up Raquel Welch and going into Brigitte Bardot, innit?" If you say so.

The original Numan/Army sound was guitar orientated fast rock; aimless and painless. The impressionable Numan constantly altered the sound, absorbing and exploring.

"Tubeway Army have always been a group on the playing side, but not the creative side. The music changes so quickly. If I have an idea, in three months time it's changed. You hear a new album, new ideas, new instruments . . . I mean, somebody bought me a piano a year ago, so I started playing keyboards — and look how much that's changed the music."

Numan's new-found love for keyboards — synthesiser and all things electronic — has deepened to such an extent he plans to drop all guitars from his next LP. The next move is to withdraw all human involvement. Then to fly off into the clouds.

MARGINALLY acquainted with his early work for Beggars Banquet — the singles 'That's Too Bad' and 'Bombers', the LP 'Tubeway Army' — and teased a little by the new LP 'Replicas', I had become intrigued if not intoxicated by the nature of the Numan pursuit. As Numan/Army had developed, and the music had begun to complement the blue-cold Numan world view, which consisted of a series of simple and savage future projections, I began to hear maybe a budding Bowie, or the stirrings of a possible wandering Eno character, or the brother spirit of John Foxx, he of Ultravox, a dealer in adolescent alienation. Wishing to sort out just which pimple Numan was squeezing, I made to interview the man. When I requested the interview Numan was unknown and unfashionable and destined to stay that way, which intrigued me even more, but by the time I came to meet him he was a real chart star, which made me smile.

I still determined to discover his sources, his future route, and how often he grins. He grins quite often, a nervous toothy sort of grin. His main modern musical likes appear to be Bowie, Human League, Kraftwerk and most especially . . . Ultravox. "I think they're brilliant, the best band in the world and no one's realised it!" he enthuses.

I drop the word pretentious into his lap. "I've never understood this pretentious bit, to be honest. As far as I'm concerned it's showbusiness. You put on a show, you dress up, create characters in your songs, you look like the characters you're creating to portray them, so that people can understand the songs better — and then people say 'Oh it's pretentious' just because you wear make-up or whatever.

"Pretentious means making claims of great importance doesn't it? Well, there's no way I'm making claims to anything. My songs are just ideas."

If Numan resents accusations of pretentiousness then he's cheerfully and slyly willing to be accepted as contrived. He had mentioned a fondness for

TUBEWAY ARMY FIGHTS ON

☐ *From page 13*

Jobriath, and I had dropped the word contrived into his lap. "Yeah, but I don't mind contrived things. Cos if something's contrived it shows that someone has gone out and thought about something and worked for it. That's what contrived is. Commendable, isn't it?" The way you say it, maybe.

A picture forms. Mix Ultravox, Jobriath, Biggles and Burroughs, add a dash of mascara and a squirt of childishness, and the dark vulnerable shadow on Numan emerges.

I ask him if he feels some kind of commitment to people who have begun to buy his records, and he's quite taken aback at the idea.

"People shouldn't expect things. If they do it isn't my fault. I make a record and then buy it, but because I make a record they shouldn't have the right to say I've got to make another record.

"I shouldn't have to play live just because I've made a record. I get lots of letters cos I'm not into the street credibility thing. I don't like that whole thing at all, I've always thought of it as a very glamorous business, the whole thing about putting on a show. All the anti-hero punk thing, it went against everything I've ever wanted to do.

"Maybe I'll be able to do the plane business *and* stay in the music business," he eventually decides. So that Arnhem trip business really is serious?

"Yeah, it's serious, it's probably childish . . . But I think there's a very good market for what I want to do.

"You imagine how many people would want to go in an old war plane, for a start just to be in an old war plane, then to actually fly in it, with the war colours, and then to fly the actual route the paratroopers took back in the war in formation with the another one, together across the ocean, low level runs. There must be an incredible market for that."

I'll be first in the queue.

"You go to Blackbush Airport every weekend where I go flying and the aeroplane that does the pleasure flights is going up with six people every fifteen minutes non-stop eight hours a day, so you can imagine what it will be like for what I want to do.

"I'll give it a go. If it doesn't work then I'll still have two Dakotas that I can play with myself. I mean John Travolta's got a Dakota."

Of all the Beggars Banquet oddities — Duffo, Lurkers, Ivor Biggun — Numan is the most endearing, and he's due a few more minutes fame than any of those people. And of the fragile freaks that have happily stained the outer limits of rock over the years, from Jobriath to Kid Strange, he is the most likeable and for whatever reasons the most popular.

But of course he has neither the stamina nor the regularity to drift like a Bowie, flirt like an Eno or even whine like a John Foxx. After our conversation, Numan dons neither goggles and gloves to take off for Arnhem, nor slips into a silver suit to swish into a distant metallic androgynous future, but climbs morosely into a taxi for a ride to the Beggars Banquet shop in Earls Court. A sad figure in black who's suddenly been thrust into the unknown. And tomorrow it's *Melody Maker.*

PAUL MORLEY

THRILLS

A grave situation . . .

Paul Morley pops up on television now and then and seems to be a personable chap. More importantly, he takes his vocation as a music historian seriously, and he's not a bad writer at all, but he did make an absolutely hilarious howler in 1981 when reviewing Numan's *Dance* L.P. for N.M.E. His monumental gaff came because he'd started to believe the nonsense the press were writing about Numan and, in doing so, he lost faith in his own intelligence and inclinations. He wrote, and I'll pause to give you leave to put your hands on your sides to stop them from splitting, (and I'm not making this up), he wrote:

"No one of any worth will be influenced by Gary Numan." *What?!* Oh, sorry, I just coughed up my breakfast. It gets me every time. Time and Prince and Trent Reznor and Frank Zappa and Neil Young and Alice Cooper and Depeche Mode and Snoop Dogg and Jack White and Kanye West, Dave Grohl and Kurt Cobain (who adored the lyrics of *Replicas*), and I could go on and on listing the worthy artists who have drawn from and acknowledged Gary Numan, but I've made my point and I don't want to kick a bright but once unthinking man for spewing out a pot of comedy gold.

Paul Morley you would have made a lesser gaff if, back in 1958, you'd have proclaimed with equal conviction: "Elvis Presley will never play Las Vegas."

LAUGHING ALL THE WAY TO THE BANQUET

FROM SECOND-HAND
RECORD SHOP TO NUMBER
ONE SINGLE AND
ALBUM. THE STORY OF
BEGGARS BANQUET
BY PHIL SUTCLIFFE

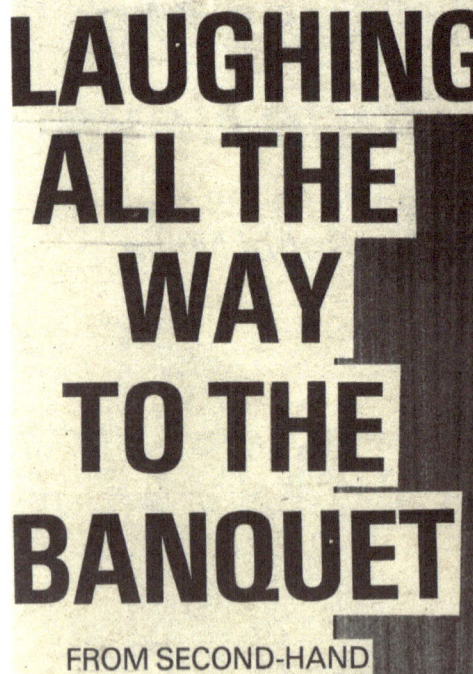

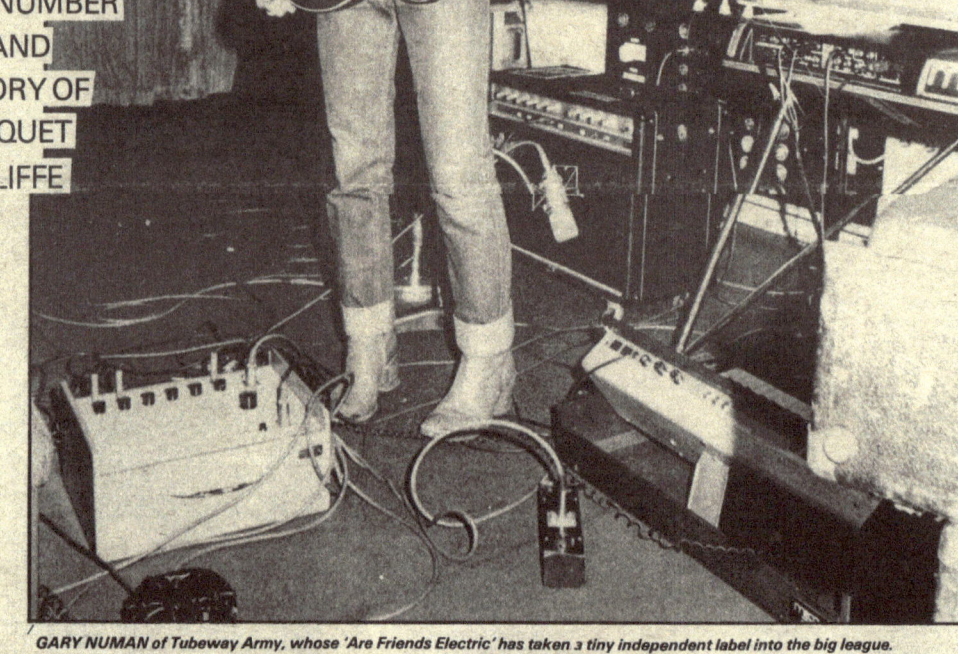

GARY NUMAN of Tubeway Army, whose 'Are Friends Electric' has taken a tiny independent label into the big league.

YOU'VE PROBABLY heard of Gary Numan by now. There's that little matter of being simultaneous No. 1 in the singles and albums charts. But what might have happened was that the first time ever you heard his voice he was singing the jingle to a Lee Cooper jeans TV advert.

Earlier this year the word came down to him through his label Beggars Banquet from WEA, the major company they are licenced to, that they would like him to consider it, or rather would implore him to, no, the managing director even would esteem it a very great personal favour if he would......

"They put me under a lot of pressure," said Numan. "Sending telegrams and telexes. Everyone was sure it would be a hit single and they were probably right. But I didn't want to do it. I thought it was totally wrong. Just to make money. I could see something like that blowing it for the rest of what we wanted to do."

Indeed there is quite a difference in quality between capturing a vast public ('Are Friends Electric?' is the way past 500,000 sales and 'Replicas' heading for 70,000) with self-written -produced and -performed music unblemished by hype or ballyhoo and riding up the charts on the back of the mind-rotting repetition of a TV jingle exploiting a ruthless commercial cycle of song-sells-jeans-sells-song-sells-jeans ad nauseam.

And Numan won. Ultimately of course he could not have been physically forced to open his tonsils against his will but he was vigorously supported, so

that the matter didn't quite reach that Gestapo stage, by Martin Mills and Nick Austin who are the founding fathers of Beggars Banquet. He seems well pleased with the way they handled it, justifying their claims to devotion to their bands' long-term artistic development. But it hasn't always been so rosy between them.

As Martin and Nick readily admit they have crossed swords often, in particular over policy on touring. It seems that when 'Replicas' was ready for release they began to set up a series of promotional gigs, the way record companies will. Arrangements were already under way before Gary heard a word about it. Result: friction.

Gary: "I didn't want to go out unless we had a big show. I don't want to just do what everybody else is doing and I've

never liked playing to a crowd that's only 50 per cent into what I'm doing. That sort of uncertainty really messes me up. Now we can go out with a spectacular show and take the country by storm — I'm sure that's what will happen."

Steve Webbon, now a director of BB management (complexities unravelled later), backed the Numan stand through a lot of shouting and evolved into Gary's 'representative' to the company: "I'd neverthink of myself as 'the manager' but I've ended up translating Gary's wishes to Nick and Martin. The thing is you have to never tell him what to do."

Now the temperamental and business factors have been shaped into a pattern that works for them all. Beggars Banquet has been making records for less

than two years and all concerned are well aware of still being learners amid the infinite variety of the commercial/artistic process.

Episodes like the above have made the Mills and Austin team more and more conscious of the fine-tuned flexibility and strength required to handle such diverse people as Numan, who wants control over everything with his name attached right down to badge design and Press releases, and the Lurkers, managed by Nick, who are happy to have someone else handle all the peripheral details and concentrate on playing.

It has been very much a person-to-person progress so far. But now it could be that change, in the shape of violent success, has them by the lapels and is about to shake them up more than somewhat. For a label

whose chief cause for rejoicing before June had been Ivor Biggun's 'Winker's Song (Misprint)' Tubeway Army's ascension must appear almost as miraculous as was JC's in his day.

When 'Are Friends Electric?' went to No. 1 they got a telegram from their big brothers at WEA saying 'Welcome to the big league.' They didn't know whether to smile or wince. Crucially Beggars Banquet are at the crossroads between retaining their character and approach as an independent and becoming part of the corporate machine......

THOUGH you wouldn't think any such portentous threats hung over them to visit the hub of the BB empire — their original record shop in Earl's

Court. Essence of independent, it's a happy tip where unless I'm much deceived people actually do go in to see their mates, line up a few things (the odd tour, recording studio, you know), and only coincidentally pick up their wage packet at the end of the week.

The office is in the basement where only two people can sit at a desk at a time and the drains stink. If you seek relief in the back room upstairs (formerly the conservatory) it's easier on the nose but conversation is punctuated by the tube which passes by a good six feet from the window. Home of the hits.

Every available surface is covered with scraps of paper bearing names and figures: phone numbers, what we owe them, what they owe us. Tubeway Army's airplay royalties and TOTP appearance fees have introduced a whole new

dimension to their accountancy and Steve and Nick (no calculations) gleefully check their sums to winkle out an extra tenner here and sixty there.

I asked what the present fee for a single spin on Radio One is and they simply didn't know. Stunning. Beggars Banquet as innocents abroad and very appealing with it. They have never employed a plugger and in fact only once sent someone, Press officer Sue, to Radio One. She hated it and never went back.

So there has been nothing spoilt yet. The feeling of the place must be much the same as when Nick finished making the first lot of browser bins for the shop, dropped a stack ofrecords in and they fell straight through on to the floor.

That was in '74 when ex-public schoolboy Austin and Oxford graduate Mills turned their back on respectability to con a bank manager into a loan to set up a shop which (the bit he didn't know) was going to run on the erstwhile 'suicide formula' of buying second-hand records and selling mainly new ones. It was precarious but both being 25 then it made a change from selling pub furniture for his father's firm (Nick) and working on statistics for the reform of the abortion law (Martin).

They had become friends in Oxford where Martin was taking an honours degree in Politics, Philosophy and Economics and Nick was 'training', working for £10 a week in a furniture shop to learn the family business from the ground. As so often applies in many ways it was a partnership of opposites although they found they were born within a week of each other (both about to be 30).

Nick is only just on the right side of chubby, full of public school bounce, even though he didn't stay long enough to learn the snobbery, and verbal in the extreme. Donkeys minus their hind legs are a commonplace on the streets of Earls Court these days. Martin is tall and thin with the forehead and specs to match his academic record and the air of someone who will always say "Now hold on, let's think about this before we take the plunge." Stereotypes, but both agree that's the general outline of their roles.

Well they made the shop work through an arcane stock control system (involving graph paper and a lot of dots) which got round the second-hand trade hazard of becoming a 'dustbin'. High prices for new records made the part-exchange idea even more popular and now they have four shops run on the same lines — that 'Tear Them Down!' message again.

But what was more important to the arrival of Beggars Banquet on the scene was that as a punk and new wave outlet

BEGGARS BANQUET label mates The Lurkers and Ivor Biggun (right).

they attracted everyone with a tape to play and their own single to do. Like Rough Trade, Small Wonder, Bruce's and others around the country they found circumstances propelling them into taking part in the making as well as the selling of music.

They discovered the Lurkers through the rehearsal rooms at their North End Road shop; trying to help them out evolved into fixing gigs and chasing record companies — they found they were in management. But the first rush of punk signings had left the Lurkers in the lurch and nobody wanted to know so they decided to make their own single, 'Shadows' — Beggars Banquet found they were a record company.

T WAS much the same with publishing and promotions. There was a large hiccup when their original distributors, Island, themselves became licenced to EMI who hurtfully took Stiff along but gave the elbow to BB but that was resolved after six months on the brink by the deal with WEA last autumn (an interesting clause preserved their right to eccentricity by allowing for release of non-WEA-approved product though it would be without benefit of their promotion staff and budget).

Their random development probably also accounts for the lack of musical identity in a roster which includes Tubeway Army and Ivor Biggun, Duffo and the Merton Parkas, the Lurkers and pub-rocking one-man-band Johnny G. It's been whatever took Austin and Mills' fancy at the time and their taste has proved decidedly freaky.

That is, on one level they have arrived at absolute zero corporate image, all-good-clean-fun individualism and innocence. On the other, to keep the edifice from laughing itself to fragments, they have become a holding company called Beggars Banquet Communications. And there is a certain similarity between that and the proper title of their ultimate parent, Warner Communications.

Again it sounds like the crack of doom for thinking small, perhaps for thinking at all. Tubeway Army have rammed the Beggars up against the irresistible force of capitalist growth.

Their artists know how

valuable BB's present style is. Gary Numan said: "I'm sure we've got more say over everything from sleeve designs to what songs we use than if we were with a big company." Danny Talbot of the Merton Parkas echoed him: "The advantage is the label's small but it's got big backing. It means we can go in and argue with the top men."

Austin and Mills know it too. Both express deep disgust at the way the majors feed on waste of people and money (though they do see their access to the WEA bureaucracy as one buffer against similar expansion within BB). They say they will plough profits back into the shops rather than futile office space and executive mahogany. Nick: "We are very conscious that we don't want to be run by accountants who will say that we must have bigger shops, bigger turnover, bigger everything, so that you end up with a monster out of control."

But all the indications are that they, like any other businessmen in the UK, will not be able to suddenly rein back development which has so far been pretty much unplanned anyway.

Already Steve Webbon has found himself needing to professionalse by working hard for artists he has no personal enthusiasm for. Shops director Ivo Watts Russell doesn't like the possibility of having to hire staff from outside the circle of friends who have so far given Beggars Banquet its life. Their Ealing shop may be threatened with compulsory purchase and demolition: would they be able to resist continuing the business in a new shopping-centre megastore?

The Merton Parkas show how attitudes are already changing on the music side. Nick described them as Beggars' "first real record company-type signing." Mod is happening so sign some. Not that he isn't passionate about the group — he described them to me as the only live band he'd seen to match the Lurkers which from Austin is the ultimate accolade — but he acknowledges the shift himself compared to the slow and dedicated build-up for Tubeway Army over the last 18 months.

That thinking has carried over into their first release, 'You Need Wheels', a rather pallid piece picked simply because it's a

scooter song. Not that Nick forced the choice on the Parkas. Danny Talbot said: "We did four or five tracks and eventually we all agreed that the one we liked least should be the single because it was the most commercial."

Careerist overrules enthusiast already. I hope it's a mistake and they score with one they realy like next time, but the airplay suggests they guessed right in cash terms though I'd rate Gary Numan's approach for longer life.

Surely this is the first sign of BBbeing trapped into 'never mind the quality feel the speed', a habit difficult to kick especially when you have to keep larger and larger sums of money flowing through the system to finance new enterprises and old. Beggars Banquet operate like a major label in paying their acts regular wages through thick and thin. It's admirable but as Martin Mills pointed out it means a four-piece band costs about £12,000 a year just to keep alive and it would take 30-40,000 albums sold to pay that off which hadn't happened to anyone before Tubeway Army.

And what does success bring? A lot of fun of course. Also the need to find £15,000 up front to launch the Gary Numan autumn tour complete with lights, lazers, robots......

S UCH PRESSURE. How can the company remain its barmy self? Austin and Mills are idiosyncratic but not really out to challenge the system on principle the way Rough Trade do. They are friendly with the Rough Trade, have affection and respect for them. But they see vital differences.

Martin: "In a lot of ways I'd like to be like Rough Trade because things are so simple for them. Make a record for very little, sell a few thousand without promotion and split the profits with the band. But either they don't go anywhere or they sign for a big company and then you lose them. We want to stay with our artists. (loyalty proven so far as much with the Lurkers and Johnny G as Gary Numan.) Though I must say Pete at Small Wonder seems delighted to do his Angelic Upstarts or Punishment Of Luxury singles and then see them taken up by a big

company."

A comparison that suits them far more is the Robert Stigwood Organisation. Gulp. Nick brought it up: "We believe in developing every aspect of the artist together. The records, publishing, management. Robert Stigwood is probably the leading example of all these things working together. We would like to develop on those lines (apoplectic noises from me) — but not get so big of course." Phew, that's all right then. Isn't it?

The aimiable Beggars Banqueteers were even so honest as to give me the number of the one band of theirs they can't somehow hit it off with though they've had some success: The Doll who charted with 'Desire Me' in January. The obvious difference with them is that they have their own manager, Lou, and are therefore at one remove from the label.

Hearing their point of view was like an icy blast of air from that 'big league' and BB's potential future unless they either fall on their faces or man the barricades against growth as no successful record company has managed to do before.

Lou: "With the rest of the bands they have it's a happy family but with us it isn't. It's more a business association. We supply the product. We have arguments the way every band has with its label and then we sort them out and then we row about the next thing.

"At one point they seemed to want to make our singer Marion became a sex symbol, wear dresses and such, but we wouldn't have that. When

"No doubt there will be confrontations always. But as long as the band and I have a say we have only ourselves to blame if there's failure. If you are happy families all the time you are going to be caught off your guard — what you have to do is never trust a record company."

Whither Beggars Banquet, that is the question. Quo vadis? And will it be the blockbusting Hollywood production or the home movie?

Record Mirror, July 21, 1979

RECORD MIRROR

GARY NUMAN
TUBEWAY ARMY

Pic
Andrew
Douglas

Graham
Stevens

Record Mirror, July 21, 1979 17

SMASH HITS

FORTNIGHTLY

June 28-July 11 1979 **25p**

Words to the TOP SINGLES including

**Sunday Girl
The Lone Ranger
C'mon Everybody
Go West**

CHAS 'n' DAVE
EDDY GRANT
PHIL LYNOTT
SKIDS
in colour

GARY NUMAN
FUTURE SHOCK
page 10

OLD SIAM, SIR

By Wings on Parlophone Records

In a village in Old Siam, sir
Lived a lady who lost her way
In an effort to find a man, sir
She found herself in the old UK.

(All the words inside)

The first Gary Numan magazine cover

OH BOY!
GARY NUMAN

gary numan + tubeway army

REPLICAS
mixes + versions

FUTURE SHOCK

If his make up don't sink him, his honesty will. Ian Cranna investigates Gary Numan and the Tubeway Army vision of things to come.

"IT'S BASICALLY what London — or any city really — will probably be like in about 10 or so years time.

"As you get more automatic cars, automatic car-making machines, automatic buses, trains, planes — so everyone that's employed with them has nothing to do, so they go back to basics which revolves round sex, violence and sleeping.

"And everyone will wipe each other out. Gang fights are going to get completely out of hand and there'll be gang battles with guns and everyone will just be destroyed. The machines won't even need to take over — there won't be anyone there to stop them. They'll just carry on running everything like they are now."

The speaker is Tubeway Army's Gary Numan, creator of one of this year's most striking and imaginative hit singles in "Are 'Friends' Electric?"

Gary's is not a pleasant vision but it's the one he's used to create a theme for the first side of his equally good "Replicas" album, now rapidly climbing the LP charts. The songs on the second side are also connected to this theme, but only loosely.

Gary's scenario is a world of personal alienation (hence the song "Me, I Disconnect From You"), run by The Grey Men who impose uniformity by means of the Quota Test. Those who fail the test (Crazies), or who commit a crime (Undesirables or UD's), are destroyed no matter what by hunting humanoids ("The Machman"). That's the creature Gary portrays on the album cover, by the way. Just to confuse matters, he's now dyed his hair black again.

To combat street violence, people are locked in after a certain time and as a deterrent to going out, there's a horrific assortment of violent machines on the loose. ("Down In The Park").

It's also a world where the end of the human race is in sight since boys and girls have now become physically unisex ("Praying To The Aliens"), and

where you now hire your "friends" by the hour ("Are 'Friends' Electric?").

"The spoken part (on the single) is private, about an incident that happened at Christmas. It speaks for itself really," Gary explains, adding that the mysterious S.U. mentioned in the song is a person.

"The rest of it is about the theme, where you can buy friends — you hire them by the hour. They're electric. You ring up and say you want a friend for

something — it can be for sex, for talking, whatever you want — and they'll send one along."

The "friends" are all identical — "a grey man in a long coat, grey hair, smoking a cigarette" — so that nobody knows what you've hired them for.

GARY REALLY believes that something like his cheerless vision (which he originally considered for an unfinished book) will actually materialise, but he's not bothered. He's got his own future all planned out.

Now 21, the quietly spoken South Londoner almost literally does live in a world of his own. A teetotaller — he gave up alcohol after years on tranquillisers as troubled teenager — he spends most of his time indoors away from people.

The start of his musical career owes a lot to his parents' enthusiastic backing. After initial gigs singing standards in pubs, Gary formed a band which ended up being called Mean Street. Internal friction over Gary's monopoly of the songwriting led

For the most part, a cut-and-paste piece pulled from the music broadsheets earlier in the month.

to him being thrown out, so he and the bass player Paul Gardiner formed their own band, The Lasers.

This time Gary planned just to play guitar and to keep in the background in order to gain stage experience. The idea was to form his own band at some future date but it didn't quite work out that way! Gary changed the name (to Tubeway Army), the songs (from punk) and, except for bass and drums, virtually *became* the band.

For the last year and a half he's been with Beggars Banquet (a small record label now marketed by the giant WEA combine), during which time he's put out four singles and two albums. Apart from the current hits, most of them are now deleted but, Gary tells us, will probably be reissued in some form in the future.

It was actually the *next* single that Gary reckoned would be the hit, according to his masterplan. Mind you, selling records isn't everything in Gary's eyes. His great ambition, would you believe, is to fly old soldiers back to old battle sites in veteran planes along the actual routes the war fighters took! Bizarre, right? But Gary reckons there's a market for it, so it's in the plan.

FLYING LESSONS are one of the few things that Gary Numan will venture out of doors for. The rest of the time he spends inside: working painstakingly over every single note in his songs, learning about record production, watching TV and listening to records for — by his own admission — ideas to steal.

For Gary Numan is probably the music business's most honest thief. He freely gives away influential information that others would do their best to conceal, for instance that his futurist scenarios are borrowed from other visionary authors like William Burroughs (through David Bowie) and Philip K. Dick.

Though you might think it would be Bowie who most influenced Gary's grippingly eerie music, Gary readily volunteers the information that it's — wait for it — *Ultravox* that he steals from!

Ultravox, in case you missed them, were basically a sound, distinctive little rock band of a couple of years back but one who had unhealthy leanings towards glam posing and pretending to be weird. Eventually they ended up so pretentious and stilted that nothing about them rang true, so it's small wonder they never caught on. And they weren't half as good as Tubeway Army.

So why idolise such a hopelessly contrived band like Ultravox, Gary?

"What's wrong with being contrived?" For the first time Gary becomes really animated. "*I'm* contrived! The whole way I look is contrived. The lyrics are contrived — they're about

something, they're thought about. That's what contrived means. There's nothing wrong with being contrived!

"It's show business when you build up an act," he continues heatedly. "The very fact of building up an act is contriving something you want to give to a public. There's nothing wrong with it. That's what show business is all about, putting on a show!"

He's mostly right, of course, but such reminders of harsh reality tend to be pretty unwelcome in the dream world of rock'n'roll. It simply isn't *done*, my dear.

Gary Numan's painful honesty about his unfashionable influences and opinions will probably get him slaughtered in the image-conscious music weeklies once his novelty has worn off. After all, they like their illusions preserved as much as anybody.

It all leaves Gary Numan in the odd position, as has been said elsewhere, of being the first honest poseur.

AND WHAT of the future? Well, any new recordings will now be released under his own name. Since the band haven't played live for a year ("Whistle Test" excepted) and since Gary virtually did everything anyway, that seems a logical step.

All that's planned in the way of tour dates (since Gary doesn't like live work) is a brief tour of 12 dates, probably in September or October. The band, Gary tells us, will consists of two keyboards, guitar, bass and drums as well as himself. He'll do some keyboard and guitar work but will concentrate mainly on singing. We gather that the show will also probably be pretty spectacular.

Oh and that Lee Cooper TV advert — you probably know by now that Gary didn't do anything except sing on it, but how had he come to do that?

"Somebody was playing the first album in the publisher's place," Gary smiles, "and Ronnie Bond — who did the advert — he just heard the voice and decided it suited his advert. So he rang up Beggars and they rang up me and we did it. It was just like one of those Hollywood films!"

That's showbiz for you.

I have nothing but gratitude for Martin Mills. He's been fantastic, a brilliant businessman. He steered that company through thick and thin. It's a very powerful company. When I started, there was only four of us on the label, it was like a little family. I've never found that again, with all the other labels that I've been with, they've never had that same vibe. The Beggars Banquet subsidiaries 4AD and XL have it now. It was such a lovely way to start out, we were all learning. Martin ran a record shop but he hadn't had any success as a label so we were all basking in that early success together. It was an amazing time. I wish I could have enjoyed it more when it was happening. The trouble was I was already worrying about what I was going to do next. I was only half enjoying it.

Classic Pop, Feb 2015

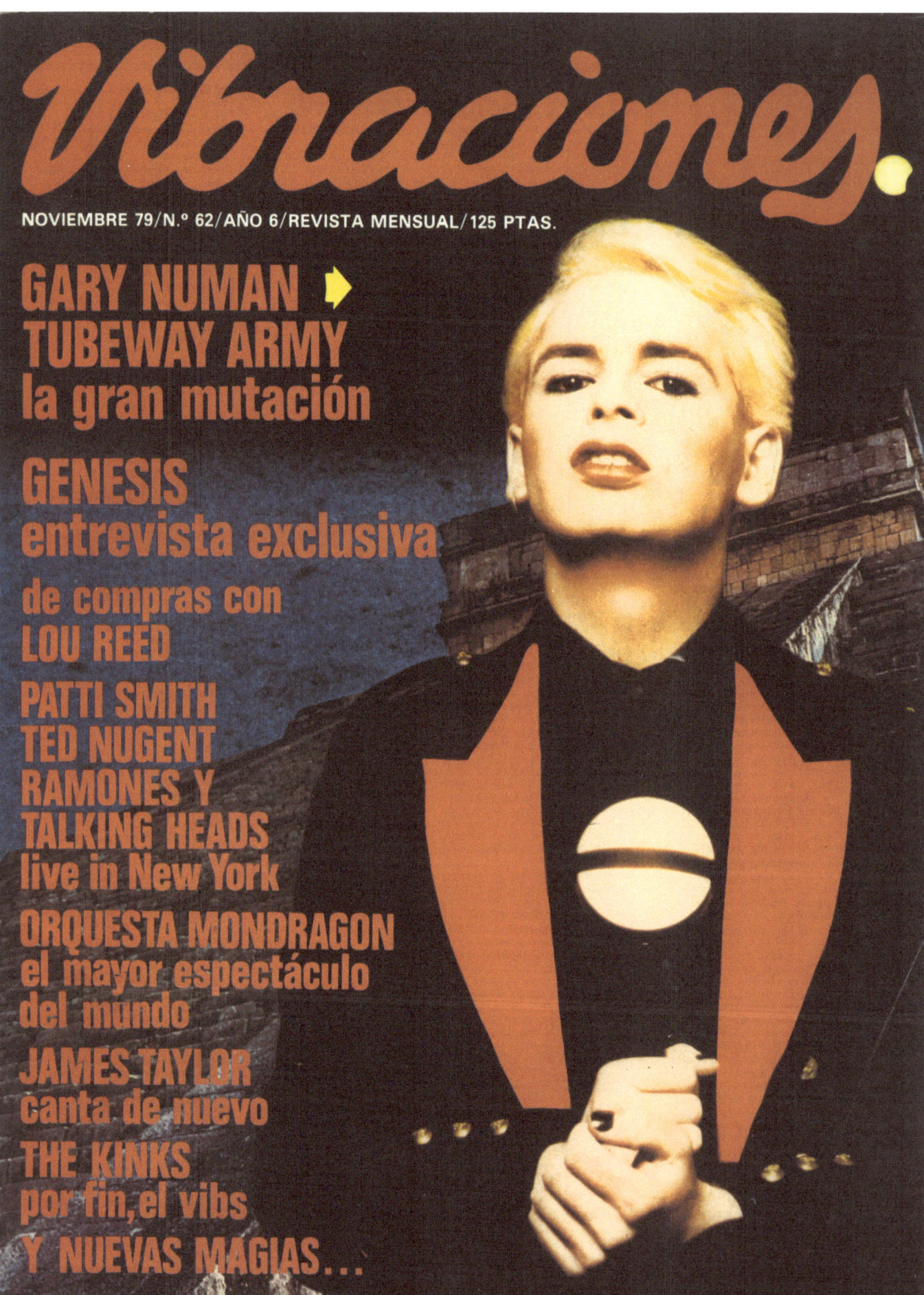

Vibraciones.

NOVIEMBRE 79/N.º 62/AÑO 6/REVISTA MENSUAL/125 PTAS.

GARY NUMAN
TUBEWAY ARMY
la gran mutación

GENESIS
entrevista exclusiva

de compras con
LOU REED

PATTI SMITH
TED NUGENT
RAMONES Y
TALKING HEADS
live in New York

ORQUESTA MONDRAGON
el mayor espectáculo
del mundo

JAMES TAYLOR
canta de nuevo

THE KINKS
por fin, el vibs
Y NUEVAS MAGIAS...

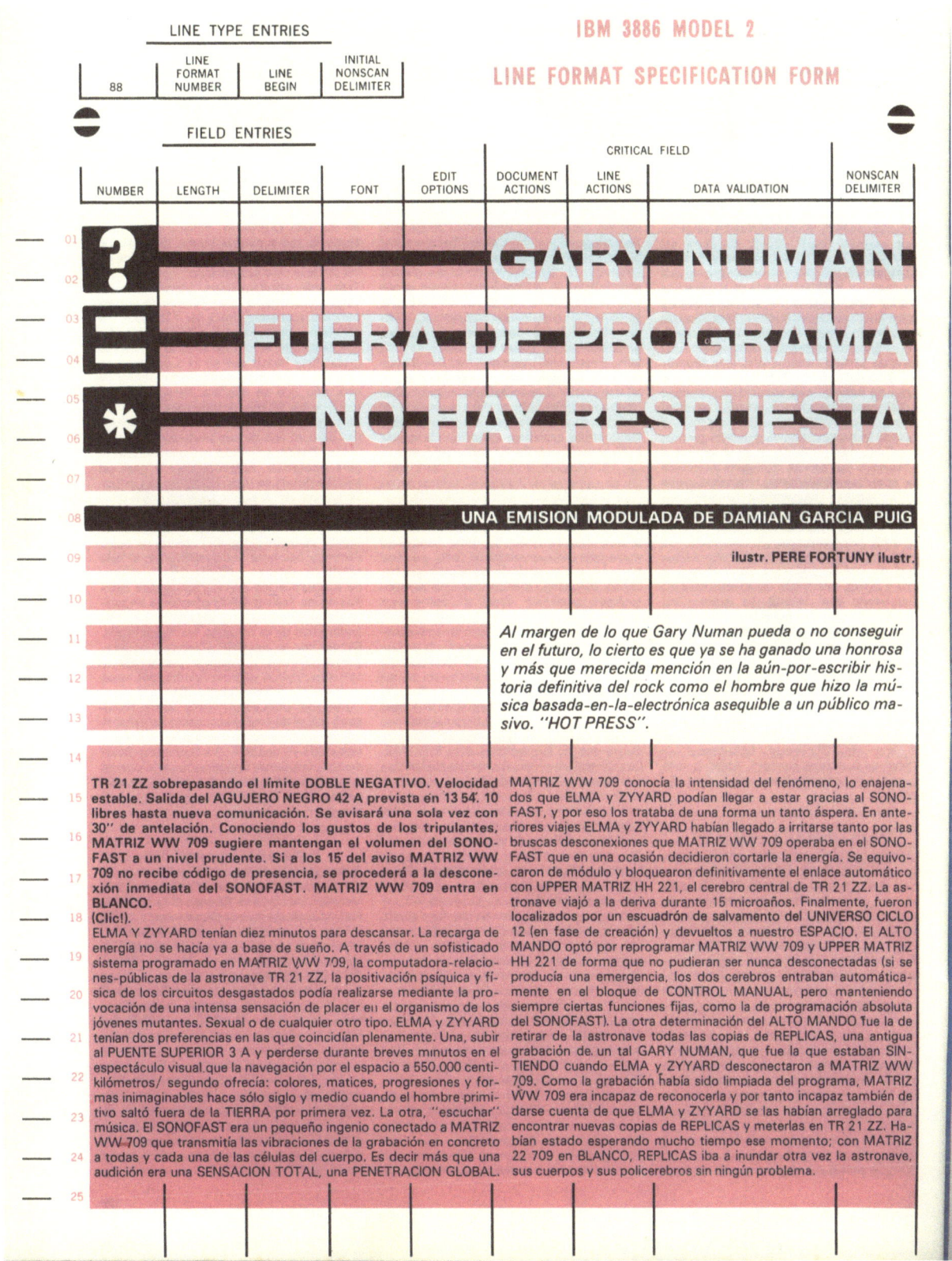

LINE TYPE ENTRIES

| 88 | LINE FORMAT NUMBER | LINE BEGIN | INITIAL NONSCAN DELIMITER |

FIELD ENTRIES

CRITICAL FIELD

| NUMBER | LENGTH | DELIMITER | FONT | EDIT OPTIONS | DOCUMENT ACTIONS | LINE ACTIONS | DATA VALIDATION | NONSCAN DELIMITER |

GARY NUMAN
FUERA DE PROGRAMA
NO HAY RESPUESTA

UNA EMISION MODULADA DE DAMIAN GARCIA PUIG

ilustr. PERE FORTUNY ilustr.

Al margen de lo que Gary Numan pueda o no conseguir en el futuro, lo cierto es que ya se ha ganado una honrosa y más que merecida mención en la aún-por-escribir historia definitiva del rock como el hombre que hizo la música basada-en-la-electrónica asequible a un público masivo. "HOT PRESS".

TR 21 ZZ sobrepasando el límite DOBLE NEGATIVO. Velocidad estable. Salida del AGUJERO NEGRO 42 A prevista en 13 54'. 10 libres hasta nueva comunicación. Se avisará una sola vez con 30'' de antelación. Conociendo los gustos de los tripulantes, MATRIZ WW 709 sugiere mantengan el volumen del SONOFAST a un nivel prudente. Si a los 15' del aviso MATRIZ WW 709 no recibe código de presencia, se procederá a la desconexión inmediata del SONOFAST. MATRIZ WW 709 entra en BLANCO.

(Clic!).

ELMA Y ZYYARD tenían diez minutos para descansar. La recarga de energía no se hacía ya a base de sueño. A través de un sofisticado sistema programado en MATRIZ WW 709, la computadora-relaciones-públicas de la astronave TR 21 ZZ, la positivación psíquica y física de los circuitos desgastados podía realizarse mediante la provocación de una intensa sensación de placer en el organismo de los jóvenes mutantes. Sexual o de cualquier otro tipo. ELMA y ZYYARD tenían dos preferencias en las que coincidían plenamente. Una, subir al PUENTE SUPERIOR 3 A y perderse durante breves minutos en el espectáculo visual que la navegación por el espacio a 550.000 centikilómetros/segundo ofrecía: colores, matices, progresiones y formas inimaginables hace sólo siglo y medio cuando el hombre primitivo saltó fuera de la TIERRA por primera vez. La otra, "escuchar" música. El SONOFAST era un pequeño ingenio conectado a MATRIZ WW 709 que transmitía las vibraciones de la grabación en concreto a todas y cada una de las células del cuerpo. Es decir más que una audición era una SENSACION TOTAL, una PENETRACION GLOBAL.

MATRIZ WW 709 conocía la intensidad del fenómeno, lo enajenados que ELMA y ZYYARD podían llegar a estar gracias al SONOFAST, y por eso los trataba de una forma un tanto áspera. En anteriores viajes ELMA y ZYYARD habían llegado a irritarse tanto por las bruscas desconexiones que MATRIZ WW 709 operaba en el SONOFAST que en una ocasión decidieron cortarle la energía. Se equivocaron de módulo y bloquearon definitivamente el enlace automático con UPPER MATRIZ HH 221, el cerebro central de TR 21 ZZ. La astronave viajó a la deriva durante 15 microaños. Finalmente, fueron localizados por un escuadrón de salvamento del UNIVERSO CICLO 12 (en fase de creación) y devueltos a nuestro ESPACIO. El ALTO MANDO optó por reprogramar MATRIZ WW 709 y UPPER MATRIZ HH 221 de forma que no pudieran ser nunca desconectadas (si se producía una emergencia, los dos cerebros entraban automáticamente en el bloque de CONTROL MANUAL, pero manteniendo siempre ciertas funciones fijas, como la de programación absoluta del SONOFAST). La otra determinación del ALTO MANDO fue la de retirar de la astronave todas las copias de REPLICAS, una antigua grabación de un tal GARY NUMAN, que fue la que estaban SINTIENDO cuando ELMA y ZYYARD desconectaron a MATRIZ WW 709. Como la grabación había sido limpiada del programa, MATRIZ WW 709 era incapaz de reconocerla y por tanto incapaz también de darse cuenta de que ELMA y ZYYARD se habían arreglado para encontrar nuevas copias de REPLICAS y meterlas en TR 21 ZZ. Habían estado esperando mucho tiempo ese momento; con MATRIZ WW 709 en BLANCO, REPLICAS iba a inundar otra vez la astronave, sus cuerpos y sus policerebros sin ningún problema.

GARY NUMAN WAS NO RESPONSE PROGRAMME "Regardless of what Gary Numan may or may not get in the future, the fact is that he has already earned a well deserved and honorable mention in the yet-to-written definitive rock history as the man who made music based on electronics accessible to a mass audience." "... ELMA And ZYYARD had ten minutes to rest. Recharging energy is no longer based to sleep. Through a sophisticated system scheduled by MARTIZ WW 709, the public relations computer of the spacecraft, TR 21 ZZ, the mental and physical cleansing of worn circuits could be made by the provocation of an intense feeling of pleasure in the body of the young mutants. Sexual or otherwise... The other determination of HEADQUARTERS was to withdraw from the spacecraft all copies of REPLICAS, an old recording by GARY NUMAN, which E & Z played when they were feeling disconnected from MARTIZ VN. As the recording had been wiped, VW MATRIX 709 was unable to recognize the programme and therefore also unable to realize that E&Z had managed to find new copies of REPLICAS and put them in the spaceship TR 21 ZZ. ...BLANK, REPLICAS is going to flood the ship again, without bodies and without police reports and without any problem."

TOTALES

**/?/ GARY NUMAN
/ = / PRIMEROS DATOS EN-
TRANDO EN PROGRAMA**

NOMBRE: *Gary.*
APELLIDOS: *Numan.*
(Desconocemos si posee otra u otras denominaciones, incluso si es ese su nombre verdadero).
FECHA DE NACIMIENTO: *Desconocida.*
(Por su aspecto no supera los 25 años).
LUGAR DE NACIMIENTO: *Islas Británicas.*

(Londres, posiblemente).
DOMICILIO FISICO: *Londres.*
DOMICILIO MENTAL: *Algún punto desconocido del espacio. (Seguramente más allá de nuestro SISTEMA).*
SEXO: *Macho.*
(Sólo de nacimiento. Su ambigüedad andrógina y mutante lo sitúa dentro de una clasificación desconocida, pero de alguna forma intuible).
PROFESION: *Artista.*
(Músico, concretando un poco más. Galácticamente famoso por sus descubrimientos en el campo del rock electrónico. Logró convertirlo en algo asequible a todas las mentes. Totalmente desligado ya de lo que se dio en llamar cultura del LSD. Rompió su decadencia, borró su siniestrismo y lo convirtió en algo sentimentalmente ordenado, modulado, cadencioso. Futurista. Influencia reconocible más cercana: David Bowie —para datos al respecto programar /?/ DAVID BOWIE—. Egocéntrico. Narcisista. Asumió su decepción ante el mundo que le rodeaba y le dio forma de concepto artístico positivista. Los textos de......

el futuro. Hilvanándolos en el más sugerente de los sonidos logró exorcizarlos).

PRODUCCION: Tubeway Army / 1979/ *Beggars Banquet/ WEA/.*
"Replicas"/ 1979/ *Beggars Banquet/ WEA/.*
"The Pleasure Principle/ 1979/ WEA/.
(Y algunos singles de éxito).
DECLARACIONES DEFINITORIAS: "Siempre he querido ser famoso y rico, pero haciendo algo por lo que mereciese la pena llegar a ese punto. Escribo lo que quiero escribir y espero que eso me haga famoso, pero nunca dejaré que el dinero o cualquier otra cosa condicione lo que hago. "Utilizo los sintetizadores para crear efectos ambientales, no sonidos efectistas, para darle a las canciones rock un nuevo concepto rítmico. "Me interesan las melodías, no los mensajes."
FUTURO: Incierto.
(Declara que posiblemente abandone el campo de la música en tres o cuatro años).

**/?/ GARY NUMAN-ESPAÑA
/ = / AVISO IMPORTANTE**

De momento en España se ha editado uno solo de los tres LPs que Gary Numan ha puesto en circulación en este año: "Réplicas"/ Tubeway Army (Hispavox). El disco es maravilloso, envolvente. Te atrapa y se convierte en un vicio inocuo. Limpia las neuronas y las pone en otra onda. Es una obra inesperada. Cuando todos presentíamos que nadie iba a ir más lejos en los sonidos electrónicos que Eno, cuando el rollo de Tangerine Dream había entrado en la fase de aburrimiento letal, Gary Numan revitaliza el asunto haciéndolo tremendamente sencillo. Como el huevo de Colón. La pieza que faltaba, algo tan evidente que nadie acertaba a descubrir. Un iluminado arranque de inspiración. Sólo me atrevo a aconsejarte que des ese "trip", que te metas en él. Verás como el rock vuelve a parecerte la más excitante de las aventuras. Olvídate de las viejas momias, regálaselas a tus padres, que por algo han de empezar. Ya somos lo suficientemente mayorcitos, ya hemos navegado por estas aguas lo bastante como para atrevernos a saltar sin traumas estúpidos a la nueva galaxia que te propone Gary Numan. Bienvenidos al futuro (Vibraciones 61-SCOPE)

REPETICION DE SECUENCIA/REPETICION DE SECUENCIA/REPETI-

REPETICION DE SECUENCIA/REPETICION DE SECUENCIA/REPETI-

REPETICION DE SECUENCIA/REPETICION DE SECUENCIA/REPETI-

REPETICION DE SECUENCIA/REPETICION DE SECUENCIA/REPETI-

REPETICION DE SECUENCIA/REPETICION DE SECUENCIA/REPETI-

COBOL-PROCEDURE

TAREA | LOTE | FECHA

NOMBRE COMPILACION
NIVEL
SELECCION
TAMANO REGISTRO
ESTADISTICA PULSACION-HORA
Traducción
Rell Reg
Relleno Bloquecinta
TIPO
FACTOR BLOQUEO
NOMBRE PROGRAMA DE ETIQUETADO
FECHA

☐ FORMATO
☐ TABLA
☐ ETIQUETAS
☐ SUBPROGRAMA
☐ COMENTA

"GARY NUMAN - SPAIN / IMPORTANT ANNOUNCEMENT So far Spain has had one of the three LPs Gary Numan has released this year: *Replicas*. The disc sounds wonderful, surround. It grabs you and becomes a harmless vice. Cleans neurons, it acts on another wave. It is an unexpected work. When we all sensed that no one was going to go further in electronic sounds than Eno, when the roll of Tangerine Dream had entered the phase of lethal boredom, Gary Numan revitalizes the matter by making it extremely simple. Like the egg of Columbus, the missing piece was something so obvious that nobody else was looking in the right place to discover it. An illuminating start of inspiration. I dare you and advise you to get into this 'trip'. For the truth is that it makes rock again seem the most exciting of adventures. Forget the mummified singers adored by your parents, you have to start something. We are already sufficiently older children, we have navigated these waters enough to dare to jump without stupidity to the new galaxy offered to you by Gary Numan. Welcome to the future."

The Catalonian journalist, Damián Garcia Puig, deduced in 1979 (decades before Puig's British counterparts) that Gary Numan revitalised rock music by moving it forward instead of looking backwards. He says Numan did this by cracking the Enigma Code of electronic music for the masses. Eno and Tangerine Dream failed because they thought the answer lay in *complexity*. Numan proved that the answer was *simplicity*.

'Veteran British rock bands alive and well.'
by John Rockwell; *New York Times, 14/9/79 p11*

THE Who's presence in town is a reminder that there are other veteran British rock bands, in greater or lesser states of togetherness. The Rolling Stones are winding up a new album... And Led Zeppelin has just released its first studio album in more than three years... The album comes in six different covers, each depicting part of the same scene and each hidden by a brown outer wrapping so you can't see what you're buying. It's hard to imagine that even Aleister Crowley, the supposed guru of Jimmy Page, the guitarist, could have been that diabolical. In any event, the music is prime Led Zeppelin ... its typical willingness to vary hard rock with folkish and exotic strains and the flashy virtuosity of Mr. Page still count for something. Not enough to rank them with the Who, to be sure. But something.

Speaking of veteran British bands, there are the Beatles. More precisely, there aren't the Beatles, but there are seemingly unstoppable maudlin public appeals for their reunion, or other reminders of their existence. One can't let the Beatles themselves off the hook on this one, to judge from John Lennon's recent full-page ad in this newspaper trumpeting his need for privacy. But Sid Bernstein's full-page "Appeal to John, Paul, George and Ringo" in last Sunday's *The New York Times* was a new extreme. Perhaps, one day, the band may get together again... But Mr. Bernstein must already have extracted every inch of mileage from his association years ago with the Beatles, when he promoted concerts by them in the mid-1960's. Maybe he's a sincere man. But his sensibility seems closer to Las Vegas charity marathons than rock-and-roll. It's enough to make any self-respecting Beatle cringe.

There are younger British rock bands with new record releases as well — two electronic and artsy, two raw and political and all four less popular but fresher than the veterans. Gary Numan and Tubeway Army are an electronically colored art-rock band that has won considerable success at home but hasn't yet made much of commercial mark in this country. (What with Subway Sect as well as Tubeway Army, the British seem to be taking the whole notion of underground rock rather too literally.) The band's *Replicas* album, released in this country on the Atco label, offers weird synthesizer effects and fashionably androidal songs and vocals over an accessibly rocking rhythm section. Not that important, maybe, but appealing in its way.

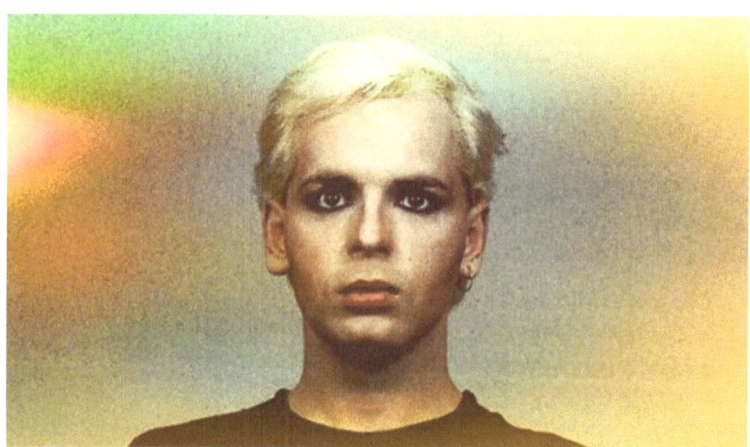

COULD YOU BE TRUSTED WITH GARY NUMAN?...TURN TO PAGE 16!

Sting:"A lot of groups have an image that is very hard to adhere to, like the stony-faced idol who can never be approached. I think Gary Numan has this, and it looks great at times, but how long can you keep it up? It's not long before people are sick of it. We get up on stage end we laugh a lot and we tell jokes and we banter with the audience, and I feel very natural. I feel very ordinary in fact. I think that will stay longer than the cold unapproachable icon. That's attractive for a short time - unless it changes all the time, like with Bowie, which is fascinating, it's a work of art. But there's a lot of pressure on him. He can do it because he's a very clever man. We don't have that problem. We're just ourselves." *NME, 1/4/80*

Tubeway Army
Replicas
BEGGARS BANQUET, 1979

Blondeness may have been pop shorthand for glamour, but it found a colder meaning around punk's occasional appropriation of Nazi imagery. Gary Numan wore black shirt, webbing and bleached hair in imitation of some futuristic replicant but the image was powerful, adding conviction to his electronic paranoia pop. Replicas, his second album (the first had guitars) imports Kraftwerk to some municipal dystopia, and Numan's robot voice reduces peroxide to its chemical formula. Like Toyah, he changed hair colour between albums.

Best Tracks Down In The Park, Are 'Friends' Electric?, Me! I Disconnect From You

Blondest Moment The unsettling, zombie imagery of Down In The Park ("You wouldn't believe the things they do")

Numan Leads Conquering Army
Briton Scores Double-Headers For Beggars Banquet

Billboard, 6 Oct 1979

By NICK ROBERTSHAW

LONDON—Double first in industry charts are like holes-in-one in golf, few and far between, mostly the province of the star names.

When the artist in question turns *out to be an unknown newcomer* like Britain's Gary Numan, recording for a minor (albeit WEA-distributed) U.K. label like Beggars Banquet, then the industry has to sit up and take notice.

That was the situation here in mid-July, when Numan's Tubeway Army topped the album best-sellers with "Replicas," and the singles charts with "Are 'Friends' Electric?"

Only 10 weeks later, he did it again, when "Cars" took over as the nation's No. 1 45, and "The Pleasure Principle" as the top album. It's a further indication of how sudden and substantial Numan's breakthrough has been that "Replicas" and his first album, reissued, are still strongly placed in the charts.

The sales action is not confined to Britain, either. His name has so far appeared on French, German and Dutch charts, and on Billboard's U.S. Top LPs & Tape listings, where "Replicas" is climbing.

Neither artist nor label are cast in a conventional mold. Rather, they're products of the new wave upheaval *in this market,* a time when hundreds of bands and retailers began to realize that they could take the business of producing and marketing records into their own hands. Numan's success typifies that shift of initiative away from the establishment.

Beggars Banquet itself started out as a West London retail store, trading new albums for old back in 1974. It was run by an Oxford graduate and an ex-public (that's private in Britain) schoolboy, Martin Mills and Nick Austin respectively. Trade prospered; today, there are four stores run on the same lines.

*At the same time, like other retail-*ers specializing in punk/new wave, the shop found itself beginning to help out some of the bands that came in with tapes to play and ambitions to make their own singles.

One such was the Lurkers, whose August 1977 single "Shadows" was the first release from the newly formed Beggars Banquet Records. The current roster of eight acts shows a markedly eccentric a&r inclination and for a while the label's only chart success was Ivor Biggun's novelty number, "The Winker's Song." Gary Numan changed all that.

The consumer press, initially lukewarm when not actually hostile, described him as an "honest poseur." He dresses in black, dyes his hair, scowls. His music is futuristic rock, latterly synthesizer-oriented, with lyrics revolving around robots, clones, aspects of a gloomy technological future.

Numan himself makes great play of unashamed plagiarism. Many of his ideas, he says, come from other people's songs. He cites Bowie, Kraftwerk, Eno and punk band Ultravox as prime sources.

From the outset, he has been an artist who demands full control over every aspect of his career. Beggars Banquet and licensor WEA tried to have him release as a single his performance of a television jingle for Lee Cooper jeans, doubtless hoping to repeat David Dundas' success with "Jeans On." Numan refused, arguing it would jeopardize all he wanted to do.

When "Replicas" was release-ready, the label wanted promotional gigs. Numan refused. Aside from tv *appearances on rock shows* "Old Grey Whistle Test" and "Top of the Pops" he has played no live concerts in more than a year. He makes no bones about being afraid of uncommitted audiences and only now, *when success guarantees crowd en-*thusiasm and finances a spectacular stage show, has he agreed to tour.

Even before Tubeway Army's first chart entry, he wanted to drop the name. The group was a fluid three-man line-up disguising *what was ob-*viously very much a one-man show, but at least it had begun to mean something to the public. Numan said frankly he preferred fame as a solo star. "Cars" and "The Pleasure Principle" both appear under his own name.

What gives Numan his present golden touch is not clear. Poor press,

(Continued on page 66)

no live gigs, comparatively little airplay—Beggars Banquet has no radio promotion staff; he hardly seems to touch any of the essential marketing bases. On the other hand, press coverage, though unenthused, has been extensive, advertising has been considerable and the combination of Beggars Banquet's astute iconoclasm with the more conventional expertise of WEA has proved a powerful alliance.

Martha Mills describes the deal as: "As good as we could possibly wish for." Originally the label was distributed by Island, till Island itself went to EMI, which opted to drop Beggars Banquet. The WEA deal was inked last fall, complete with "eccentricity clause" allowing the label to release non-WEA-approved material, without benefit of the major's promotion.

Beggars Banquet has one or two overseas deals predating WEA: with CNR in Holland, and Aves in West Germany, for instance. In America, a special relationship has developed with Atco. Mills comments: "We're very happy with them. Doug Morris is a very respected figure; it's a good label to be with. Now the intention is for Beggars Banquet become a custom label, and we are looking into the possibility of having our own people, our own setup there, maybe early in the New Year."

It is by no means a one-act label. Seven Beggars Banquet signings have released singles; six have had U.K. chart entries. But it is the sudden volume of Numan's sales—gold single, gold album, one of each silver going gold all in the space of a summer—that has turned it into a significant industry force. Observers wonder whether its fresh, astute style of operation will suffer from large-scale commercial success, but there is no question of holding back. Mills and Austin will push hard for international success, and Numan is the spearhead.

A 15-date U.K. tour is currently in progress. When it ends, Numan flies to the States for promotional appearances, and if the promise of "Replicas" is fulfilled, there will be a U.S. tour in the New Year.

It will be interesting to see how commercial pressures are reconciled with the label's alternative strategies and with Numan's clear determination to control his own destiny. Still only 21, he is no easily manipulated record biz innocent. He made this clear after signing his first contract, when he said: "If I'd started by playing the stuff I do now, I'd never have got anywhere. Get signed, and then you're in and can do what you want."

Numan in 1979 with the car his record company gave him as a present. "I've made money. I'm not ashamed of that. I'm not a true blue Tory, but I'd rather drive a Ferrari than a Mini."

Robert Ellis

Daniele Baldelli: "Until 1978, disco was a good sound. But then they started to mass produce records, and it became different. It wasn't as beautiful as before. But I think Gary Numan, Depeche Mode, Klaus Schulze, Brian Briggs, Jean-Michel Jarre, Phil Collins, Mike Oldfield or Sky Records—they didn't make music for the dance floor; they made music just to make music. So this is how music came to me, and once I had it, I played it in the Cosmic club." electronicbeats.net

RM 21/7/79

NUMAN'S LOOMIN'

IN DEFERENCE to our female readers (a small, but loud mouthed bunch) we've called a halt to the stream of Deb Harry pix and brought you instead Sting (last week) and Gary Numan (this week), Here's why . . .

Gorgeous Gary

PLEASE PRINT a picture of gorgeous Gary Numan 'cos I was going to save the last one but a teacher nicked my Record Mirror. She said he looked like a girl but I bet she fancied him really and now she's got her sweaty hands on my picture.

J. Wallace, Southend On Sea, Essex.

PS. I hate Mick Jagger.

● LP winner (not for hating Mick Jagger, but to make up for having a teacher that fancies Gary Numan).

How dare you

HOW DARE that Juicy Luicy say that 'Are Friends Electric' is awful. It's the best single of 1979. It's fantastic. It's the most original sound out. Maybe you lot are just too damn thick to understand it. Anything you don't understand you just destroy. And don't take the piss out of Gary just because he wears make up. You're only jealous cos I bet you wish you were as good looking as he is and anyway, Gary's already explained why he wears make up on stage. he sings about a machman (What? Mailman) so he has to look like a machman. So you just leave Gary alone. He's brilliant.

Lynn, Manchester.

● When did they plug you in?

GORGEOUS GARY

ESTATE 1979
(chart USA + UK + Germania, giugno-luglio-agosto)

#	TITOLO	INTERPRETE	Score
1	RING MY BELL	Anita Ward	1307,76
2	HOT STUFF	Donna Summer	1137,50
3	BAD GIRLS	Donna Summer	1021,53
4	GOOD TIMES	Chic	702,48
5	BOOGIE WONDERLAND	Earth Wind and Fire With The Emotions	620,75
6	WE ARE FAMILY	Sister Sledge	595,84
7	POP MUZIK	M	577,11
8	BORN TO BE ALIVE	Patrick Hernandez	549,13
9	ARE 'FRIENDS' ELECTRIC	Tubeway Army	507,43
10	MY SHARONA	The Knack	491,71
11	SUNDAY GIRL	Blondie	488,38
12	CHUCK E.'S IN LOVE	Rickie Lee Jones	460,23

GARY NUMAN & TUBEWAY ARMY REPLICAS

REPLICAS gary numan tubeway army

ATCO CS 38-117 DOLBY SYSTEM

□ **TUBEWAY PATROL** are a new group, marking the re-formation of some original members of Gary Numan's Tubeway Army. They make their live debut at London Marquee tomorrow (Friday), and will have their first record released by Carrere next month.

ME-Hits/Leser

1. Pink Floyd, The Wall (2)
2. Police, Regatta De Blanc (1)
3. The Ruts, The Crack (18)
4. The Specials, The Specials (5)
5. Talking Heads, Fear Of Music (14)
6. Police, Outlandos D'Amor (4)
7. Neil Young, Live Rust (8)
8. Boomtown Rats, The Fine Art Of Surfacing (3)
9. Fleetwood Mac, Tusk (9)
10. B-52's, Play It Loud (6)
11. Clash, London Calling (NEU)
12. Supertramp, Breakfast In America (7)
13. No Nukes, (NEU)
14. The Headboys, The Headboys (NEU)
15. Nina Hagen, Unbehagen (NEU)
16. Madness, One Step Beyond (NEU)
17. Rory Gallagher, Top Priority (17)
18. Scorpions, Lovedrive (12)
19. Tubeway Army, Replicas (NEU)
20. Jam, Setting Sons (NEU)

GARY'S GONE TO THE DOGS!

Can you picture this?! Gorgeous Gary Numan, all done up in his best boiler suit, singing 'Tie A Yellow Ribbon' down his local pub?

"It's difficult to imagine," smiled Gary, "but that's exactly what I had to do a few years back, 'cos it was the only way I could practise my singing. Apart from bath-time, natch!

"Y'see, my dad used to moan if I sang too loudly at home.

"So I'd nip down to the local every night and practise there."

All this is a million miles from Gary's current brand of synthesised sounds, which have been such a smash success for him! And surely he must be a bit too well-known now, to try out his tonsils down the local?

"Sad to say, I suppose I am," sighed Gary. "So I have to practise at home now. And I *still* get complaints! This time from my two dogs who sit and howl every time I start singing!"

CAN SOMEBODY please tell me what the hell has gone wrong with this country? Are we all mad? I am talking about the crap that has reached number one in the last year. First, it was that overrated couple Olvia Newton John and John Travolta screeching 'You're The One That I Want' for two months and then that dreadful song 'Summer Nights'. Since then we've been treated with dribble from the Boomtown Rats (especially 'I Don't Like Mondays') Gary Numan, Village People and much worse (ie, Blondie the Bee Gees etc).

Groups like the Electric Light Orchestra, Thin Lizzy, Queen, Wings and Supertramp have brought out singles far superior to 'Sunday Girl' and 'Are Friends Electric'.

Will there never be a decent number one?
Andrew G. Maxwell, Glasgow.
● As long as you remain an idiot and a bigot, NO.

Terminal bad taste

I HAVE just returned from holiday in Italy, only to be informed by a friend that while I was away it was announced on Radio One that Gary Numan is suffering from a terminal disease. I was horrified and cannot believe that it's true, because Gary is so young and talented.

I hope you don't think that I'm being over emotional, but Gary Numan is the first artist whose music I have been able to relate to in any way. Until recently I showed only a general interest in music with no strong leanings towards disco, punk or any other type of music. I even shocked my friends with statements like "who are Sham 69". Then one day I turned the radio on and heard 'Are Friends Electric' for the first time and I was totally mesmerised. I know you often poke fun at Gary but please be serious for once and print the truth about the situation. I'm living in the faint hope that it's all a sick joke on the part of Radio One. Please help, I am genuinely upset.
Helen Moffatt, Newcastle.
● With a friend like that who needs enemies? Gary is fine and healthy.

Marc lives

I FIND it hard to believe Marc Bolan has been dead for two years and I want to get a message across to all other rock, pop, soul or whatever fans. While your fave idol/group is still alive go and see them at every concert you can. Buy their records while you can or it could be too late. I didn't go to half as many T Rex concerts as I would have liked (and could have). Then it was too late because Bolan was killed. I can't get into another rock star like I did with Marc.
Freddie Garnwell, East Worsley.
● Take heed gentle readers.

Are Friends Electric

By Tubeway Army on Beggars Banquet Records

It's cold outside
And the paint's peeling off of my walls
There's a man outside
In a long coat, grey hat, smoking a cigarette

Now the light fades out
And I wonder what I'm doing in a room like this
There's a knock on the door
And just for a second I thought I remembered you

So now I'm alone
Now I can think for myself
About little deals
And S.U's
And things that I just don't understand
Like a white lie that night
Or a sly touch at times
I don't think it meant anything to you

So I open the door
It's the 'friend' that I'd left in the hallway
'Please sit down'
A candle lit shadow on a wall near the bed

You know I hate to ask
But are 'friends' electric?
Only mine's broke down
And now I've no-one to love

So I find out your reason
For the phone calls and smiles
And it hurts
And I'm lonely
And I should never have tried
And I missed you tonight
So it's time to leave
You see it meant everything to me

Words and music by Gary Numan. Reproduced by permission Andrew Heath Music Ltd.

SMASH HITS 5

Beryl and John Webb celebrate with their son.

78

tubeway army

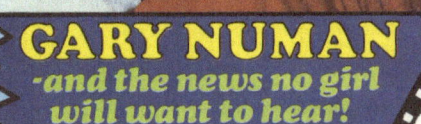

Heute habe ich mal wieder einen Text aus den englischen Charts für Euch.

Song
BRAVO-DISCO 49
ERWOCHE

Gary Numan

Tubeway Army:
Are „friends" electric?

It's cold outside
And the paint's peeling off of
My walls
There's a man outside
In a long coat, grey hat, smoking
A cigarette

Now the light fades out
And I wonder what I'm doing in a
Room like this
There's a knock on the door
And just for a second I thought
I remembered you

So now I'm alone
Now I can think for myself
About little deals
And Su's

And things that I just don't
Understand
Like a white lie that night

Or a sly touch at times
I don't think it meant anything
To you

So I open the door
It's the "friend" that I left in the
Hallway

"Please sit down"
A candle lit shadow on a wall
Near the bed

You know I hate to ask
But are "friends" electric?
Only mine's broken down
And now I've no one to love

So I find out your reason
For the phone calls and smiles
And it hurts
And I'm lonely
And I should never have tried
And I missed you tonight

So it's time to leave
You see it meant everything to me

Sind „Freunde" elektrisch?

Draußen ist es kalt
Und die Farbe schält sich von
Meinen Wänden
Ein Mann steht draußen
In einem langen Mantel
Mit grauem Hut, und er raucht
Eine Zigarette

Nun verlöscht das Licht
Und ich frage mich, was ich in
Einem Zimmer
Wie diesem verloren habe
Es klopft an der Tür
Und für eine Sekunde
Glaubte ich mich an dich zu
Erinnern

Nun bin ich also allein
Jetzt kann ich nachdenken
Über kleine Geschäfte
Und Mädchen wie Su
Und Dinge, die ich nicht verstehe
Wie die gutgemeinte Lüge in
Jener Nacht
Oder eine zarte Berührung hin
Und wieder

Ich glaube nicht, daß dir das je
Etwas bedeutet hat
So öffne ich die Tür
Es ist der „Freund", den ich im
Gang warten ließ
„Bitte setz dich"
Die Kerze wirft einen schwachen
Schatten
an die Wand nahe beim Bett

Du weißt, ich hasse es zu fragen
Aber sind „Freunde" elektrisch?
Nur meiner ist „unterbrochen"
Und jetzt habe ich niemanden
Den ich lieben kann

Nun finde ich auch den Grund
Für die Anrufe und das aufgesetzte
Lächeln
Und das tut weh
Und ich bin einsam
Hätte ich es doch nie versucht
Ich habe dich heute nacht verloren
Nun ist es Zeit zu gehen
Du siehst
Für mich hat es alles bedeutet

Natürlich meint Gary Numan das „elektrisch"
hier nicht wörtlich – er meint damit, daß man Freunde
nicht an- und abschalten kann wie elektrisches
Licht. Alles klar? Also dann bis nächste Woche

Ever Saulto

80

The Australian picture cover has warmer colours than the original picture disc.

Commercial posters from 2015 (left), 1979 (by Jeremy Soar, above) and 1980 (by unknown artist, bottom right). The 1980 poster places Numan within a landscape inspired by H.R.Giger (*Alien*) and *Close Encounters,* three elements that had a profound impact on sci-fi imagery of the period.

The Secret Ingredient in transforming *Do Android Dream of Electric Sheep?* into *Blade Runner* was Gary Numan and *Replicas*.

It was possibly the first ever science fiction film with a synthesizer score. The score starts in a style not dissimilar to the song, *Replicas* (particularly the Wembley intro version), a solo keyboard playing a grand but simple melody, one-held-high-note at a time. This plays over *Telekon* red titles on a *Telekon* black background in a *Telekon*-style font.

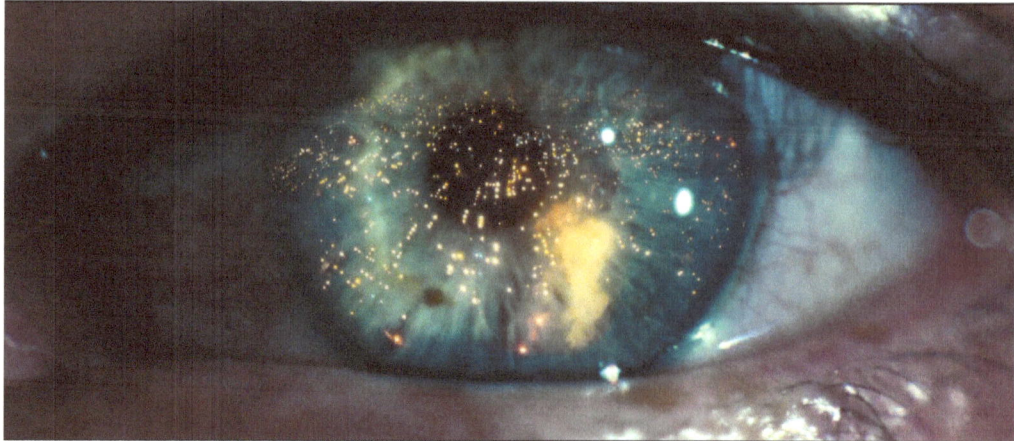

In Dick's novel, the man-machines are called 'andys'. The word Replicant to describe a man-machine is not used in the novel. The inspiration was Numan's album, *Replicas*.

The first 'human' image is strange lights reflected in the close-up of an eye. The two prominent white dots on the right-hand side reference the two left-side lights on the *Replicas* eye on the back of the album cover.

In the novel, the lead android, Roy, has Mongolian features and wears "a rumpled shirt and stained trousers, giving an air of almost deliberate vulgarity." For *Blade Runner* they used instead the cover image from *Replicas*, a cool uber-Ayran white-haired android dressed all in black.

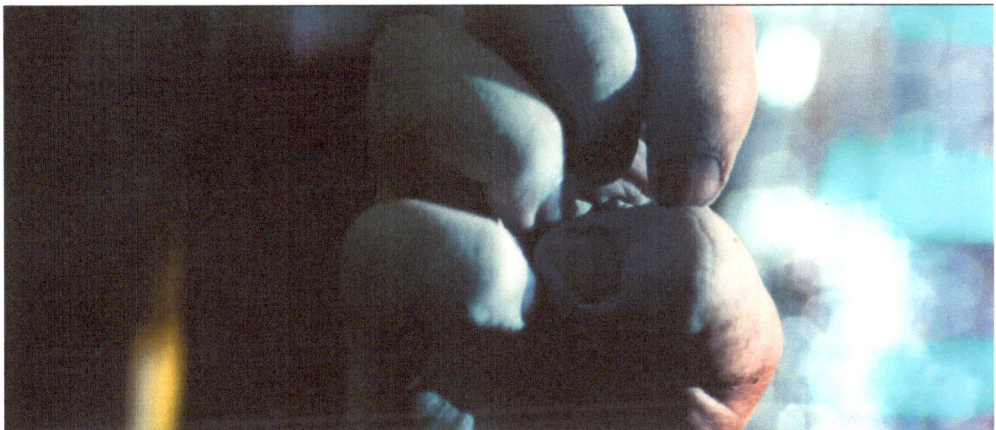

Like the android on *Replicas*, the androids in *Blade Runner* mostly have black fingernails. The first live image of the Roy is of his 'black' fingernails.

At the start of *Replicas*, Numan sings: "I couldn't recognise my photograph." Photographic recognition is a major sub-theme of the film. Photographs play no part in the novel. The Blade Runner's search begins by him looking at photos. The photo which starts the investigation, and provides a set-piece, is one of a brown-coloured interior with "a bed near the window" and strange reflection in the mirror. These are ideas and images from *Replicas*.

In the film, Dekkard falls in love with an android who uses a photograph of her mother to 'prove' that she is human. There is no mention of this in the novel. On the *Replicas* album, Numan sings: "They want to relive all my memories/ Give me the service daily/ Maybe it was mother / I can't seem to remember much at all these days."

In the book, the replicants gather by chance at the flat of a man with a low IQ called John Isidore. In the film, they gather by design at the flat of a genetic designer of genius who had a hand in making them, "There's some of me in you," he says to Roy. His name in the film is changed to J. F. Sebastian, a name that rings so loud with echoes of J(ohann) S(ebastian) Bach that the filmmakers are confessing that their film was made partly by ideas from a pioneering musician.

So why has there been no official acknowledgement of Numan's imagery and inspiration? Perhaps it's as Rutger Hauer says in the film: "It's not an easy thing to meet your maker... I've done questionable things." It's possible that like the failure of Grace Jones's cover version of *Me! I Disconnect From You* to make the first cut of *Nightclubbing*, Numan's name had been so tarnished by press abuse and mockery that artists with narrower shoulders were scared of the burden of association. That and the fact that Warner Brothers own both copyrights.

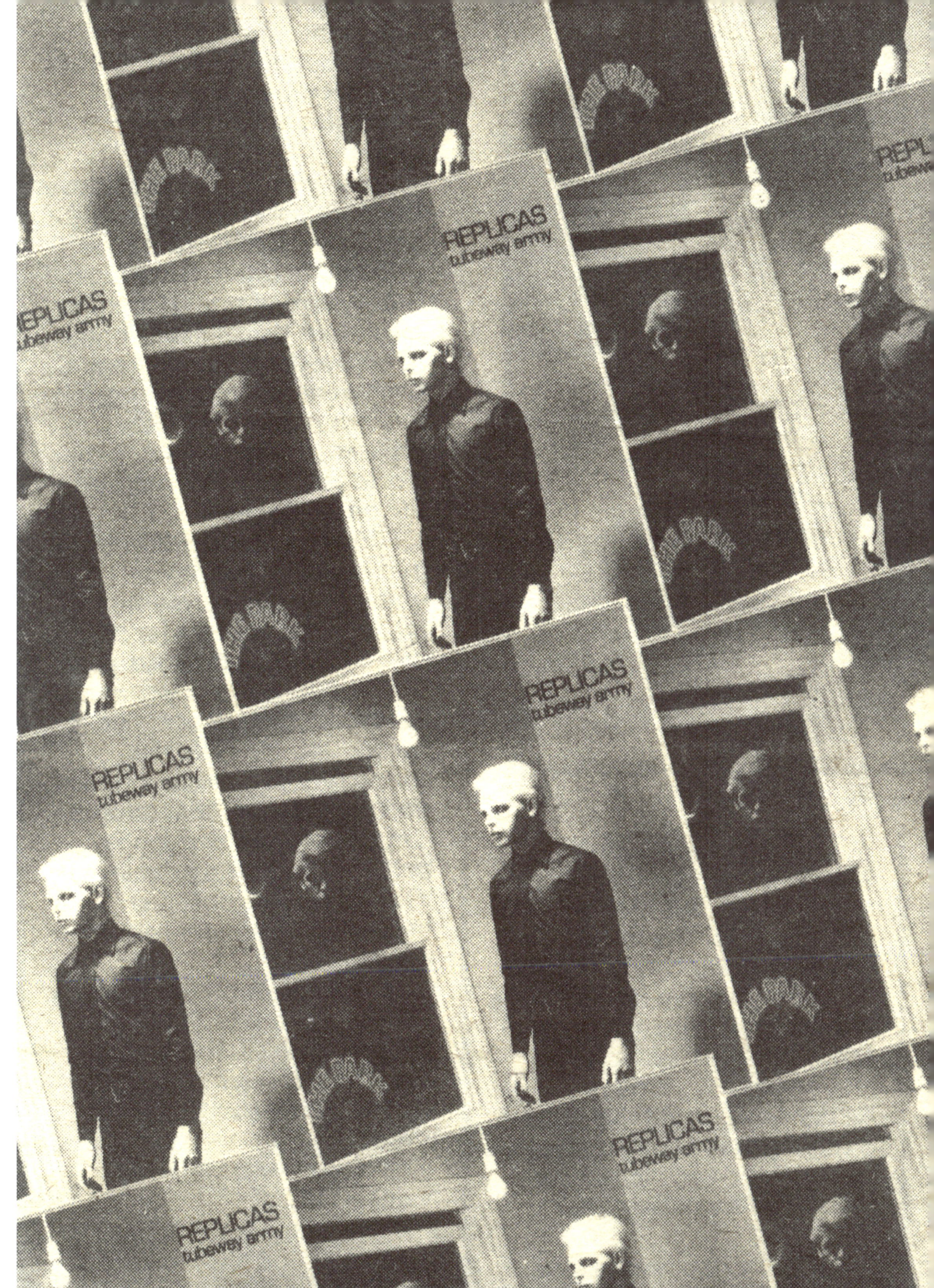

Numan paid tribute to the *Replicas* cover on the picture disc release of *The Plan*, the collection of Tubeway Army demos.

The copyright breach of Numan's *Replicas* imagery wasn't challenged because Warner Brothers owned the distribution rights of both records, though *Replicas* was released on Atlantic Records' offshoot in the States.

Prince: "You know, his album *Replicas* never left my turntable... there are people still trying to work out what a genius he was." *Prince in the Studio* by Jake Brown

Television This Week; OF SPECIAL INTEREST

12:9i(11)The FBI l ai(4)Secortd City TV (>n Ladies Pro Golt 1:J6(4)Don Kirshner's Rock Con cert: Pink Floyd, Pat Benetar, **Gary Numan**, Toto, Prince, Diane Nictwld, Richard Robinson, guests (11)News 1:48(t)News

May 04, 1980 - - Print Headline: "Television This Week; OF SPECIAL INTEREST"

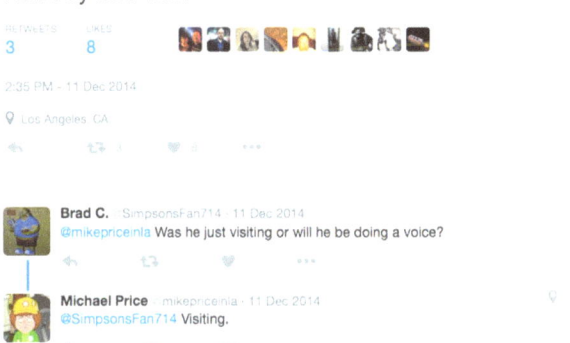

Michael Price Follow
@mikepriceinla

Devastated to learn that Gary Numan was at our Simpsons table read this morning and nobody told me.

RETWEETS 3   LIKES 8

2:35 PM - 11 Dec 2014

Los Angeles, CA

Brad C. @SimpsonsFan714 · 11 Dec 2014
@mikepriceinla Was he just visiting or will he be doing a voice?

Michael Price @mikepriceinla · 11 Dec 2014
@SimpsonsFan714 Visiting.

My compliments to the artist who created this homage. Homer sang *Cars* in the tenth episode of the 15th season. Numan was a guest of *The Simpsons* producers in 2014.

The Pleasure Principle

Airlane

Metal

Complex

Films

M.E.

Tracks

Observer

Conversation

Cars

Engineers

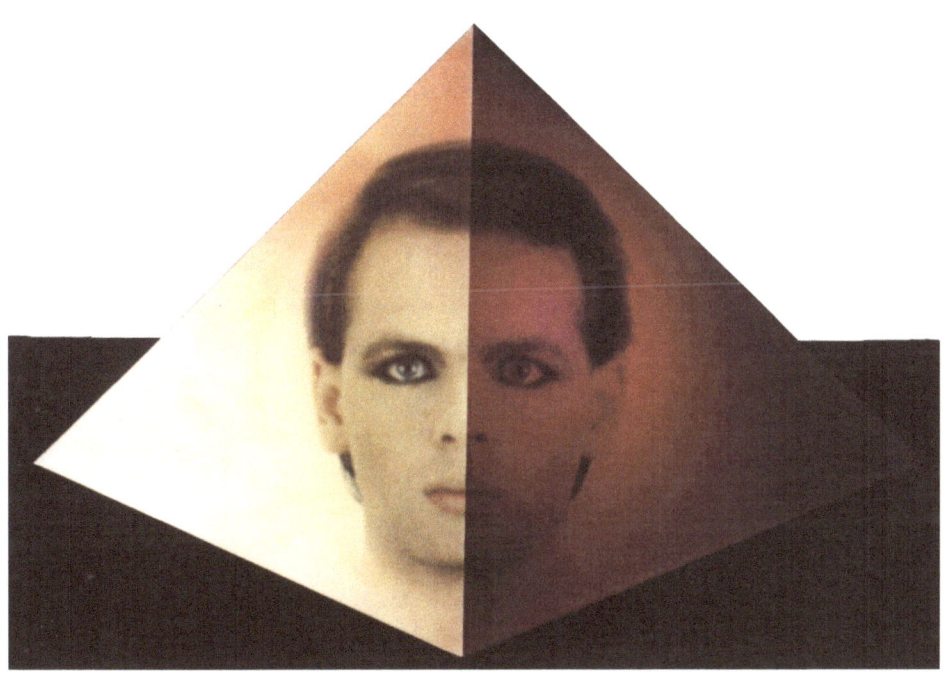

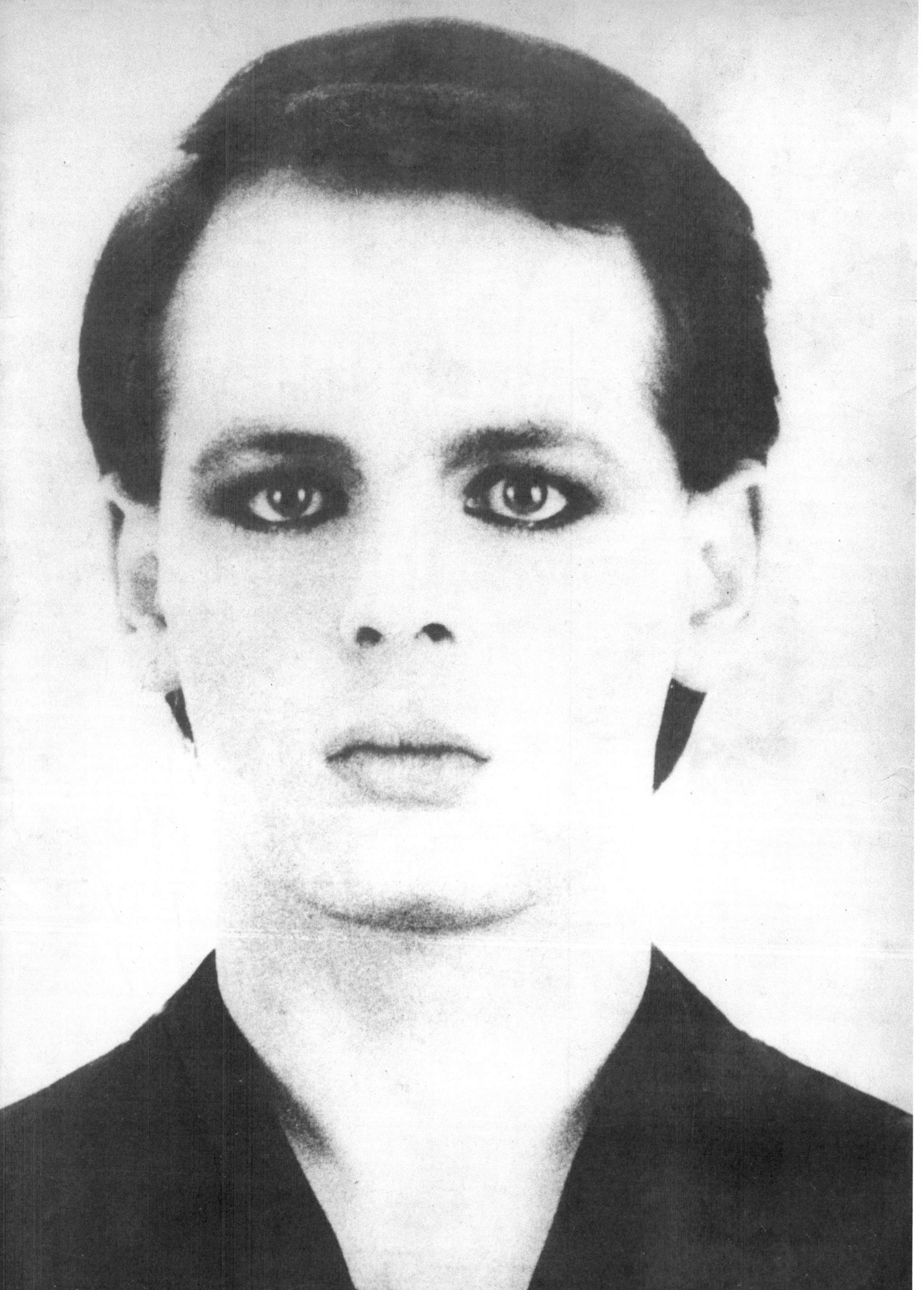

...Or At Least Some Sort Of Soul

GARY NUMAN
The Pleasure Principle
(Beggars Banquet)

And people seethe at the Golden Boy.

Let's forget the threadbare rock'n'roll bitch that it's all been done before by 'proper' artists — Bowie this, Kraftwerk that — because, although the groundwork was laid down by lots of clever folk long ago nobody has done what Gary Numan is doing right now. Outside of Moroder, electronic music has always avoided commercial success with its accent on extended aural think pieces 'hi, Tangerine Dream', or indulgent student pranks (hey, Orchestral Manouevres In The Dark or, perhaps, Telex!).

But Numan is knocking out a bunch of important sounding moog anthems that never threaten to stray from ABC pattern, gives them a traditional rock backline and stammers through the most obvious of 'futuristic babble' lyrics — and thus lulls the punter to believe that their musical tastes are taking leaps forward.

Simply, Numan is making intelligent music for people who aren't intelligent. (And, unless you're the most guilty liberal, you know just how many folk just aren't too sharp).

This outlook I have confirmed by the amount of people, mainly boys, who will trot up to my DJ podium and ask for something by 'The Tube'. When I have to decline their requests, they invariably step back and with the look of a conqueror on their face say "What, is he too weird for this place?" then stride away with the air of a person of great discernment.

And Gary is their Hero. I think Numan is harmless enough. I certainly don't believe the man himself is overly smart, which is probably his biggest selling point. After all, anyone with a bit of suss would shrink from penning anything as embarrassing as ninety per cent of the lyrics on 'TPP'. Example: *"These are no faces/This is my complex ... Am I a photo/I can't remember..."* Very witty, Numan. Very very witty.

No, the signs point to old Gal being a bit of an intellectual earwig by anyone's standards, but this aspect is what causes him to have a bottle to be free from all yearnings of 'critical respect' that all rock/pop crossover acts so desperately try to maintain. He sincerely believes in that 1984/Modern Man pantomime and his introduction of riffing synthesizers has tapped a very, ah, rich vein.

'The Pleasure Principle' is pure Big Brother Status Quo.

The lyrics are rarely more than duosyllabic and, by picking out the middles of sentences, they try hard to remain obscure — not that they are about much in the first place. I imagine Gary would love to be the subject of large 'in-depth' features where he could be quizzed as to What It All Means, and then he could be even more tight-lipped and spin his bluff out even further.

But at the moment he seems to have forgotten that it is a bluff at all. Like, National Lampoon couldn't have got together a better 'futurepose' sleeve than this. (In which we see Gary Numan asking questions of a small red pyramid). No, our Gary is just a ham with a synthesizer and, by God, the British public does love a ham.

The music on this LP is easy and listenable — albeit not for too long — and the production — by Gazza himself — is excellent. Only 'Metal' (and didn'tcha know all the titles were but one word) is as good as 'Are Friends Electric?', but it will certainly be a number one record; its faultless inanity is irresistible.

It's ironic, too, that this is the chap who advertised to us all *Don't be a dummy*.

It seems to me that the instant Gary Numan wises up — well, that's when he stops selling records.

Danny Baker

Pic: Chris Horler

Norman: "Do you think this pose is intense enough?"

Danny Baker would soon find success as a pleasant comedy D.J. and as a longtime writer for Chris Evans, including on the 2016 multicoloured swop show: *We Haven't Got Clarkson's Talent But, Hey, We're P.C. (Can You Hear Me At The Back)*, so it is surprising to see him strike such a nasty cheap-jibing tone in his review of a 20th Century masterpiece. Believe it or not, Baker's piece is one of the most perceptive British articles about Numan published in 1979. He identifies the commercial shortcomings of the famous Moog doodlers who tried and failed where Numan succeeded, and his attributing Numan's success to playing "Big Brother Status Quo", is perceptive, witty and essentially true.

Baker is bold enough to say that *Metal* is "as good as *Are Friends Electric?*" (it isn't but it is a musical landmark), and his final prophecy that "the instant Gary Numan wises up" is "when he stops selling records", alas proved to be true.

Of course, hacks and the public didn't know about Asperger's Syndrome in 1979. No one would read *The Curious Incident with the Dog* (or whatever it is called) and learn to be all sympathetic and kind to young men on-the-register for another twenty years or so. So Baker, and his ilk, were clearly feeling threatened by Numan's original intelligence, by his music-without-nods-and-winks, by the seriousness of something palpably so simple it could almost be called childlike if it wasn't so dark and so disturbed and so serious.

(Isn't 'simplicity' a definition of genius?).

It's human nature to feel threatened by things that can't be understood. Baker's defence mechanism for failing to understand the simplicity-complexity paradox of Numan's music-and-book is to kick out and mock what he sees as failings in Numan's intelligence. The question of Numan's intelligence is an interesting one. In conversation it is clear that Gary Numan is not an educated man. He may have quoted Magritte on the album cover, and he'd referenced Burroughs and Ballard in his writings, but a glance at the Me-My-and-I of his lyrics tell us that he was too deep inside his own thoughts and fears, and his own originality, to care to cultivate a close interest in the work of others (unless he saw the work of others as food for his own art, and that's exactly the wrong kind of approach to understanding anything). So one knows that Numan doesn't spend his evenings watching European art films with John Foxx or foraging the drawers of world culture with David Bowie. To do so would have made him a more rounded man, and that would have made him, at that time, a lesser Gary Numan. There is a relationship between education, cultivation, and intelligence but those qualities of The Higher Man are not interdependent, nor are they any kind of measure of *genius*.

I think of Gary Numan when I see that early scene in the film of *Amadeus*, when Salieri enters the Mozart household and looks around, excitedly, for his first glimpse at the young man who has been writing such music as the world has never heard before. To his horror, it dawns on Salieri that the genius is not a Golden Boy of fine manners and noble bearing, but a vulgar youth playing silly games with girls under the table. Salieri learns that God's gifts come from God.

GARY NUMAN
'The Pleasure Principle'
(Beggar's Banquet BEGA 10)***

Sounds 8/9/80

I COULD be unkind and say I saw this album coming. A fluke number one single hoiking the album up the charts, the demise of Tubeway Army and the promise of a lucrative solo career and, courtesy of one of the biggest record companies in Britain (WEA), an upcoming nationwide tour playing large venues and with a stage presentation alleged to make HAL from '2001' look like Robbie The Robot.

But this isn't one of those 'Queue here for the Gary Numan backlash' numbers. Most of 'The Pleasure Principle' was under wraps before 'Are 'Friends' Electric?' and 'Replicas' peaked in the charts, so I can't accuse Gary of contriving a formula for chart success.

I am, though, worried by the uniformity of the ten tracks on this album. Okay, it's now Gary Numan, not Tubeway Army, and he's dropped the guitar (which gave the previous two albums their edge) completely; but there must be some explanation for the feeling you get at the end of side two of having heard ten unvarying musical clones.

Excepting the inclusion of ex-Ultravoxer Billie Currie's violin on 'Tracks' and 'Conversation', 'Pleasure Principle' consists of ten slices of fuzzed synthi-bass, fluttering, trebly synthesiser lead and Gary's slightly nasal voice intoning over futuristic marches and dirges. Superficially, you might describe 'The Pleasure Principle' as floating in a stasis field bordered by Jean-Jacques Burnel, Pink Floyd (circa 'Meddle') and Bowie.

The main disappointment is that it shows little progression on from 'Replicas'; there's little space between the more simplistic parts of 'Replicas' and the bulk of 'Pleasure Principle'. Gary's the first to admit he's no synthesiser technician, but he's become less adventurous with his use of sound. He's jettisoned the variety of synth effects, opting for a smooth, homogeneous sound.

Lyrically, he's pared down the sci-fi tension of 'Replicas'. There are no threatening androids, no loss of sexual identity and no recognisable symbols of paranoia (a recurring Numan theme); just an understated neurosis with no real victims or aggressors. And that clipped machine-syntax reads just a mite too self conscious.

To be fair, though, it'll go down very well with those fans won over by 'Are 'Friends' Electric?' and stands up well alongside 'Replicas', even though overshadowed by the latter. I just expected a little more variety, a few more risks taken.

Merely in passing, as it were, but did you know the 'This Heat' album is going for the bargain price of £3.50 at Rough Trade and other alternative outlets?

JOHN GILL

臆病な自分を素直に認める潔さ
よさに妙なシンパシーを

平沢　ようするにバッキングでもあんなふうに　代わりにバッキングでありながら、

く狙れ合うことを拒絶するゲイ

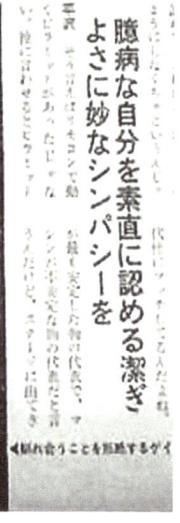

Gary Numan

18 Record Mirror, September 8, 1979

PAIN IN PLEASURE

GARY NUMAN: 'The Pleasure Principle' (Beggars Banquet BEGA 10)

I'M WARY of anything that is as calculated and cold as this. Every tiny detail has been carefully planned and inspected with a clinical detachment, leaving nothing to chance.

'Are Friends Electric' was brilliantly original, but the formula is repeated here again and again.

The thing that disturbs me most about Gary Numan is how perfectly he realises musically what Fritz Lang predicted back in the twenties with his film 'Metropolis'. Lang's vision was of an industrialised world of tedious repetition and oppression — Numan would have been able to provide the perfect musical score. As in the film, individuality has no place in Numan's music, neither does freedom of expression or movement. There is no heart.

Numan adopts the stance of observer, of an outsider. As he impersonally intones on 'Observer': "Watching you, and waiting always/I could observe you all." As well as this sense of alienation, 'The Pleasure Principle' has an overpowering sense of claustrophobia, of being trapped. And all the time you are being observed by dead, impassionate eyes.

Detachment and distance are painstakingly sewn

into every track: 'Complex', 'M.E.', 'Observer', and the single 'Cars'. Numan's affected android voice and his lumbering synthesiser infiltrate your mind, leaving you numbed and clogged. And just when you think it might be leading somewhere, as with 'Complex', an overweight dirge in the form of 'Films' drags up and almost suffocates you. 'M.E.' is as narcissistic as it sounds, opening with a syn-melody strikingly like 'Amazing Grace', although it almost goes without saying that all the life has been drained from it. 'M.E.' fills you with a sense of intense desperation and depression, with which Numan manages to whip himself on to ever more extreme limits: "But there's no one left to see/And there's no one left to die/There's only me."

They say familiarity breeds contempt, here the contempt stems from similarity instead. You could play this album backwards, sideways or even upside down and it would still sound the same, which is a tragedy. Numan has an enormous talent, but it is obscured by a desperation and musical insecurity. This in turn makes it impossible for him to realise the potential just beyond reach.

Obsession with your own phobias and neuroses, apart from running up a heavy bill with the shrink, can make you narrow and unbending. This album creaks and groans with just such fears, waiting to unload themselves on the unsuspecting. You have been warned. + + **SIMON LUDGATE**

Like the infamous John Gill of *Sounds*, whose uncharacteristically balanced review is on the opposite page (see page 278 for Gill's self-reveal), Ludgate is uneasy with Numan's very un-English perfectionism. Of course, it was the exactness of Numan's music that made it so attractive to the godfathers of Hip Hop and EDM.

95

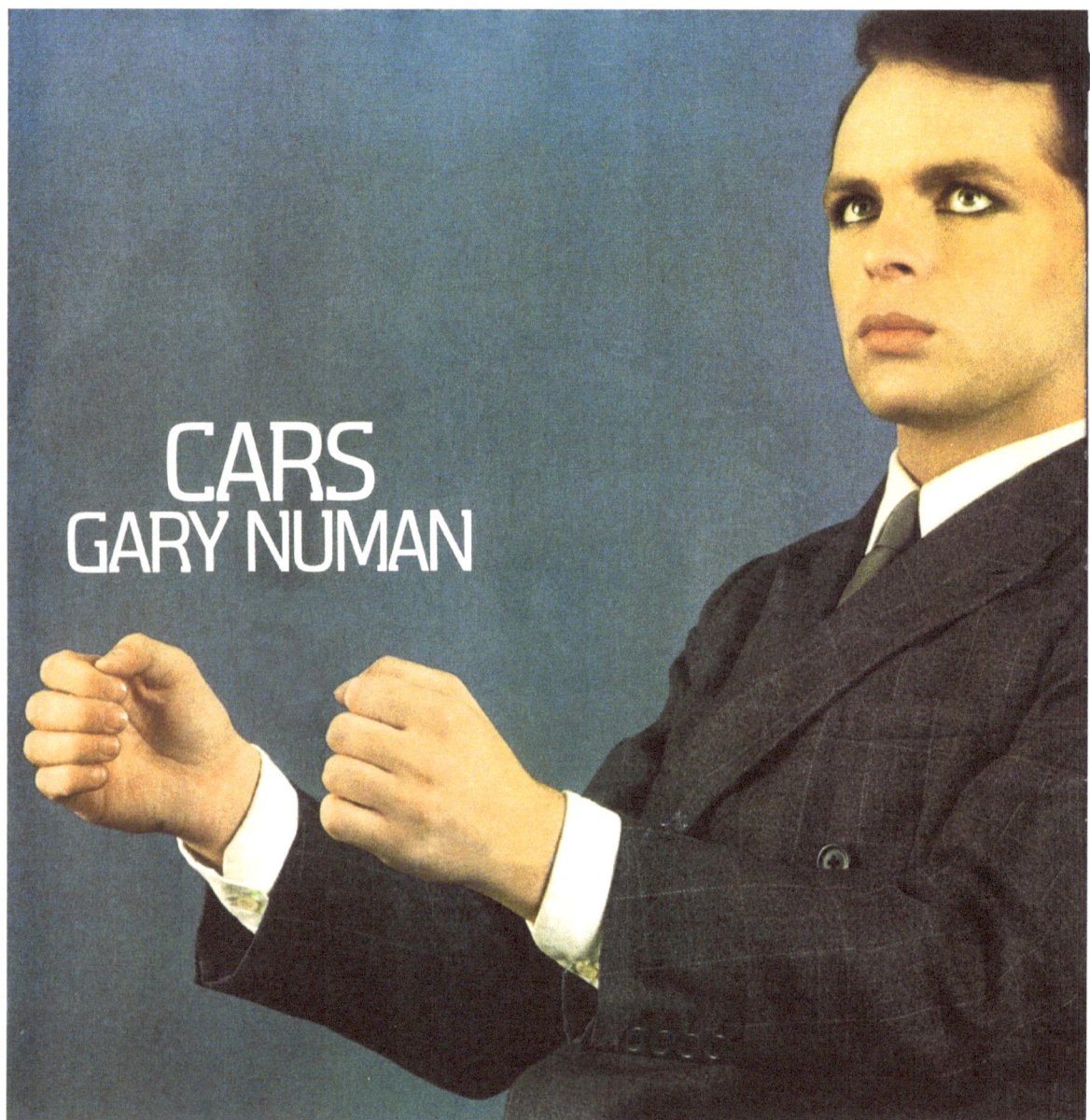

CARS
GARY NUMAN

The genius of simplicity. Bowie tied himself up in knots and painted himself, wore crazy mime costumes, trained with always wonderful Lindsay Kemp, and worked himself down into a drugged-out shell whilst, unfortunately, often looking ridiculous. Numan knew that mime could be rendered 'cool' only when stripped so far back to basics that a Zen master would be obliged to bow to him. On the picture sleeve of *Cars*, Gary Numan uses mime to construct a masculine *image*, and a universally understood symbol, as opposed to the kind of obfuscatory feminine *posing* that had long brought mime artistry into disrepute. The bold use of full colour in combination with the gorgeously subtle tint of steel in the eyes, to suggest the machine-man (a theme of three songs on *The Pleasure Principle*), is in full chime with the machine music of the song itself, music that advanced the art-form by its aural palette and by its very *simplicity*. The result, of course, is a design masterpiece.

Cars topped the British charts on 22nd September 1979 and spent ten weeks in the top 50. It was a hit in Japan but it spent only one week on the German charts, peaking at number 45 on 12.11.1979. In New Zealand, it reached number 18 and spent 14 weeks on the charts. It topped the Canadian charts, the Philippine charts (I think), and the city charts all across America. On the U.S. *Variety* charts (sales in big cities) it peaked at number 3. On the *Billboard* charts (sales and radio plays combined) it reached number 9. *Are 'Friends' Electric?* had sold more than two million copies in its first year on release. *Cars* sold two-and-a-half million copies that very same year. It has continued to sell healthily for almost half a century. The first A-list musician to do a cover version was Frank Zappa, soon followed by Robert Palmer, William Shatner, Fear Factory, Snoop Dogg, Nine Inch Nails, The Leisure Society and very nearly every other rock/garage/electro band.

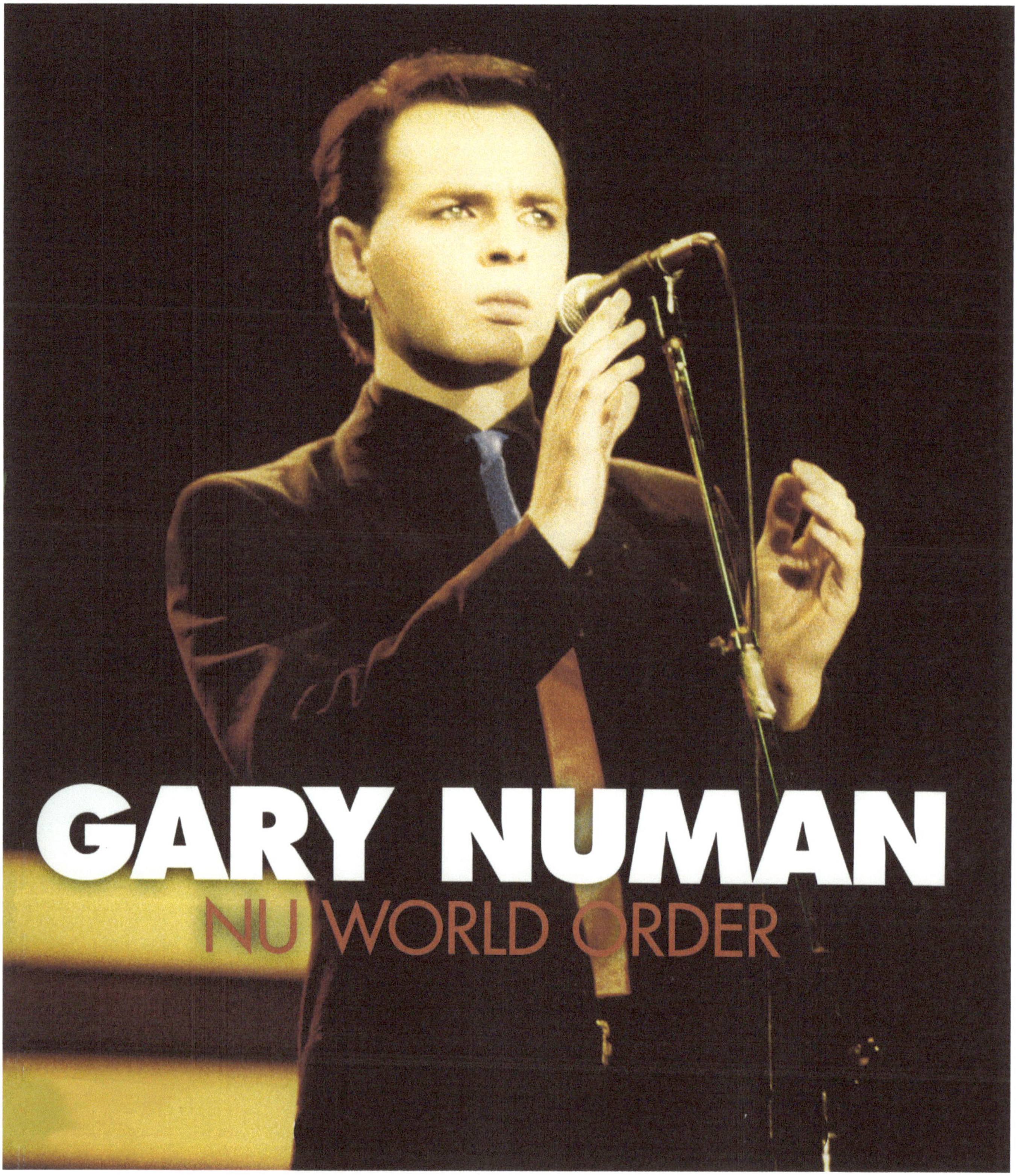

GARY NUMAN
NU WORLD ORDER

He hasn't changed a winning formula. The callous, digital memory backing is as smooth and soullessly seamless as ever but there is none of the McDowell tension that made **Down In The Park** so compelling. A hit, of course. **Max Bell, NME, August 1979**

Tubeway Army (L-R): Duffo, Ivor Biggun, Gary Numan. Pic: Chris Horlicks.

GARY NUMAN

★★★★★★★★★★★★★★★★★★★★★★★★
★ Numan competition coupon ★
★★★★★★★★★★★★★★★★★★★★★★★★

"The songwriting just comes from somewhere deep in the back of my head"

Within months of 'Friends' topping the U.K. chart, Numan had disbanded Tubeway Army and set out on his own. His first solo release, 'Cars,' gave him a second British Number 1 and his only U.S. Top 10 hit. Like its predecessor, 'Cars' has a bleak, post-modern lyric – in this instance inspired by a road-rage incident – but is set to a somewhat lighter musical backdrop. In the U.K. it has charted in three successive decades: first in its original form in '79; then with an 'E Reg' remix in 1987; and again in 1996, after its use on TV ads for beer.

The first performance of
Cars on Top of the Pops
30th August 1979

© Jill Furmanovsky

CARS

By Gary Numan on
Beggars Banquet Records

Here in my car
I feel safest of all
I can lock all my doors
It's the only way to live
In cars

Here in my car
I can only receive
I can listen to you
It keeps me stable for days
In cars

Here in my car
The image breaks down
Will you visit me? Please?
If I open my door
In cars

Here in my car
I know I've started to think
About leaving tonight
Although nothing seems right
In cars

I know I've started to think

I know I've started to think

Words and music by Gary Numan
Reproduced by permission Beggars
Banquet/Andrew Heath Music

PIC: CHRIS HORLER
BACKGROUND PIC: JILL FURMANOVSKY

THE HUMAN ALIEN

Gary Numan is normal.
Sometimes he feels different.
Today he feels nervous.
CHRIS WESTWOOD
calms him down

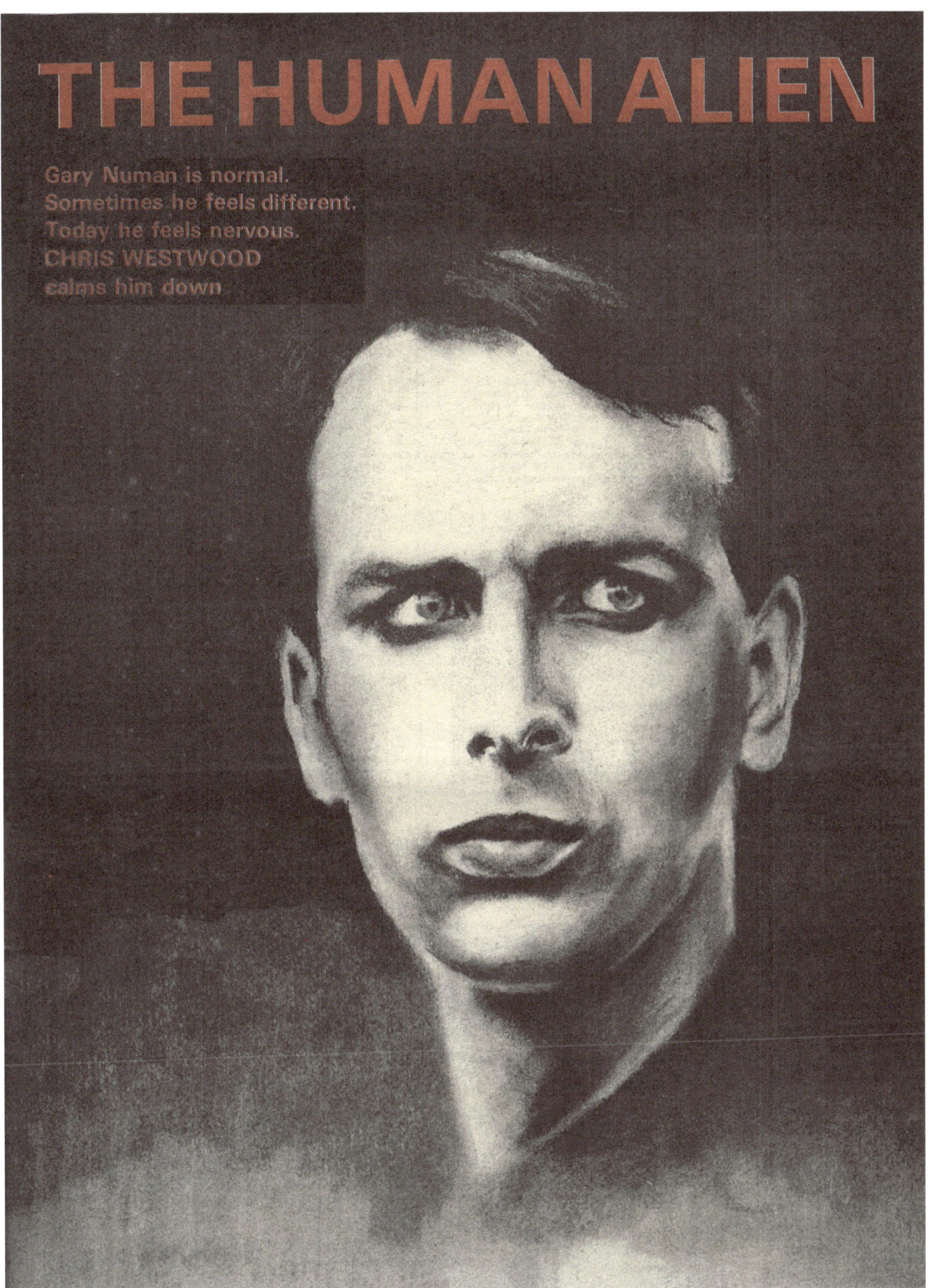

A BRISK jaunt from the Broadway station, along High Street, Ealing, and Beggar's Banquet lies before a new car-park site, down the road from Crusts and War On Want. Further on still is The Park — not necessarily *that* Park, but it's called The Park nevertheless.

Come early, early evening, Ealing is a quiet, blank place. Pubs don't open till seven on Sundays, but that's when it happens. That's when the cans get kicked through the streets until the frustrated constables feel inclined to intrude, and that's when the Safeways trolleys get sprung loose. Ealing is strict boozer-territory, 10 pints of Fullers a night and ripped-off burgers from Crusts.

In Beggar's Banquet, Gary Numan is playing 'The Lodger' and fiddling with a TV control unit. He's relaxed, smiling, perfectly affable and he tells me he knows someone with a control unit that even adjusts the treble and bass on the set. Gary Numan is not the inverted Alien I'd perhaps anticipated, and I disregard the multitude of delving technological questions I've equipped myself with.

Numan happens to be a genuine nice-guy who confines himself to the shade through lack of trust and security; it's "paranoia," in his own words. He's trapped between two poles, I feel: influenced and motivated by the rock and roll sparkle, the flash of a Hank Marvin guitar on sixties TV, entranced by the breadth of Bowie and Burroughs; he relishes his success, but at the same time feels inclined to withdraw from the limelight which that success naturally bestows.

It's obvious when we parade down the local burger pit for a take-away that Numan is uncomfortable: all those heads turn in his direction and he's swift to make a retreat. Later he explains, though his music is sufficient to suggest a recluse character — Gary Numan of 'Replicas' is more a breed of Real-Life-Gary-Numan-Alter-Ego than anything else.

But we're back at Beggar's and he starts by explaining his exploits pre-Tubeway Army . . .

"The only relevant stage, I suppose, was leaving school around '73, and working. First thing I did was about two and a half weeks putting air conditioning in — had to give that up 'cause it meant real hard work in basements . . . with freezing water coming down, walking round in ice particies. I got pinned against a wall by a big giant tube, the main air-conditioning tube . . . and that was it.

I ran home that day and never went back. And after that, it was mainly air-freight for two years, working as an import clerk.

"I think the first time I got interested by music was when I was four, and I saw Hank Marvin. It wasn't the musical side — just the look of the guitar, flashing in the light."

THEN there was a band. Numan and his current bass player were part of an outfit which eventually evolved into Mean Street, before which Numan was slung out. There was Tubeway Army, initially pubescent-punk mainstream, until Kraftwerk, Bowie and, in particular, Ultravox made their respective marks. Tubeway Army's last live performance was in early 1978, an Acton White Hart gig shared with The Skids.

"There was always that thing about Hank Marvin's guitar," enthuses the passive interviewee, "the knobs and gadgets — I found that fascinating. But I was starting to get fed up with guitars, being through the Punk thing and realising it wasn't going anywhere. It wasn't changing, wasn't getting any better . . . and I couldn't write songs on guitar anymore — it was boring; I realised there was nothing you could do that hadn't gone before. And then I saw Ultravox. I became aware of the depths you could get, the changes you could put them through — like a dozen instruments rolled into one . . . they were like toys."

There's some foundation to the comparisons people have made with Bowie and Ultravox?

"Yeah, a certain ammount — but no-one mentioned Ultravox 'till I mentioned them in interviews. So when I see things like that now I lose interest in their opinions."

Why did you drop the Tubeway Army monicker and revert to Gary Numan?

"Well . . . I wanted it to be Gary Numan before the first album, really, but Nick and Martin from Beggar's wouldn't let me because of the comparatively good little following we had then. But really, when you read what the press have said about it, it's obvious to them that it's not a group effort . . . I can't work with other people — their ideas and mine are always separate — I like to be in control. So I'm lucky to be in this position."

'Replicas' was where things began to gell: it was part-successful world of science, alienation, solitary figures in dark, dull rooms. It was Numan's highly, vaguely, personalised feelings locked in a different context — impenetrable, futuristic ideas provoking charges of almost-justified pretentiousness. But all he'd done was to approach the album as Ballard approaches a novel; his imagination had produced a living, breathing society of the future, indirectly born through today's possibilities and realities . . .

"I wouldn't have thought it was difficult to understand but apparently most people seem to have trouble with the lyrics . . . but, anyway, I've always seen machines as being powerful and cold — and, for me, the only way to be successful is to be cold. And the successful nations have always been essentially cold — the Romans and the Germans. I don't think I'd ever enjoy being that, but — Gord, look at that!" he beams, wheeling his gaze round in the direction of the TV screen. "Gord . . . I love Grand Prix.

"Aw, sorry . . . I was saying, I don't think it's too far away from the stage where they'll be constructing a machine which is superier to us . . . but the 'Replicas' thing wasn't about machines taking over, destroying us — well, it may be in a sense, but the thing I was thinking about when I wrote it was that machines wouldn't need to take over, since we'd get rid of ourselves. Because they were doing everything we wouldn't need to work. The unity's going . . . there's total lack of unity. The terraced houses are disappearing, the neighbours don't talk anymore . . ."

I enquire as to whether The Park was hemmed into 'Replicas' as a pure escapist alternative to his mechanised society.

"The Park? Aw, The Park is simply something very frightning. I don't walk alone in parks anymore at night, I don't think many people do. I saw this programme about Central Park — they were saying 'All this violence thing is completely overblown' and in the background there all these sirens going — it was stupid, I just couldn't believe it. They were saying how you don't get drug smuggling there, and they were actually dealing right out in the open. It really does happen."

Numan's writing process — which generally involves taking a particular line from, say, Burroughs, then converting and writing around it before discarding the original line — is obviously more heavyly connected with an authoristic approach than with standard rock lyricism.

"'Replicas', the album sleeve — the main part of it where I'm standing by the window — represents a Machman. Really, the album's all about . . . well, I was writing a book, which I dropped because I'm better with short stories . . . but I'd started with an attempt at what London would be like in 10 or 20 years . . . and what happened was that the Government made a machine which made all the decisions — like a dictator — but the people weren't allowed to find out.

"The machine decided that the only thing holding back the State was the people themselves, so they decided to stage a quota test under the pretence that if you weren't up to quota-standard, you were taken and re-educated. Where, in fact, you were simply got rid of.

"The people who sat the quota test were the Crazies, the people who set it were the Grey Men, and people collecting the ones who'd failed the test . . . were The Machmen, who were used as a special police force. The cover is a Machman looking through a window at a friend, and 'Are Friends Electric?' is about friends . . ."

It seems to suggest the loss of friends.

"I wrote it because I lost friends when I was younger: I didn't *lose* them so much as them getting rid of me. Which bothered me quite a lot because it was unnecessary . . . like getting thrown out of Mean Street.

"A lot of the songs are about friends — losing me girl at one time."

So do you feel alienated?

"I suppose that's the case. I can say I don't like mixing with people one day, and it'll be completely true. Another day it might be different, but there are days I can't go out and walk down the street. Doing what we did then, going to Crusts, I get nervous doing that. It's only 'cause there were four of us that it was OK — but I wouldn't do it on me own. It's not that I feel I don't fit in, so much as I stand out — and it's not so much egotistical as paranoid.

"Things have happened that way as I've grown up, since my mid-teens,

initially because, deliberately, I wanted to be very different . . . and since, because other things have happened, emotionally or otherwise. Like, I may grow out of it — I may not. I may commit suicide or I may, one day, be completely alright. I don't really enjoy being like it any more. I did at one time, when I thought I was really different, but now . . ."

Were the songs written in this particular frame of mind?

"Most of them are concerned with me, or me putting myself into another place — and perhaps how I'd react in that situation. The songs still are that way. They're still about me — not me as me — but me as a figure, a kind of underground figure which is always there, always ominous."

BZZZZ Click. The tape recorder has been observing us. It is promptly switched off and stashed away and 'The Pleasure Principle' is played. Written post-'Replicas', its studio completion coincided with 'Are Friends Electric's first week at number one. Numan is pleased with the result: it represents perhaps his most stable, professional recordings to date, still very much in the mould, but with a face-life.

Numan isn't exactly gambling with 'The Pleasure Principle', he's not treading tight-ropes and he's not staring commercial disaster in the face. Merely, he's sticking limpet-tight to his little box and improving what he's got. He enthuses about the Polymoogs he's acquired and employed — £1,500 a shot — and eagerly points to their role in the scheme of things as the music progresses.

He explains away the arsenal of visual effects he'll be touring with — robots, computerised newsreader, the works. At this stage — the tour is already guaranteed a 25 grand loss, and no-one seems to be too worried by it all.

Numan is as personally *un-stable* as he is financially *stable*. But for all the cold, distant exterior, for all the inverted complexities of his music, the little recluse has *something*. There's no way his work can be branded "emotionless" — it's just powered by emotions of a very personal, inhibited nature; it never contrives to be anything it isn't. There's another level, too, and the one which looks like rooting Numan at the top of the tree for some while yet: he's producing some of the most optimistic, forward-facing Pop of the

seventies, no matter what you may design to throw in his direction.

He may be as irrelevant as you wish him to be, but Gary Numan's time seems to have come.

As I prepare to embark on my brisk jaunt to the Broadway Station, along the High Street, he invites me to turn up at rehearsals and investigate the great delicacies of his Polymoogs. If there's one way to a poor critic's heart . . .

One of those articles that tells of the unpleasant London streets, full of anti-social drunks, which inspired Numan's dystopia, and which shows how far we've since come as a society in understanding mental health. It was written in the era when 'mental health' meant *mental* and a lifetime locked away in a Victorian asylum. Therefore it was wise for the millions who suffered from common mental health conditions to hide their thoughts and feelings and illness.

By openly talking about his agoraphobia, paranoia and anxiety, mostly because his Asperger's prevented him from telling lies, Numan was a whole generation or two ahead of his time. The problem with being ahead of your time is that you are not understood. And if you are not understood you will be feared and ridiculed.

Gary Numan
von Tubeway Army

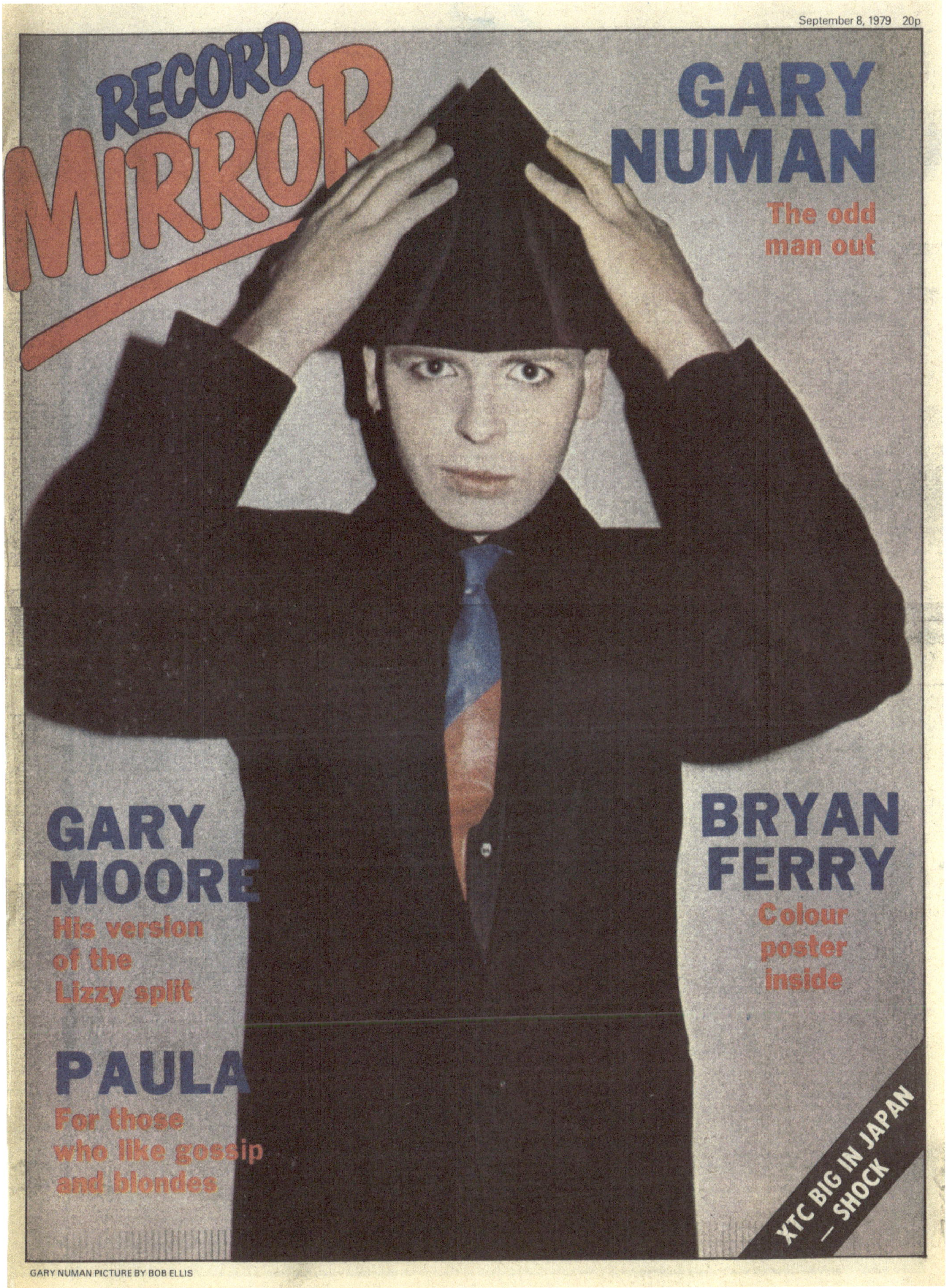
September 8, 1979 20p
RECORD MIRROR
GARY NUMAN
The odd man out
GARY MOORE
His version of the Lizzy split
PAULA
For those who like gossip and blondes
BRYAN FERRY
Colour poster inside
XTC BIG IN JAPAN — SHOCK
GARY NUMAN PICTURE BY BOB ELLIS

Albums

1 (1) **THE PLEASURE PRINCIPLE**
Gary Numan, Beggars Banquet
2 (—) **REGGATTA DE BLANC**
Police, A & M
3 (11) **EAT TO THE BEAT**
Blondie, Chrysalis
4 (13) **THE RAVEN**
Stranglers, United Artists
5 (3) **OCEANS OF FANTASY**
Boney M, Atlantic
6 (2) **DISCOVERY**
Electric Light Orchestra, Jet
7 (6) **ROCK 'N' ROLL JUVENILE**
Cliff Richard, EMI
8 (4) **IN THROUGH THE OUT DOOR**
Led Zeppelin, Swan Song
9 (10) **OUTLANDOS D'AMOUR**
Police, A & M
10 (5) **STRING OF HITS** Shadows, EMI

GARY NUMAN: The Pleasure Principle (Beggars Banquet). Pens ready, Gary Numan Defence League? Then tally-ho, because I'm not greatly sold on this. It's not bad, mind you — a smoother, almost discoish version of "Replicas" — but much too similar to it and not as adventurous, though Numan worshippers will doubtless adore it anyway. Good lyrics, but more musical and vocal variety next time please. Includes "Cars". Best trax: "Metal", "Engineers". (7 out of 10).

GARY NUMAN: 'Cars' (Beggar's Banquet) Music to computer date by. Pale, sickly Gary, beaming in from planet Zombie with 'Son Of Are Friends Electric', tucked safely in his cosmic handbag. The whiny weedy vocals are surpassed only by the monotony of the relentless rhythm.

ROBERT ELLIS

"I NEVER AGREED WITH COMING ON AND BEING THE SAME AS THE AUDIENCE. I THOUGHT IT WAS VERY FALSE . . ."

The Pleasure Principle by Rene Magritte, painted in 1937, is a portrait of the English poet and art patron, Edward James. James's most famous poem begins: "I have seen such beauty as one man has seldom seen", which sounds pleasantly like the start of the Rutger Hauer's replicant elegy in *Blade Runner*.

6 **OMD: "Messages"**
"THAT record reminds me of the time I became famous. They supported me on my first tour. I used to hear it when I was in the dressing room, with my mum putting my white and blue make up on me. You know this Take That-mania? It was like that. People jumping from balconies onto the PA, people stowing away in the boot of the coach, every bizarre offer you could imagine . . . At one show, people were climbing 80 feet up the side of the theatre to get in! F***ing hell! *No one's that good. I sure as f*** wasn't!" (Loud buzzer goes off in background. Numan waves hands between legs, as though he's farted)*

7 **ROBERT PALMER: "Addicted To Love"**
"HE used to do 'Cars' and 'Me, I Disconnect From You' in his live set. There's nothing guaranteed to make you more proud than someone else covering your song. We've co-written a few songs. On the sleeve of his Greatest Hits, he says that I'm painfully shy. And I am!"

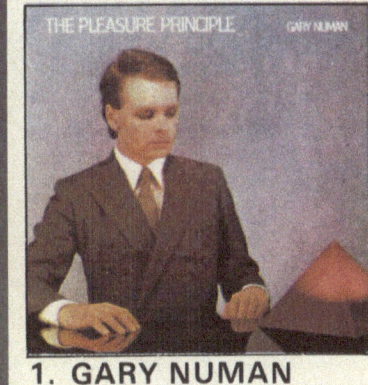

1. GARY NUMAN

It's been Gary Numan's year. After his Number One single and album under the name Tubeway Army he has crashed to the top of the charts with *Cars* and his album *The Pleasure Principle*. His brand of eerie, contemporary pop music with its heavy use of synthesisers has swept him to the top but his composing and production talents are sometimes not appreciated by people who point to his gimmicky image. His moody stance, clipped vocals and eye make-up are nothing new. The music, though, is something else. What was the title of Tubeway Army's first single hit? Was it (A) *I Nearly Married a Human*, (B) *The Life Machine*, (C) *Are Friends Electric?*

THE FINAL stimulus to change came towards the end of last year when OMD were invited to support Gary Numan (gasp!!) on his first British tour:

"Gary heard our single at Beggar's Banquet (the record shop/label that Numan is on) and really liked it, came to see us play at the Nashville and liked that too, so he got his manager to ring us up and ask us to do the tour.

"We did really well on that tour. His fans seemed to take to us very easily, which surprised us 'cos our music is very different.

"We travelled in the same coach as him between gigs. He's a very shy person. He thought we didn't like him for the first week and didn't talk to us. Once he realised that wasn't true, he was very friendly. He's a really nice person; we like him a lot."

The exposure that tour gave OMD around Britain was certainly positive enough to send their album bobbing into the LP top 30 and set their current single "Messages" on its way chartwards. They've since played in Paris, Amsterdam, Germany and Belgium and are on their way to the States in June.

Can they think of any reason why they have had such rapid success in an area where other bands — The Human League for instance, with whom they shared a Top Of The Pops recently — have been struggling?

"We don't particularly like being put in the same league as the John Foxxs and the Gary Numans; they're into a cold robotic image that we don't want to be a part of at all. We like to think our image is quite warm, the warm side of electronic music."

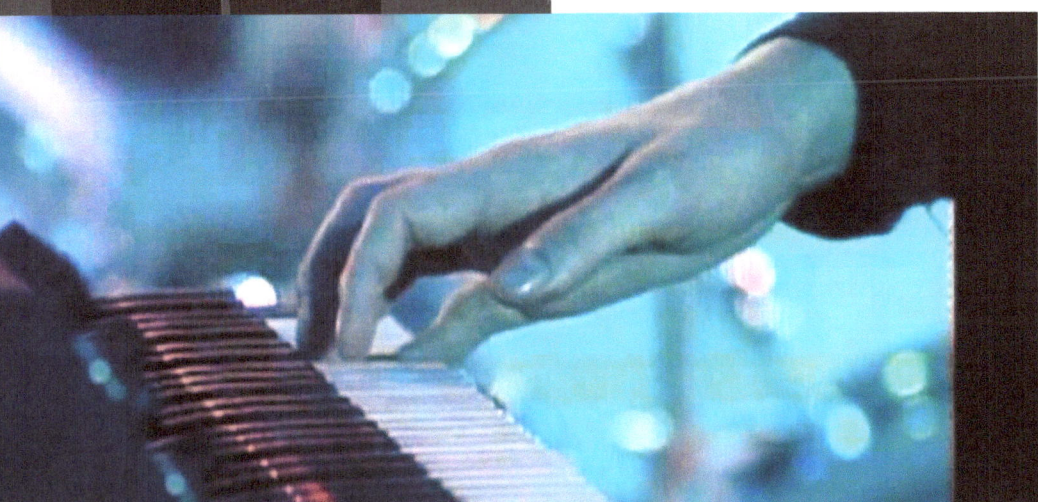

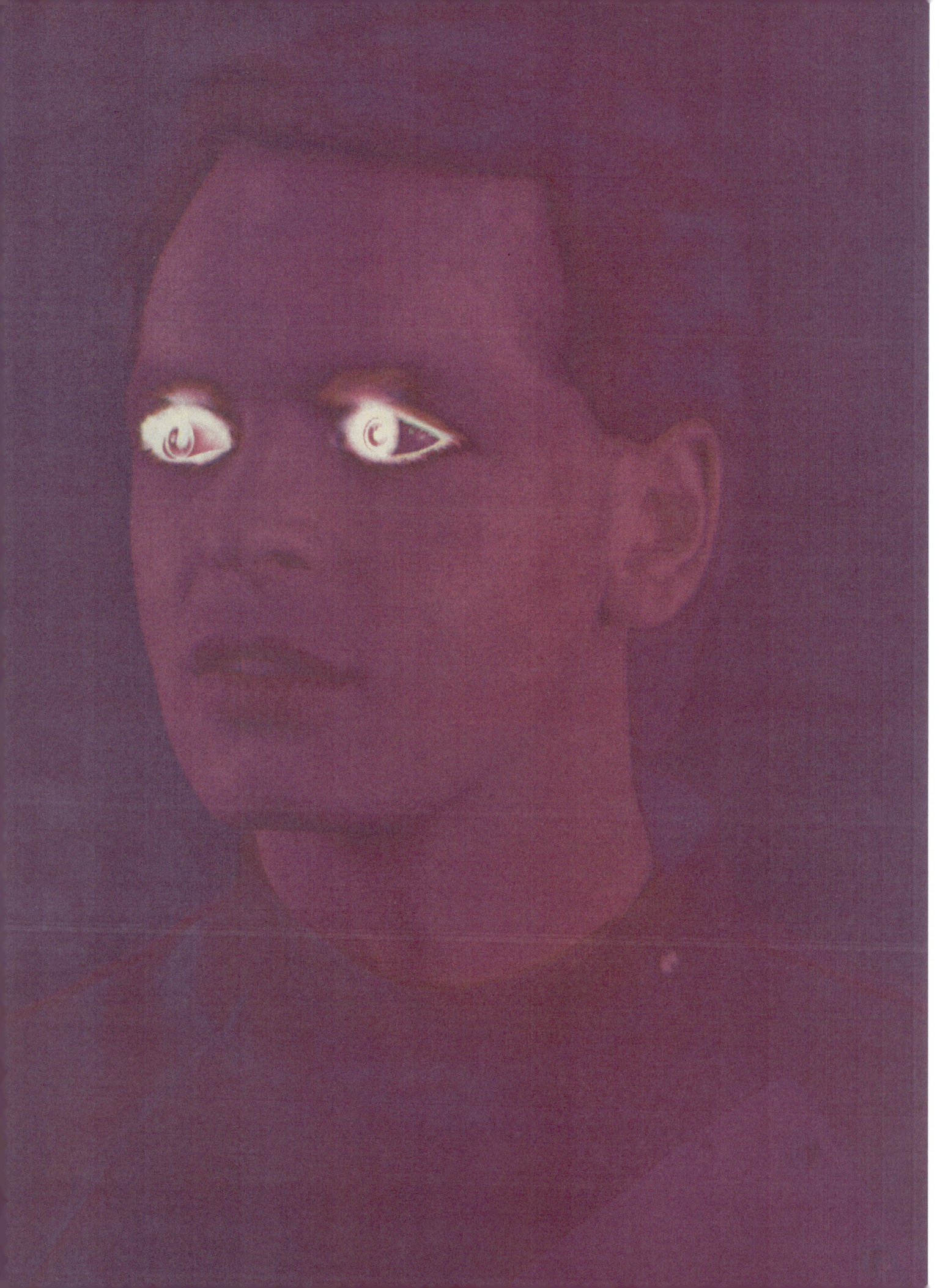

PLAYING TO THE ALIENS

John Savage finds out what success means to Gary Numan.

IN THE space of a few months, Gary Numan has emerged from complete obscurity to having two number one records, "Are Friends Electric?" and "Cars", two no. 1 albums, "Replicas" and "The Pleasure Principle", and, at one stage, three LPs in the Top 20 at once. Clearly, Gary Numan is a phenomenon.

The background to his rise to fame is by now quite well known. What's most interesting (now) is his reactions to his fame; whether, now that he's got it it's what he wanted; and what he feels about performing.

ON OCTOBER 8, Gary Numan finished his first tour since becoming a star. Fifteen dates earlier, at Glasgow's Apollo, he'd played his first live gig since a tiny pub date in Acton (London) in mid-78.

The tour was a complete sell-out but even allowing for £3,000 given to 'Save The Whale' from one of his Hammersmith London dates, Gary still lost £30,000 or so on the tour.

By his own admission not a natural performer, he decided to do the show as it was and lose money, because . . .

"I thought there was no point in going out unless you were going to give people something to remember and to make it worthwhile. There's no point in being top of the pile unless your show's going to be top of the pile as well."

Some people have said that the lavishness of the show was to distract attention from his (understandable) inexperience.

"You mean to take the limelight away from me a bit? No, it wasn't really. To be honest, the show was put together to be something to look at. I merely thought that being new at it, I wouldn't be very interesting to look at for one and a quarter hours.

"I don't think I am: I can't do enough different things or look in enough different ways to keep people interested for that time — apart from the real diehards who'll gaze at me for hours. Obviously the majority of the audience isn't like that — especially at this early stage. Half of them are just going to see what the fuss is all about."

Fair enough, but what was, say, the point of the pyramids?

"On the cover? It was image. On stage, the robots are pyramid-shaped — that's to tie in with the cover, and also because I thought that robots . . . you say a robot and people think of something that does this (gesticulates mechanically) and

PIC: GERARD McNAMARA

clanks about, and really that's the most unpractical shape you can think of because it's so unstable. It keeps falling over all the time.

"A pyramid is, I think, the most stable shape you can have. It really is hard to budge. Talking about a straight-thinking machine, it'd have to be that shape where it didn't fall over and damage itself.

"So I thought — well, if I'm going to do it, let's do it realistically, in the proper shape of what they'll be and not go for the image. We had enough impact in the show itself — it'd be nice to put some realism into it.

"I also think that the panels, the walls, it looks like they just light up. I think that one day probably we'll have buildings like that where you don't have street lights, but the walls of the buildings themselves light up outwards, so it's not like street lights and shadows and little quiet corners that you could get mugged in . . ."

The shows were certainly beautifully staged, but it's difficult to see them without being reminded of the difference between Numan's lavish showmanship and the ideals of the punks through whom he seems to have emerged. Did he want the new kind of relationship with his audience?

"I think . . . no, I'm not really interested in a new relationship. I'm sure what can be done. I've really no idea . . . apart from the fact that you talk to the audience and claim to be one of them, or admit that you're not one of them, which is why you're

singing and they're not, and get on with it, which is what I've done . . . I've very little to say to them.

"They know what the songs are, I'd imagine. I really wouldn't want to tell them what the songs are about before each number: there's no need to tell them what they are, because they already know. There really isn't much more to say — you can't have a conversation — it's very false with between two and four thousand people . . ."

This is certainly very different from many of the new groups, who just want to be "one of the people".

"I think it's just taking it back to cabaret — showbiz for showbiz's sake more than anything. That's trying to explain

114

what we're on about, and use this as a visual expansion of our songs.

"To be honest I used to hate all that stuff (cabaret), but fairly recently I've got to really like Bing Crosby and now I like Frank Sinatra. I never did before, but the way he just breezes among his crowd as if they're in a circle and not on stage, and he's so relaxed."

AS YOU may have gathered, Gary Numan is very honest. If you ask him a question, provided it's put clearly, he'll answer it as clearly and as directly as he can. It's a quality very rare in most pop stars, who, when asked a difficult question, will for some reason evade the point or get angry. Perhaps they're afraid.

From being unknown, Gary has suddenly become very famous. He's prepared to talk with as much honesty about what it means to him, and what it's doing to him.

It's a Monday afternoon in a small room in a Sheffield hotel. Gary answers the questions, carefully and quietly, with some humour. While he's talking, he teases his newly washed hair in a mirror opposite.

The same day, one of the national papers has done a story on him, pronouncing his image as "cold and aloof". Is he really, and what does he feel about the article?

"Most of what I said had been blanded out. I didn't actually say what he wrote down; he took the gist of it only. It wasn't done in a nasty way, so I didn't mind it — it was a bit sweet and sickly. I'm not like that.

"The image doesn't worry me. From an outsider's view, it's probably accurate. I think I'm quite strong-willed and know exactly what I'm doing — which is mistaken for arrogance. The 'aloof' bit is my wish not to get too close to the audience . . . which isn't being aloof. It's more survival, really."

WHAT DOES Gary feel about all the people who come to see him?

"It's very awkward — to be honest about it without giving the wrong impression. I don't feel any . . . I won't say loyalty, I don't feel that I owe them anything. I made the records and they bought them. They owe me as much as I owe them, so they cancel each other out, really.

"I don't now have to make another album. I get very annoyed when I hear these things like, oh, people saying, 'We made you.' They really didn't, they really didn't make anybody at all. We made ourselves, they simply bought the records."

What sort of hero does he think he is to the people who come and see him?

"It's a bit difficult to answer. I think possibly to a lot of people I'm a symbol of something new

PIC:
ANDRE CSILLAG

Incredibly rare pic of Gary Numan smiling.

— I wouldn't venture any more than that.

"The . . . *pose* element is an image. They'll see that, and then they'll go home and imitate it in a mirror and do G. Numan handclaps. That's thought out the same as the image is thought out, to give people something to latch onto.

"It's taken everything I did when I was young and when I was a fan — and using that, knowing that other people somewhere must be similar to me: I'd like them to do what I did to my heroes."

When he was listening to his heroes, Gary was, he says, a lonely, troubled adolescent. The spoken parts in "Are Friends Electric" was about one of his experiences before he was famous. At the time, he was hanging around with a group of friends, and they:

" . . . got rid of me because . . . I was singing in a group and they didn't want me writing the songs any more, so I said, 'It really doesn't bother me.' I didn't intend at that time to become a big frontman pop-star anyway — I was just doing it to gain experience, but they weren't writing any songs.

"So I said, 'Well, write them then, I don't mind,' but that wasn't very good. And so they got rid of me, then went out and did their own set.

"It took them about six months to write their set, and they had a couple of my songs in it anyway — there was only about a 30-minute set, and it really was awful. They group? It was Mean Street. They were on the Vortex live album.

"I was disgusted. And all my so-called friends at that time would follow them around religiously, and pogo at every gig. It was like rent-a-crowd. And they dropped me completely from parties, from anything at all.

"And then obviously being deserted made me very paranoid in my attitudes towards friends. I

often tended to write 'friends' in inverted commas in a lot of the songs."

IF HE was lonely before, being a star doesn't always help. It's a lot of pressure, even more so because Gary tries to manage as much of his own career as possible, from writing the songs to performing and producing them, working out his finances and designing the stage set.

Many of his songs are about this loneliness, this distance between people put just a little into the future: was this how he lived?

"I used to live it out quite a lot before, really, because I didn't go out much, I've never gone to parties. If I go out, I normally go out on my own, in the car, driving . . ."

Is he treated as an object?

"Completely. As a product, yes."

Would this encourage him to treat others in the same way?

"I think it would do. I think it's a bit early yet for me to change my personality to that extent. I find it difficult when the audience meets you, because when they do they're obviously nervous or edgy because they're not sure how you're going to be.

"Most of them you meet are completely unnatural. They're not giving you their real personalities at all, and you have to accept that.

"Obviously a lot of them are impolite because of that, and a lot of them try to give the impression that they're not bothered a bit about meeting you, and put on this big air of indifference. That upsets me a bit, because it's unnecessary, as well."

Does he *feel* under pressure?

"Not consciously, but all of a sudden things get on top of me for no reason whatsoever, and really it can come on within minutes. I feel as though I have to do something, but I don't know what it is, and nothing you do seems to be it.

"I'd imagine it's like getting stuck in a lift, it's the same sort of helplessness. It's very frightening, sometimes."

IF THE pressures of touring are now over for a while, others begin. The next day, Numan and the band are going into the studio to begin demoing the new album, "Telekon", which is about:

" . . . a man who can finally harness the power of telekinesis, who can move things by thinking about it. He realises he can do it, and it just increases and snowballs. Because of his power he ends up destroying everything, including himself.

"That's planned, but it's not definite yet."

Then it's Europe, America, Japan, the world.

Complex

By Gary Numan on Beggars Banquet Records

They won't come back
You know it's always the same
And they're sure to forget
Saying "Everyone lies"

So I'm down to this
I'm down to walking on air
And you're here by my side
With all your waving and smiles

Please keep them away
Don't let them touch me
Please don't let them lie
Don't let them see me

*Words and music by Gary Numan.
Reproduced by permission
Beggars Banquet/Andrew Heath Music Ltd.*

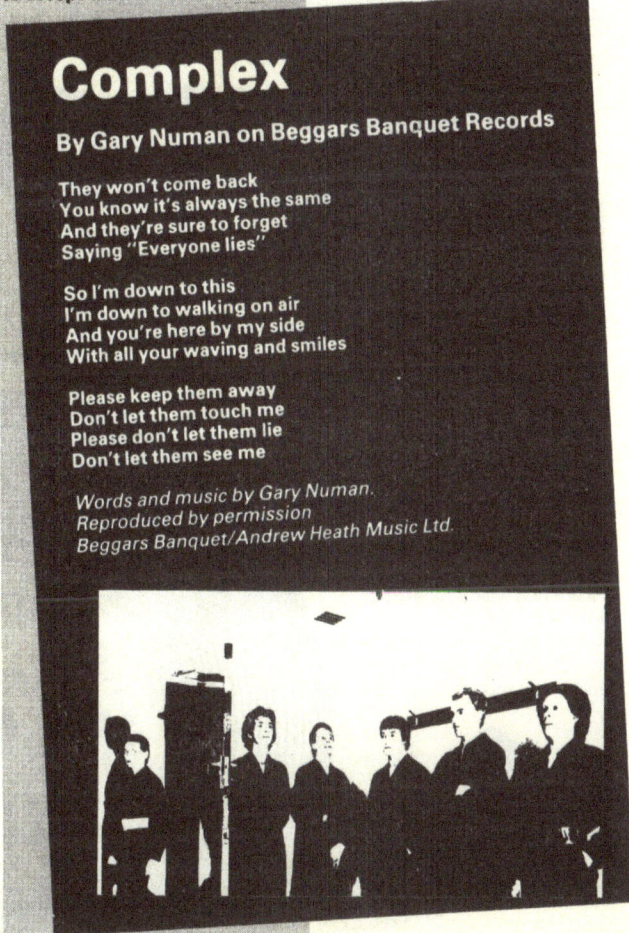

Magpie 1979 with Derek Burbidge (right), the director of the *Cars, Complex, We Are Glass* and *I Die You Die* videos.

THE BAND

RRUSSELL BELL
Born on 15th September 1955, Rrussell plays guitars, synthesisers and other bits and pieces. He started having classical training on the violin at the age of 9 and two years later took up his first guitar. Six foot tall, Rrussell is the tallest member of the band and holds a brown belt in karate. He has a very dry sense of humour and claims to have been born in "Kent, Great Yarmouth and London". his ambition is to play the first gig on the moon but admits to being worried about the size and nature of the audience.

CHRIS PAYNE
Before joining Tubeway Army in the February auditions, Chris was with a classical rock group called Crucible for four years. He plays both keyboards and viola. His worst experience in life was being knifed at a football match. Born in Penzance, Cornwall on 1st February 1957, Chris likes tennis, squash, football and walking in the country as only some of his many likes. His favourite solo artists is Gary Numan and his ambition is to cross the Andes.

PAUL GARDINER
Age 21, born in Hayes, Middlesex and still lives there. He's played bass in Tubeway Army and is the only original member to still be with Gary Numan. Paul's ambition is to be a well known musician in his own right. He describes himself as a quiet person who may not say much but thinks an awful lot. Paul really enjoys music and loves playing live, seeing and listening to other groups and making music in studios. He plans to play more of his own material one day and work sessions with other bands as well as forming his own record label.

CEDRIC SHARPLEY
Born in Cape Town on 2nd July 1952, "Ced" plays the drums. He auditioned to join Tubeway Army in February 1979. He had the total sound that Gary Numan was seeking and he was offered the position. Before he joined the band, Ced was a full time musician in a band calling themselves Druid and after a few years joined another band called the Blazers for a while. His favourite solo artists are Elton John and David Bowie. Ced has a great sense of humour and bubbling personality.

Billie Currie: "I went to see Magazine at Drury Lane Theatre and there was this guy called Steve Webbon from Beggar's Banquet. Nice bloke, too nice to be in this business, and he just comes up to me and says, "Hello Billy," a really charming bloke and, after a while, I notice this guy sort of hiding behind him and it was Gary. He was so shy. And he says, "I'd like you to meet Gary", and he drags Gary onto the scene. This was in the bar, on the stairs, in fact, at Drury Lane, and we sort of had a chat and I think he mentioned straight away, or rather Steve Webbon did, about doing this tour that was coming up. I remember meeting up with him in a rehearsal room, it's a bit of a distant memory now, doing some rehearsing to see if we all fitted together. But I got on with him pretty much straight away, with Gary because he was a fan. I mean, I could get away with murder in a way. It was quite nice for me not to be in Ultravox and just have some fun, because he was a big fan of Ultravox. But I remember him giving me a lift back home and he showed me the *Are 'Friends' Electric?* picture disc and I was a bit like. "Mmmm, that's very nice." I didn't really know what to say. I was tired. I just wanted to go home and, like two weeks later it's massive (laughs), successful. I suppose I was a bit snobbish in some ways, I was so into Ultravox that I found it difficult to get into other people's things, because I'd found that artwork slightly garish, in other words, that's what I'm saying, I found it a little bit tasteless. Ced (Sharpley) was good for Gary because he made his songs groove, otherwise they could have been a bit too deadpan." *Extreme Voice, 14*

**Gary Numan
Born 8.3.58**

PEOPLE BORN on this date are romantic, sensitive and shy, but they do make faithful friends and can always be relied on. Gary is very artistic and has many new ideas which he successfully puts into practice (when he's not busy crashing his 'plane). He works hard and gets the most out of his exciting life.

GARY NUMAN

50p

INTO THE 80's by
Peter Gilbert & Francis Drake

Bound within card covers, and given away to the first subscribers to the fan club, this was the first book about Gary Numan. Gilbert and Drake were the John Peel of print and prints, photographic journalists who sought out and promoted new musicians. They were the first to interview Numan.

SPECIAL THANKS TO: TONY & BERYL WEBB - SU & STEVE AT BEGGARS BANQUET & GARY NUMAN.

GARY NUMAN

DESIGN & LAY-OUT by FRANCIS DRAKE. TYPESET by PETER GILBERT.

119

THE NUMAN INTERVIEW

We had just been shown the stage-set for the Gary Numan tour and had listened as the band had run through a couple of numbers. We had both worked the remote contols of the robots to be used on stage and now we were perched high up on an outside balcony of the recently closed ('For Alterations') Roxy in High Street, Harlesden in north-west London. The Roxy was being used as a rehearsal venue for the Gary Numan tour and it was here that we decided to interview Gary Numan for this booklet. With the traffic roaring below us we asked Gary how he had felt when he first heard that 'Are 'friends' Electric' had reached number one?

"When I first heard about it, Martin from Beggars Banquet rang me up at home and said; "It's done it!", and I went into the front room and leapt up and down because I thought I was supposed to leap up and down. It was a big anti-climax in one way though but it was very nice in another. There was a nice sense of satisfaction and pride inside, but nothing I could actually put my finger on. I didn't want to go out and celebrate for weeks on end or anything like that, I just wanted to keep on going on as before but with 'all that' under my belt."

Pic:Peter Gilbert.

What sort of person is Gary now, since everything has happened? "I'm pretty much the same sort of person as I was before really. I expect a little bit better treatment now though, which I suppose is just ego really. Now that I am famous I think I ought to be treated as such but that doesn't get out of order at all. It's just that if I go out to eat at a restaurant, I don't expect someone to tell me to wait outside. I expect them to respect me more and be more polite, just as I expected them to have treated me before but now I think I'm more aware that I don't have to put up with people being impolite and things like that anymore." Gary assured us that this attitude doesn't spill over into his private life though, he doesn't expect anything more from his own family or close friends for example. In this respect he's convinced he hasn't changed at all.

We wanted to seek out the Gary Numan that is usually hidden from his fans and asked him
if he was easily hurt by people? "I have been in the past but not for a long, long
time because now I won't let anyone get close enough to hurt me." We mentioned that
his first hit single 'Are 'friends' Electric' was really about that feeling of detachment as a result of being hurt by someone? "It's about what happened to me, really
feeling cut off .... it's strange really, I mean there's this person now who I don't
want to name but I'm very very close to them, yet a little while ago we had a row and
that was it, I could stop and it didn't bother me at all." Gary frowned and looked at
the busy street below before continuing. "I don't know whether it didn't really bother me because I could stop or whether it didn't bother me because I knew that this person would always be there - I'm not sure to be honest - I wouldn't really want to put
it to the test either because I wouldn't want to be hurt again."

One thing is for sure anyway, Gary Numan hasn't lost his ability to be honest with his
answers. When we first interviewed Gary, he told us that he always drove around in his
car with all the doors locked because he was really nervous. We asked him if his latest
single 'Cars' meant that he still did this because the song seemed to confirm this?
"Yeah I do, y'see it started with me just being frightened I suppose. Like, if I was
down in the high street below, I'd be nervous but I'm up here so I'm ok and if somebody
comes in here through this door   (he points to a door on his left) I know I can get
out through that one - Y'see I always need a way out." We told him that we get a lot
of letters from people saying what he needs is someone to look after him, someone to
protect him. Is this what he felt he needed?   "No!, I don't want someone to feel as
if they want to protect me. No, I don't want protection at all. I do need somebody that
I can scream at, someone that won't vanish the very first second I start screaming, a
person that won't disappear for good. I need that kind of person, y'know, someone to
moan at but I think that most people need someone to moan at, it's just that I moan a
little more energetically than most people do."   What about marriage? Does Gary need
someone he can devote his life to or does his past experiences make him feel that he
wouldn't want to get in that situation?   "Until a short while ago, I very much wanted to get married but I really don't feel I want to at all now. I don't feel a bit like
getting married, I don't feel like I want to have children or have anything to do with
anybody - (he looks down at the floor) - These feelings might all be gone tomorrow, to
be honest with you I haven't really thought about this very much until you just asked
me."   Was it the feeling of being 'tied-down' that bothered Gary?   "No, I don't mind
being tied down at all, I don't think being married does tie you down. If you get married, you get married because you want to stay with one person. You wouldn't want to
sleep around or do anything anyway, so it wouldn't tie you down because you wouldn't
want to do these things if you got married for the right reasons. I believe in doing
things for the right reasons. I don't know why I don't want to get married anymore,

maybe I've just lost interest."   Gary looked a little sad and we asked if success
had given him this attitude?   "I don't know, I've only just this second thought about
it."   He pauses and swallows.   "It must be that but I don't know how or why it's
done it......... I just haven't met anybody that I'd particularly want to stay with
permanently. Although I've never met anybody in my life, apart from 'Jo' and at that
time I really did want to get married."   We pointed out to Gary that the music business has both its 'ups' and its 'downs', he may not feel the need to have anybody
close at the moment because things were looking 'up' but what about when the 'downs'
come along?   "Well I'm hoping to be out of this business before the 'downs' come
anyway." Does this mean that Gary won't carry on until he's not as popular? Will
he quit while he's still on top?   "I'd rather leave when I get fed up and if that
happens while I'm still at the top, so much the better. Actually, thinking about all

this, I wouldn't leave unless I saw that things were starting to decline and I could see that I wasn't interested enough in putting out better songs or at least working at putting out better songs."

Gary doesn't think that the Gary Numan on stage is any different to the ordinary, everyday Gary Numan, he doesn't think he has seperate identities. We pointed out that in our opinion, the Gary Numan on, for example, 'Top Of The Pops' was very different from the Gary Numan that we were now interviewing. He always seems so ultra-confident when he's on the stage? "It all depends really. When I'm out there I'm amongst that lot (he points at the people in the street below) and I'm just one of a thousand billion people and being famous isn't going to stop a knife going in me, that's not going to stop anyone punching me to the ground. On stage however, there is no worry of that happening, the only thing I can do is what I actually do and I am very confident in that respect." Was this type of show, with all the visual effects and robots etc; the sort of thing that Gary always wanted to do? Was this the sort of show he liked to see when he went to see someone like Bowie on stage? "Yeah, shows like what I'm doing are the ones I've always liked - Big shows - I'm very into that. I'm not really into the clubs at all. I've never understood why people have wanted to stick to sweaty little clubs where you could never really see anything......"

We explained to Gary that we felt that places like Earls Court were just too big? Would Gary ever consider playing bigger places than those on this tour, stadiums for example? "I think stadiums are a bit silly really, especially for a visual act, because in stadiums and those sort of places there are no visuals. Earls Court is good but if you are at the back of the place the distance from where you are to the actuall stage is too far but then again, if you're at the front of the stage or if you are actually performing on the stage, you can look out and see all these people and the atmosphere is amazing. There are good and bad things about playing the larger venues, the bad thing is that three quaters of the way towards the back, the visual side drops quite a bit. The good side is the atmosphere, it's better and at least people can get to see you."

What about the very early Tubeway Army fans who have now turned against Gary because he is now famous, does this hurt him at all? "It did at first but I didn't so much feel hurt as I did helpless. There's just nothing I can do about that, there is just no way that they should turn against me that I can understand." What are his feelings for those at the dressing room door that want to get his autograph but won't be allowed in for obvious reasons? He can't be let loose among hundreds of screaming girls but would he like to go outside and talk to them properly without being mobbed and seen as a 'superstar'? "If there were a few outside then I would speak to them but I'd rather not speak to too many because it all gets a bit silly. Out of all the people that I've met, less than half of them I've enjoyed meeting because of their bad manners. It's either that or they're so shy that there's no point but there have been a few that are shy but nice and grown-up at the same time. There again there are those that are silly and grown up as well." Is Gary embarrassed by this sort of thing? "Yeah, I get quite embarrassed sometimes especially if it happens in public. I don't think I always will be though, it's just embarrassing because it's new to me at the moment." Gary seems to be confused. "I feel very much as if I don't quite belong to being famous at the moment, I haven't quite got used to it yet - (Gary grins as he continues) - I don't know if I'll be famous long enough to get used to it either!"

We changed the subject at this point to ask Gary a question that has been asked by so many people who we have received letters from. What exactly is a 'Machman'? "A Machman! I stole that name from a little article that I read and this machman in the story made love to machines. In the lyrics to my songs, a 'Machman' is like a part of a special police force, it's a humanoid, an android, completely perfect in appearance, very striking and very tall and very, very powerful. It simply collects the 'crazies', I got the idea of the 'crazies' from a book that the 'Replicas' theme came out of. They are similar to commandos but they're in ordinary, everyday streets." Our minds were just buzzing at this stage, what on earth are 'crazies'? "Well, this goes back to the Replicas thing. The 'crazies' are humans who have failed the quota-test and who have made a run for it. That's what 'Down In The Park' is all about. Y'see, the 'crazies' can hide in the park where nobody goes or in the underground where they can't get found" Did you think, like us that 'Down In The Park' was about humans? Well, like us you are wrong! At least according to Gary Numan, who wrote the lyrics. "Down In The Park" is about the park. And around the park there is a place where the 'Machmen' go to watch both the park and the machines chomping through the 'crazies'. Where they watch the 'crazies' trying to fight the machines and also watch the other machmen going there to to beat up the 'crazies' who they could see were beating the machines." This explanation was all too much for us to take in at once but if you think about what Gary says, it all makes sense in a strange kind of way. (read it through again).

GARY SIGNS AUTOGRAPHS AT 'TOP OF THE POPS' — AUGUST 1979.

The first two albums by Tubeway army were very depressing but the third album by Gary Numan 'The Pleasure Principle' isn't the same, why is this? "I've probably got fed-up with writing depressing songs." But you told us in our first interview with you, that you could only write when you were depressed? Does this mean that has all changed now? "No, not really. Now I seem to be writing songs when I'm in quite a state. I mean, if I get myself worked up into a state or I get angry or anything like that, then I start writing. When my mind is ticking over and I'm doing a thousand different character changes a second, that's when I'm able to write." We referred back to the earlier part of the interview and the matter of insecurety. Where does Gary feel at ease and what does he feel secure doing? "Nothing" he answered. But doesn't he feel safe and secure in his car with all the doors and windows locked? "I feel safe providing it keeps going but there's always that nagging suspicion that the engine's going to break down and I'm not going to be able to get away. There is always something that can go wrong - Always!"

Gary went on to explain that even on stage, there's that same fear that something's going to go wrong, a microphone could pack up for example."There is really nowhere where I feel one hundred per cent safe and secure, I do when I'm at home with my family of course." We asked if this was a sort of refuge for him? "I thought you said 'refuse' for a minute." A rare smile crosses Gary's face at this remark, which is quickly replaced with his usual serious expression. "Yes I do see home as a sort of refuge but even at home I'm not safe nowadays. We get people ringing me up all the time, people knocking at the door and things being thrown into the garden." Gary added that he was disillusioned by people's reactions to him. The press reaction however, doesn't really disillusion him, it was no worse than he expected. He admitted that the press had mis-quoted him on a number of occasions and he imagined that they would have shown more of an interest and treated his ideas with more respect? "I thought they would have been a bit bored writing about punk and mods etc and I just thought it would have been refreshing to have something different that they could show an interest in." We suggested that they may not be showing much interest because they hadn't discovered Gary themselves?

"Well, somebody told me the other day that they aren't as interested in us as they could be because they missed us at the beginning and they're not really into us because they never 'made' us. They resent us really, because nearly all journalist's in the music press like to feel that they've done it all, then they can boast with, "I discovered this and I discovered that." But none of them can say that about us, y'see when we did become popular, everyone wanted to interview us. All the people that came to do the interviews said; "Well, I was the only one that was interested in you years ago but I just couldn't get an interview with you!" The truth is, the only people that were really interested in us at the beginning was Chris Westwood and yourselves." We asked Gary why he thought it was that people liked his music so much? What is it that they have seen?

"Something different I think. Everybody in the music press seems to hate us and I think that this type of person feels sort of special not liking us. But I think the special people are the ones that <u>do</u> like us - I think it takes a lot of intelligence to like us when everyone in the music press is telling you that we're <u>not</u> intelligent. The fact that people can see through these journalist's that are trained to fool them, well I just think that's great! Everyone in the music papers is trying to tell these people that they're stupid for not seeing through me but let's face it, I'm the most obvious person you could wish to meet." We spoke next about the future, would the bands line-up be changed when the tour ended? "Well, obviously Billy Currie will be going back to join Ultravox and the emphasis is to go back to guitar and violin for the fourth album, the synthesiser element is being dropped. The drummer is going to stay, the bass player's going to stay, RRussel plays guitar so he's going to stay, Chris plays violin so he's going to stay too, and I'm going to stay (Gary grins). So I'd imagine it will drop down to five people."

By using different instruments in the future, the sound is obviously going to be a lot different? "That's another good reason for doing it really, I'm getting a bit fed up with synthesisers. I think there's more that can be done with guitars than I realised. Now I've made some money I've been able to buy some gadgets which can do all sorts of things to the sound of guitars and I think I can do a lot of other things as well, to make them sound different." Finally Gary was asked about the third album 'The Pleasure Principle'. When we first did an interview with him he explained that he took ideas from other people and was one of the few people honest enough to admit to this. But is he intending to do this in the future as well? "Well, this is going to be embarrasing because I didn't steal 'The Pleasure Principle' from anybody and having said before, that I steal things all the time it now sounds as if I'm denying it. I admit that the second album 'Replicas', was taken from Ultravox and the first album was taken from almost everybody that I've ever heard. They were both heavily stolen from people that were around, both lyrically and musically. 'The Pleasure Principle' however, wasn't taken from anybody else, y'see Ultravox weren't doing anything at the time and there just wasn't anybody else to steal from."

We both looked at each other and smiled, one thing about Gary certainly hasn't changed, his outspoken honesty. And judging by his last answer you definitely can't get any more honest than that!

INTERVIEW BY **FRANCIS DRAKE** & **PETER GILBERT** : IN THE CITY FANZINE.

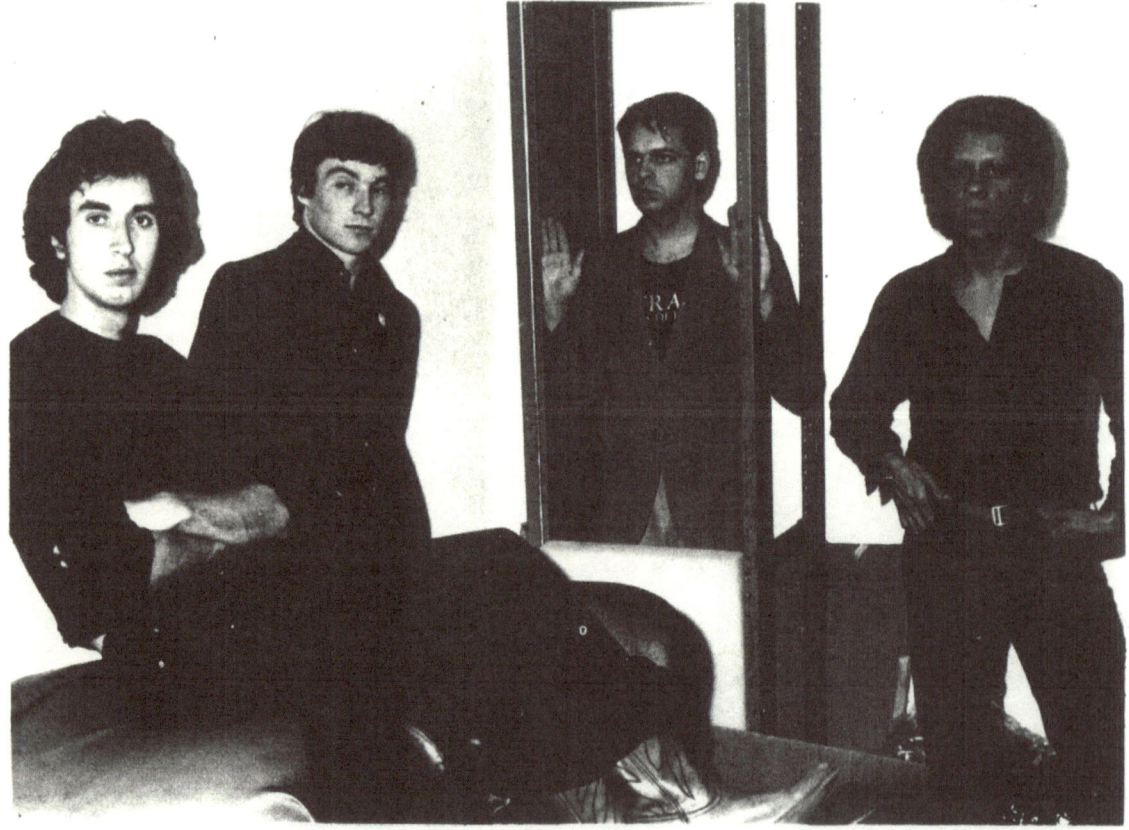

Pic:Peter Gilbert.

GARY NUMAN, who topped the singles & album charts with his band **TUBEWAY ARMY,** finally goes out on tour in his own right this month, playing at Glasgow, Newcastle, Bristol, Liverpool, Manchester, London (H'smith Odeon) & Birmingham. From October 1 he is at Guildford, Southampton, Ipswich, Brighton, Aylesbury, Wolverhampton & Sheffield. After his initial chart impact as **Tubeway Army** with the hit single "Are 'friends' Electric?" from the 2nd album **"Replicas"** on Beggars Banquet BEGA.7, the show is being billed purely as **Gary Numan**—as is his new single "Cars"/"Asylum" on BEG.23 & the new album **"The Pleasure Principle".** Meanwhile, Beggars Banquet are making re-available all early **Tubeway Army** records which were previously deleted & for which a tremendous demand has arisen. The 1st album, known as the Blue album, has been re-released, along with the early singles "That's Too Bad" & "Bombers" twinned as a double pack selling for £1.60.

Until **Tubeway Army** was seen on 'Top of the Pops' only a cult minority were aware of **Gary Numan's** provocative talent & his positive & individual approach to his music. It's not easy in today's pop world to create a vital new music style, but such was the power & chilling feel of Gary's images on that all-important No. 1 single & top selling album that he has rocketed to instant fame! Now his hypnotic compelling music style is established & the cult following has enlarged beyond even the expectations of Beggars Banquet, the record company who signed **Tubeway Army** on the strength of a demo tape which with a little re-mixing became their debut single, to be almost immediately followed by a debut album which was the result of only 4 days in a demo studio!

All material is written & produced by the prolific **Gary Numan** who is a remarkable & uniquely talented 20-year-old who plays keyboards & guitars as well as delivers the vocals. His backing musicians on tour are virtually the same as on his TV appearances, namely **Paul Gardiner** (bass), **Chris Payne & Billy Currie** (synthesisers & keyboards), **Ced Sharpley** (drums) & one other guitar/synthesiser player. A spectacular monochrome stage set has been designed, featuring twin 20ft towers for

NUMAN MAKES MORE FRIENDS

THE AUTUMN tour by Gary Numan's Tubeway Army — exclusively revealed in Record Mirror last week — has undergone several revisions, and all ticket prices and booking details have now been finalised.

The complete date sheet now reads: Glasgow Apollo September 20, Newcastle City Hall 21, Bristol Colston Hall 24, Liverpool Empire 25, Manchester Apollo 26, London Hammersmith Odeon 28, Birmingham Odeon 30, Guildford Civic Hall October 1, Southampton Gaumont 2, Ipswich Gaumont 3, Brighton Dome 5, Aylesbury Friars 6, Wolverhampton Civic Hall 7, Sheffield City Hall 8.

Tickets will cost £3.75 in London, and £3.00 at provincial venues, and will be available at box offices and usual agencies from this Friday (July 20).

Meanwhile Numan's follow-up album will be 'The Pleasure Principle', set for release on September 7, with a single available at the same time. Beggar's Banquet are also making available again all the early Tubeway Army recordings which had been deleted. The first album, 'Blue Album', is re-released on August 4, along with a double pack of the early singles — 'that's Too Bad' and 'Bombers' — selling for £1.60.

21/6/79

© Boris Spremo

© William Wright, 2016

NUMAN GOES INTO SPACE

Numan's predicament similar to that of Kate Bush. Both artists were rich and successful, well established in careers built entirely on records and TV appearances. The problem was to contrive an impressive original live show with little or no experience, save the advice of experts. One chose a daring line in specious mime; the other has decided on a brief selection of basic, aloof poses to camouflage his nervousness, and superficially 'modern' decor to go with his swooping, bombastic, space, cartoon music.

The PA is white and looks like Habitat / Design Centre approved for functional elegance. From here a roaring cathedral hum swells through the hall in great sustained surge. Dry ice, posing as deadly vapours, swirls amidst fantastic architecture of alien origin (actually two four foot pyramids flanking the stage), like a *Dr. Who* setting for druids from Metabellus 3.

Most of the chaps stroll quietly on stage, and array themselves in assigned positions: bassist Paul Gardiner: the other first album veteran; Russell Bell on guitars, devices and irritating synthesized percussion which sounds like your auxiliary reserve tanks being struck by meteorites. Behind them is the kind of framework once favoured by *Supersonic*: a high platform holding Cedric Sharpley and his drums - almost as distinctive a part of Numan sound as the voice itself. On either side great pillars of parallel bar-lights flash through limited permutations. Electrical Supervisors (keyboards) Chris Payne and Billy Currie, occupy symmetrical insets.

Neatly groomed, impassive in black, they're like model citizens of a technician-controlled megacity in a '50s space movie. They play one of their indistinguishable instrumentals; music to accompany hostile mermen on amphibikes attacking *Stingray*; drifting into space-vortices with *Fireball XL5*.

Numan walks on slightly too fast like a model's catwalk debut, feigning nonchalance, and sings *Me, I Disconnect From you*.

I only saw the TV film, but with the distinctive light show, the blatant mimicry of Numan's movements, it's *exactly* like Bowie's Thin White Duke tour some years ago, the simulations too pronounced for coincidence. Surely they must realize how many people will notice? In timing and precise body angles, Numan's replica is fastidious; Bowie's ultimate, untouchable star persona, revered throughout galaxies, evoked well. Considering promises of robots and dancing cubes, I'd expected a *Thunderbirds* puppet tutored by Kate Bush and *The Jetsons*.

I'd also expected to enjoy the music more. Only *Down In The Park* approached the mystery and atmosphere I'd hoped for. Impressive lights can't retain interest indefinitely when the music is little more than pleasant with a veneer of majesty.

During instrumental breaks Numan strides around striking ludicrous Gary Glitter poses; stands, arms folded in death repose / Tralfamadorian masonic salute; or leaves the stage altogether. His voice, strongly reminiscent of Bowie's early Newley-bleat, is a perfect extension of the music - echoing with images of machine-age, *Brave New World* factories and technological wastelands. All fine apart from *On Broadway*, done as a creeping march where the normal detached tones are exchanged for an attempt at conventional singing. It is a disaster.

Most effective are the slow, stately melodies, which hint at greater subtleties for the future. *Everyday I Die* works quite well, as does *Bombers*, despite the simulated laser attack (ho-hum), and a few others.

Finally the dancing cubes! During *Down In The Park*, the pyramids, with muted lights glowing mysteriously within, start to revolve and shuffle awkwardly like fused Daleks - the whole ridiculous spectacle provoking memories of Busby Berkeleys famous movie sequence with dancing pianos, each propelled by a hidden dwarf. Golddiggers of '79? Fortunately Gary Numan doesn't seem to take it too seriously either.

For the moment, if Numan is acting as the vanguard for a million SF enthusiasts with *Practical Electronics* subscriptions, and *Vogue*-endorsed austere androgyny in fashion, he's about to be supplanted in the flood. But he's still young, and basically sincere I believe; he may yet create something essential.

Prominence has been thrust upon him, after all. Amazing he's coping so well, really.

ROBERT ELLIS

Gary Numan doesn't trust people much, and he won't let them get too close. JON SAVAGE observes the Seventies' last star.

A HERO IN THE MIRROR

. . . thinking of it now, a television documentary would be preferable. On a commercial channel, so it's nicely broken up. A working title could be "Some People Need The Heroes": it's a line from one of the subject's songs which seems to fit.

After the station ident, there'd be a short piece of film before the titles start running. This section would consist of two short, contrasting clips.

The first would show the subject (Numan) on stage in mid-performance, just out of reach of scores of hands which wave like sea-anemones (nice simile—beguiling but deadly): he darts, suddenly, to brush a few of them lightly. There are a few sharp, clipped screams.

The second clip would show Numan talking, white T-shirt, wary eyes, soft voice, in a hotel room: he doesn't really understand human nature, or even like people very much — he worries about not getting close to people, becoming a product.

The clips (perhaps melodramatically, but That's Entertainment!) would take Numan's pop stardom as granted, and go further to pose a series of questions: did he choose to become a star? what kind of star is he? what does 'star' mean? and what is he going to do with this peculiar but pressured position? In short, to try and sort out, a little, what is this thing called Numan.

Which, it not being an ideal world or even America, will have to comprise the parameters of this article.

AT the time of writing, Gary Numan's first tour since becoming a major "pop" attraction has just finished. He has played to — roughly — 40,000 people in 16 capacity venues throughout the country: by the last date, at Sheffield's City Hall, he has lost about £30,000 on the tour (including the £3,000 or so given to Save The Whales from one of the Hammersmith nights) which has, nevertheless, confirmed Numan in many people's eyes (including pop columnists on the national tabloids) as a new pop star. It can be said to have been very successful.

The writer is to join the tour for the last two dates — Wolverhampton and Sheffield. In adapting to the different time scale of the touring party, he will become a different person: The Journalist. In writing about it, he will swap lived experience for self-conscious experience. As The Journalist, he will interview The Pop Star: perhaps they'll both be able to crash through their roles a little.

The writer's motives: he's interested by the fact that the music press have so consistently got Numan completely wrong; he likes the last two singles enormously (but worries about the albums) and is interested enough to have quite a lot of theories about the phenomenon.

The facts about Numan's success are obvious if you flick to the charts pages. They don't need reiterating. Like other recent developments — the mod thingy, the recurrence of "teen-style" following for figures as diverse as Geldof and Sting, and the emergence of political groups far more explicit than the TRB ever were — this success illustrates a concerted stylistic shift further away from the last and current stylistic revolution (punk) and its more directly-related products. As far as the mass market is concerned, passion — being an uneasy fashion — is being hesitantly or otherwise discarded as a new breed of heroes (as opposed to anti-) emerges.

The strands contained in the "original" groups and followers (which compression enabled them to make such an impact) are now being unravelled further and further and turned into careers by groups who are trying to extend the ideas even further than imagined. The context is lost. Whether you approve or not, it's inevitable. In this confusion, the writer, more by accident than design, becomes involved with documenting this particular strand: a post-punk mutation (rather than plagiarism) of certain Bowie and Roxy Music elements, made new, different, attractive and successful.

TO the narrative. Armed with all this speculation and more, the journalist arrives at the Walsall Crest Hotel in time to meet the mediator between him and the star, Su Wathan, and to be transported to the concert. He meets Numan, tentatively, helps himself to some food, and watches the event, attentively.

It reinforces his earlier impression: it is A Spectacle. Numan takes his environment around with him: tonight it's set up in an ugly, functional Thirties hall, more suited to school speech-days than any kind of celebration. Conceived with an architect's megalomania, the stage set dominates and frames both audience and performers alike: impossible to escape or ignore, exactly contemporary in its practical futurism. Measuring time by decades, we look spuriously to the new to bring up new things: to a considerable section of the pop audience, Numan is it, a successful percentage of new information grafted onto old.

From inside the towers, fronted by banks of lights, the five-piece band — clockwise from bottom left: Paul Gardiner on bass, Chris Payne on keyboards and violin, Ced Sharpley on drums, Billy Currie (Ultravox!) on moog, and Russell Bell on guitar and noises — and Numan, stage-centre, run through 20 songs to tumultuous applause.

The audience is a mix of archetypes and individuals: some "punks", some electric friends, some who've paid Numan the ultimate accolade of exact imitation (the "Replicas" phase) and quite a few who are non-aligned but who've simply come to see what this thing called Numan is about.

A common factor is their youth: a large number are under 21 — a generation too young to have seen Bowie or Roxy Music, or even later heroes or anti-heroes from the Sex Pistols onwards. Some people need the heroes, and Numan is the one they seem to need: they don't dance, much, but watch intently. The ones at the front stretch their arms out with palms open, like drowning men: these gestures of innocence turn to ones of danger when the star gets closer — they'd tear him apart if they got the chance.

The quality of the material is variable, but they don't seem to notice. The performance suffers from a sag in energy after the initial impact of the opening: some of the songs, too, sound remarkably similar to one another. The band play the material better than they did at Glasgow, and Numan's performance is more confident, able to encompass a relaxed spontaneity.

But what's missing in Wolverhampton is a sense of occasion. It's special enough for the audience, but not for the band: the same old story of what the audience sees once, the group plays scores of times. This time they're professional enough — remarkable, considering their inexperience as a unit — to maintain a standard, but there's little extra.

The journalist gets a bit bored and concentrates more on the audience. What is strange about the event is their relationship to Numan: it's peculiarly passive, bereft of direct contact (bar the hand-to-hand brushes) — as if there's an invisible wall between them. He's up *there*, they're down there: it's a more formal relationship than the journalist is used to, made perhaps more obvious because of Numan's comparative inexperience and the particular performer-mode he's chosen.

"I THINK . . . no, I'm not really interested in a new relationship: I'm sure what can be done. I've really no idea . . . apart from the fact that you talk to the audience and claim to be one of them, or admit that you're not one of them, which is why you're singing and they're not, and get on with it, which is what I've done . . . I've very little to say to them. They know what the songs are, I'd imagine. I really wouldn't want to tell them what the songs are about before each number: there's no need to tell them what they are, because they already know. There really isn't much more to say — you can't have a conversation — it's very false with between two and four thousand people.

Captured on CRO2, Numan's voice plays back to the writer a few days later. At the time he remembers being impressed by Numan's candour and directness, whether or not agreeing with all of what he said. As the journalist, he'd chaperoned a helpful, courteous Numan to the tape in a hotel room in Sheffield, the day after Wolverhampton.

By this time he'd met the rest of the band, the support band (Orchestral Manoeuvres in the Dark) the tour organiser, the security people, Numan's parents and others whose presence is necessary for the tour, and had been impressed by the subtle sanity of this operation under strain.

Although by now locked with each other into the different time schedule that constant travelling and the long, peculiar hours induce, those on the bus retained an air of innocence even when winding-down from the adrenalin of the performance: the more traditional " rock 'n' roll " methods of alleviating the strain — both chemical and attitudinal — were, mostly, conspicuous by their absence, much to the journalist's relief.

Continuing: " That kind of performance suits me. I don't like being very close to them. I don't like standing gigs at all: I get very

worried when they get near the front. I know it's very flattering that they rush the stage but it does worry me when they get that close. I like there to be a gap, I like theatres where there's an orchestra pit. It isn't that I don't want to talk to them, meet them, or anything like that, it's just that I don't feel safe with all those people trying to get there. . . ."

WE'RE eavesdropping on the tape again. At this point, the journalist is easing the interview in by discussing the previous night's performance, commenting on that gap he'd noticed between performer and audience: as he suspected, it has something to do with the quick, massive pressure of the situation in which the "star" finds himself. Numan is sitting, concentrating on the replies as hard as the journalist is on the questions, at the same time watching his reflection in a mirror as he nervously teases his recently-washed hair.

They've both established enough of a rapport to attempt communication: by prior arrangement, both have driven up from Wolverhampton to Sheffield in Numan's shiny, white, expensive American sports car — a present from WEA Records to induce Numan to enter into a fresh five-year deal.

The drive is uneventful, pleasant — through the West Midlands to the M1, then North — as the journalist gradually forgets the incongruity of his position in the careful, respectful attempts to find common ground. Naughahyde, red on white, Neu, Bowie and Roxy Music tapes, stunning acceleration — a complete sense of unreality in the Indian summer, amplified by lack of sleep. Here, in his car, Numan appears safest of all.

By his own admission not a natural performer, he decided to do the show as it was, and lose money, because "I thought there was no point in going out unless you were going to give people something to remember and to make it worthwhile. There's no point in being top of the pile unless your show's going to be top of the pile as well."

Was the lavishness not also to cloak his inexperience?

"You mean to take the limelight away from me a bit? No, it wasn't really. To be honest, the show was put together to be something to look at. I merely thought that being new at it, I wouldn't be very interesting to look at for one and a quarter hours.

"I don't think I am: I can't do enough different things or look in enough different ways to keep people interested for that time — apart from the real diehards who'll gaze at me for hours. Obviously the majority of the audience isn't like that — especially at this early stage, a lot of them — half of them are just going to see what the fuss is all about."

What was the point of the pyramids?

"On the cover? It was image. On stage, the robots are pyramid-shaped — that's to tie-in with the cover, and also because I thought that robots . . . you say a robot and people think of something that does this (gesticulates mechanically) and clanks about, and really that's the most unpractical shape you can think of because it's so unstable, it keeps falling over all the time. A pyramid is, I think, the most stable shape you can have: it really is hard to budge. Talking about a straight-thinking machine, it'd have to be that shape where it didn't fall over and damage itself.

"So I thought — well, if I'm going to do it, let's do it realistically, in the proper shape of what they'll be and not go for the image. We had enough impact in the show itself — it'd be nice to put some realism into it.

"I also think that the panels, the walls, it looks like they just light up. I think that one day probably we'll have buildings like that where you don't have street lights, but the walls of the buildings themselves light up outwards, so it's not like street lights and shadows and little quiet corners that you could get mugged in. . . ."

The journalist demurs. It transpires that Numan was actually beaten up in a 'quiet corner': that would account for it.

THE journalist then mentions that the show lacks an edge of provocation that he's become used to, and likes in his 'entertainment'.

"I think it's just taking it back to cabaret — showbiz for showbiz's more than anything. That's trying to explain what we're on about, and use this as a visual expansion of our songs. . . . To be honest I used to hate all that stuff (cabaret), but fairly recently I've got to really like Bing Crosby and now I like Frank Sinatra. I never did before, but the way he just breezes among his crowd as if they're in a circle and not on stage, and he's so relaxed."

To compound the impression, Numan performs a reasonable version of "On Broadway" in his current set: it's a song he's always liked, and featured in the lyric of "You Are In My Vision". The journalist finds this conservative aspect a little hard to take, and wonders how Numan felt about the atmosphere in which he moved in late 1976 and early 1977, seeing the Sex Pistols early on (at Notre Dame Hall) and playing the Roxy in June 1977.

"I always thought it was a movement, especially so in the early days before it came fashionable. I don't feel part of it, no. I don't think I'm doing what I'm doing now because of it, I think I'm doing what I do now *quicker* because of it, if you know what I mean. The business side of it changed: people got signed up, so I went out, crashed away for a few months, got a contract, and then away we went on our own tack. Which is because of punk, but I didn't get into it and evolve into what I'm doing now, I just simply used it."

ROBERT ELLIS

It fits. In moving the audience away from the last fashion, Numan mustn't appear to identify too much with it. For good or ill, his preoccupations are different.

"I did use it solely as a means of getting a contract. I didn't see it as going anywhere, I don't think it has gone anywhere. I was excited by the thing as a whole, that all of a sudden there was something that was completely new — new fashion, new music. Hopefully when it got started, something really great would come out of it, but it sort of got destroyed by its own ideas. The anti-hero thing could never happen because this country has always had the heroes, it always will do — I think it's a very English thing to make heroes."

He replies, to another question: "I never agreed with coming on and being the same as the audience, I never liked that side of it. I never liked it as a personal taste. Also I thought it was very false: you'd see bands as they got more and more well known get more and more distant. Half of it is necessity, really — you have to. . . ."

THE phone rings, interrupting the journalist's question. After it's finished, he tries to pick up the thread, remembering his Socratic dialogues; he suggests that Numan's lyrics project a nightmare, depressing view of the future . . .

"It's an extreme view of the future . . . from what's happening now, but only one view. It's not necessarily the only one I have, the only view I think there could be — it's possibly the most interesting to write about. It's what I see around me. I'm obviously very affected by things — the violent side of human nature. Human nature itself is quite interesting to write about, if you take it to its extremes."

The journalist agrees. Does he think they'll get more extreme over the next decade? And if so, what can he see himself doing in that case?

"Hopefully I'll have enough money, whatever, to get away from it. . . ."

Wouldn't he try to do something about it, even if it was merely banging his head against a brick wall . . .

"I haven't got the interest to want to prevent it or stop it — I tend to be much more selfish and think how I can get out of it, rather than help other people out of it — that may change as I grow older and hopefully grow up a bit more. I know a lot of things I do are very selfish — there must be a word stronger than selfish to cover it— something I'd imagine really isn't quite right."

Numan's honesty, at least, is refreshing. Like many who are in control of their own destiny, who've struck lucky at an early age, he often seems impatient of those weaker than him, heartless perhaps. He's done it *himself:* why shouldn't others?

His business instincts are acute: apart from having as much control over his career as is possible — he writes the songs, produces them, designed the stage set, hired the band— he's recently entered a favourable deal with WEA, through licensees Beggars Banquet. The deal is for a five-year period, with an advance of £17,000 for the first year.

The deal, further, binds him to seven albums over the five years: "But we did write into it that if any time I wanted to, I could stop — we talked a lot about this, and it's quite important — that any time I wanted to I could stop and they can't withhold the royalties, but the agreement is that if I ever do go back to writing I go back to them and finish off that deal. I've signed up for albums, but not for any special time — I don't have time schedules to meet. It's quite nice."

Earlier he'd mentioned his appreciation for the down-to-earth aspect of WEA, their honesty about the nature of their involvement with the music business (cash). It is suggested that he's extremely fortunate in his relationship with them — in being in a position to dictate his own terms: they need him more than he needs them.

He ponders, and replies: "I think on a straight fifty-fifty basis, that's true ... because we could go elsewhere, and they couldn't go and just nip out another number one."

His position is even stronger because of the current comparative weakness of the music business: "No, no. They need everyone they can get (laughs). WEA have got Rickie Lee Jones and. ... God knows ... Fleetwood Mac, the Eagles ... they're all right. They're doing quite well at the moment, but these people may not be going for another five years, and they think I will."

THE white sports car with red naughahyde is an illustration of that strength, that bargaining power. The journalist enquiries whether Numan thinks it's a toy.

"It's a toy for a little boy, to keep him happy, that's the feeling I get ... It doesn't bother me. It appeals to that side of me ... 'Oh wow!' that sort of thing. Also, it's a good move on their part to make sure I didn't bugger off to CBS: it's a good little lever they had to make sure negotiations went on in a semi-friendly fashion. I found it flattering that they gave it to me, I don't think they've done anything like that for quite a while.

"I was told that when they heard that I'd been talking to CBS — it was only really to find out what the going rate was — it got back to WEA and they thought, 'Oh my God, he's signed to CBS,' and — this is what I've been told, mind you, it's not me shooting off my own trumpet — I was told that they said, 'Get him whatever he wants, just make sure he doesn't go'—which is fair enough, 'cos I suppose I make a lot of money for them."

All isn't entirely roses, however: "It's easier for me to dictate now than it was before ... to say we want to do this, we want to do that. Before we used to have big arguments about it, now I sort of say, 'That's what we're doing,' and then make sure that they do it — but that's half the problem, to get them to do what they say they'll do, because they say OK to keep you happy and then worm their way around it. They need constant watching.

"But ... I don't know if this is true, but they seem to have a respect for my intuition, if you like, in what's to be done. I think they're realising I know more of where I'm going than anyone else does, because they've no idea of what I'm going to do until I have. Problems haven't arisen."

Numan's known where he's going for a long time. Is 'being a star' what he'd always wanted?

"Yes, very much so, that's why I went into it. It's the only thing I've wanted, you know, for such a long time. I ... always thought I'd do it — looking back on the material I based that opinion on, I'm very surprised. It really is awful. That was when I was 15, 16, hadn't even written a song, still thinking I was going to be a star.

"There was something about the atmosphere of the business that interested me — I can't really give a definite thing that gave me that atmosphere, I just remember reading about it. I had a cousin about seven years older than me who was really into it — and an uncle, Jess (Lidyard) on drums, who I ended up working with — and obviously being around this side of the family, I'd read their papers, I'd watch RSG, and I just got the atmosphere from it, really from when I was quite young. I thought: Well, that's for me, even though I didn't really do anything constructive about it until I was 18."

Often becoming a 'star' is as much an act of will as of talent: some have the talent, few the *will* to enter the marketplace in the manner that being a 'star' demands, and then to hold on to what you've got: the consolidation is even more of an effort than the initial rise.

At one stage, Numan admits that he's sometimes at present holding on by his fingertips. The pressure is intense, and increasing: "I didn't plan on it being this early"

GARY Numan is 21. He still lives with his parents in Wraysbury, near Slough. His father, who works for British Airways, sank all his savings to enable Gary to continue without a record contract. The family are obviously very close.

The journalist asks Numan about his adolescence, seeking clues. Numan admits he was a very isolated child, by choice: "I wasn't bothered trying to meet other kids. It didn't bother me ... to meet other people and talk to them."

He left school at 16: "I went to a grammar school: that's the one that sent me to a psychologist. I was expelled from there, eventually. ... I was a disturbing influence. They did try to help me, they were quite nice: they let me stay an extra year — they didn't expel me — even though I should have been. I went into the top class, the A stream. The next year, I was demoted to the bottom class."

Numan's 'problem' was irrational fits of violence, which came on quite suddenly, without warning. In the next couple of years, he went from school to school.

"I then went to — I had a talk with my dad who said (in "Summertime Blues" voice) 'You really need an education, son,' (laughs) so off I went to technical college and ... it happened again. I had some really weird experiences there ... I was just sitting down, and all of a sudden you feel like a bubble forms and people's voices stop making sense.

"I couldn't understand what people were saying, and I could feel myself actually moving back into it, and my head became the bubble and I was going inside that. It only happened about three times: it made me feel quite strange, occasionally — it really did affect me quite a bit."

On playback (and at the time) the writer wonders whether Numan hasn't swapped that bubble for the society-approved bubble of stardom. Numan continues:

"I left college and went straight into work. In the daytime I put air-conditioning into buildings, I was a driver, a clerk, really just everyday jobs, all the time planning as well as writing. I was always intending that it was just for now, so it was about bearable. It was enjoyable if I enjoyed the people I was with — one job I had, I was there exactly for a year from birthday to birthday, and it was the worst time of my life — horrible. Horrible people. They hated me because I dyed my hair: they used to call me 'Wally Wanker' — that was my nickname."

It is guessed that this might be one of the reasons why he doesn't like people very much....

"Obviously this is where ... at various times I met people, particularly when I was younger, and I've taken it all in. Another thing that affected me a lot was when I split up with the girl — that was quite some ago, about two years ago in September, or three years ago. It was very painful. That possibly affected me more than anything, particularly in terms of me getting close to people. It was the one and only time I've ever loved someone outside the family."

Still, it happens to a lot of people and they survive.

THE journalist asks whether he has any of his old friends left. Numan comments with a certain objective humour:

"No, they dropped me long before I become famous. Quite some time ago. They got rid of me because ... I was singing in a group and they didn't want me writing the songs any more, so I said, 'It really doesn't bother me' — I didn't intend at that time to become a big front-man pop-star anyway — I was just doing it to gain experience, but they weren't writing any songs.

"So I said, 'Well, write them then, I don't mind,' but that wasn't very good. And so they got rid of me, then went out and did their own set — it took them about six months to write their set, and they had a couple of my songs in it anyway — there was only about a 30-minute set, and it really was awful. The group? It was Mean Street. They were on the Vortex live album."

The journalist dimly remembers hating it.

"I was disgusted. And all my so-called friends at that time would follow them around religiously, and pogo at every gig, it was like rent-a-crowd. And they dropped me completely from parties, from anything at all. ... I had one other one, called Gary Robson, who's the only friend I've got ... the only friend I trust completely."

Presumably that's where "Are 'Friends' Electric" came from?

"Yes, it was based on that. And then obviously being deserted made me very paranoid in my attitudes towards friends. I often tended to write 'friends' in inverted commas in a lot of the songs."

The journalist mentions that he seems to have had a lot of unpleasant experiences ....

"I don't think any more than most people, I just think that I take them .... badly (laughs). I find it hard to accept that and understand it — I find it very hard to understand human nature a lot of the time, which is part of the problem."

THE same day, in the Daily Star, Numan is given the honour of a centrespread: "'Gary — We Love You! But Numan Is So Alone". The image machine revs into higher gear; Numan is typecast as "aloof and arrogant" ....

"Most of what I said had been blanded out — I didn't actually say what he wrote down, he took the gist of it only. It wasn't done in a nasty way, so I didn't mind it — it was a bit sweet and sickly. I'm not like that.

"The image doesn't worry me. From an outsider's view, it's probably accurate. I think I'm quite strong-willed and know exactly what I'm doing — which is mistaken for arrogance. The 'aloof' bit is my wish not to get too close to the audience ... which isn't being aloof. It's more survival, really."

His audience?

"It's very awkward — to be honest about it without giving the wrong impression. I don't feel any ... I won't say loyalty, I don't feel that I owe them anything. I made the records and they bought them. They owe me as much as I owe them, so they cancel each other out, really. I don't now have to make another album; I get very annoyed when I hear these things like, oh, people saying, 'We made you.' They really didn't, they really didn't make anybody at all. We made ourselves, they simply bought the records."

What kind of hero does he think he is to them?

"It's a bit difficult to answer. I think possibly to a lot of people I'm a symbol of something new — I wouldn't venture any more than that. The . . . pose element is an image: they'll see that, and then they'll go home and imitate it in a mirror and do G. Numan handclaps. That's thought out the same as the image is thought out, to give people something to latch onto. It's taken everything I did when I was young and when I was a fan — and using that, knowing that other people somewhere must be similar to me: I'd like them to do what I did to my heroes."

As the pressure mounts, and the demands increase, Numan's attitude to his audience, like most stars before him, becomes all the more equivocal. But then, this attitude is, as well, an extension of his attitude towards people in general — wary, mistrustful.

Most of Numan's songs are about alienation, distances between people, failures to communicate. By becoming a star, he's given societal approval to live out those states without attracting attention, as he used to in school . . .

"I used to live it out quite a lot before, really, because I didn't go out much, I've never gone to parties. If I go out, I normally go out on my own, in the car, driving . . ."

Is he treated as an object?

"Completely. As a product, yes."

Would this encourage him to treat others in the same way?

"I think it would do. I think it's a bit early yet for me to change my personality to that extent. I find it difficult when the audience meets you, because when they do they're obviously nervous or edgy because they're not sure how you're going to be. Most of them you meet are completely unnatural: they're not giving you their real personalities at all, and you have to accept that. Obviously a lot of them are impolite because of that, and a lot of them try to give the impression that they're not bothered a bit about meeting you and put on this big air of indifference. That upsets me a bit, because it's unnecessary, as well."

Does he feel under pressure?

"Not consciously, but all of a sudden things get on top of me for no reason whatsoever, and really it can come on within minutes. I feel as though I have to do something, but I don't know what it is, and nothing you do seems to be it. I'd imagine it's like getting stuck in a lift, it's the same sort of helplessness. It's very frightening, sometimes."

The journalist empathises. He's noticed previously, as one by-product of this tour, numbers of stray females making their way in a very determined fashion into the hotels where the group are staying. Numan finds this hard to cope with.

"I find it very unnerving when people come back to the hotel, because being a 'rock 'n' roll star' you're obviously expected to pull the lot — so you've got to come out with the smooth talk, and I'm just not like that. I don't chat people up at all. I find that, trying to get the role right — my 'position' — that what they expect me to do and what I want to do aren't the same. I find that possibly the most difficult part of it."

NUMAN has to go to a sound-check. The journalist packs up the tape and goes off to visit some friends. During the sound-check, the tension rises: Sheffield is the last night, with all that entails.

The gig is superb — the journalist is, wittingly, quite riveted by the spectacle: on top of the edge given by the knowledge that this is the last time that these songs will be played so, the road-crew are dicing with the robots and dry-ice, up-staging Numan whenever possible. Numan enjoys it, perhaps relieved of the burden of his image, and rushes round the stage like a boy let out of school.

While it's the best performance out of the three that the journalist has seen, out of a tour whose staging is such that all others will be measured against it for some time, he still worries (he likes to, really) about the sameness of much of the material and the spectacle's ultimate reinforcement of passivity, of one-way experience. There's no doubting, however, its objective success: the crowd go tapioca.

Back at the hotel, there's an end-of-term party, featuring band members, WEA functionaries (including a recognisable but definitely sleeker Dave Dee: the irreverent journalist thinks of "Bend It" and smiles) and assorted liggers, with a chastened Human League in tow.

It's brought home here to the journalist what a cruel game the music business can be, for both those at the top and the bottom of the pile: one is fawned over, the other is ignored, excluded. Both involve a dehumanisation. The journalist, as voyeur/vampire, submits and watches. He argues amicably with the classically-trained Chris Payne (about noise), talks to the careful Paul Gardiner, and discreetly slips out of the circus, early.

THE next day, he ties up some loose ends with Numan. Gradually he finds out that, last night, Numan finally buckled under the strain.

"I like it exactly as I am at the moment, except that there's still too many people geting to me after gigs and before gigs. Last night there were too many people that I didn't know and that I didn't want there, but I was just too polite to say 'Get them out,' so I ended up having rows again.

"There was another scene last night: during the last two or three days I finally decided that I'm fed up with trying to be nice to people, because it isn't respected or appreciated for what it is. I don't think they realise the effort that's needed for somebody in my posiion to constantly be nice all the time and sign every little bit of scrap paper they stick under your nose . . . I think there should be quite a change of attitude from now on.

"If people are rude to me because of nerves, or anything else, then I'm really getting into the frame of mind that I really won't put up with it, which isn't getting . . . tired, already, of their attitude. I don't want to be treated like a product any more. I think it's about time I put my foot down, make people realise that they can only get so much before you get fed up like any normal person."

The journalist supposes that it's the pressure.

"I think, finally, yes. I was really surprised — I was completely calm, and then something happened and then I went off . . . ."

But surely that's a direct function of his wishing to become a star, which is what he always wanted . . . .

"Yeah .... but then I don't have to take it when I get it, I can adapt."

It transpires that the straw which broke the camel's back was a pair of professionally stray females, shrink-wrapped in lurid turquoise, who gained admittance to the hotel and then settled in. Apart from harassing Numan at a particularly vulnerable point, they attacked his assistant, Su. These irritations were compounded by further annoyances, until . . .

".... I finally said — this is the first time in six months I've done that — I just said, very loud, 'Get off my back', and just shrugged them off, walked away. And then I walked past this woman and she goes: 'Temper, temper' — and that was the last straw. I started slamming doors and throwing things.

Then I calmed down a bit, but it then flared up again later on and I wrecked a radiator — threw a fire extinguisher and smashed a radiator — and a phone and a chair .... then I was all right. I was completely calm ...."

It reminds the journalist of Numan's description of his schooldays, a little unnervingly.

IF the pressures of touring are now over for a while, others begin: the next day, Numan and the band are going into the studio to begin demoing the new album, " Telekon ", which is about:

".... a man who can finally harness the power of telekinesis, who can move things by thinking about it. He realises he can do it, and it just increases and snowballs: because of his power he ends up destroying everything, including himself. That's planned, but it's not definite yet."

.... and mixing live tapes recorded at Hammersmith for an EP: one of the tracks included will be the live version of "Bombers". Then it's Europe, America, Japan, the world. Ad infinitum.

The journalist looks at the fragile, incredibly determined youth and wonders. He's impressed by Numan's candour, humour, directness and willingness to communicate, and respects the sweep of his vision and his nerve in carrying it out. He thinks, later, that Numan might still be seeing only part of the overall picture, and that, although young, fast, bright, and learning on his feet, the pressure of his chosen position is going to give him severe problems. Numan is controlled to a "t": it makes the break all the harsher when it occurs.

The writer later flicks lazily through a Burroughs/Gysin volume, "The Third Man", for lateral illumination: he reads a piece about coincidences, synchronicity. On transcribing the tape he finds it's broken off in mid-sentence, with Numan finally saying, hesitantly: "I ... don't know ...."

Some people need to be the heroes: but what does it do to them?

This piece on Numan is worthy of preservation because it is written with style and with a serious analytical intent. Jon Savage gives an honest portrait of Numan on his first concert tour, and he reaches conclusions that are thoughtful and fair. And that's not surprising. Savage was one of the two or three best music journalists in Britain; a would-be Capote or Mailer or Thompson or Wolfe, though his achievements are a long way from the Class of Four who inspired him. That's no slight on Savage because those four Cornerstones of New Journalism were so far ahead of everyone else they were a different species, a new form of man. I'm holding off from playing New Journalism games by bringing that Foxx-ian quote poetically back round to *Numan*, because I'm running out of space so I'll get on.

Savage writes of himself in the Third Person and calls himself The Journalist. This is pretentious, though an oft-used conceit of New Journalism, and it detracts from the impact of the writing, partly because of its pretension and pomposity but mostly because Savage misuses it. In Norman Mailer's great Documentary Novel, *Armies of the Night* (1968), Mailer steps outside of himself and writes of himself as a character in the novel, in order to provide a more three-dimensional account of the documentary narrative he is telling. He does so, aptly, because he is writing of events in which he often plays a leading part, i.e. he is at the centre of the narrative (he starts by giving an account of his arrest), he is not merely a fly-on-the-wall. Jon Savage cannot successfully step outside of himself to become a once-removed character in the narrative because he is not a character in the narrative-of-the-subject, he is a spectator, a journalist. The subject is *not* Jon Savage it is Gary Numan.

Despite that almost serious failure of approach, Savage's article is valuable and entertaining. Before I pull out two points of particular interest, it's useful to note that Savage's own musical heroes were the Anderson/Wakeman Yes. Savage had flown the Atlantic for a cold-shouldering 15-minute meeting with Anderson (oh, and to see their Wedding Cake Show at Madison Square Garden) and he wrote almost fawningly that he would follow their British tour. Then he became the historian for Punk. That's quite a leap, impressively taken.

The first point of interest is the tag-line, accurately describing Numan as the last star of the Seventies. This Truthful Fact was widely known in 1979 but it has been forgotten by the public at large, mostly because *Cars* was a one-off novelty hit in the rest of the world one year-decade later, and novelty diminishes stature. Numan's music and appeal are timeless but it is time to re-establish the fact that, in Britain, Gary Numan *was* the first big star of the post punk era in music and, more importantly (for people interested in pop cultural Truth), the last star of the Seventies in any medium. In film terms, he was *Star Wars*. He completely changed the game. His work in this end-of-the-seventies era is still being copied and referenced ad infinitum.

On the first page of his article, Savage's observation that "Numan takes his environment around with him" and his description of the contemporary practical futurism of Numan's stage set "conceived with an architect's megalomania" and placed within a municipal Thirties building, where it frames the performers and the audience, is brilliant. It makes subtle connections with the totalitarian aspects of Numan's performance art and is drawn from the strident powerful hypnotic repetitive aspect (i.e. the core) of the music that Numan was playing, music that chimed completely with young working class people in a Broken Britain, whose neo-fascist leader would infamously (and increasingly accurately) declare that "There is no such thing as Society". That ugly functional municipality of environment (and mind) had bred this man and this music but, and this is the vital ingredient for Numan's success, and Savage almost reaches this conclusion in the article: Numan wasn't the machine, the oppressor, he was the oppressed, the awakening soul, angry and afraid, strident and lost, maniacally adored and all alone. And yet he went on record saying he didn't want to overthrow the Establishment, he wanted to be a part of it. Numan was a compound of delicious sparking contradictions. An impossible balancing act, emotionally and creatively, and therefore doomed to fall, and to fall hard. As Jon Savage concludes, with a fine twist on Numan's own lyric: "Some people need to be the heroes: but what does it do to them?".

Melody Maker

October 20, 1979   20p weekly   USA: one dollar

DATES: QUEEN TOUR, WHO IN BRIGHTON

ALBUMS: RATS, SPECIALS, F. MAC, E. JOHN, MOTORHEAD

GARY NUMAN:

ROBERT ELLIS

IN EVERY DREAM CAR, A HEART-THROB

by JON SAVAGE (p.31-33)

ELLEN FOLEY IS NO MEATHEAD

by MARK WILLIAMS (p.18)

GARY NUMAN and friends: the Reginald Dixons of the 1980s?

Sounds 29/9/79

Are pin-ups electric?

Gary Numan
Newcastle

"HOW BORING and predictable!" concluded a southern accent with a backstage pass pinned to his jacket as he exited his way past me halfway through the second date of Gary Numan's first ever tour.

Being an altogether more reasonable chap I wouldn't go as far as the unknown dissenter, but he did have a point. 'Are Friends Electric?' is one of the classic singles of the year, but herein 20 variations one after another didn't make for the most exciting of musical menus.

As Dr Phibes' church organ tootles in the background, black curtains swishes open to reveal two synthesiser players, a drummer, a bass player and a general handyman who quadruples on synth, syndrums, guitar and tambourine. They are arranged in an H-shape amongst scaffolding covered in revolving flashing strips with a glowing neon triangle in the middle and two small mobile pyramids at either side.

After the static five have electronically droned for several minutes the strips stop revolving, shine even more intensely and young Gaz strolls on. Dressed in black, he meanders around, waves, folds his arms across his chest and has the general look of a man with a well-used mirror.

Being an overnight sensation obviously tickles Numan pink and this appreciation shines through the carefully rehearsed poses every so often. He says very little, perhaps because like David Bowie (whose last tour all of this irresistibly reminds me of) he knows that it's a lot easier to maintain a facade of mystery if you keep your trap shut. When he eventually speaks and says "This has all happened rather quickly" he sounds more surprised than anything else.

The performance started high, with 'Cars' as third one in and finished high with 'Electric' as a penultimate, but samyness apart, there's a couple of clumsy touches, leaving your super-duper smasheroo out of the main set to make sure of an encore is a cheap trick and one that Numan certainly didn't need to resort to as the audience were in raptures anyway. But 'Electric' only showed up after Gary's gang had done the obligatory troop backwards and forwards.

The middle section of the show was a bit flabby, with Numan spending a good three to five minutes off as the band (are they or aren't they Tubeway Army?) juddered their way through a nondescript instrumental.

The golden boy doesn't play anything on stage himself so rather than attempt a prolonged period of calisthenics he disappears. His re-entries were a bit anti-climactic and lacked the drama needed to pull out of the lull that he'd left behind.

The only non-Numan number, 'On Broadway' was less predictable than the rest of the set, but still not the most unexpected of choices, what with its references to neon lights and all. Imagine the George Benson arrangement with synthesiser instead of guitar, and Numan's rigid vocal intonations (which were the same for every song) and you've just about got it.

There's no doubt in my mind that the crown Gary Numan is after is David Bowie's. If Bowie is God, Numan is Jesus. But if Bowie is John the Baptist, Numan is still Jesus. He's gonna need more than this to do it with. In the space of three albums and one tour, Numan has taken android rock as far as he seems capable of. Which isn't to say that someone else couldn't take it further.

If he's able to synthesise, Bowie's chameleon qualities as well as he's absorbed his theatrics, Gary Numan will live long and prosper. If he can't he's shunted himself up one hell of a blind alley.

IAN RAVENDALE

A generally positive review but, seeing that 'neutrals' tend only read the first paragraph, it seems daft, or calculated, to start with such a negative precis. Ravendale points out the points of influence of Bowie but sensibly notes that they are very different performers, and makes the fair point that Numan musically and visually may have 'shunted himself up one hell of a blind alley' i.e. peaked with this new genre and this Bowie-inspired style. Ravendale was wrong, of course. He reviews the Teletour on page 230.

The touring principle

THE TOURING PRINCIPLE

As I sat in 'The Dome' theatre, Brighton, on the evening of the 5th of October 1979 I had no idea of what to expect as I had never seen Numan before, although it was to be the first of many occasions.

At the time I was just as interested in OMD as in Numan so their support act was excellent in musical content, although they performed sparcely in front of the stage curtain (with only their tape computer for company) behind which lay numan's massive stage set, a spectacular alien landscape on which he was to mesmerise us from for most part of the evening.

Before long a deep humming synthesizer frequency was being felt in our ears, heads and stomachs, all over the theatre. Being amongst the people in the front row I suffered the worst of the 'dry throat' effect of the dry ice pouring from the side of the stage.

As 'Airlane' got in to full swing bouncers filled the alleyways and front stage, although they were not needed. The audience, dazzled and dumb-struck by the brightness, speed and size of the light show, sat glued to their seats for most of the show.

From the right hand side of the stage

The old theatre buzzed with excitement and anticipation as the lights went up; OMD had done their job as the warm up act. The stangely dressed audience were ready for Numan and willing the curtain to go up.

appeared a solitary figure, a dark silhouette in the haze. Slowly walking towards the microphone as 'Airlane' reached its final notes, the figure took the microphone and the audiences' attention with the cold steely

A very rare piece from *The Park* fanzine. Sue Jackson kept the home fires burning by hosting Numan discos in Brighton in the years following Numan's emigration, and his retirement from live performances.

glare with which he was to successfully hold us for the whole of the evening.

Having such a close view, I distinctly remember Numan as he repeatedly stood in front of me on the edge of the stage. Black suit, red and blue tie, jet black hair, young white face, ear ring and the steel blue eyes, which were enough to give anyone a nightmare if you looked into them long enough.

No one dared to get up and touch Numan, although he seemed to be teasing and defying us to; standing only one or two feet away, although within touching distance he was not real, did not exist, just in our immagination.

The concert featured tracks from 'Tubeway Army', 'Replicas', the newly released 'Pleasure Principle' and a few surprises. Some of the highlights of the show were 'Praying to the Aliens', 'Me I disconnect from you' 'Down in the park', 'Metal', 'Conversations', 'Films' and undoubtedly 'Are Friends Electric ?','Cars' and 'Tracks'.

We were pleased to hear 'b' sides such as 'We are so fragile', and 'On Broadway' served as the novelty number in which Numan embarrassingly tried to bring an animated element of humour into the show, frequently looking up at Su Watham for support, who was sitting in the side balcony amongst the audience.

Numan was taken back by a pair of knickers thrown at him by a girl a few rows back, but he used them to wipe his forehead with, then threw them back with a glare.

Then, grinning for the first time, his teasing became too much and several screams could be heard from emotional Numanoids.

This started off what was to be a noisy ending to the show - it was obvious Gary was coming back for an encore as 'Are Friends Electric ?' had not been played. To the enthusiastic and emotional cries of "Numan, Numan" the man himself returned, shirtless, with 'Tracks' and the legendary 'Are Friends Electric ?'.

By this time the audience were clambering to get to Numan ; one unfortunate Numanoid was manhandled away by the bouncer, as she made a leap at Numan.

Members of the band, particularly Paul Gardiner, were sweating in front of the lights and seemed to be struggling to keep on playing in the heat. So as the final notes came from Billy Currie's fingertips, Numan's hand came up to signify it was the end of the show. The 20 foot towers of strip lights slowed down their flashing effects and the two glowing pyramids stopped dead.

Dissappearing in a final flurry of dry ice Numan exits stage left, the whole evening was over as quickly as it had started.

Outside, amongst the massive crowd at the stage door, little did I know Gary Numan was going to affect my life so strongly for the next five years.

Sue Jackson.

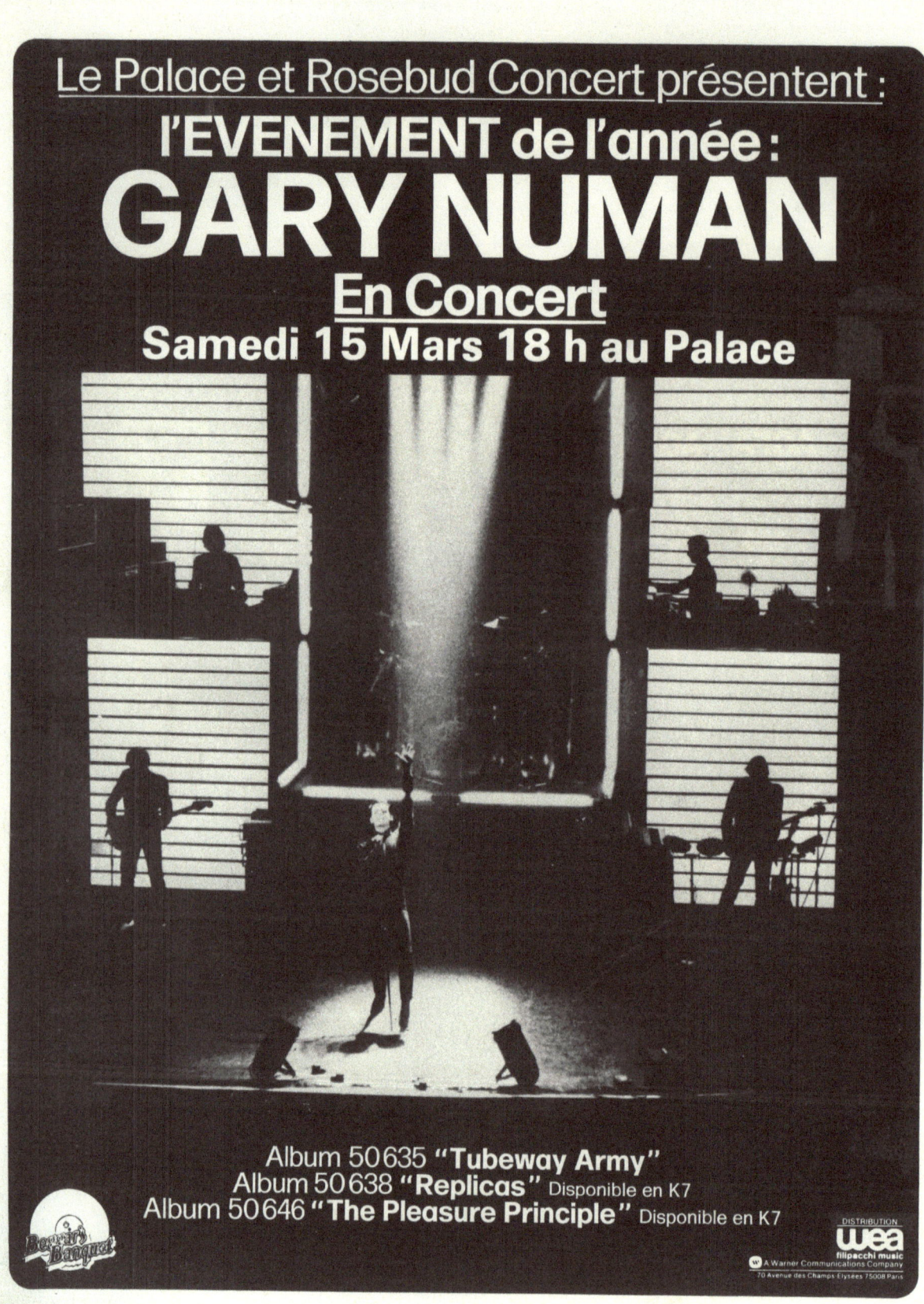

Le Palace et Rosebud Concert présentent :
l'EVENEMENT de l'année :
GARY NUMAN
En Concert
Samedi 15 Mars 18 h au Palace

Album 50635 "Tubeway Army"
Album 50638 "Replicas" Disponible en K7
Album 50646 "The Pleasure Principle" Disponible en K7

Pic Robert Ellis

The man-machine turns off

Gary Numan

Paris

TO A Marxist, Gary Numan must represent the apotheosis of the theory that the Industrial Revolution turned workers into 'a mere appendage of flesh on a machine of iron'. Not only does Numan flaunt his interdependence on his synthesizers, but he's also the most commercially successful musician whose work centres on the theme of alienation.

The effect of this man-machine on his audience seems contradictory — for most of the gig they stood rapt and statuesque, more entranced than emotional; yet at the end he received exceptionally enthusiastic applause.

Parisian rock fans are a non-sectarian bunch and Numan is as fashionable as The Specials or The Police, but this hardly explains tonight's fervour. "Je m'en fous" (I don't give a damn) is one of the most frequently-used expressions in Paris, and it's not considered hip to show enough enthusiasm to make an encore obligatory.

What made the reaction even more surprising was that this was a reasonably mature, young adult audience, not the band of teenyboppers you might have expected.

Perhaps the fans appreciated the trouble and expense that had gone into the presentation of the show. Numan's attention to detail is manifest, and although his image is that of an automaton, he smiles enough to suggest that he might have a likeable personality.

All this makes it difficult to be too harsh about a gig which struck me as tedious. The central failing was that Numan seemed to have tried to maximise the impact of each individual song, while ignoring their cumulative effect. This was epitomised by the use of a mass of varied lights. They gave an excellent initial impression, and were no doubt perfect for the cameras filming the show for French TV, but ten minutes of multi-coloured beams, huge flashing panels and ultra-violets had me covering my eyes. The occasional introduction of dry-ice came more as a relief than as an imaginative use of variety.

One function of the lights may have been an unconscious attempt to compensate for the greyness of the music. There were some nice touches such as the drumming and coda on 'Down In The Park', a couple of instrumentals and the odd funkier number, but these were overshadowed by the monotonous thrashing of electronic percussion and Numan's limited nasal droning. 'Cars' (a perfect replica of the single) and 'Me! I Disconnect From You' were as dynamic as anything produced all evening.

Visually, Gary Numan is as successful as you would expect a robot to be. For all his cool stylishness, the same fixed snarl, vacant stare and carefully rehearsed slow motion chops did little to enhance the music. Only the jokey way he dispensed with 'Are Friends Electric?' and a few occasions when he played guitar indicated any depth of human talent. It came as quite a shock when, not having spoken all evening, he took the trouble to thank his road crew at the end of the show.

If it had been spread out as a dozen cameo performances on *Top Of The Pops*, this set would have been innocuous enough, maybe even enjoyable. As an evening's entertainment it was excruciating.

Frazer Clarke

The Paris concert on 29th March 1980 holds a special place in the hearts of Gary Numan fans. *Replicas, I Die You Die* and *Are 'Friends' Electric?* were filmed and broadcast across Europe, including France, Germany and Italy. Numan's vocals, the Moog sounds, and Numan's guitar playing, with his gorgeous controlled feedback solos at the end of the first two tracks, is a very high highpoint of his career. It's a defining performance. The programme was presented by Antoine de Caunes and directed by Don Kent for Antenne 2. Francis Juneck was the photographer and he and his cameras are markedly better than the team that photographed the London show for *The Touring Principle* film. Alas, the greed and stupidity of the production company means that the broadcast is only available as a bootleg. Numan failed to capitalise on the moment. He didn't play Paris for another eighteen years, and then only a low-key gig at a sparsely attended Le Divan du Monde. The attendance was better when Numan played La Locomotive nightclub, attached to the Moulin Rouge, in 2006. I know because I there. In the expectant crowd outside was a rare black fan dressed in the *Dance* trilby outfit complete with make-up. I wonder what he thought of the jagged industrial metal that Numan played that night?

デビュー・アルバム

めくるめくシンセサイザー・サウンドの開花により一躍スーパー・ヒーローとなったゲイリー・ニューマン。人気爆発の基盤となった噂のデビュー・アルバムの登場！ゲイリー・ニューマンの足跡を知る上でもマニア必携、ロック・ファン必聴のアルバムである。●P-10779A ¥2,500（1/25発売）〔歌詞対訳付〕

エレクトリック・ショック！
●P-10755A ¥2,500
（好評発売中）
〔歌詞対訳付〕

幻想アンドロイド／チューブウェイ・アーミー
●P-10729A ¥2,500
（好評発売中）
〔歌詞対訳付〕

〈シングル〉

コンプレックス

A面45回転、B面33回転という異色のシングル。●A面 コンプレックス ●B面断ち切られた絆～ボンバーズ（ライヴ）
●P-527A ¥600(1/25発売)

カーズ
●P-500A ¥600（好評発売中）

エレクトリック・フレンズ
●P-466A ¥600（好評発売中）

'79年度 M・M紙「ブライテスト・ホープ」No.1！

ゲイリー・ニューマン

Draw In!

Ooh! A nice pic of that Numan being, Gary! It's been done by Jean from Derry. Well done, chum, definitely a Mates Masterpiece!

QUOTE OF THE WEEK

"I don't like alcohol," says the super-cool Gary Numan. "There's no sense in getting a taste for something that's going to make you forget most of what you're enjoying! I can relax or get excited just through *me*. And I have a great time — watching the drunks!"

DM 8,— ISSN 0343-5601 1F 21747 E Juni 6/1980

DON
Deutschlands Magazin von Männern für Männer

GARY NUMAN, EIN STAR DER 80ER JAHRE

STORIES & NEWS INTERESSANTE NACKTE VIELE KONTAKTE

ゲイリー・ニューマン
エレクトリック・ボーイからダンサブル・ボーイへ

145

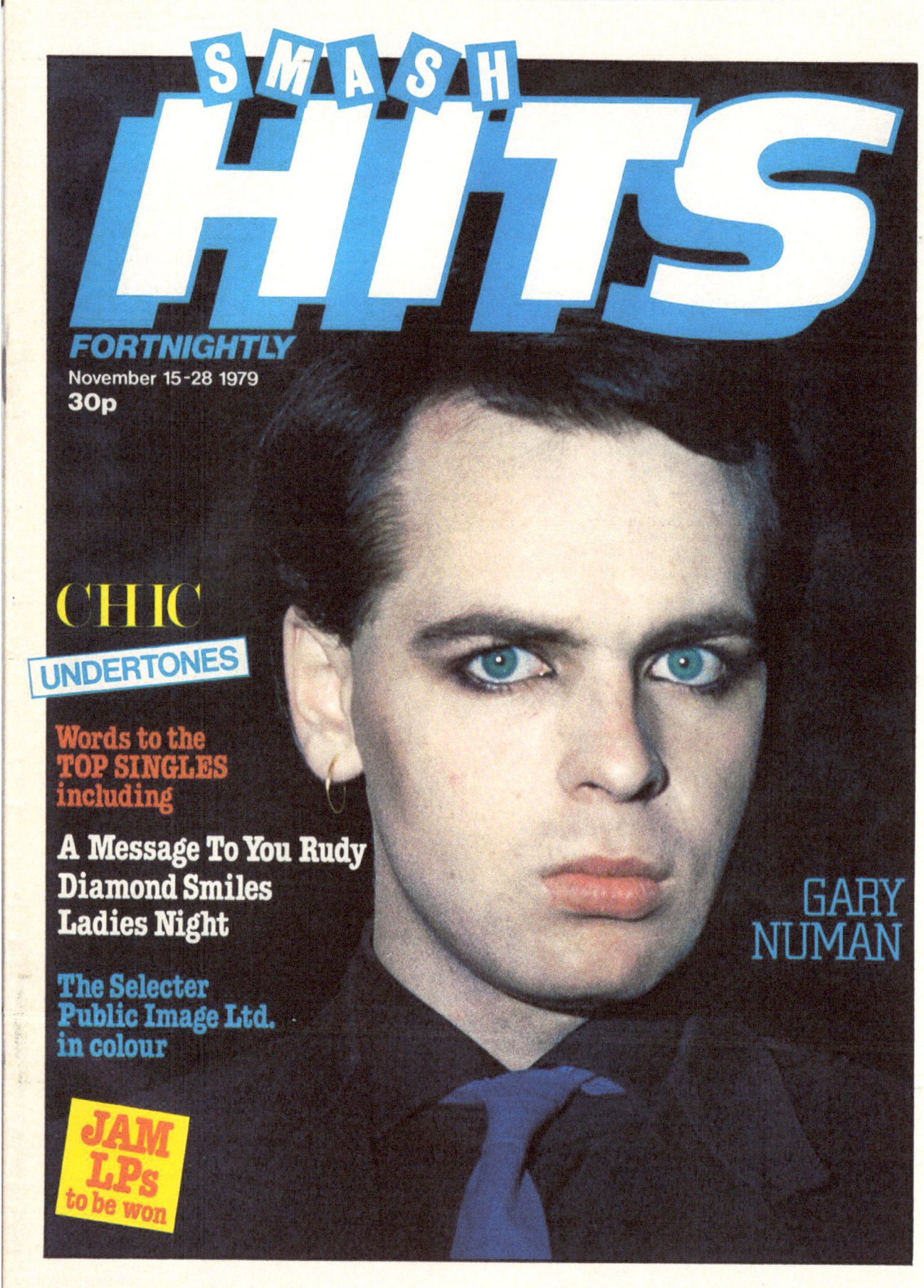

SMASH HITS

FORTNIGHTLY

November 15-28 1979
30p

CHIC

UNDERTONES

Words to the
TOP SINGLES
including

A Message To You Rudy
Diamond Smiles
Ladies Night

The Selecter
Public Image Ltd.
in colour

JAM
LPs
to be won

GARY
NUMAN

Er sieht super aus, er singt toll, er ist mächtig schüchtern und wer ihn jetzt in der 'Szene 79' gesehen hat, weiß, daß er das Zeug zum Superstar hat. Und mit Sicherheit wird er einer von der angenehmen Sorte der Superstars werden, denn Gary Numan ist mit seinen 21 Jahren schon ein pfiffiges, sympathisches, ausgebufftes Kerlchen...

Den Job bei Tubeway Army bekam Gary eigentlich nur, weil er der Einzige war, der damals vorspielte. Das liegt gut zwei Jahre zurück. Die Band suchte einen Gitarristen, Gary war auf dem Instrument Zuhause und ergriff seine Chance. Doch es dauerte gar nicht lange, und er hatte die Fäden von TA in der Hand. Er komponierte, textete, bediente Gitarre und Keyboards – kurz er setzte seine musikalischen Vorstellungen durch. Es entstanden so zwei Alben, „The Blue Album" und „Replicas", von dem auch sein Superhit „Are 'Friends' Electric" stammt.

„Mit dem Hit habe ich eigentlich gar nicht gerechnet", erzählt Gary POPFOTO bei einem Gespräch in Berlin. „Der kommt mir auch viel zu früh, denn ich habe richtig Angst, mich schon einem großen Publikum zu zeigen. Ich bin echt verwirrt um den Wirbel, der plötzlich um mich gemacht wird."

Aber kaum ist er beim Erzählen, packt er auch schon voll aus: „Tubeway Army ist wirklich ein Fantasie-Name. Alle anderen, die da was reindichten wollen, sind auf dem Holzweg. Außerdem gibt es die Band nicht mehr, da ich jetzt nur noch als Gary Numan auftreten werde. Natürlich mit einer festen Band im Nacken, aber nur mit dem Namen 'Gary Numan'. So haben wir auch die neue LP, sie wird rechtzeitig zu meiner ersten Tournee im November rauskommen, schon mit den neuen Leuten eingespielt. Das erste Konzert machen wir übrigens am 28. September im Hammersmith Odeon in London. Daß der Riesenladen gleich zweimal ausverkauft ist, und das schon Wochen vorher, ist für mich auch ein Wunder. Übrigens habe ich auch schon wieder neue Pläne und Ideen. Ich möchte einmal die Songs einer Platte nicht nur als LP rausbringen, sondern gleichzeitig den Inhalt der Songs als kurze Filme auf einer Cassette dazu!"

David Bowie hat es ihm angetan. Wenn man Bowies Namen ins Gespräch wirft, fangen seine Augen gleich zu leuchten an. Und mit John Foxx (Ex-Ultrafox) will er auch gemeinsam was machen.

Gary Numan ist ein total ausgeklinkter Typ: Teenager-Lächeln und irre Ideen in der Birne. Unser Superstar des Monats wird sich bestimmt zum Superstar auf Dauer entwickeln. Wir bringen in POPFOTO jedenfalls im nächsten Heft eine große Special-Story mit Gary...

'He looks great, he sings great, he is able, shy and everyone who has now seen him on the show *Scene 79* knows that he has the makings of a Superstar. And certainly he will become one of the pleasant variety of Superstars, as Gary Numan, with his 21 years, is already a smart, sympathetic, savvy guy... Gary got the job at Tubeway Army because he was actually the only person who applied. That was more than two years back. The band was looking for a guitarist, Gary had been practicing the instrument at home and seized his chance. But it was not long before he had the strings of Tubeway Army in hand. He composed the music, wrote the lyrics, played the guitar and operated the keyboards - in short, the band carried his musical ideas through onto two albums, *The Blue Album* and *Replicas*, from which his smash hit *Are 'Friends' Electric?* comes.

"I did not really expect it to be a hit," Gary told *Popfoto* in an interview in Berlin, "It struck me as being too soon, because I'm afraid to show myself to a large audience. It's made me really confused about being me. Tubeway Army is truly a made-up name. The band is no more, because I will now only release records as Gary Numan." *Popfoto*, Oct79

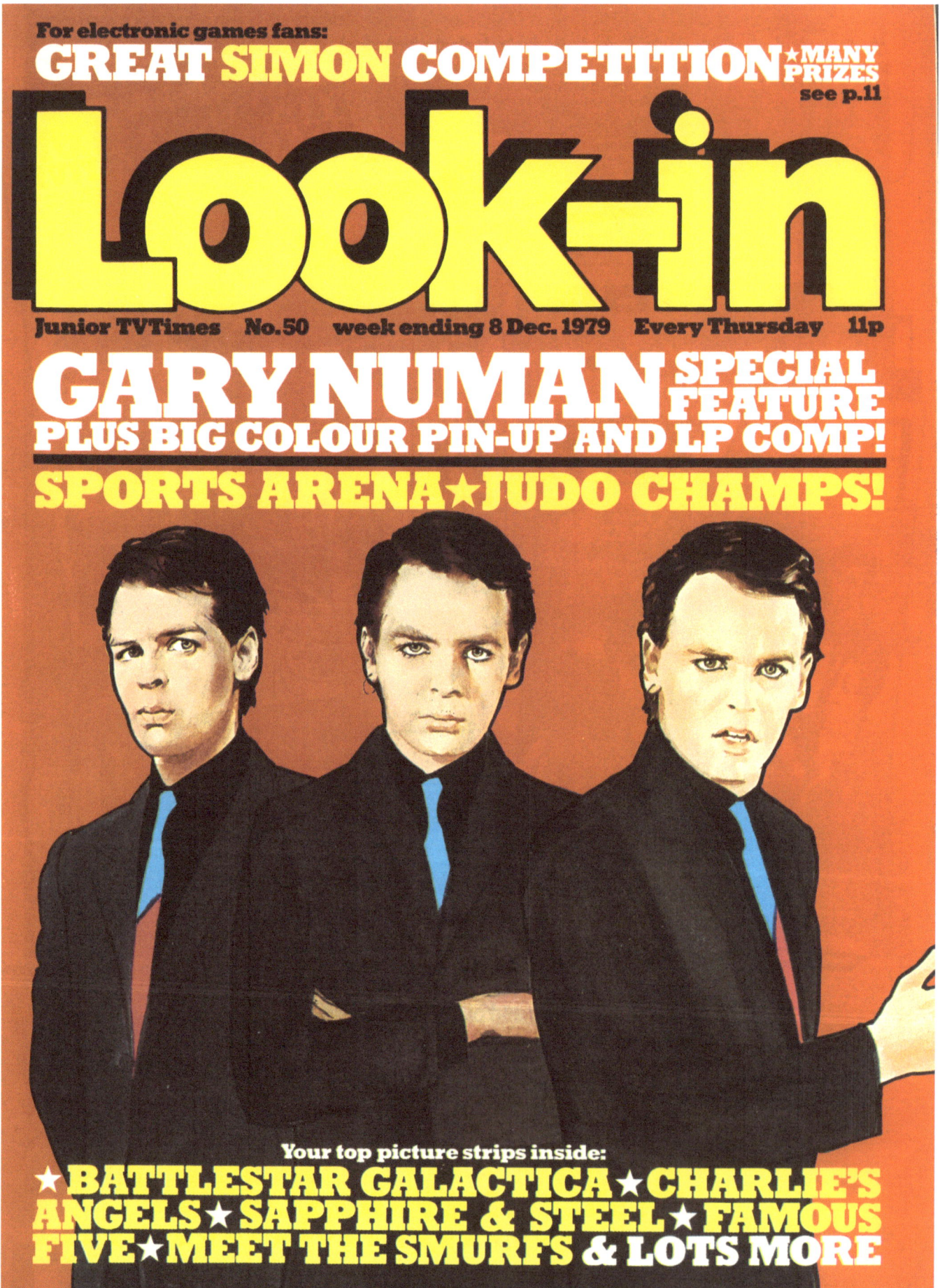

For electronic games fans:

GREAT SIMON COMPETITION ★MANY PRIZES
see p.11

Look-in

Junior TVTimes   No.50   week ending 8 Dec. 1979   Every Thursday   11p

GARY NUMAN SPECIAL FEATURE
PLUS BIG COLOUR PIN-UP AND LP COMP!

SPORTS ARENA ★ JUDO CHAMPS!

Your top picture strips inside:
★**BATTLESTAR GALACTICA** ★ **CHARLIE'S ANGELS** ★ **SAPPHIRE & STEEL** ★ **FAMOUS FIVE** ★ **MEET THE SMURFS** & **LOTS MORE**

A MYSTIQUE has quickly grown up around latest pop hero Gary Numan — the voice behind Tubeway Army, and now a hitmaker in his own name with his song *Cars*, on the Beggar's Banquet label.

Yet is there anything particularly strange about a 21-year-old who prefers the peace and quiet of the country and the company of his pet dogs to the bustle and crowds of London? The big city may be the centre of the pop world, but Gary still lives at home with his parents near Slough.

The reasons why he has acquired an air of mystery and seems a weird character to some, are partly because of his almost robot-like appearance — he almost never smiles on stage and his eyes are fixed in a stare — and the mechanical sound of his records.

And he used to wear nothing but black, to contrast sharply with his bleached hair, and this gave him a sinister look. These days he dresses with more variety, and his hair has returned to its natural light brown.

Gary's distinctive voice has been likened to that of David Bowie, and he freely admits the influence. The first songs he wrote were modelled on Bowie's *Ziggy Stardust* album.

Backing his voice are several thousand pounds worth of synthesisers — versatile instruments he treasures — which at times sound like machines droning and beating in the background.

It all blends together into the sort of sound that people tend to either love or loathe. Fortunately, enough fans clicked to the singular sound to rocket *Are Friends Electric?* to the number one spot.

Not That Simple

Success hasn't been that simple for Gary, and the first Tubeway Army single, *That's Too Bad*, lived up to its title.

The first job he tackled after leaving school was installing giant air-conditioning tubes in freezing cold basements. That must have provided plenty of inspiration for his stark musical compositions, but he didn't turn to music straight away. He stood the job for just a few weeks and then became an import clerk for a freight company.

He was dabbling in bands, and one musical memory is of playing *Tie A Yellow Ribbon* in a pub. Then Tubeway Army got caught up in the punk boom, playing high energy material a million miles away from the slick, calculated feel of the current Numan sound.

The style changed when Gary lost interest in guitars

and placed all his faith in keyboards and synthesisers. His songwriting became more complex, and the music business — particularly the Beggar's Banquet label — began to take notice of this talent.

Replicas, the first great album success for Tubeway Army, from which *Are Friends Electric?* was taken, was never intended to end up on record. It started out as a book!

It was going to be a frightening futuristic look at London, but as the story developed Gary realised that the episodes were more suited to songs.

The story contained such weird and wonderful characters as Crazies, UDs and Machmen, all involved in a conspiracy by the State to control the population by machine. It seems almost a pity he didn't finish the book as the storyline seems fascinating.

Something Special

After the success of *Replicas*, Numan and his record company felt confident enough to reveal the force behind Tubeway Army and

launch Gary on a glittering solo career.

Gary's rapid success has rather startled him, and appearing on television for the first time was a nerve-racking experience. Yet even with that sort of experience behind him, he remains essentially shy.

Gary has total control over his music, and seems to know in exactly which direction he's travelling. He is content to concentrate on his music — and that bodes well for the autumn tour he's making. He is promising a monstrous, extravagant stage show, which is expected to make a financial loss for him. The special lighting effects alone will cost thousands of pounds.

Yes, Gary Numan is special, and he aims to prove it!

MUSICAL MYSTERY MAN

His stark compositions and futuristic presentation have made Gary Numan someone special — who you either love or loathe!

視覚的要素が要求されだしている

現在のロック・シーン

美しいものに引かれるのは

いつの時代でも同じこと

ここに登場する8人の美男こそ

新しい時代の

ROCK'N'ROLL AESTHETICS

したたかに あくまでも美しく

新しいセックス・シンボル

GARY NUMAN
ゲイリー・ニューマン

　80年代ポップ・ミュージックの若き旗手、ゲイリー・ニューマン。新しい世代のための新しいセックス・シンボル——。彼の持つ、無機質な感覚は、一種異様な催眠効果でボクたちをひきつけてしまう。まるで未来人を見るように、ボクたちの目は彼にそそがれる。

Pic : Robert Ellis

むかし異端児　いま英雄
ゲイリー・ニューマン

All photos by Robert Ellis

Gary Numan on stage

衝撃のデビュー・アルバムがやっと日本でも発売される
ゲイリー・ニューマン。先に発売された2枚のアルバムで
すでに彼の魅力は十分伝えられている。ニュー・アルバム
は来年までおあずけ。1年間かけて精神統一し充実したア
ルバム創りをすると発表したばかりのゲイリー・ニューマ
ン。やはりやることがどこか違う…。

アンドロイドの覚醒

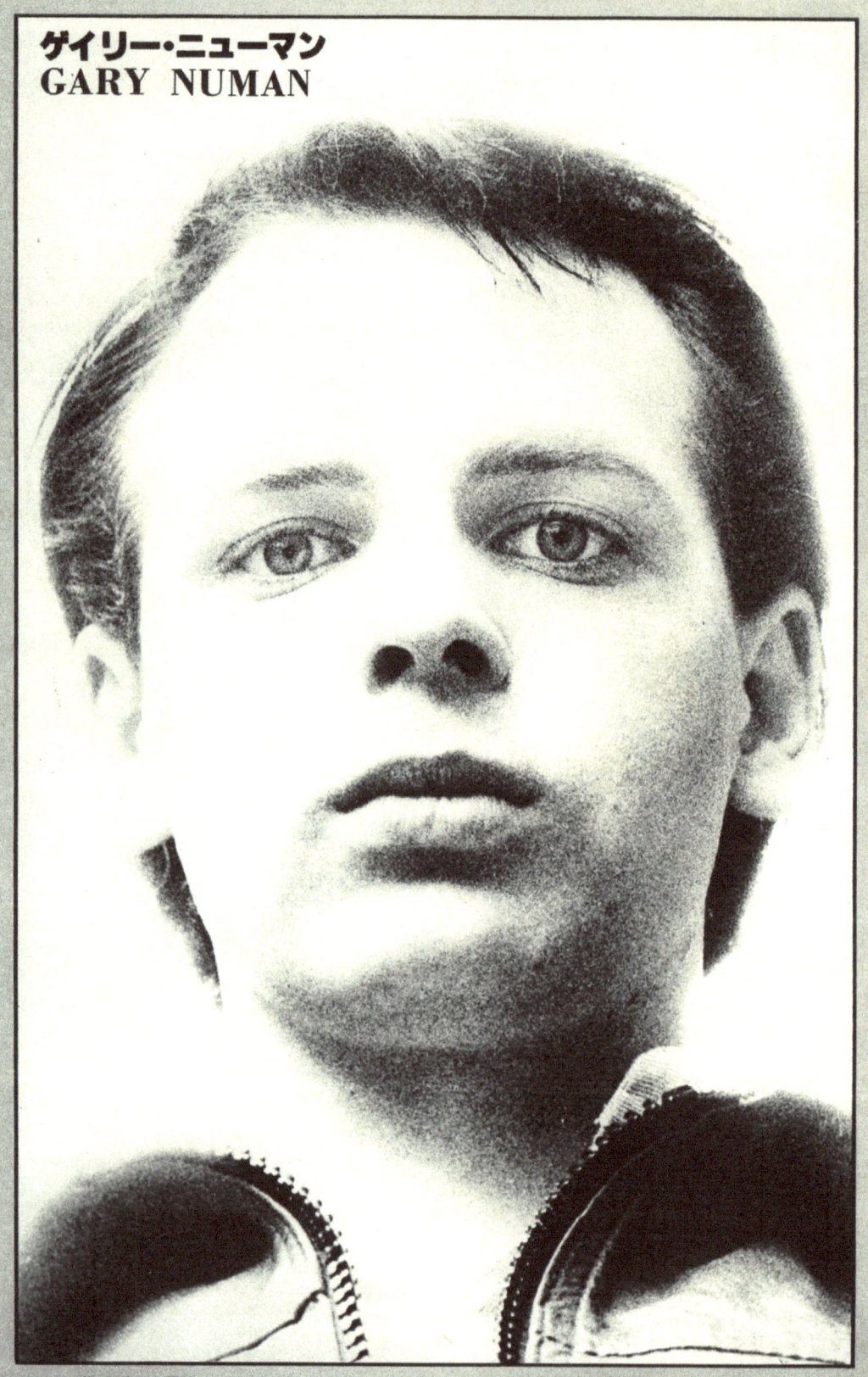

ゲイリー・ニューマン
GARY NUMAN

シンセサイザーを駆使したエレクトリック・サウンドでロック・シーンに登場して来たゲイリー・ニューマン。あっという間に大きな人気を獲得した彼は英国メロディ・メーカー紙の人気投票でブライテスト・ホープNo.1、本誌でも4位に選ばれるなど、世界じゅうのロック・ファンの期待と注目を集めている。

Gary Numan
at the turning point of his life

転機を迎えた孤独なアンドロイド
ゲイリー・ニューマン　インタビュー

インタビューと文：山田道成　**by Michinari Yamada**

pix:Koh Hasebe / Music Life

FOR ALL READERS OF
MUSIC LIFE
THANK-YOU AGAIN FOR YOUR WELCOME
SEE YOU SOON
Love.
Gary Numan
X.

　"ミック・カーンをゲストに迎えてニュー・アルバムを制作……" というニュースが伝わってきてから間もない 2 月中半、何ともタイミング良くジャパンの来日とほぼ同時にゲイリー・ニューマンが突然日本を訪れた。4 月を契機にコンサート活動を中止、しかも音楽アプローチの面においても過去を捨てて新たに再出発をはかるというゲイリー……。一体何が彼をここまで変えたのか？　その真相を探ってみると……。

　「今回はホリデーのつもりで日本に来たんだ。本当はコンサート・ツアーを行なう予定もあったんだけどキャンセルになってしまってネ。まあ、昨年来た時はあまりの忙しさに遊ぶことも出来なかったし……」
　買ったばかりのトランシーバーを箱に入れて大事そうに抱え、部屋に入ってくるなりゲイリーはこう話してく

れた。確かに今回の彼には、昨年コンサートのために来た時にあった異常なまでの緊張感のようなものは全くない。ただ「日本に着いて以来ショッピングもしたし、クイーンやジャパンのコンサートにも行ったヨ」と楽しそうに話しながらも、ゲイリーのその表情には何かしら暗い影のようなものが感じられる。それはなぜだろうか。

153

Beware of The Machine Civilization, Or You'll Be Man-machines!!

GARY NUMAN

自らの機械化に挑む コンクリート社会の 落し子

Photo by Robert Ellis

レッド・ツェッペリンの「イン・スルー・ジ・アウト・ドア」を1位の座から引きずり降ろした「エレクトリック・ショック」は、キング・クリムズンの「21世紀の精神異常者」がビートルズの「アビー・ロード」を引きずり降ろした時と同じ衝撃だった。まるで、アンドロイドかサイボーグ人間のようなゲイリー・ニューマンが奏でる冷たいサウンドは、現在のロック・シーンにおいては、逆に暖かさすら感じてしまう。

Replicas was released in Japan as *Genso Android* (*Fantastic Android*). *The Pleasure Principle* was called *Electric Shock!*. Both albums were very successful. Of the other albums, *Telekon*, *Dance*, *Warriors* and *New Anger* enjoyed strong sales; the later's success prompted the release of the *Asylum* box sets.

ゲイリー・ニューマン インタビュー

An Exclusive Interview, Gary Numan

僕の心は車の中でのみ解放される

インタビュー■立川直樹

▼マネージャーである父に甘えるゲイリー。

撮影■長谷部宏／本誌
All photos by Koh Hasebe / Music Life

Gary Numan: "We sold out three dates in Tokyo, one in Osaka and one in Nagoya. They were all 2,000-3,000 seaters, so I'd achieved a very healthy position for a Western artist."

PATCHES

GARY NUMAN

© Fin Costello

50

GARY NUMAN

His unique musical vision of the future is machine-dominated, paranoid and eerie. And those are the good parts. By LOU STATHIS

Ask a typical American record buyer what the name Gary Numan means to him/her, and chances are you'll get a blank look for an answer. While Numan is a virtual unknown in the U.S.A., he was Great Britain's rock success story of 1979. His singles "Are 'Friends' Electric?" and "Cars" were both number one on the U.K. charts for extended periods, while the albums *Replicas* and *The Pleasure Principle* each in turn monopolized the top LP slot and followed it with a criminally near-permanent stay in the top ten.

Numan's success, if not overnight, has certainly been meteoric. Two years ago his name was known to no one—not even himself. At that time, while still a teenager, he played in an unremarkable band called Tubeway Army and used the nom de rock "Valerian" (after a French SF comic hero). The band released two singles in the winter of 1977-78, "That's Too Bad" and "Bombers," a pair of straightforward hard-rockers that, as was the fashion, relied heavily on Valerian's wall-of-sound, power-chorded guitar. The records went nowhere, as did the band, and they promptly dissolved. In August of that year, Valerian changed his name to Numan, and with the assistance of Army-men Jess Lidyard (drummer, and Numan's uncle as well) and Paul Gardiner (bass), recorded some songs he had been writing. Though never intended for release, the result was issued shortly thereafter by Numan/Tubeway Army's record company, Beggars Banquet, as *Tubeway Army* (though essentially it was Numan's first solo album). Musically, the LP was still limited by its traditional rock trio format, but as the song lyrics clearly indicate, Numan's bleak vision of a paranoid, machine-dominated future was beginning to take shape.

This vision, fed by Numan's prodigious reading of William Burroughs and Philip K. Dick, reached its first stage of maturity with the April, 1979 release of *Replicas*, Numan's second album. Gary himself feels that the change measured by the two LPs was a natural one. He says, "I was getting fed up with guitars; going through the Punk thing and realizing it wasn't going anywhere. It wasn't changing at all, and I just couldn't write songs on the guitar anymore—it was boring. I realized that there was nothing you could do that hadn't gone before."

In the fall of '78 two things happened to change Gary Numan's musical outlook—first, he acquired a synthesizer, and second, he discovered Ultravox, a seminally important group of avant-rock hybridizers. Numan discovered, while teaching himself to play his

Left: Numan feels a chill onstage. **Above:** Bless its pointy little head.

newly-acquired instrument, what a truly limitless potential the machine possessed. "I became aware of the depths you could get," he remembers. "The changes you could put them through—it's like a dozen instruments rolled into one. Synths have far more feeling than guitars. They are probably the most human of all machines, as variable as humans—different every time you play them." Numan willingly acknowledges the debt he owes Ultravox for their exploration of new avenues of expression. As he describes it, "Ultravox influenced me to use synths not as a squiggly noise or rhythm instrument, but for atmospheric effect and for putting a whole new rhythm into a rock song—sort of taking the place of the rhythm guitar." On *Replicas* Numan uses the synthesizer to add depth and texture to his science-fictional vision—giving "Down In The Park" an unmistakable air of eerie malevolence, and songs like "Replicas," "Are 'Friends' Electric?" and "Me, I Disconnect From You" the feeling of hopelessness and melancholy that pervades much of his work.

Replicas, as originally conceived, was to have been a collection of short stories exploring Numan's vision of a near-future England, a world that mixes *A Clockwork Orange*'s random violence, the despair and furtiveness of Burrough's junkie underworld, and the paranoid struggle for humanity contained in most of Dick's novels. "I suppose it's a bit bleak," Numan admits. Tentatively titled *Praying To The Aliens*, the book told the story of a time, "in ten or 20 years when the government creates a machine that makes all decisions—like a dictator—but the people aren't told of its existence. The machine decides that the only thing holding back the State is the people themselves, so a quota test is staged under the pretense that if you weren't up to quota-standard, you would be taken away and re-educated. In fact, you were simply gotten rid of. The people sitting the test are the 'Crazies,' the people who set it are the 'Grey Men,' and those collecting the ones who've failed are called 'Machmen.' " The cover of *Replicas* has Numan dressed as a Machman—black uniform, bleached hair, pale lifeless skin—staring at the reflection of a 'friend' in the window ('friends' are mechanized companions). The idea for this nightmarish image of repressive authority came from an old war book Numan remembers seeing as a child. "There was this picture of an SS man, wearing all black, just standing —his eyes bloodless and staring. It struck me as the perfect vision of terror."

Many of the songs on *Replicas* have meaning on at least two levels—one, as part of Numan's SF scenario, and also as personal statements on present-day reality. Songs like "Me, I Disconnect From You," and "Are 'Friends' Electric?" are touching, plaintive stories about the pain of feeling in a cold, depersonalized world. " 'Friends' is about complete alienation behind a facade of normality. It's about not having real friends anymore, where you ring up a 'friends' agency and they send 'round a mechanical sort of friend—something that's devoid of problems

and any real feeling." He adds, by way of comment, "People don't really talk to each other or make real friends any more. I wrote the song because I lost friends when I was younger; I didn't *lose* them so much as them getting rid of me. It bothered me quite a bit."

Obviously, this young man feels alienated from, and apparently fearful of, the rest of humanity. He describes himself as an "over-the-top paranoid," and professes a distrust of crowds. "There are some days when I just can't go out and walk down the street. I don't like being in crowds where you're so close to people that, if anything happens, you can't get away. I like to see who's near me, so I can look at them and decide whether they're going to do anything or not." From this fear grew "Cars," Numan's second number one single and probably the best song he's recorded. " 'Cars' is about feeling safe—being protected by metal, by a big engine, locked doors, seat belts, etc." Numan's statements betray a marked ambivalence in his feelings toward technology, seeming at the same time fearful of it and looking to it for protecton

and as a sort of role model. "I've always seen machines as being powerful and cold—and for me, the only way to be successful is to be cold. I don't think I'd enjoy being that way, but . . ." He leaves the thought unfinished. "I don't really think machines threaten us the way most people think. They won't have to take over our lives because we're getting rid of ourselves. Machines have given us more leisure time, and because of this people are reverting to their primal instincts—that is, being violent."

The release of *The Pleasure Principle* came in September '79, when "Cars" was the U.K.'s reigning single. One week after the LP hit the stores, it too was holding court from the top. Musically the album is a complete step beyond *Replicas*—more confident, mature and refined. All guitars have gone, and reliance on synthesizers is almost complete. The songs are still structured traditionally, leaning heavily on the driving rock-rhythm foundation and the simple melodic interplay of the synthesizers. The sound is clean and efficient, almost spartan; mesmerizing, but never mechanical. Again, despite the looming specter of loss and hurt, the songs make superior pop music.

On the heels of *The Pleasure Principle* came Numan's first major world tour—his first live appearance since the early Tubeway Army days and the first time he would appear in the U.S.A. and the Far East. The show's scale and spectacle reflected Numan's desire to create larger-than-life images with a striking, visually stimulating performance (in the

tradition of Pink Floyd and David Bowie). His studied stage presence, and the role-playing he adopts like a protective mask, reinforce the feeling that Numan wishes to keep the audience at arm's distance. He concurs, but sees it more as a necessary part of the illusion he is enacting for the audience. "As far as I'm concerned it's show business. You put on a show, you dress up, create characters in your songs, you look like the characters you're creating in order to portray them, so that people can understand the songs better. I don't see the point in singing about things which are happening every day. I don't want to go out and listen to a bloke prattling on about how terrible it is living on the dole. I'd rather go and see somebody on stage with big high towers and little robots moving about, than somebody in jeans and an old mac in the back of a pub."

The stage-setting that accompanied Numan around the world did indeed feature the aforementioned high towers (which served as dual keyboard command posts for band members) and scurrying, diminutive pyramids. The robot, due to the limited stage space available, never made it out of the crate. Numan emerged at the show's beginning from the darkness, standing amidst a swirling mist, outlined by a luminous wedge of light directed at him from the huge towers. Watching him stalk the stage with studied grace, you can't help but wonder about the rumors that Numan was actually cloned from accidentally irradiated Bowie cell-matter, or that he is a simulacrum constructed in some underground automated factory. His deep-set eyes and pale-skinned face call up the image of Klaus Kinski as Dracula in Herzog's *Nosferatu*. The two share a predatory, ambisexual aura; a chillingly feral, prowling presence that is positively unnerving. Numan shows little emotion on stage—when he smiles his lips pull back toward his ears while an inhuman, anthropophagus glint ignites in his eyes (a bit like Godzilla readying to stomp Tokyo into the ground).

The key to Numan's success is his facility to synthesize the ideas of others into compelling, memorable popular music. His talent is in manipulating symbols and concepts, exploiting the resonance they produce with all the technology available to him as a modern artist, and producing a visual, aural and visceral entertainment. He will eagerly point out his sources of inspiration for you, and self-deprecatingly calls his method of creation "parasitical." He says, "I take phrases that I like out of books and such, twist them until they are unrecognizable and then write songs with them." He uses the accessibility of the rock song the way a science fiction writer uses a strong, involving story-line. The result in both cases feeds your mind and body simultaneously. Numan claims he is not long for the music business. He expresses interest in writing SF stories, and says he is studying to obtain his pilot's license. "I really love to fly," he tells you with a grin. His goals? "I've always wanted to be famous and rich, but I wanted to do something that would make it worthwhile to get there." 🔲

NUMAN TOUR—Atco artist Gary Numan right, above, meets with KNAC-FM Long Beach, Calif., DJ Steve Snyder left, as Atlantic West Coast artist relations director Tony Mandich looks on. At right, Numan makes a point to KWST-FM Los Angeles jock J.J. Jackson. Both meetings took place during an appearance by Numan at the Forum in Los Angeles.

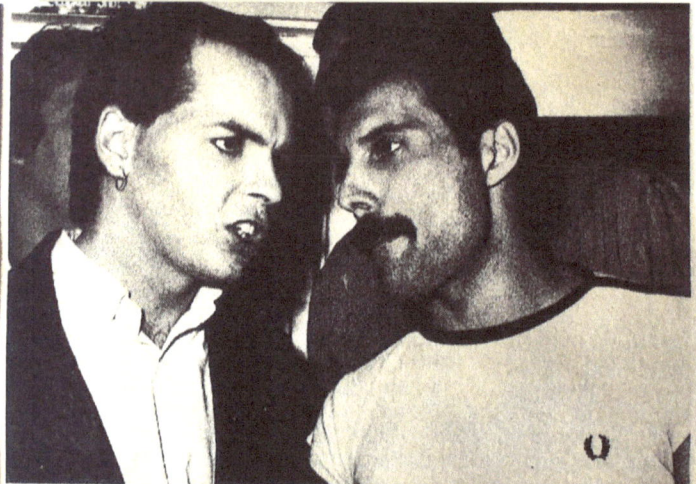

STARS MEET—British rock stars Freddie Mercury, right, and Gary Numan converse during a party held at London's Legends club after Queen's recent concert in the capital. The occasion also celebrated the release of Queen's soundtrack album for "Flash Gordon."

Billboard 10/1/81

Auditoriums (Under 6,000)

1	ELTON JOHN/JUDIE ZTUKE—Avalon Attractions, The Forum, Inglewood, Ca., Nov 6&7 (2)	2,800	$7.50 $12.50	$312,900
2	BEATLEMANIA—Feyline Presents, Aud. Theatre, Denver, Colo., Nov 5-9 (8)	11,921	$9-$15	$175,632
3	TEDDY PENDERGRASS—Alive Enter., Mill Run Theatre, Niles, Ill., Nov 5-19 (6)	10,292	$14.75 $16.75	$159,540
4	JETHRO TULL/MICHAEL DES BARRES—Avalon Attractions, The Swing Aud., San Bernardino, Ca. Nov. 7	5,982	$8.75 $9.75	$52,712
5	THE B-52'S—Ron Delsener, The Bacon Theatre, New York, N.Y., Nov 8&9 (2)	5,200	$9-$10	$50,150
6	GARY NUMAN/GARY MYRICK & THE FIGURES—Perryscope Concerts, Queen Elizabeth Theatre, Vancouver, B.C., Can., Nov 9	5,662	$8-$9	$49,616
7	MOLLY HATCHET/MICHAEL SCHENKER—Don Law Co., Springfield Civic Center, Springfield, Mass.	4,000	$9.50 $10.50	$37,763

AC/DC moved over to Atlantic, but the reborn Atco continued to thrive. The logo returned to the top 10 of the Hot 100 in 1980 thanks to Gary Numan's electronic opus "Cars." A re-formed Yes gave the label its first No. 1 title on the Hot 100 in 13 years with "Owner Of A Lonely Heart."

Look to the future of rock 'n' roll with GARY NUMAN.

Gary Numan makes rock 'n' roll with his eye on the future, collecting thousands of fans on his way.

"The Pleasure Principle," his new album, has already topped British charts, spurred on by the #1 success of an amazing single, "Cars."

Gary Numan's "The Pleasure Principle." Rock 'n' roll the way it will be.

On Atco Records and Tapes. Includes the single, "Cars."

Produced by Gary Numan.

GARY NUMAN
THE PLEASURE PRINCIPLE

GARY NUMAN LIVE

A new series of American concerts for the BBC ROCK HOUR kicks off with ATCO recording artist Gary Numan, captured live at the Santa Monica Civic Auditorium.

Sept. 7

Over 130 major radio stations coast to coast!

Produced by
ReelTime PRODUCTIONS

for London Wavelength

Pic By Chuck Pullin

GARY NUMAN

FROZEN ROBOTS

GARY NUMAN
Warfield Theatre, San Francisco

GARY NUMAN'S rise to success has been meteoric — though he would probably prefer a mechanistic image, maybe rocket-like. So here he is, on his 22nd birthday, playing to an almost sold-out theatre in San Francisco, the penultimate date of his first American tour.

Unfortunately, as Gary explains apologetically at the end of the show, there's no robots. They were damaged somewhere in the snow on the way to a sold out but cancelled show in Vancouver. Maybe they ran out of anti-freeze.

There's already a lot of interest in Gary in the States, enough to have sold out most of the tour, even in towns like San Francisco where there's been

a distinct lack of airplay. Who is the Numan? He's the comfortably numb man, the post human new man. But nothing gets cliched quicker than visions of the future.

On stage, he's all arrogance, strutting away, a puppet king ruling a puppet world that includes the audience, the observer watching the observers watching the image. It's a circular argument just like his emptiness — if I'm empty, how can I show emotion? Actually Gary's version isn't scary or even sad; in fact it's rather soothing.

So here we are in Numan's world, a second hand science-fiction composite. He's a real flirt, a Garbo Hollywood walk as he wanders the stage, unworldly staring eyes, a pouting mouth, a sexuality completely liberated from emotion.

The audience waits expectantly. A screaming comes across the sky, a dark hall, filled by pompous synthesisers, all grandeur without soul, a sense of seriousness and doom unjustified by content. The stage is as futuristic as a tower block. There are two lines of strutted lights, the two synthesiser players high above in their windows, the bass and guitar players directly beneath them. A rectangle with Gary in the middle. The lights flash on and off in various patterns throughout the show, brilliantly and repetitively. It's a combination of Top Of The Pops, a gay disco and a Santa Claus grotto, quite impressive actually.

Gary raises his hand and they're off into an hour's election from the 'Replicas' and 'Pleasure Principle' albums, starting with 'I Disconnect You'. Periodically, smoke swathes the stage — not exactly mysterious, rather, one of the oldest tricks in the book. By the third time, you're beginning to wish the robots weren't stuck in the snow. The band stay in place while Gary moves around striking poses, deadly serious as only a true showman can be. He performs like one of those fake fortune tellers, lots of mysticism and prophetic stares, oodles of mumbo jumbo.

The band and Numan are all dressed in black, the drummer invisible behind his drums, 15 feet off the ground. They all wear the same ties and they don't move — except the guitar player who is periodically allowed to thrash a strange looking drum. Nothing stands out.

'Metal' sounds like Egyptian snake charmer music and that's the effect. The audience clap vigorously but sit transfixed, hypnotized, passive. Until the end that is when they all stamp and cheer and run up to the front of the stage.

Gary's birthday is announced and for the first time the pose is dropped. Gary comes on blushing, the band swigging beers. Almost human silhouettes come to life.

'Coldest Way to Zero' is the encore and Gary looks the part in an open leather jacket. And then he's off, despite a persistent crowd. For all his conservatism, Gary may be a little far out for American radio, but who knows? He's a comfortable cult. **MARK COOPER**

HEN Gary is talking about himself, his music and his ideas, he seems to be a series of contradictions. He admits to being shy and quiet, and a hater of big crowds — preferring to stay at home with his dogs or to go for drives in the country in his car. He is a loner who has few friends, trusts few people and is openly hostile to the glitter of the music business.

Yet he is one of the biggest pop stars to emerge this year; the stage show on his recent British tour was one of the most magnificent visual spectacles to be seen in ages and his pessimistic songs of doom bring joy and happiness to thousands of fans!

So why does he do it? *"Being a star is the only thing that I've ever wanted to be,"* he says. *"There seemed to be an atmosphere about the music business that attracted me. But if I was going to make it, I wanted to do it with something worthwhile.*

"Now I'm in it, you see the other side, and it's not as glamorous as you imagine. It's only fun while it's new. Now I'm interested in it for my own enjoyment, and if it doesn't last, I'll carry on until I think that I've run out of songs and interest — which I think could be in about three or four years." For someone who is only 21 now, that seems quite a gloomy prediction. And it is ironically in keeping with the mood of his songs.

His second album, **Replicas**, with its science-fiction songs and cover, sums up his ideas: *"The man on the cover"*, says Gary, *"is*

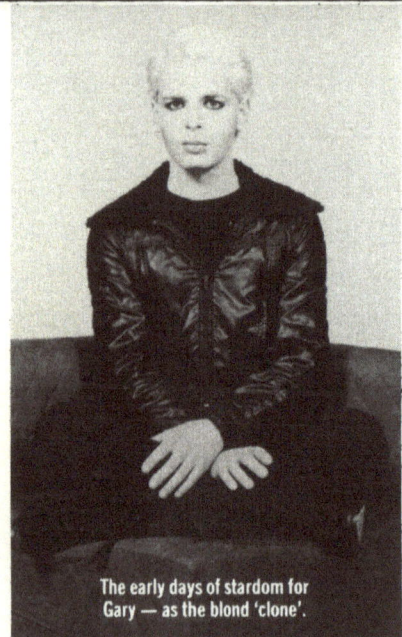
The early days of stardom for Gary — as the blond 'clone'.

Gary Numan is as mysterious in real life as he looks and sounds on record, and that unearthly and untouchable image is not all that far removed from the character of the man himself, as John Palmer discovered when he investigated . . .

a Machman — a robot covered with a kind of human skin — and you see him in a mirror because all Machmen are the same, like clones."

One of the most realistic aspects of his view of the future is that he sets his songs only ten or twenty years ahead, which is a period we can all identify with.

"People are already dominated by machines, everyone is getting more leisure time because of machines, and hand in hand with technological development there is an upsurge in violence," he says.

"The songs tell stories", he explains, saying that in **Replicas** he was making the point that it is not machines which will destroy us, but ourselves. **The Pleasure Principle** album took that theory a little farther, to show our reliance on machines for protection; just listen to the lyrics of **Cars,** for instance.

He admits that the greatest sci-fi influence on him has come from two authors, Philip K. Dick and William Burroughs . . . and that originally, **Replicas** had been planned as a book.

"It started as a full length book, then I changed it to short stories, but finally felt that it would be much more effective to interpret the stories through music," he says.

But the type of music was developed almost by accident. *"The major musical influence is a band called Ultravox,"* he explains (and Billy Currie from Ultravox was one of the musicians during Gary's recent tour). *"The music may not sound the* ⟫⟫⟫

THE NUMAN COMPLEX

Latter day Numan — the Complex superstar.

Gary leads Tubeway Army into the eighties with a studio chart!

>>>> same as that of Ultravox, but we use synthesisers in the same way, to create an atmospheric effect rather than just sound effects."

And here, really, is another contradiction. For someone who has such a pessimistic and gloomy view of the influence of machines, he has chosen the most advanced technological machines available to create his sound.

SYNTHESISER SOUND

That discovery was almost accidental, because it was while he was recording his first album **Tubeway Army** (which is guitar-based) that he started playing around with a mini-moog synthesiser and found that the possibilities for development were endless. Having experimented on the **Replicas** album, he let his imagination run even further, to produce **The Pleasure Principle**, which is made up almost entirely of synthesised sounds.

"You can produce whatever you want from synthesisers", he says *"A lot of people think that they limit the sound you can achieve, but in fact the opposite is true. We tried to create a synthesised sound which would be acceptable to a wide audience."*

The next album will take that synthesiser sound even further. For he is now working on a way of producing a guitar sound by playing it through a synthesiser, and of even using a synthesised viola!

But before the results of these experiments become available on an album, Gary is likely to have taken his present sound on a tour of America.

"We will probably be going in February, and we will be taking the same show which toured here — only better," says Beggar's Banquet, his record company. "There are a few adaptations which we have made with the experience of British shows behind us."

A lot of people have compared the stage presentation, and also the music, of Gary to that of David Bowie, but Gary dismisses these comparisons: *"I don't see him as a musical influence at all, but I admire the way*

he has projected himself, and the way he has planned his career. His approach has been very important to me, and I did learn from his movements, but that's where the similarity ends,"* he claims.

Until his recent tour, he had never played any large venues, but all those who know him agree that his preparations stood him in good stead, and he coped well with the strain of being thrust so quickly into the role of a pop super star.

Yet it wasn't just Gary who caught the eye, it was the astonishing array of flashing fluorescent lights, pyramid robots and stunning stage effects.

"I wanted the show to be a spectacle, to keep the audience fascinated", he says. *"I didn't necessarily want them looking at me all the time — that would have been boring — so we presented a visual show."*

His performance was deliberate, with as little communication with his audience as possible — which again seems strange when you consider how much the audience wanted to see him. But he has his reasons: *"I don't think that audiences necessarily want to see someone who identifies completely with them — they like their heroes to be distant and aloof, they want to see someone who is different.*

"And, really, I've very little to say to them. You can't have a conversation between one

"Now where've I seen you before? Gary's exact replica . . .

person and two or three thousand. The audiences know the songs and I wouldn't want to tell them what each song is about before each number. They already know, so there isn't much point in saying any more."*

Perhaps that is an honest answer, but could it also cover his shyness, and a desire to be a star without always being in the limelight?

U.S. DEBUT

Gary's record company, Beggar's Banquet is looking forward to that American debut. His personal assistant, Su, explained: "The **Replicas** album is being played on a lot of American radio stations, and there is quite a buzz about Gary over there.

"But now a tour has become necessary, because — as all of those who saw the shows over here will know — the visual aspect of his work is very important, and the Americans are not yet aware of it."

The large American venues dwarf the halls in England which we regard as gigantic — like the Hammersmith Odeon and the Manchester Apollo — so Gary should be optimistic about playing them, for he does not like playing small venues. He feels there is less control over the audiences' responses and reactions. He likes them to watch the show and concentrate on what's going on on stage.

LIVE VERSION

If you were unable to see what was going on during his stage performances, you can at least hear him live on the B side of **Complex.** For on the seven-inch single there is a live version of **Bombers** — which was his second single — recorded at the Hammersmith Odeon, while the 12-inch version also has another track from the Hammersmith shows, **May I Disconnect From You.**

With the success of the latest single, Gary really is flying high, in more than one sense, for he is keen on flying aeroplanes, and is on the verge of qualifying for his pilot's licence, so the sky really could be the limit for Gary 'uman . . .

NUMAN NEWS

THOSE OF you who sent off to the Gary Numan Fan Club after our last issue (£2.50 plus SAE to PO Box 14, Staines, Middlesex TW19 5AZ for new readers) shouldn't worry if you don't hear ahything for a while yet.

We understand from Beggars Banquet (Gary's record company) that actual operations won't be starting until January 1 1980. The reason for the delay is to prepare for the huge demand expected and because Gary and Beggars Banquet are determined to make sure that everybody gets a really good deal from the club.

For your money you'll be getting (eventually!) three newsletters per year, membership cards, badges, and autographed photos, plus extras like opportunities to get exclusive T shirts etc.

Sounds like a good deal — if you've got the patience to wait.

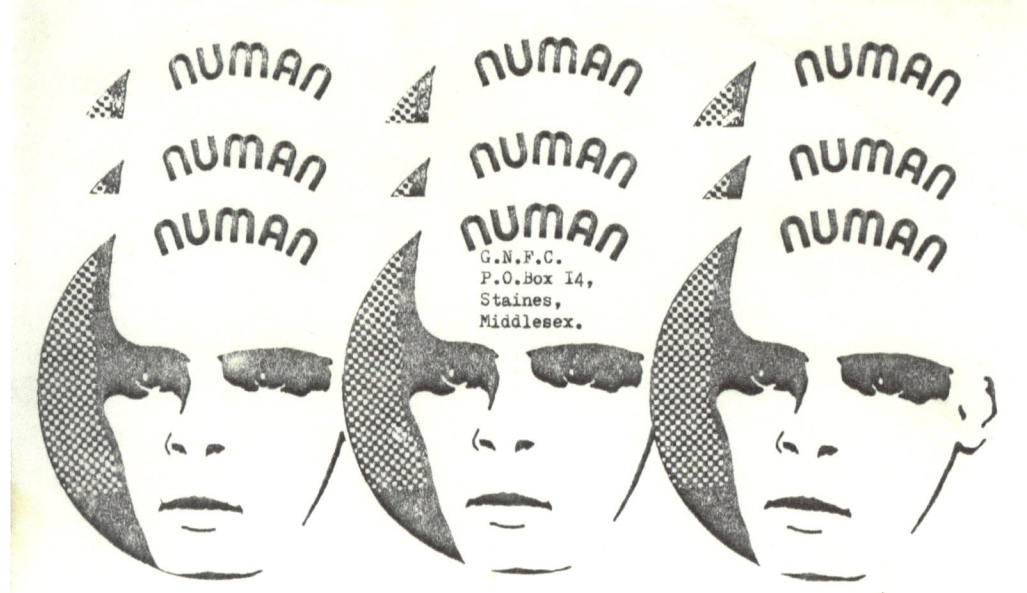

G.N.F.C.
P.O.Box I4,
Staines,
Middlesex.

NUMAN — NEW TOUR

All Gary Numan fans will be pleased to hear that Gary is embarking on another British tour in September of this year.

In the spring, Gary visited America for a tour and was an immediate success. It's not many British artists who can fill a 3000-seat hall on their first tour of the States and pull if off. So Gary is well-pleased with the way that things went and looking forward to seeing all his British fans on the tour — don't miss it!

Thank you for your subscription - yes, we have received it and do know who you are! At the moment we are busy preparing your fan pack. We would be grateful if you could send in a stamped addressed envelope when ever you write to us about anything as this would ensure that you do get a reply and save a lot of time. We have had such a lot of response from all of you that there will obviously be some delay, but hope to get your pack to you in the not too distant future.

Me! I disconnect from you.

Television This Week; OF SPECIAL INTEREST

12:9i(11)The FBI I ai(4)Secortd City TV (>n Ladies Pro Golt 1:J6(4)Don Kirshner's Rock Con cert: Pink Floyd, Pat Benetar, **Gary Numan**, Toto, Prince, Diane Nictwld, Richard Robinson, guests (11)News 1:48(t)News

May 04, 1980 - - Print Headline: "Television This Week; OF SPECIAL INTEREST"

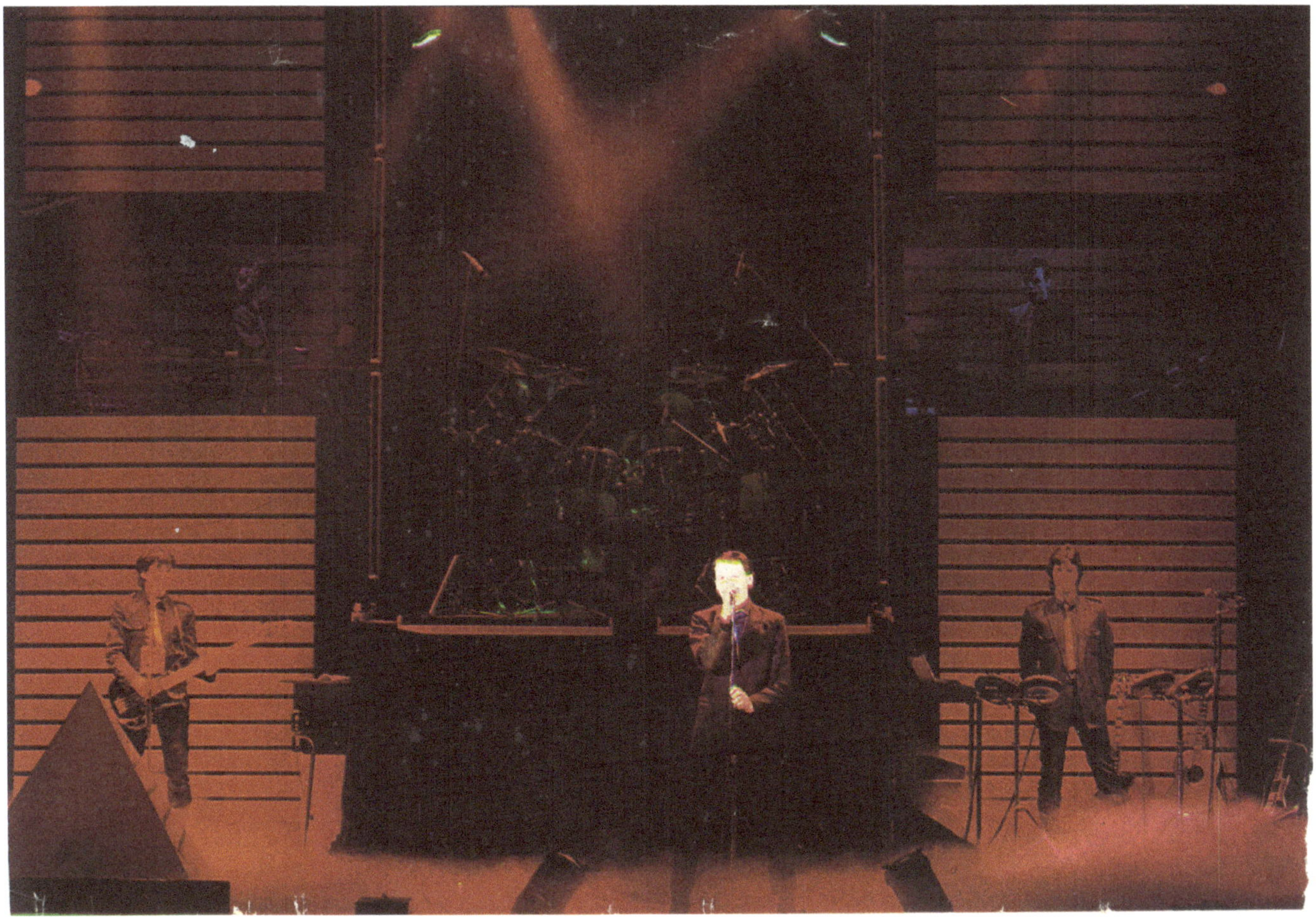

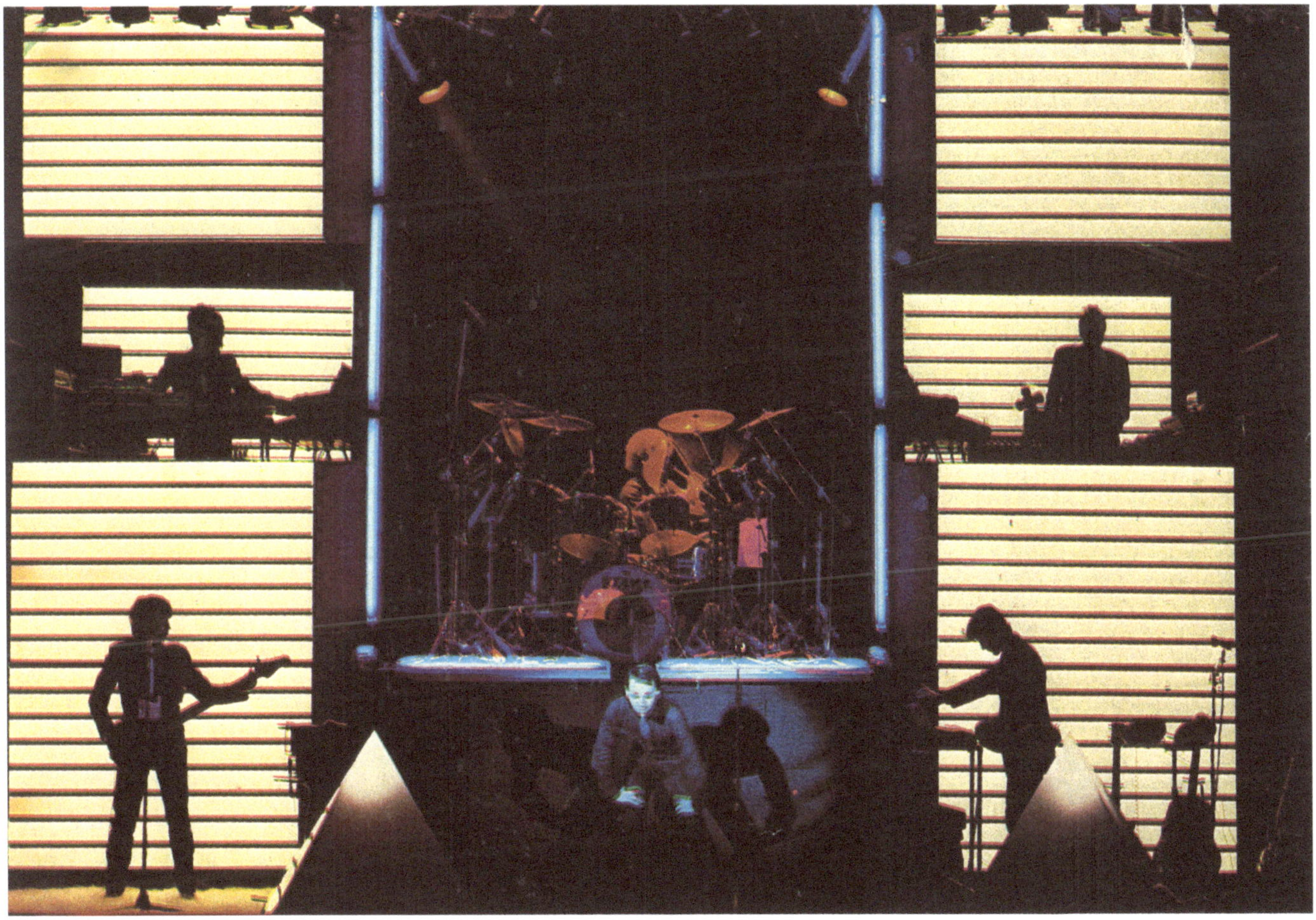

GARY NUMAN did for the boys last year what Kate Bush did for the girls in 1978: he gave them someone to copy, someone to watch, a hero on a pedestal. He is a lone, frail figure on stage, with a unique presentation, impossible to ignore, who doesn't look quite strong enough to cope with words like "remarkable", "superstar" and "hot property."

Two startling, innovative singles, *Are Friends Electric?* and *Cars*, both No. 1s, pushed Numan and Tubeway Army into the relentless spotlight — and brought the inevitable comparisons.

As soon as Numan appeared, it was obvious he would be compared with David Bowie: the flat, nasal voice, the stance, the pose, the aloofness, and even the face. "A David Bowie clone", one critic dubbed him. Numan is tired of hearing about it.

He has never met Bowie, but word has filtered through that Bowie is aware of, and interested in, Numan's work. Flattering? Yes. Numan lists Bowie and the late Marc Bolan as two of his greatest influences. They made him conscious of the importance of the visual image — "I'm certain I wouldn't have been a success if I'd worn jeans", he says.

Black clothes, white make-up and white lighting. Stark, revealing, with no shadows. There is very little grey about Gary Numan, except for grey matter. He has a sharp, analytical brain and an unusual, disturbing honesty. He's quiet, polite and more vulnerable than he appears on stage, but very cool and very shrewd.

"My show is calculated," he admits. "It has to be. I'd watched the music scene for many years and while there were lots of successful groups, there were no solo stars, and that's what the public likes. The kids want to relate to one person, not a group of people."

But he ignored the easy route to acceptance, the frenzied "Kids are united" approach of the new-wave bands. Instead, he surrounds himself with high-tech. scaffolding, his movements are robotic, unspontaneous, he rarely speaks and never smiles at his audience. He doesn't see that as a contradiction, because what might look like

Gary Numan's role as one of life's loners is reinforced (above) by the presentation of his stage act. As for the cold, almost hostile image he projects (beloww) he maintains: "It's the only way for me to be successful. "And he's been proved right . . .

arrogance, is, in fact, a basic shyness — fear of contact. "I don't like being very close to them," he explained. "I know it's very flattering, but I get worried when they rush the stage. I like there to be a gap.

"It isn't that I don't want to talk to them, meet them, it's just that . . . . ." he glances at his image in a wall mirror, smoothes down his hair slowly and continues: "It's very unnerving. Being a 'star' you're supposed to come out with the smooth talk, and I'm just not like that. I don't chat people up at all. I find that what they expect me to do and what I want to do aren't the same. That's possibly the most difficult part of it."

He often refers to "me and them" and explains: "Of course I'm different from the people who come and see me. If I was like them, I'd be sitting in the audience rather than appearing on stage." True: yet, if he wants them to relate to him, why create barriers, like all that stage paraphernalia? "To be honest, the show was put together to

be something to look at. I can't do enough different things to keep people interested for an hour and a half. I want to give people their money's worth, something they will accept and remember."

Numan is no stranger to rejection. Expelled from three schools — grammar, secondary modern and technical college — he has always been a loner. Few people get close to him, he avoids large crowds and is frequently disillusioned by "fair weather friends" and hangers-on. It's one reason why he distrusts and is vaguely frightened by this sudden mass acceptance.

"Originally, I liked the idea of being famous; now I know what it's like, I don't enjoy it very much," he has said. "They have parties for me after some of the shows, but I don't know many people there, so I don't stop long. A lot of my fans aren't very polite when they ask for autographs. They try to give the impression that they're not bothered about meeting you, and they put on an act of indifference. That upsets me a bit, because it's dishonest."

He trusts only his family. Until recently, he shared the family home near London's Heathrow Airport. Now he's having to move out, not because he wants to — "but it's hard for them having the phone ringing at four in the morning and girls knocking on the door all the time." His mother cuts his hair and looks after his clothes. His father, a British Airways bus driver, acts as his manager and takes care of business. It was his father who listened when Numan told him, at the age of 11, that he didn't want to go to school anymore, just wanted to be a star. "When I was 18, my father said: 'You haven't done anything about it yet.' That decided me."

He taught himself keyboards from a second-hand piano, found the name Gary Numan in the Yellow Pages, had a brief brush with punk and then, with the futuristic Tubeway Army, marched into an Ealing record shop which had its own label, Beggar's Banquet, and played them some tapes. They were impressed enough to sign the band, initially billed as Tubeway Army.

"I wanted it to be Gary Numan before the first album, but Tubeway Army had a good little following, so I let it go at first. But I can't work with other people. Their ideas and mine are always separate; I like to be in control."

Still only 21, Numan writes fast and is never worried about running out of ideas. His fears and fantasies for a technological future, and his own helplessness within it, provide an endless kaleidoscope of drama and inspiration.

Many of his songs are about loneliness, a failure to communicate, and he himself has an aloofness, a single-mindedness. It is not surprising that he is successful — but can he hang on to that remarkable self-control indefinitely?

His new album *Telekon* is about a man who can move things by the process of thought. His power finally increases and snowballs until it destroys everything, himself included. Numan admitted: "Most of my lyrics are concerned with me putting myself into another place and how I'd react in that situation. They are me as a figure, a kind of underground figure, which is always there, always ominous. Most people seem to have trouble with the lyrics, but I wouldn't have thought they were difficult to understand. I've always seen machines as being powerful and cold and, for me, the only way to be successful is to be cold."

It might not win friends, but it influences people — and that, for the moment anyway, is the **Numan Principle**.

NUMANS COMPLEX

妖艶アンドロイド｜ゲイリー・ニューマン

Fascinating Android Gary Numan

To compound the impression Numan performs a reasonable version of 'On Broadway' in his current set: it's a song he's always liked and featured in the lyric of 'You Are in My Vision'. I find the conservative aspect a little hard to take, and wonder how Numan felt about the atmosphere in which he moved in late 1976 and early 1977, seeing the Sex Pistols early on (at Notre Dame Hall) and playing the Roxy in June 1977.

"I always thought it was a movement, especially in the early days before it became fashionable. I don't feel part of it, no. I don't think I'm doing what I'm doing now because of it. I think I'm doing what I'm doing now I'm doing quicker because of it, if you know what I mean. The business side of it changed: people go signed up, so I went out, crashed away for a few months, got a contract and ten away we went on our own tack. Which is because of punk but I didn't get it and evolve into what I'm doing now. I just simply used it."

It fits, in moving the audience away from the last fashion, Numan mustn't appear to identify too much with it. For good or ill, his preoccupations are different.

"I did use it solely as a means of getting a contract. I didn't see it as going anywhere. I don't think it has gone anywhere. I was excited by the thing as a whole, that all of a sudden there was something that was completely new — new fashion, new music.

Gary's whales

GARY NUMAN'S Tubeway Army are to join the forces with the 'Save The Whale' campaign . . . by playing a special London benefit concert.

Tubeway Army, who already appear at the Hammersmith Odeon on September 27 as part of their British tour, have added an extra concert there on September 27.

All proceeds will go to the campaign, and tickets are available immediately.

Numan is a committed supporter of PETA.

WAS GARY A GURU?

Gary Numan was born on March 8th under the star sign of Pisces.

Subjects born under this sign are well known for their tendencies to dream. They plan great things but seldom follow through with them!

In love they are equally unsure of themselves. They need someone to guide them. Left alone they are often incapable of making decisions.

In a previous existence Gary may have been a Guru. A man involved with the mystical qualities of life, far removed from everyday life. Gary would have loved the life 'cos he certainly looks like he's from another planet!

Gary Numan
Clean, clean, clean sind alle meine Bilder

'All my pictures are clean, clean, clean.'

„Listen to the Sirens", warnte unser Held schon auf seiner ersten langen Platte. Vor einem guten Jahr war das. Nun haben wir den Salat. Sage niemand: „Das habe ich nicht gewußt". Jetzt haben wir ihn, den neuen Super-Star, auf den wir die ganze schnöde Punkzeit über gewartet haben.
Überall ist er: Nummer 1 der Single-Charts, Nummer 1 der LP-Charts. Und die zweite LP ist auch noch drin. Aus dem Fernseher glotzt er. Und jetzt bereitete mir seine deutsche Plattenfirma auch noch das Vergnügen, ihn live zu sehen. Danke schön.

Gary im Chevy – ein Geschenk seiner Plattenfirma

Von Alfred Hilsberg

Gary Numan ist 21. Den Pilotenschein hat er voriges Jahr, also mit 20, gemacht. Als er in die Luft ging, wurde ich auf den Boden gedrückt: REPLICAS, sein zweites Album, kam mir vor wie ein Trip ins Nichts, eine einzige Abschlaff-Orgie, ein nutzloser Sprung in längst überwunden geglaubte l'art-pour-l'art-Vergangenheit. Dieses düdel-dum, simpelste Synthesizer-Harmonien, nett untermalt von simpelsten Schlagzeug/Gitarren-Rhythmen, bedeutungsschwanger stilisiert durch melancholische Gesänge, dieser klinische Sound-Brei sollte die von den Sex Pistols geläuterte Jugend interessieren?

Der Junge ist Nummer 1 in England. Der Knabe ist in den bundesdeutschen Hitparaden. Und er wird es nicht schwer haben, die Welt zu erobern. Hat er ja auch vor einem Jahr in seiner Bio bereits verkünden lassen: „Die Welt wartet auf Gary Numan". Ungläubigkeit auf den Gesichtern in der SOUNDS-Redaktion, als ich auf das Phänomen Numan hinweise. Fassungslosigkeit, als ausgerechnet *ich* mich interessiert zeige, Herrn Numan zu besuchen. Na gut, irgendwas muß ja daran sein. Es ist.
Als schüchtern, sensibel, schwer zugänglich haben sie ihn beschrieben, die Plattenfirma und die Gazetten. Er könnte nur schreiben, wenn er depressiv sei. Der muß oft

eine Depression haben, um seine Blicke so oft in die Zukunft richten zu können. Im hermetisch abgeschirmten Roxy-Theater im Norden Londons bereitet er sich auf seine erste Tournee mit den neuen Songs vor. Er ist die Nummer 1 geworden ohne Live-Auftritte. Und von seiner Firma Beggars Banquet hat er kaum Unterstützung bekommen. Das Vertriebsnetz der WEA mag geholfen haben. Die netten Leute von Beggars Banquet stellen ihn mir vor.
Das Gespräch beginnt etwas mühsam, Gary hat noch einen Apfel zu kauen. Ab und zu blickt er kontrollierend zur Bühne, wo sich die Techniker abmühen, seine Vorstellungen eines modernen, zukunftsweisenden Bühnenbilds zu realisieren. Licht ist seine Zauberformel: „Ich habe das alles selbst ausgedacht, es war schwierig, eine Firma dafür zu finden." Eine Laser-Genehmigung hat er nicht bekommen, so hilft er sich mit gigantischen Stahlrohr-Gerüsten, an denen ganze Batterien von Neon-Röhren, Scheinwerfern und Spots befestigt sind. Zwischen den bald zehn Meter hohen Gerüsten, auch etwas erhöht: das Schlagzeug. Links und rechts vor den Lichtbauten: die Gitarristen. Gary selbst, als Sänger, vorn in der Mitte.

Der Augenaufschlag ins Nichts

Die beiden Synthesizer-Spieler thronen fünf Meter über dem Bühnenboden, wie in Zimmern, inmitten der Lichtanlagen. Gary weiß, was er tut: „Es ist das erste Mal, daß die Synthesizer derart im Mittel-

punkt der Bühne sind".
Ja, das ist schon sein Verdienst, das werte Publikum mit einschmeichelnden, süßen Harmonien zu bezirzen. Ich bekomme nicht den Eindruck eines schüchternen Knaben, für den andere eine Werbekampagne erfunden haben, den sie nach ihrem Willen verwursten. Gary Numan ist selbstbewußt. Seine Helfer hören auf seine Kommandos. Es muß so klappen, wie er sich's vorstellt. Ab und zu geht er aus der Probe raus, spielt Autorennen am Automaten, streichelt einem Girl über den Kopf, wechselt ein paar Worte mit dem Mixer. Keine auffällige Erscheinung; Jeans hat er an, dunkles Hemd, ungeschminkt, eher etwas zu klein geraten für einen Mann, der Erfolg bei Frauen hat. Und den hat er, meint er lächelnd: „Meine Fans sind mehr Frauen als Männer, aber nicht die jungen Teenager, mehr die etwas Intelligenteren so um Zwanzig herum." Eine „feste" Freundin hat er nicht, ans Heiraten denkt er schon gar nicht, wie mir später Bob Ellis erzählt, der für die exklusive fotografische Verbreitung seiner Live-Auftritte bestellt ist. Ich darf nicht fotografieren, denn das von Gary verbreitete Bild darf nicht angekratzt werden.

Keine Werbekampagne, und auch nicht in erster Linie die Musik ist Numans Erfolgsgeheimnis. Das Image macht das Geld. Das gibt er auch zu: „David Bowie ist für mich das Vorbild, von ihm habe ich

A tatty bit of German journalese: *'Listen to the Sirens* our hero warned on his very first LP. That was over a year ago. Now we are in a fine mess. And let nobody say they didn't expect it. Now we have him, the new superstar, for whom we have been waiting for through the whole vile period of Punk. He is everywhere: Number One in the single charts, Number One in the album charts. And now we've got the second LP as well. He's staring at us from the TV.'

sehr viele Image-Sachen gelernt". Wer als Pin-Up an der Wand hängen will, der sollte nicht ungepflegt aussehen. Der darf die Träume junger Frauen nicht zerstören mit einem Rocker-Image. Eine starke Persönlichkeit ist gefragt, eine, zu der man aufblicken kann. Wie zu einem Führer. Bilder gibt es von ihm, da erinnert er mich mit seiner Fantasie-Uniform, seiner leicht breitbeinigen Haltung, seinem Pokerface und dem leicht verschleierten Blick fatal an Gestalten aus deutscher Vergangenheit. Ich kenne keine Bilder, auf denen er lacht. Immer schaut er ernst aus der dunkel gehaltenen Wäsche, geheimnisvoll und düster, unnahbar, aber umso begehrenswerter. Ein wenig wie die Feuerwehr-Leute in Truffauts „Fahrenheit 451".

Gary wartet nicht bis 1984, Science Fiction ist heute „in". Aus Sci-Fi-Büchern bezieht er Ideen für Songs und Image, und sogar den guten William F. Burroughs spannt er — vermutlich ungefragt — in seine Verführungs-Dienste ein, wie im Programm zu seiner Tour zu lesen ist. Die Jugend hört auf seine Sirenenklänge und sein cleanes Image. Es ist ja nichts da, worüber es sich aufzuregen lohnt. Das Bild ist die Botschaft. Und das sagt nichts. Kostprobe von Numans Zukunfts-Visionen gefällig? *Where are the tracks?/ Where are the lines?/ Where are the tracks?/ Where is the time?/ You were so cold/ You were so slow/ And we were so old/ And we were unsure/ And I want your lines/ And I want your time/ And I want your face/ And you can have mine/* („Tracks" vom Album THE PLEASURE PRINCIPLE)

Der Bowie hat das Jahre früher alles schon besser gemacht, erinnere ich mich. Gary Numan weiß seine Chancen gut zu kalkulieren: „Seit Mitte der 70er Jahre hat es eigentlich keinen Superstar mehr gegeben. Elvis Costello hat es nicht geschafft, andere werden es auch nicht bringen." Aber er, mit seinem sowohl maskulinen wie auch femininen Identifikations-Image. Ich frage mich, wie ein Billy Currie, der Ultravox-Geiger, an dieser Dekadenz Gefallen finden kann. Vielleicht war es Garys erklärte

Vorliebe für die Ultravox-Musik. Aus ihr, auch das gibt er zu, hat er reichlich geklaut. Nicht die aggressiven Elemente, eher die wohltemperierten; von Brian Eno lieh er sich die einschmeichelnden, hohen Synthie-Töne.

Roßtäuscher

Kein Star für die schmutzigen Punk-Keller in London. Gary will damit nichts mehr zu tun haben: „Mit Tubeway Army war ich schon in der Punkzeit Abend für Abend in den Clubs auf der Bühne. Aber was hat das gebracht? Ich mag es nicht, diese engen Clubs mit den schwitzenden, tanzenden, spuckenden Leuten. Ich meine, daß die Leute meiner Musik besser zuhören sollten, wie in einem Konzertsaal". Das taten sie dann auch ausgiebig im Hammersmith Odeon, dem Ort des Geschehens um Nichts. Ob Punketten, Mods oder Immer-noch-Hippies, ein Jubel bricht los, als sich der Sicherheitsvorhang hebt — und nichts zu sehen ist.

Denn erstmal — nachher noch öfter — wird die Bühne mit Nebel vollgeblasen, vom Band wabern die wohlbekannten Numan-Brummereien aus weißen Lautsprechertürmen in die ergriffene Menge; dann ein „Ah!" und „Oh" vieltausendfach, als die Lichtorgie einsetzt und das ersetzt, was nicht kommt, weil es nicht da ist: Substanz, Spaß, Gefühl. Spontaneität. Bei der Probe im Roxy (glücklicherweise nicht das legendäre Punk-Roxy) hatte ich schon den Verdacht, einer Gigantomanie ausgeliefert zu werden. Gary äußert auch Zweifel: „Ja, es ist schon kalkuliert. Und ich hoffe, daß es mir auf der Bühne noch Spaß bringt".

Das Pärchen rechts vor mir hat sich in einen Numan-Zwilling verwandelt, ganz in rot, die Haare noch in blond. Dabei hat Gary jetzt wieder einen dunklen Schopf. Verantwortung für sein Publikum will er nicht haben: „Jeder kann das heraushören und empfinden, was er will. Das kann ich nicht beeinflussen." Also gibt er's ihnen, per Picture-Disc und niedrigen Eintrittspreisen. Drei Pfund sind

wirklich nicht viel für eine gut eineinhalbstündige Schau, die 35 000 Pfund gekostet hat. Das kommt bei der Tour nicht wieder rein, auch wenn alle 16 Konzerte bereits sechs Wochen vorher ausverkauft waren. (Und das ohne jede Plakatwerbung, wie Nick von Beggars Banquet mir immer wieder strahlend erzählt.) Die englischen Musikzeitungen werden von einem „Desaster" sprechen, wenn sie die Schau kritisieren. Das macht alles nichts. Gary Numan geht seinen Weg, unbeirrt von den Verrissen der neunmalklugen, bösartigen Journalisten. Er hat einen Vater, der ihn bedingungslos unterstützt, er hat neue Pläne, will mit Video arbeiten, mit John Foxx (Ex-Ultravox) ein Buch machen, arbeitet bereits am nächsten Album („es wird wieder mehr Gitarren haben") und denkt an Amerika: „Aber auspressen lasse ich mich nicht".

Die Katastrophe neigt sich dem Ende zu: die bisher statisch links und rechts auf der Bühne stehenden weißen Pyramiden beginnen zu leuchten und sich zu bewegen. Fasziniert starren alle auf die sich drehenden Konstruktionen. Ach, hätten sie's schon früher getan, ich hätte meinen Blick woanders hinwerfen können als auf den nichtssagenden, aber umso böser blickenden *black boy* am Mikrofon. Wo Nichts ist, müssen Licht und Sound und Image und Rauch undundund her. Ein uralter Jahrmarktstrick, der in diesem erschreckenden Fall wichtige Impulse wie sie von Ultravox oder Devo kamen, auf das Niveau von Roßtäuschern gebracht werden. Numan betreibt kein erneuerndes, kein faszinierendes und auch kein naives Spiel mit Zukunftsängsten, mit Maschinenmusik, mit Bühneneffekten. Als ich mich erschlagen aus dem Gestühl erhebe, fällt es mir schwer, mehr als „Nichts" zu registrieren. Oder ist es Numans Verdienst, Synthie-Klänge in Discos zu etablieren? Die Technologie wohnzimmerfähig zu machem? Anpassung – nein danke! Gary hat den größten Teil der Vortrags-Einnahmen für die Kampagne „Save The Whale" zur Verfügung gestellt. Danke, Gary. ♣

'I remember Bowie has done everything better years earlier. Gary Numan knows how to calculate his chances well: "Since the mid-70s, there hasn't actually been a new superstar. Elvis Costello has not managed it." But Numan, with his dual masculine / feminine identification image might. I wonder how Billy Currie, Ultravox's violinist, came to find favour at this decadence? Perhaps it was Gary's declared preference for Ultravox's music. From them he admits he has stolen plenty. Not the aggressive elements, rather the well-tempered bits; from Brian Eno he borrowed the high synth tone...

Although all 16 concerts were sold out six weeks in advance (and that without any advertising posters, Nick of Beggars Banquet tells me again and again with a beaming smile). The critics reviewing them in the English music newspapers will talk of a "disaster" when they review the show. That does not matter anyway. Gary Numan goes his own way, undeterred by the panning from the smart-aleck, malicious journalists.

The disaster is approaching its end: the white pyramids standing on the left and right of the stage are beginning to gleam and move. Everyone is staring with fascination at the rotating constructions. If only they had done this earlier, I would have been able to cast my glance elsewhere than at the insignificant but all black boy with the evil eye at the microphone. Where there is nothing, light and sound and image and smoke must come forth. An ancient carnival trick by means of which the Impulses, like those that came from Ultravox or Devo, are clothed in new colours and brought down to the level of deception found in horse-trading. ...

With Machine Music, with stage effects. Numan operates an unrefreshing, unfascinating and an un-naive game of playing with fears about the future.'

'And now his German record company has given me the added pleasure to see him live. Thank you very much.' ... I know no pictures in which he laughs. He always looks serious, mysterious and gloomy, unapproachable, but desirable. A bit like the fire brigade people in Truffaut's *Fahrenheit 451*. ...'

"One day my image will kill me, because five years of success means five years of depression!"

Gary Numan:
„Eines Tages wird mich mein Image töten! Denn, fünf Jahre Erfolg heißen für mich: Fünf Jahre Depressionen!"
Fotos: Robert Ellis

Superstars sind offenbar wieder angesagt: Gary Numan in seiner gigantischen Konzert-Kuliss

Ist Gary Numan elektrisch?

Die Über-Nacht-Sensation Englands betritt die Bühne des Hammersmith-Odeon in London: kaut er etwa noch Kaugummi? Gary Numan, der neue Superstar. Frenetischer Beifall. Seine erste Tournee war, ohne jede Plakatwerbung, bereits sechs Wochen vor Beginn ausverkauft. Seine neue LP und die Single „Cars" sind beide Nummer 1 der Charts. Dabei hatte die Punkbewegung doch endgültig für das 'Aus' der alten Superstars sorgen wollen. Heute sind die Punk-Mädchen, die Fans im Numan-Military-Look, die Hippies in ihren Gewändern und die Mods friedvoll vereint, ihren neuen Helden zu feiern. Ein Phänomen aus dem Nichts.

Ganz in Schwarz, das Blond seiner Haare ausgewaschen, mit kalkulierten Gesten, manchmal etwas unsicher, trotzdem aber kontrolliert, konfrontiert der Selfmade-Man die angetretenen Gläubigen mit einer kostspieligen, bombastischen Licht- und Soundorgie. Fünf Meter über dem Superstar thronen die Synthesizer-Spie-

ler im Lichtgerüst, sie bilden die Grundlage für den Numan-Sound, eine clevere Mischung aus eingängigen eintönigen Harmonien. Numans kalte Stimme paßt sich dem monotonen Klanggebilde an. Kein Witz, keine Emotion, allenfalls ein knappes Lächeln kommt von der Bühne. Aber die Fans sind's zufrieden. Beim letzten Stück springen sie von den Sitzen auf: zwei leuchtende Pyramiden kreiseln neben dem Bowie-Schüler. Ob die Vorbilder Bowie (für den musikalischen Teil) und Ultravox (für die 80er Jahre) ausreichen? Numan genießt den Beifall der Menge. Er ist erst 21, da kommt noch einiges. Vielleicht kann er seine Science-Fiction-Visionen dann mit Leben füllen. Clever ist er, aber ob es zum Genie reicht?

PS: Seiner englischen Schallplattenfirma, ist Gary allerdings einiges wert. Für den Erfolg seiner Single „Cars" schenkte sie ihrem Star einen weißen Corvette Stingray!   A. Pank

Musik Express Nov79 p2

"England's Overnight Sensation enters the stage of the Hammersmith Odeon in London: yet he is chewing gum? Gary Numan the new Superstar. Frenetic applause. Without any advertising, his first tour was sold out six weeks before it started. His new LP and single *Cars* are both Number 1 in the charts. The punk movement had wanted to bring an end to 'superstars'. Today punk girls are fans dressed in Numan-military look. The hippies in their robes and the mods peacefully unite to celebrate their new hero. A phenomenon out of nowhere.

He is all in black, the blond washed from his hair, and with calculated gestures, sometimes a little uncertain but still controlled, this Self-Made man confronts and competes with a costly and huge orgy of lighting and sound. Five meters above the Superstar are synthesizer players enthroned in light stands. They form the basis for the Numan sound, a clever mix of catchy monotonous harmonies. Numan's cold voice adapts to the monotonous sound structures. He tells no jokes, shows no emotion, at most a brief smile comes from the stage. But the fans are satisfied. For the last song they jump up from their seats: two glowing pyramids gyrating next to the Bowie pupil. Will the models, Bowie (for the musical part) and Ultravox (for 80s), be enough? Numan enjoys the applause of the crowd. He is only 21, and yet there is something still to come. Maybe he can build his science-fiction visions and fill them with life. He is very canny man but does that amount to genius?"

the keyboards, radio controlled robots, laser guns
& direct focus lighting effects.
But most spectacular, most electrifying is the one-
time blond now dark-haired Mr Numan, who mes-
merises his audiences with his magnetic stage
presence & his highly original music.
Credit: Cover Photo is the copyright of **Robert
Ellis**, who took the photographs for the **Gary
Numan** Tour Brochure.

*GAZZA NUMAN'S feet land on the ground and the boards starting at Birm-
ingham Odeon on Thursday and Friday*

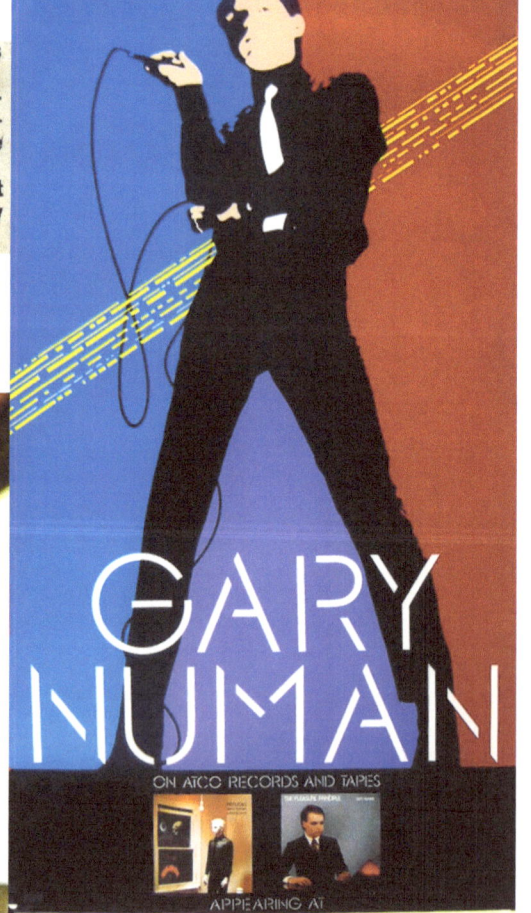

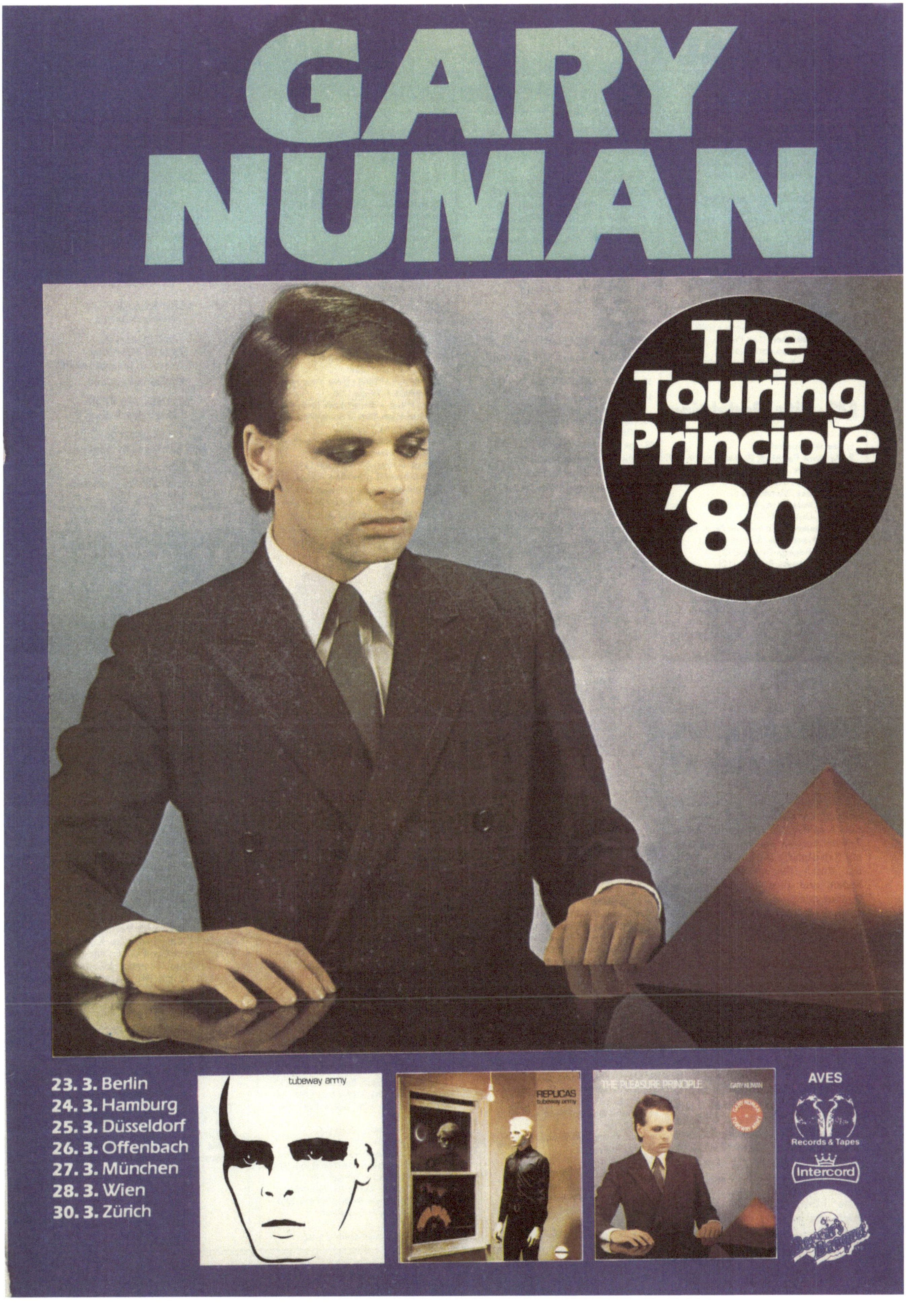

GARY NUMAN

The Touring Principle '80

23. 3. Berlin
24. 3. Hamburg
25. 3. Düsseldorf
26. 3. Offenbach
27. 3. München
28. 3. Wien
30. 3. Zürich

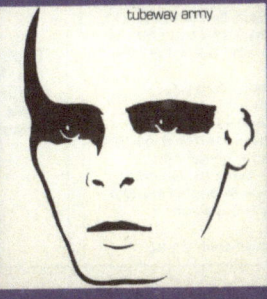
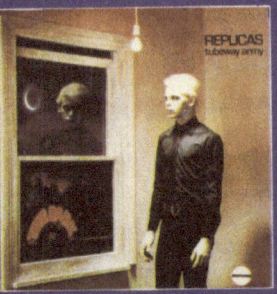

AVES

Records & Tapes

Intercord

COMMANDER NUMANS ·STAR TREK· BAND

Gary Numan genießt es, berühmt zu sein. Posters, Pin ups, kreischende Teenager streicheln sein Ego, das gibt er unumwunden zu. Trotzdem, so sagt er, habe er schon längst die Nase voll vom Ruhm. Er will aussteigen und warum, das werden seine Texte auf der kommenden LP erzählen, die ungefähr im September fertig sein soll. Diese widersprüchliche Einstellung erläuterte er nachts nach seinem Auftritt in der Hamburger Musikhalle.

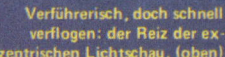
Gary Numan auf der Bühne — ein argwöhnischer Sonderling, ein absurder Superstar.

Verführerisch, doch schnell verflogen: der Reiz der exzentrischen Lichtschau. (oben)

Für alle Fans, die jetzt weiche Knie bekommen: Gary wird es noch ein paar Jahre aushalten. Aber eines ist klar: Spaß macht ihm der Job auf der Bühne nicht. Das Miniatur-Monster, das er darstellt, sei so etwas wie sein Alter-Ego und angesprochen auf seine offensichtliche Bowie-Affinität meint er: „Bowie tanzt, ich nicht. Bowie bleibt im Gegensatz zu mir auch nicht immer auf einem Fleck stehen". Seinen modisch-roboterhaften Bewegungen mißt er auch keine tiefere Bedeutung zu. Das Thema Mensch/Maschine hat er auf seiner zweiten LP, REPLICAS, abgelegt, auf hochtrabende Interpretationen seiner Darstellung (von wegen Symbolik aufgrund der Idee von geklonten Rockperformern) reagiert er gelassen: „Das

kommt allein daher, daß ich nicht tanzen kann".

In England wird bei Gary Numan-Gigs gepogot, auch in den Staaten soll es in den Konzerten hoch hergegangen sein. Hierzulande war die Stimmung eher gemischt. Der Kartenverkauf erreichte – vorsichtig ausgedrückt – keine Rekordziffern.

Gary Numan versteht es durchaus, dich spontan zu beeindrucken. Doch dieser momentane *flash* hält nicht lange vor. Wenn du seinen Nr. 1-Hit „Are Friends Electric" kennst, und vielleicht noch „Me, I Disconnect From You" dazunimmst, dann bist du mit seiner Musik vertraut. Ich mag „Friends. . ." sehr. Ich war auch zunächst gefesselt von der exzentrisch flackernden Bühnenarchitektur. Rechts und

links im Neon-Turm je ein Synthie-Mann plaziert, in der Mitte der Bühne Garys eigene elektronische Kommando-Zentrale, die allerdings ziemlich selten besetzt ist: Eine Entertainment-Zelle aus dem Raumschiff Enterprise, ausgestattet mit gleichförmig programmierten Puppen, die den Menschen der Zukunft in angenehm relaxtem Dämmerzustand hält. Doch wer noch nicht ganz zum Valium-Zombie mutiert ist, wehrt sich irgendwann gegen dieses monotone, klinisch perfekte Spektakel. Bestechendes Blendwerk, dessen vielfarbiger Glanz sich nur viel zu schnell abnutzt.

Dazwischen Gary Numan: dünn, klein; kajalumrandete Augen signalisieren so etwas wie den Wunsch nach mystischer Überhöhung. Aber: „Ich

stehe nicht über den Dingen. Ich bin immer noch ängstlich genug, um alles von mir fernhalten zu wollen. Das ist auch der Grund, warum ich nie richtig lächele. Lieber schaue ich nach unten, um den Kontakt zu vermeiden". Hat er Angst? „Irgendwie ja, ich bin nervös". Dort oben auf der Bühne fühle er sich jedoch relativ sicher vor dem Publikum. „Ich beobachte die Zuschauer ganz genau – *like a suspicious freak*".

Ein Schuß Paranoia also. Und ein wenig Schizophrenie ist auch dabei. Als die englische New Wave noch weitgehend nach der *non hero*-Philosophie ausgerichtet war, stilisierte er sich zum Superstar. „Ich habe es nicht versucht – *I did it*", korrigierte er meine Fragestellung. „Überall Pin ups und Posters, kleine Mädchen die krei-

schen. Darum macht mir die Sache auch Spaß. Diese Arie des Punk Rock: ,Wir wollen nicht berühmt werden!' war doch eine einzige Lüge. Alle wollten berühmt sein".

Ich wittere den Widerspruch. Aber Gary: „Ich habe gesagt, daß es mir Spaß mache, berühmt zu sein aber daß es mir keinen Spaß mache, aufzutreten. Live spielen ist ein Job, berühmt sein ist ein Zustand." Doch, so erklärt er weiter, es würde ihm nichts ausmachen, wenn man ihn eines Tages nicht mehr auf der Straße erkennt, denn eigentlich würde ihn gerade das doch ziemlich nerven. „In England kannst du nicht mehr aus dem Haus gehen; du bekommst alberne Anrufe, man droht, dein Gesicht zu zerschneiden oder deinen Wagen zu zertrümmern, dich zu verprügeln. Und das nur, weil du berühmt bist und sie nicht, aus Eifersucht. Ich verdiene eine Menge Geld, deshalb werde ich auch noch eine Weile weitermachen. Ich will noch einige Platten machen, weil ich glaube, daß es da noch ein paar Dinge gibt, die ich verwirklichen kann. Aber nach ein paar Jahren werde ich aussteigen".

Noch weniger wird Gary Numan offenbar mit der Feindseligkeit der englischen Presse fertig. Ein weiterer Grund dafür, daß ihm das Showbiz nun doch nicht so viel Spaß macht, wie er sich ursprünglich vorgestellt hatte. „Sobald du berühmt bist, merkst du plötzlich, daß dich unheimlich viele Leute nicht mögen. Also höre ich lieber damit auf. So sehr imponiert mir dieses Geschäft sowieso nicht mehr. Gut, es ist nicht alles negativ. Ich habe einige sehr nette Menschen getroffen, denen ich sonst wahrscheinlich nie begegnet wäre. Wie gesagt, ich verdiene viel, und es tut dem Ego gut. Aber es gibt so viele negative Begleiterscheinungen, die längst nicht dadurch aufgewogen werden".

Gary macht zur Zeit seinen Flugschein. Und in ungefähr acht Jahren, wenn – wie er heute meint – seine Möglichkeiten, LPs und Videos zu machen ausgeschöpft sein werden, will er sich ganz der Fliegerei widmen, vielleicht einen Aeroclub aufziehen. Im Moment scheint es ihm damit sogar ernst zu sein. Sein teures Spielzeug, jene aufwendige Lichtarchitektur im Werte von 200.000 Mark, die ihn pro Abend zwischen zwölf und 16.000 Mark kostet, hat bis dahin hoffentlich nicht das notwendige Startkapital verschlungen.

Gabriele Meierding

Fotos: Rainer Drechsler

Musik Joker,
November 1979

This article captures the annoyance of the German press when Numan dropped the Tubeway Army moniker, a name that, to a large part of the general population, is probably still more famous today in Germany than 'Gary Numan', on account of the one genuine hit that Numan had there.

Gary Numan: Ich war Tubeway Army

Numan: „Je depressiver ich bin, desto besser wird die Show"

Wer bei einem London-Aufenthalt zufällig im Record-Store der Hogarth Road in Süd-West 5 seine üblichen England-Plattenkäufe tätigt, muß sich nicht wundern, wenn plötzlich der Tubeway Army-Boß Gary Numan aus den hinteren Räumen auftaucht und bei den Scheiben von Ultravox und Bowie rumkramt. Was hier nur aussieht wie ein ganz gewöhnliches Plattengeschäft, ist die Zentrale der kleinen – aber sehr erfolgreichen – Plattenfirma Beggar's Banquet. Und damit Hauptsitz Gary Numan's und seiner inzwischen verstorbenen Tubeway Army.

Wieso verstorben? Ganz einfach: Auf der Spitze des Erfolges (die LP „Replicas" und die Single „Are 'Friends' Electric?" waren beide auf Platz 1 in England) hat General Numan seine Armee aufgelöst, um als Zivilist seinen weiteren Weg zu gehen. Gäbe es im Guiness Buch der Rekorde eine Sparte für Introvertierte, man fände Numan bestimmt unter den ersten. Kein Musik-Journalist, der nicht ohne das „herzliche Beileid" seiner Kollegen nach London gefahren ist, um Mr. Unknown Numan zu interviewen.

Bitte umblättern

Gary Numan: I was Tubeway Army. At the height of his success, General Numan has disbanded his army to go as a civilian into the future. If there were a Guinness Book of Records section for introverts, you would find Numan determined to be listed as the first.

Gary Numan

Ungeachtet der zahlreichen Beileidstelegramme fuhr auch ich in die englische Rock-Metropole, um sage und schreibe vier Tage in den Hinterräumen von Beggar's Banquet zu verbringen, in der Hoffnung auf ein paar druckreife Zitate von Monsieur 110 Volt.

Um es gleich vorweg zu sagen: am vierten Tag gelang es mir endlich, mit ihm etwas „warm" zu werden. Doch vorher – ob bei einem Dinner mit ihm und seinem Stab von B. B. oder bei Treffen mit seinen Firmenkollegen The Lurkers & Merton Parkers hatten alle etwas – manchmal sogar sehr Bedeutendes – zu sagen – nur Mr. Numan nicht.

„Wie fühlt man sich denn so, wenn man nach fünf erfolglosen Jahren auf einmal einen No. One Hit hat?"

„Ganz gut!"

„Warum hast du Tubeway Army aufgelöst?"

„Nur so!"

„Du willst auf Tour gehen. Was passiert auf der Bühne?"

„Einiges!"

„Was heißt ‚einiges'?"

„Sehr viel!"

Nach drei fruchtlosen Tagen war es dann soweit: Numan und ich verdrückten uns am vierten Tag in einen im Umbau begriffenen Raum über dem B. B.-Geschäft. Für ein paar Stunden die totale Ruhe. Kein Fotograf, der ihn ablichten wollte, kein Kollege, der um ein Gespräch bat.

„Weißt du, es ist nun wirklich kein Vergnügen für mich, mit vielen Leuten schlecht auszukommen. Nur, wenn ich diese depressive Phase habe, bei der ich auch nur einzig und allein meine Songs schreibe, dann kann ich nun mal nicht mit irgend jemandem sprechen – geschweige denn lachen." „Aber warum hast du in Gottes Namen die Tubeways aufgelöst?"

„Paß auf! Ich bin und das hängt mit meiner Selbsteinschätzung zusammen, lieber ein Solist, als der – wenn auch bestimmende – Teil einer Gruppe. Die ganze Zeit seit Anfang '77 war ich es, der die Songs geschrieben hat, der den Sound kreierte. Und genau das sollen die Leute wissen. Tubeway Army ist Gary Numan !!! Druck das bitte!"

„Bedeutet das, die anderen Jungs sind mehr oder weniger Studio-Musiker?"

„So ist es!"

„Wie meinst du das?"

„Tubeway Army war und ist für mich nur ein Sprungbrett nach oben gewesen. Ich war Komponist, Texter, Arrangeur, Produzent, Gitarrist, Keyboardspieler und Sänger in einem. Ich hab' also nur den Namen geändert. Tubeway Army ist Gary Numan!"

So macht dann auch zur Zeit nicht Tubeway Army eine Tournee durch Europa, sondern General a. D. Numan. Eine Tour, bei der sich der deutsche Laser-Schoener noch einiges abgucken kann. Ob die Tour auch erfolgreich ist, wollte ich zum Schluß von ihm wissen. „Eine Tour, bei der man „sold out" schon in die Plakate drucken muß, ist glaub' ich schon ganz erfolgreich."

„Welche Plakate? Du oder Tubeway Army?"

„Ist doch klar: Gary Numan ist Tubeway Army !!!"   nick

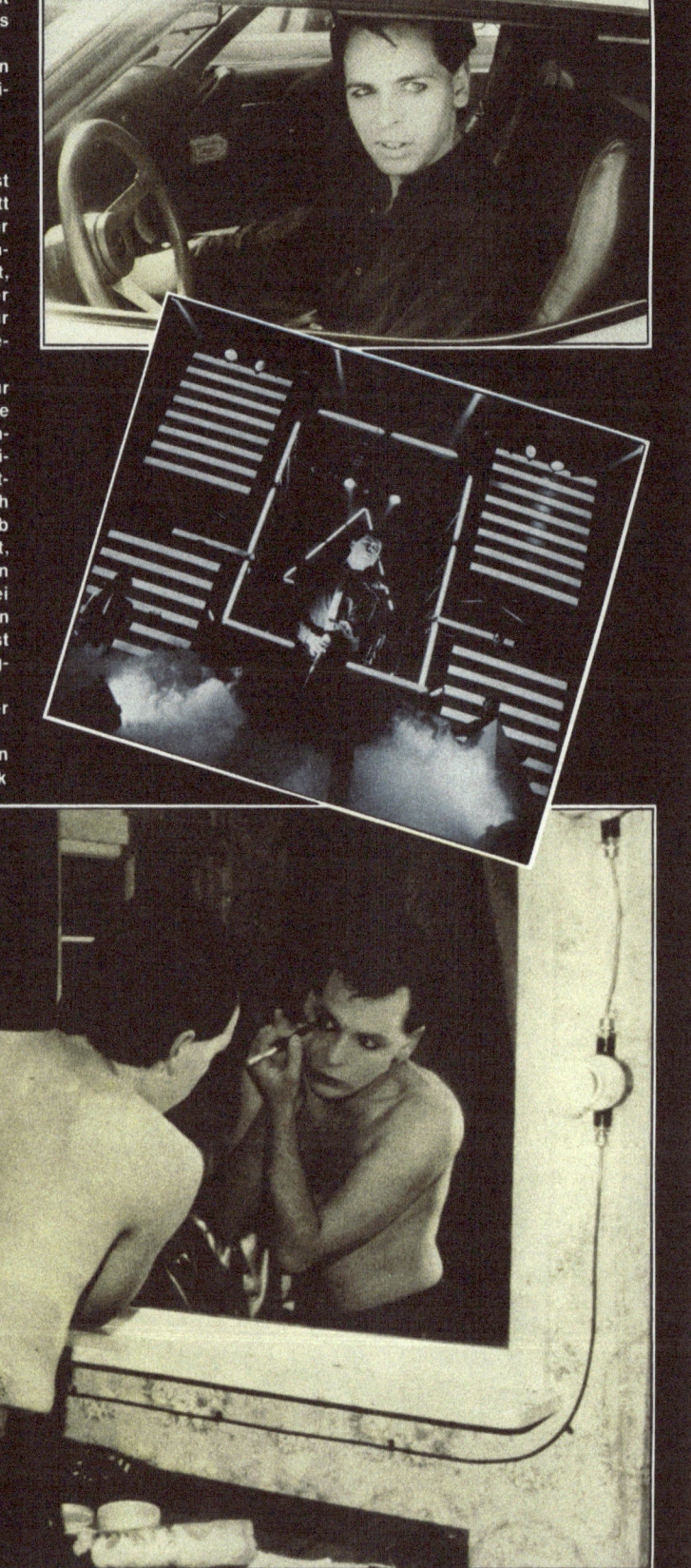

Numan: „Ob privat im Auto, beim Schminken in der Garderobe oder live auf der Bühne: Mit meinem wahren Gesicht käme ich mir völlig nackt und entblößt vor"

"But why in God's name have you absolved the name of Tubeway Army?". "I've been a soloist since the beginning in 1977, albeit as the decisive part of the group. I wrote the songs. I created the sound." "Does that mean the other guys are more or less studio musicians?" "That's the way it is!" "How do you mean?" "Tubeway Army was just a stepping stone to the top for me. I was the composer, lyricist, arranger, producer, guitarist, keyboard player and singer in one."

Gary Numan + Tubeway Army

Die Mensch-Maschine

Gary Numan ist 21 Jahre alt und sehr schüchtern. Als er vor zwei Jahren bei seiner späteren Band vorspielte, konnte er noch nicht ahnen, daß er mit der Zeit zum Produzenten, Komponisten, Sänger, Keyboardspieler avancieren sollte. All das neben seiner ursprünglich vorgesehenen Rolle als Leadgitarrist, versteht sich. Es war ein glücklicher Zufall: „Als ich vorspielte," gesteht Gary, der mittlerweile wieder von weißblond zu seiner natürlichen dunklen Haarfarbe zurückgekehrt ist, „war ich der einzige, der aufkreuzte, darum bekam ich den Job. Nach einer Woche hatte sich das Konzept der Gruppe total verändert, weil ich den Jungs älteres Material von mir vorgespielt hatte."

Es ist nicht gerade leicht, Gary auf Anhieb zu verstehen. Sein Hang zu Science Fiction und Depressionen ist so stark mit seinem Privatleben verstrickt, daß eigentlich nur eine Figur aus einem Orson Welles-Film ihn so richtig begreifen könnte. Außerdem verabscheut er Tourneen und mißtraut den meisten Leuten seiner Umgebung; will sie gleichzeitig aber mit seinen musikalischen Ideen unterhalten und darüber hinaus populär und berühmt werden.

„Es hängt mit dem Ego zusammen," erklärt er ungerührt, wenn die Sprache auf den Split von Tubeway Army kommt. „Ich bin lieber Solist als Teil einer Band, obwohl ich ja immerhin das Rückgrad von Tubeway Army ausmache." Naja, seinen Willen bekommt er im Herbst, wenn er als Gary Numan auf Tournee geht. „Ich will, daß man Tubeway Army einzig und allein als mein Sprungbrett betrachtet. Ich kann nicht mit Leuten zusammenarbeiten, die mir vorschreiben, was ich zu tun habe. Ich arbeite lieber mit Leuten zusammen, denen ich erkläre, was sie machen sollen. Davon abgesehen dreht sich in der Band sowieso alles um mich. Keiner kommt mal mit einem Song oder anderen Initiativen."

So wird es also bei zwei Tubeway Army-Alben bleiben: Das erste war einfach bekannt unter dem Titel „The Blue Album", das zweite war dann das erfolgreiche „Replicas". Die neue LP, „The Pleasure Principle", erscheint bereits unter Gary Numan (in England im September). Aber wer bitteschön ist eigentlich Herr Numan?

„Der Name ist nur ein Bühnen-Pseudonym. Ich hab ihn im Branchenverzeichnis entdeckt unter der Rubrik 'Haushaltsgeräte'. Mein eigener Name ist nämlich so gewöhnlich wie der Staub auf der Straße." Als Gary Numan kennt man unseren Mann erst seit den Anfangstagen von Tubeway Army. Diese Formation durchlief zahlreiche Reinkarnationen. Nur Bassist Paul Gardiner hielt sich immer an Garys Seite. „Ich stieg mal in eine Band ein, die sich The Lasers nannte," berichtet Gary. „Nach einem Gig im Roxy hatte ich Krach mit dem anderen Gitarristen, weil der mit irgendeiner blöden Ausrede einen Übungstermin abgesagt hatte. Es war mir klar, daß es schwer sein würde, mit ihm zusammenzuarbeiten. Ich ging und Paul kam mit, weil er auf meine Songs stand."

Ehe sich hierzulande so richtig rumgesprochen hatte, wer oder was Tubeway Army eigentlich ist, wurde der Begriff schon wieder liquidiert. Denn nach dem immensen Erfolg der Single „Are Friends Electric?" von der LP „Replicas" (siehe ME 8/79) will *mastermind* Gary Numan das Projekt nur noch unter seinem eigenen Namen weiterführen.

Tubeway Army wurde im Frühjahr '77 gegründet. Gary: „Mein Vater gab uns 24.000 DM für das Equipment. Und mein Onkel Jess Lidyard spielte bei uns Schlagzeug. Zunächst hat er versucht, uns mit Wirbeln und allen möglichen anderen Kunststückchen zu imponieren, verzichtete dann aber schnell darauf, nachdem ich ihn mit New Wave-Material ver-

Kleines Foto: Space-Commander Numan inspiziert seine Live-Truppe.

16

traut gemacht hatte. Punk und New Wave waren damals unheimlich angesagt und wir haben natürlich immer gepogot. Als wir dann bei Beggar's Banquet unterzeichneten, änderten wir das Konzept, und Jess verließ die Band. Für ihn kam ein Drummer namens Gerald, aber es stellte sich heraus, daß er wegen seines festen Jobs nicht auftreten konnte. Später nahmen wir noch einen zweiten Gitarristen dazu: der hieß Sean, und sein Freund Barry spielte Schlagzeug. Zu unseren Gigs kam nie jemand. Die beiden zogen auch bald wieder ab, weil sie das neue Material nicht mochten, an dem Paul und ich arbeiteten. Also holten wir wieder Uncle Jess ins Studio, um „Replicas" aufzunehmen."

Für „Pleasure Principle" gilt dasselbe *line up*; für die bevorstehende Herbst-Tournee werden allerdings noch fünf weitere Musiker angeheuert. Numans Sci-Fi-Trip wird sich im Bühnenbild weiterspiegeln. Geplant sind zum Beispiel sechs Meter hohe Türme für die Keyboards, ferngesteuerte Roboter, Laserkanonen und spezielle Lichteffekte. Eine besondere Überraschung noch: Bill Currie, Ultavox-Keyboardmann wird mit auf Tournee gehen. Eine Tatsache, über die Gary mehr als erfreut ist, um es mal mit typisch englischem Understatement auszudrücken.

Ultravox gehört neben Bowie und einer neueren englischen New Wave-Band namens Human League zu Numans absoluten Favoriten. „ 'Replicas' bewegt sich ja auch völlig auf der Ultravox-Linie," gibt er zu; „sie hat mich stark beeinflußt. Ultravox-Songs sind teilweise richtig unheilverheißend, und das ist genau mein Stil. Und dann Bowie: Als ich 16 war, schrieb ich eine Menge Songs, die sich alle auf Ziggy Stardust bezogen; jeder war vom Ziggy-Album geklaut. Ich mache es heute in Wirklichkeit noch genauso, aber ich vertusche das natürlich jetzt besser. Ja, ich stehe auf Ziggy's Image. Ich bin noch immer ein Bowie-Fan, obwohl ich mit seinen Texten heute nicht mehr viel anfangen kann. Ich wünschte, er hätte damals in dem Stil weitergemacht. Eine bessere Beziehung habe ich zu Kraftwerk und Eno und natürlich zu Ultravox."

Wohinter Gary Numan sich auch immer verstecken mag, sein Hang zur Depression wird ihn immer verraten. Da macht auch seine dritte LP keine Ausnahme. „Das ist beabsichtigt.

Die meisten Songs werfen die Frage auf 'Was wäre wenn?'. 'Are Yor Real' von der ersten LP zum Beispiel dreht sich um das Herstellen von Duplikaten (Clones) nach menschlichem Vorbild; "My Love Is A Liquid' handelt von Retortenbabies. In 'The Machman' geht es um einen Mann, der es mit einer Maschine treibt. 'The Life Machine' handelt von diesen Lebenserhaltungsmaschinen, die die Ärzte nicht einmal dann abschalten, wenn der Patient den Wunsch hat zu sterben. Ich beschäftige mich sehr viel mit derartigen Dingen und versetze mich in die Situation anderer Personen. Darum benutze ich auch oft die ich-Form in meinen Texten wie in 'Life Machine' zum Beispiel. Da denke ich mich in die Situation eines Menschen, der sterben will. Ich finde, wenn jemand tot ist, dann sollte man abschalten. Es gibt keinen Grund dafür, das Herz länger am Schlagen zu halten, wenn der Betroffene gar nicht mehr merkt, daß er noch lebt. Auch wenn es meine Mutter wäre. Das ist deprimierend...zumindest für mich."

Gary ergeht sich gern in Selbstzerfleischung: „Ich bin ein erbärmlicher Typ. Immer wenn ich mit anderen enger zusammenkomme, bereite ich ihnen auch nur Elend. Mit 17 nahm ich Valium; das machte einen Zombie aus mir! Es stoppte meine Gefühle, meine Emotionen, überhaupt alles. Gleich danach fing ich an, diese deprimierenden Songs zu schreiben. Aber das war schon okay, denn ich kann nur schreiben, wenn ich deprimiert bin. Also das heißt: wenn meine Karriere als Musiker noch fünf oder zehn Jahre dauern sollte, muß ich solange als elende Kreatur weitermachen. Ich bin auf eine gewisse Weise glücklich, wenn ich deprimiert bin, so ironisch das auch klingt. Zum Beispiel, als ich den Schallplattenvertrag mit Beggar's Banquet bekam: Meine Familie hat sich wirklich gefreut und sie fragten mich, wie alles kam und so weiter, und ich war richtig mies zu ihnen. Ich habe mich ihnen gegenüber wie ein Schwein aufgeführt. Ich verstehe selbst nicht, warum ich mich manchmal so benehme. Ich bin übrigens kein religiöser Mensch. Ich glaube an Geister. Ich glaube, daß da irgendetwas vor sich geht, aber ich kann es nicht so richtig packen. Es ist wie das All und das Universum, also schwer zu begreifen..."

Genau wie Tubeway Army und Gary Numan eben.

Ray Bonici

Gary Numan war die Überraschung 1979. Mit „Are Friends electric" hatte er den Super-Hit. „I die, you die" ist sein letzter Treffer

BRAVO 14

The article *Die Mensch-Maschine* by the Maltese journalist, Ray Bonici, published here in German in September 1979, was reprinted in the Italian magazine, *Rockstar Uno* in April 81. The Italian version is overleaf. My partial translation is on page 184.

Mutant PoP

'The creator of Tubeway Army looks like an alien being. For some time he left the name of the band and went on his earthly mission releasing work as Gary Numan.'

Rockstar Uno April 81

RAY BONICI ——————————————— & ——————————————— RED RONNIE

Foto: Jaserarts

L'artefice di Tubeway Army assomiglia ad un essere alieno. Da qualche tempo ha abbandonato il nome della band ed ha continuato la sua missione terrestre soltanto come Gary Numan. Anche John Foxx ha abbandonato il gruppo base, gli Ultravox, perché li considerava soltanto un esperimento. Ora, entrambi rincorrono la loro vita sul filo di un... sibilo elettronico.

Foto: Red Ronnie

1 Quando questo timido chitarrista ventunenne fece un'audizione per la band, non pensava neanche minimamente che il suo ruolo si sarebbe in seguito sviluppato in quello di produttore, compositore, cantante, tastierista è chitarrista solista all'interno del gruppo. Per lui fu un colpo di fortuna, ma era anche evidente che avrebbe dominato il futuro di Tubeway Army.

«Quando feci l'audizione», ha detto Gary, che dopo molte tinture si è ora deciso per gli usuali capelli neri, «ottenni il lavoro soprattutto perché non si era presentato nessun altro. Dopo una settimana, suonai agli altri alcune mie cose, e tutto cambiò.» Gary non è certo una tra le più facili persone da capire. I suoi concetti di scetticismo, fantascienza e depressione sono così confusi nella sua vita personale che soltanto un personaggio uscito da un film di Orson Welles potrebbe forse capire. Detesta fare i tours, diffida di quasi tutte le persone che lo circondano, ma vuole diventare famosissimo.

«È tutta una questione di ego», spiegò per nulla imbarazzato, quando venne fuori la questione della spaccatura all'interno dei Tubeway, «preferisco esser un famoso solista che esser parte di un gruppo famoso. Anche se sono la spina dorsale dei Tube-

way, voglio sempre essere un performer solista». La sua determinazione si è infatti sviluppata molto tempo fa. «Vorrei che i Tubeway Army fossero conosciuti come il mio terreno iniziale», comanda piuttosto seriamente, « e niente di più; sono sicuro di quello che dico. Non ha nulla a che fare con il nome, è soltanto che voglio stare da solo. Non so lavorare con un mucchio di gente che dice quello che bisogna fare. Vorrei lavorare con gente che sia disposta a fare quello che dico io. E poi la band ruota intorno a me, che mi piaccia o no. Cioè, nessun altro del gruppo tira mai fuori una canzone o una delle cose che faccio io.»

Finora Numan si è attribuito il merito di quattro albums. Il primo è semplicemente conosciuto come «The Blue Album», il secondo è «Replicas», che ha ottenuto un grande successo. «The Pleasure Principle» si è immediatamente piazzato al primo posto. Sebbene sia stato attribuito a Gary Numan, il riferimento a Tubeway Army era inevitabile. «Telekon» ha completato il successo. Dopotutto, puoi chiedere, «Chi è Gary Numan?»

«È un nome d'arte. L'ho scoperto sotto la voce "elettrodomestici" delle Pagine Gialle, perché vedi, il mio vero nome è molto ordinario», ha rivelato.

Come musicista, il suo nome risale soltanto al pe-

riodo della formazione di Tubeway Army. La stessa band attraversò diverse reincarnazioni, ma vicino a Gary c'era il sempre fedele bassista Paul Gardiner Gary spiega:

«Entrai nel gruppo dei Lasers e facemmo un concerto al Roxy. Finii per azzuffarmi con l'altro chitarrista perché aveva cancellato una prova con delle stupidissime scuse. Sapevo che sarebbe stato duro lavorarci insieme, e allora me ne andai. Paul venne via con me perché gli piacevano le mie canzoni. I Tubeway Army si costituirono nella primavera del 1977. Mio padre mise 6000 sterline per l'attrezzatura del gruppo. Poi chiamammo mio zio Jess Lidyard a suonare la batteria con noi. All'inizio cercò di impressionarci rompendo tutto e rullando dappertutto, ma cambiò subito appena gli insegnai le cose di new wave molto semplici. A quell'epoca il punk e la new wave stavano diventando popolarissimi e infatti ballavamo il pogo, ma quando firmammo con la Beggars Banquet, cominciammo veramente a cambiare e cambiò anche la formazione. Jess se ne andò e al posto suo venne Gerald, ma scoprimmo che non poteva fare gli spettacoli dal vivo perché aveva un lavoro fisso. Quindi lo sostituimmo con Bob, che ha suonato nel nostro primo singolo. Poi decidemmo di ampliare la formazione con un chitarrista che si chiama Sean e il suo amico Barry alla batteria, ma le cose non funzionarono. Facevamo dei concerti che nessuno venica a vedere. Poi Sean e Barry decisero di andarsene, perché non volevano fare le cose nuove che stavamo preparando io e Paul; ci dividemmo di nuovo. Dopodiché chiamammo di nuovo mio zio Jess per un lavoro di studio ed è così che abbiamo fatto gli ultimi albums».

Gary ha portato a termine una specie di tour mondiale per il quale saranno chiamati cinque musicisti. Ancora basata sulla fantascienza e la musica elettronica, la costosa apparecchiatura del concerto era composta di due torri di 6 metri per i tastieristi, robots radiocomandati, pistole laser e speciali effetti luce. Insieme a Gary, al sintetizzatore, ha lavorato Bill Currie, degli Ultravox. Gary è felicissimo di questo perché insieme a Bowie e Human League, gli Ultravox sono le sue guide. Gary ammette apertamente di trarre la sua musica da quegli artisti, specialmente da John Foxx (ex Ultravox) e David Bowie.

«"Replicas" è quasi completamente Ultravox», ha detto Gary, che è stato recentemente accusato di copiare Bowie, «mi hanno influenzato sui dischi e sul palcoscenico. Alcune delle cose che quelle persone hanno fatto sono cariche di distruzione e quello è esattamente il mio stile. Infatti, a 16 anni scrissi una serie di canzoni basate su Ziggy Stardust. Ognuna di quelle canzoni è un furto dai pezzi dell'album di David Bowie. Lo faccio ancora adesso ma cerco di camuffarle di più. Mi piace molto l'immagine di Ziggy. Avrei voluto che Bowie continuasse. Credo che Bowie sia una delle persone più creative che siano emerse nell'ultimo decennio. Bowie mi piace ancora molto, sebbene non mi interessino più i suoi testi. Ora mi interesso più a Eno e ai Kraftwerk, e naturalmente, agli Ultravox».

«Si può dire che queste persone che ho nominato ed io abbiamo qualcosa in comune, oltre alla musica elettronica», ha aggiunto, «è l'immagine visiva. Trovo sia molto importante adesso che stiamo entrando nell'età del video perché il pubblico può far riferimento a te in entrambi i modi, quello musicale e quello visivo.»

In scena si dipinge e si veste come un assessuato. Sembra che per le sue aperte ammissioni sulla influenza di Bowie, egli abbia ora due tipi di pubblico. I fans di Bowie e i suoi veri fans.

«Quando ho fatto uscire il mio secondo album pensavo che ci avrebbe messo un po' di tempo per arrivare ai primi posti, ma nel giro di pochi giorni ventò il numero uno. Io avevo fatto un piano ma andò più veloce di quanto pensassi. Ero sulla lista della critica. Ora sto prendendo le cose con più calma e facendo così, so esattamente quello che mi succede».

In qualsiasi band Gary cerchi di mimetizzarsi, c'è sempre un fattore dominante in lui... la depressione. Proprio come «Replicas» e «The Blue Album». «Pleasure Principle» e «Telekon» non fanno eccezione.

Per esempio, "Are You Real", nel primo album, parla della clonazione. "My Love Is A Liquid" parla dei bambini nati in provetta. "The Machman" delle macchine che mantengono in vita quando dei dottori non le disinseriscono, anche se è la stessa persona che vuole morire. Io mi rifletto in queste situazioni o mi metto nei panni di un altro. È per questo che uso un mucchio di "io" e "me" nei testi. Come in "Life Machine", mi metto nella posizione della persona che vuole morire. Penso che se una persona è morta, esse dovrebbero esser spente. Non c'è ragione di continuare a far battere il cuore, se quella persona neanche sa di essere in vita. Anche se accadesse a mia madre.»

Se Gary dice questo di sua madre, significa che è un ragazzo molto attaccato ai genitori. Infatti vive ancora nella casa dei genitori, a Staines. Ma non è stato sempre così. La sua depressione lo aveva reso un animale per i suoi genitori.

«Sono una persona tristissima. Sono sempre molto depresso e se mi avvicino a qualcuno, li rendo tristi la vita. Sono molto timido, non bevo e a volte divento inaspettatamente violento. Di solito gridavo e rompevo le sedie. Sai, a 17 anni dovevo prendere molti Valium e questo mi ha trasformato in uno zombie. Mi impedivano di sentire qualsiasi emozione. Subito dopo cominciai a scrivere queste tristi canzoni, ma va bene perché riesco a scrivere canzoni solo quando sono triste. Sono influenzato da tutte le cose deprimenti. Diciamo che se conti-

Foto: Jaserarts

Gary Numan, dopo una serie di concerti trionfali tenuti nel 1980, ha deciso di interrompere la sua carriera di performer. Mai più un concerto, a quanto dice, o almeno non prima di aver esaurito tutto il lavoro che lo attende in studio. E per lui, invischiato com'è nelle produzioni elettroniche, non sarà un lavoro da poco.

nuerò la mia carriera di musicista per altri cinque o dieci anni, dovrò essere triste per tutto questo spazio di tempo. Sono quasi felice quando sono depresso, è ironico. Quando, ad esempio, feci il contratto con la Beggars Banquet, tornai a casa e i miei genitori erano così contenti che mi fecero un mucchio di domande in proposito, ma io ero estremamente triste. Fui molto scortese con loro. Io non so

proprio perché a volte mi comporto così. Malgrado questo, non sono una persona religiosa. Credo nei fantasmi. Credo ci sia qualcosa di nascosto, cui non riesco ad arrivare. È come lo spazio e l'universo, è difficile capirli».

Sì, proprio come Tubeway Army e Gary Numan. Chi ha detto che i pazzi si trovano solo nei manicomi?

trad. Valentina Gentili

183

Gary Numan's music and name are known to the cognoscenti in Italy but his songs didn't chart there because they weren't widely played on the radio. Italian radio, and the Italian charts, are rightly dominated by Italian acts singing in Italian. The Italians had already fused electronics with rock with the band, Goblin, who topped the charts in 1975 with their score for Dario Argento's film, *Profondo Rosso*. Anglo synthesizer rock and pop didn't get a look-in until March 1980 when (of all things) *Video Killed The Radio Star,* by the novelty act The Buggles, topped the charts in Italy for TEN weeks. Thereafter replaced by Toto Cutugno, Lucio Battisti, Katia Svizzero Alan Sorrenti, etc. The closest Numan came to mainstream success in Italy was in July 1980, when he became the first Englishman ever to take part in Italy's most famous music show, *Saint Vincent Estate,* a three-hour televised competition for the year's best song. It was watched by something like half the country. But Gary Numan didn't play a concert in Italy until the Jagged Tour of 2006, when he played clubs in Cesana, Turin and Milan. The concerts were not well attended.

The *Mutant Pop* article is a reproduction of *Die Mensche-Machine* but with additional saracastic asides that give the game away that Bonici was a London-based journalist.

From *Mutant Pop*: 'When this shy twenty-year-old guitarist auditioned for the band, he did not have even the slightest thought that his role would be later develop into that of band's producer, composer, singer, keyboardist and lead guitarist. For him it was a fluke, but it was also evident that would dominate the future of Tubeway Army. "When I did the audition," says Gary, who after many shades of hair has now decided to go with black, "I got the job largely because nobody else showed up. After one week, the concept of the group had totally changed because I had the other guys playing all my old material." Gary is certainly not one of the easiest people to understand. His penchant for science fiction and depression is so strongly entangled with his private life that only a character from an Orson Welles movie could really understand him. He hates to do tours, mistrusts almost all the people around him, but wants to become famous, and is happy to chat about his musical ideas and beyond.

"I was once in a band called The Lasers," says Gary. "After a gig at the Roxy, I had a row with the other guitarist because he had cancelled a scheduled rehearsal with some stupid excuse. It was clear to me that would it be difficult to work with him. I left the band and Paul came with me, because he was on my songs." ...

"You can say that these people I mentioned and I have something in common, in addition to electronic music," he added, "and that's the visual image. I think it's very important now that we are entering the age of the video because the public can refer to you either way, the musical and visual."

The image he projects is asexual and it seems that for his open admissions on the influence of Bowie, he now has two audiences, fans of Bowie and his true fans. "When I released my second album I thought it would take a bit of time to reach the top spot but, in a few days I become number one. I had made a plan but everything went faster than I thought. Now I'm taking things more calmly so I know exactly what happens to me."

In any band Gary tries to create, there is always a dominant theme in his work ... depression. Just like *Replicas* and *The Blue Album*, and *The Pleasure Principle*, *Telekon* is no exception. Gary Numan likes to hide his tendency to depression in his songs. "That was intentional. From the first LP to the third, most songs ask the question, Are You Real?"... In the song, *The Life Machine*, I put myself in the position of the person who wants to die. I think if a person is dead, they should be turned off. There is no reason to continue to make the heart beat, even if that person knows they are alive. Even if it happened to my mother.". If Gary says that about his mother it means the guy is very attached to his parents. In fact, he still lives at home with parents in Staines. It was not always so happy. His depression did make him an animal for his parents. "I am a very sad person. I am always very depressed, and if I get close to someone I make their life sad. I am very shy. I do not drink and do not smoke and sometimes I become unexpectedly violent. When I was 17 I cried and I smashed the chairs at home. For many years, I had to take Valium and this has turned me into a zombie. It prevented me from feeling any emotion... Let's say that if I continue my career as a musician for another five or ten years, I'll be sad for all that space of time. Ironically, I'm almost happiest when I am depressed. When, for example, I signed the contract with Beggars Banquet, I came home and my parents were so happy and asked a lot of questions about it, but I was extremely sad. I was very rude to them. I do not know why I sometimes act like that. Despite this, I am not a religious person. I believe in ghosts. I think there is something hidden, which I can not reach. And as to space and the universe, it's difficult to understand them."

Yes, it's just Tubeway Army and Gary Numan. Who said that the lunatics are found only in asylums?'

A *Saint Vincent Estate* photo-sheet pulled from an ebay listing, low-res and covered with an unsporting dealers's false copyright notice. He has no claim to these photos of the rehearsal and the performance. Numan is probably singing *I Die You Die*. A recording of the performance hasn't surfaced, but youtube clips of Italian singers performing that night indicate that it was mimed. The show was broadcast on July 5 and directed by Antonio Moretti. The following year, after Numan's pioneering example, the floodgates opened. Phil Collins, Joe Dolce, Grace Jones, OMD, Visage and Toyah all took part. The OMD and Visage performances are on youtube. The show ran from 1964 to 2003.

Gary Numan/ Tubeway Army
L'amico elettrico

SONO INIZIATI GLI ANNI OTTANTA ANCHE PER IL ROCK? GARY NUMAN DICE DI SI: IN INGHILTERRA E' IL NUOVO EROE DELLA MUSICA FUTURISTA. UN ROCK PESSIMISTA E GLACIALE CARATTERIZZA IL SUO GRUPPO E I SUOI DISCHI. OGGI IN ITALIA ESCE "REPLICAS" MENTRE IN TUTTO IL MONDO ESCE "THE PLEASURE PRINCIPLE"

Nel giro di pochi mesi, quasi dal nulla, i giovani adolescenti inglesi hanno costruito un nuovo eroe. O forse, come molti pensano, il nuovo eroe ha costruito se stesso attraverso i giovani adolescenti inglesi. Ma andiamo con ordine: l'eroe in questione si chiama Gary Numan, ed è conosciuto nella sua qualità di leader indiscusso del gruppo after-punk dei Tubeway Army.

Benché siano nati nel 1977, la vera consacrazione dei Tubeway Army è avvenuta quest'anno, grazie al 45 giri "Are friends electric?", il cui successo ha imposto ai vertici delle classifiche l'album "Replicas", il secondo del gruppo. Subito dopo, ai primi posti delle classifiche è stato recuperato anche il primo album, intitolato "Listen to the sirens" (o più semplicemente "Tubeway army"). In questi giorni, infine, il terzo album appare intestato al solo leader, Gary Numan: si intitola "The pleasure principle", e immediatamente si è imposto come l'album del momento.

Ma insomma, chi sono i Tubeway Army? e soprattutto, chi è Gary Numan? I Tubeway Army sono nati tra il 1976 e il 1977. Sulla scia delle esperienze moderne dei Roxy Music, di David Bowie dei Kraftwerk, comincia a svilupparsi una nuova scena: è la scena del rock glaciale, elettronico e sintetico, del rock after-punk. In questo nuovo underground post-moderno, si muovono dunque a Londra, a partire dal 1977, nomi come Human League, Cabaret Voltaire, Tubeway Army.

● **STAR DEL 1980**

Già il primo album dei Tubeway Army contiene, sia pure in maniera non sempre coerentemente sviluppata, i germi del loro suono sintetico, che li ha successivamente imposti come il nuovo attuale fenomeno di massa del rock inglese. Ma i vari brani risentono ancora di un sensibile aggancio con il passato, con lo psichedelismo

"I always thought that punk was a real movement, especially in the early days, before it became fashionable. But I only used punk rock as a way to get a record contract. …. It's hard to answer questions about fans honestly without causing a bad impression. For me …. I do not have any loyalty towards them … I make the records and they buy them. It bores me very much to hear people when they say: "We made you." It's not true. They can not 'make' anyone. We do it alone. They simply buy the records… I think for a lot of people I am the symbol of something new. The pose, the image are important. The fans see me and then they go home and imitate me in the mirror. They are like me when I was a fan. I give them exactly what I wanted from my heroes."

elettronico degli anni Sessanta, degli Electric Prunes, dei primi Pink Floyd... Autore di tutto il repertorio è il leader, Gary Numan: la sua figura è inquietante e androgina, come e più di un David Bowie (ma con oltre dieci anni di meno: nel 1977, Numan ha appena diciannove anni). Anche in concerto, è sempre distante, glaciale. In scena come nella vita, mima e rappresenta il lato "disumano" dell'uomo-robot metropolitano del XXI secolo. Non solo Numan è autore dei brani: ma è anche produttore del gruppo, disegnatore delle futuristiche scenografie industriali dei suoi spettacoli dal vivo, nonché proprietario della piccola etichetta discografica dei Tubeway Army (la Beggar's Banquet, della quale Numan ha ceduto per cinque anni la licenza di distribuzione alla WEA, per una cifra considerevole).

Insomma, un gelido costruttore del proprio successo, padrone di se stesso e del proprio destino, esattamente come Eno e Bowie, i prototipi della star moderna. Proprio Bowie, nonché i Roxy Music e i Kraftwerk, sono alla base del suono di "Replicas", il secondo album dei Tubeway Army: robotici ritmi elettronico-germanici, voci disperse e distanti, parole di fredda disperazione, di grigio futuro, di alienazione. L'album è un puro prodotto moderno:

il rock elettronico e sintetico, pur rimanendo su strutture di avanguardia progressiva, fonde felicemente questa dimensione con quella consumistica. Avanguardia elettronico-sintetica e consumismo industriale sono infatti le due caratteristiche, apparentemente opposte, che il novo-rock dell'afterpunk fonde per la prima volta insieme.

E infatti, "Replicas" vola in cima alle classifiche e ci resta per mesi e mesi. E il 45 giri "Are friends electric?" diventa il nuovo inno elettronico dei ragazzi moderni.

● THE PLEASURE PRINCIPLE

Il terzo stadio della ascesa di Gary Numan come nuovo eroe di massa giovanile proposto dai media elettronici, si intitola "Tre pleasure principle": questo album (che esce in questi giorni anche in Italia), pur essendo stato realizzato da tutti i ragazzi dei Tubeway Army — Paul Gardiner al basso, Chris Payne alle tastiere e al violino, Ced Sharpley alla batteria, Billie Currie, ex Ultravox, al sintetizzatore, e Russell Bell alla chitarra — ha questa volta il solo Gary Numan come titolare.

Si tratta del suo album più maturo e completo. Gary Numan prende per mano l'ascoltatore, e gli fa attraversare il ponte che separa gli anni Settanta dagli anni Ottanta. Titoli

scarni, asciutti, metropolitani ("Metal", "Complex", "Cars", "Tracks", "Films"...), e parole altrettanto asciutte, sintetiche, imbevute di una sorta di agghiacciante "realismo futurista". E la musica è un piccolo compendio della modernità: un rock elettronico, post-moderno, un po' wagneriano e un po' barocco, che fa propria e fonde con grande perizia la lezione di quasi tutti i campioni del suono degli anni Ottanta: da David Bowie ai Roxy Music, da Eno a Todd Rundgren, dai Kraftwerk a Giorgio Moroder. Un suono che ha qualcosa di vecchio e qualcosa di nuovo: "qualcosa" che, probabilmente, è destinata a durare.

● LA PAROLA A GARY NUMAN

D.: In che misura devi qualcosa al punk-rock?

R.: Ho sempre pensato che il punk fosse un vero e proprio movimento, specie nei primi tempi, prima che diventasse moda. Ma non mi sono mai sentito parte di esso. Mi sono servito del punk-rock solo come un mezzo per ottenere un contratto discografico. Certo, ero eccitato da ciò che aveva portato: una nuova musica, una nuova moda... ma poi il punk è stato distrutto dalle sue stesse idee. Il "trip" dell'anti-eroe non avrebbe mai potuto realizzarsi, perché questo

paese ha sempre avuto degli eroi. Credo che sia tipicamente inglese il creare degli eroi.

D.: I testi delle tue canzoni rappresentano il futuro come un incubo...

R.: E' una visione piuttosto estremistica del futuro, derivata da ciò che accade ora, ma è solo una delle varie visioni possibili. E' ciò che vedo intorno a me... la parte grigia della natura umana, e poi la parte violenta. La stessa natura umana è un argomento interessantissimo se la consideri nei suoi lati estremistici.

D.: Che rapporto hai con il tuo pubblico?

R.: E' difficile rispondere onestamente senza suscitare brutte impressioni. Per me... io non devo loro nessuna lealtà... io faccio i dischi e loro li comprano. Mi annoia molto il sentire la gente quando dice: « Noi ti abbiamo fatto ». Non è vero, loro non possono "fare" nessuno: ci facciamo da soli, loro semplicemente comprano i dischi. Credo che per molta gente io sia il simbolo di qualcosa di nuovo. La posa, l'immagine sono elementi importanti. Loro mi vedono, e poi vanno a casa ad imitarmi davanti allo specchio. Io so che loro sono simili a me, quando ero un fan: e dò loro esattamente ciò che io desideravo dai miei eroi.

Manuel Insolera

Look-In 23 June 1980

GARY NUMAN

ROCK STAR

No. 1 45p

AN INTIMATE PROFILE

THE SEMI-DETACHED STAR OF SUBURBAN STAINES

Alsatian dogs lurk in the bushes. A tall, white gate stands between the neat, red-brick house. The barking dogs give their warning and Gary Numan's father appears from the side of the house to pull them away. Numan Jr is at home in his fortress, his cage. A product of the rock and roll machine age, his dazzling success — with both singles and albums topping the charts within the last three months — has all the neon-bright, cold-edged trappings of synthesisers, video, supercars and technological toys.

22-year-old Numan (real name Gary Webb) is 5ft 9in high, and dresses in tight jeans and black-heeled boots. His hair is dyed coal black s (whereas it was once bleached blonde, it's naturally brown) and brushed behind his ears. It is reputed to be suffering from the onslaught of chemicals. he can't use aftershave or anti-perspirants because they bring him out in a rash. He still exists on a diet composed almost exclusively of junk food like "chips and hamburgers".

"Hi," he says and the handshake is firm. But he seems shy, waiting for me to speak first. He tucks himself into an armchair and a mock fire burns behind mock logs. His mother brings us a cup of tea.

"I don't drink alcohol or smoke," he volunteers. "I made up my mind I wouldn't and I've never put a cigarette to my mouth.

"If I'm feeling upset about anything, I go for a run in the car," he says, jerking his head towards the back window and a gleaming white Corvette.

Doesn't he sometimes wonder if he'll wake up one morning and find it gone, that none of this ever happened to him?

"I did to begin with," he agrees. "Just like when we first went to number one, I couldn't believe it.

"I had a carefully worked out plan But it went wrong. Everything happened faster than I thought it would. We never thought 'Are Friends Electric?' would go to the top. I thought it wouldn't happen until 'Cars', the second single — and by that time I would have had more experience with performing."

In fact, the first time he fronted the group, Tubeway Army, was the first time he appeared on TV's 'Old Grey Whistle Test', in June last year.

He did that programme and 'Top of the Pops' in the same week and he credits his entire meteoric streak to the top to that one thing: television exposure.

"It's what sells records in this country," he says. "Visual image is important, because it gives the kids something to latch on to."

So on stage he dresses in tight leather, paints his face white ("I started doing it to cover my spots. I only eat burgers and chips so they never seem to get any better") and rings his slate grey eyes with black pencil. His fans are already beginning to dress like that, but Numan appears to derive little satisfaction from that.

"Being a success is a lot different than I thought it would be," he says wrying. "I thought it would be fast, hectic, glamorous; wild parties and lots of flashy women. I got into that briefly but I didn't like it. It's all very false."

He finds the other members of his band helpful as sound in boards for his musical direction, and describes the relationship between them all being "not so close as brothers — it's more like being in the Army and they are the other blokes in the barrack room.

"I wouldn't trust them not to leave me for another group that paid more money," he says realistically. "We get on very well, but it is a business arrangement."

When he gets bothered by people on the road the others help him escape. It is rudeness wich bothers him the most.

A key to Numan's work and character lies in his attitude to David Bowie.

"If it wasn't for him I would never have got into theatre and movement and putting on a big show," he admits quickly. "Bowie made it obvious to me what I could do."

He first saw Bowie perform live during the 1976 'Station-to-Station' period, when he slicked back his hair, wore a dinner jacket and started to experiment with white light.

Two years later Numan attended the Earls Court shows where Bowie straddled, with consummate ease, all the phases of his development, welding them into a coherent whole.

Criticism of Numan's stage show stems mainly from the fact that many music writers found it monotonous rather than cohesive, and Numan unable to sustain the pace and excitement needed for performance to build to a climax.

"I knew that would happen," he says angrily. "I designed an enormous computer news-screen to create images behind the drum kit, from thousands and thousands of tiny light bulbs. It was obvious to me that the audience would be used to the special effects by about 20 minutes into the concert. The computer was supposed to start lighting up then, to avoid a slump.

"I worked it out so carefully," he says, slamming his fist into the palm of his hand. "They didn't tell me 'til the day we were going on the road that it wouldn't be ready on time. I put £10,000 of my own money into it and it's still not ready."

Bowie and Newman have never met, so it is worship from a distance.

"I think he is one of the most creative people. to come out of the last decade," says Gary. "I'd like to be able to change as much as he does. But you must remember he didn't try to change his image until he had established himself."

Bowie is a star of the sixties going on seventies; Numan is a star of the seventies going on eighties and all its technology.

He writes all his own conflict into his lyrics.

But unemployment, bad housing, bad drugs, bad company are far cries from the Numan crouched before me in a comfortable armchair. Glancing at the normality of his home, it seems ridiculous for him to be writing about, and for, punks and their problems. A bit like Oscar Wilde writing about the indignities of manual labour — a double standard.

He simply shrugs this off and says: "You can feel things strongly enough to write about without having to actually live them."

"My family has lived in this area since I was two months old." His arm desribes a wide arc, embracing what seems to be the whole of this Thames-side area, from Staines to Windsor. "I guess a lot of people would hate it," he says wryly.

He is seriously considering moving around a bit more now that he has some money of his own. H explains that he gets very stuck in his ways. For years the furthest away from home he ventured was Weymouth, for an annual summer holiday. Then somebody suggested Cyprus, so he went there every year.

"Now, what I'd really like to do is buy an island in the Pacific. I was reading about one the other day. It's only £150,000 and that's quite cheap, isn't it?"

I smile and try to work out how much money he must be making — or about to make. The tour won him acclaim, not money. All of £30,000 of his own money went into creating a spectacular stage production. Royalties are now pouring in for publishing and for the last three albums and singles. Massive sales of the third single are worth untold thousands.

I ask how it all began and learn that at eleven he started to play with his schoolfriend's electric guitar. But all he really wanted to do was to be a pilot.

"That was until I was 13. Then we had a careers talk at school and they told us only one in a thousand ever gets to be a pilot. It stopped me there and then. I looked around at the thousand people in my school and I knew I wasn't the cleverest. So I weighed up the odds and decided to go into something else pretty quick."

Now he can say: "There's a lot of commonsense involved with success in the rock and roll business. You have to be very shrewd in terms of deciding what you're going to do and when you're going to do it."

5

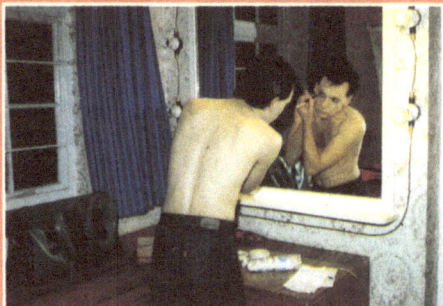

Gary reflects on his belief that he attracts (or causes) poltergeist activity.

His method of song-writing is to compose several songs, then chop them up, and put different chunks from each together into one song. But he does it by verses.

It is not the same as the cut-up method favoured by Bowie and taught him by William Burroughs, which involves writing lines, then cutting up the words and sticking them back together again in whatever pattern they fall.

"It's meaningless," says Numan dismissively. "Too random. If you've got feelings you want to write about there's no point in doing cut-ups because it makes no sense to you or the person hearing it. Apparently, my lyrics are hard enough to understand as it is."

There is a bitter lemon twist to the statement which comes out of a kind of wounded disbelief that anyone could or would criticise or misunderstand his work. He claims people do that all the time and basically he does not like people.

So, he admits, his ultimate reason for remaining in the musical rat race is fair and square, money.

"I want to take as much as I possibly can," he says. That day he had been out buying a 200mph go-kart. A few days previously, an enormous screen and slide projector were added to his possesions. Flying lessons are also part of his lifestyle. He has no feeling of betraying his 'art' for gold. Gold is simply one of the goals.

Closer dreams or ambitions include considering a film version of his 'Replicas' album. He is also preparing plans for a series of four-minute videos. This projected 'Replicas' film is likely to have a similar story line treatment to 'Soylent Green', which was set in an over-populated future. "I would like to hav robot machines winning, the bad is getting badder and badder but a machine could handle life perfectly."

Then there's his coast-to-coast tour of America which he started in February 1980. If he breaks there (in the world's biggest record market) and the records start selling, he can look forward to a sizeable fortune.

"If I got that island in the Pacific," he says, pursuing the immediate fantasy, nobody would tell me I coudlNt. ride my go-kart

because it was making too much noise. And that I can drive my car at only 30 miles an hour through the town. I could do what I wanted and that means a lot to me. Money can buy me freedom."

But not necessarily satisfaction. To me, he seems very confused beneath the controlled exterior. "I used to go into shops, and if what I wanted took too long to say, I wouldn't even ask for it," he says. "I couldn't talk in front of a queue of people. I'd just get tongue tied. I'm still shy, but not on stage.

"I don't feel nervous playing to thousands of people. Yet when we were just playing to 10 or so I used to get so frightened I would almost be sick."

"The power of the mind fascinates me," he says. The album he is working on now, called Telekon, is concerned with telekinetics and telepathy. He reads R D Laing, science fiction and books on psychology. "I started reading them to find out about myself. I used to have a problem when I was younger."

Until six years ago, while he was still at the local grammar school, he used to have blackouts or fits and became unexpectedly violent.

"I'd be perfectly normal," he explains. "Whatever might be bothering me I would simply take in and behave as though nothing was. Then one thin would happen that was no more or less than any of the others, but it would just trigger me, and I'd be off. I'd flare up and catch everybody by surprise, including me.

"I wasn't violent towards people, but things. I just had to smash things. I would smash chairs and scream."

This uncharacteristic lack of control is the one area where he cannot confide in his parents. "I can talk to them about almost anything else. Sex can be a bit of a problem when you're growing up, but I talked to my Mum completely openly."

He has had one serious love affair, which broke up two years ago. "It affected me very badly," he admits. "It made it very hard for me to get along with other people. No matter how long someone is around, I never believe that they won't up and leave the next day. I put very little value on people's promises.

"She went very suddenly, without any breakdown in the relationship. One night she just said 'That's it' and left. I could never do that to someone I loved."

Yet in a way that is what he is planning to do with his millions of fans, most of whom are in the six to 16-year-old age range.

He is not prepared to develop his stage performances through voice training or movement tuition.

Rather, he will expand the theatre of the show as a whole, and then stop performing completely.

"I'm not going to be in it long enough to take classes," he says. "Next year I want to have a huge stage show. Take it on the road for a world tour. Then pack up completedly and never go on the stage again."

Perhaps it is instinctive self-defence. He is more guarded than anyone of his age should be. Outside the dogs prowl, ready to scare off the carloads of teenagers who sometimes descend on his house in the dark of night and sometimes hurl milkbottles through the windows. Indoors, his parents, ever attentive, make tea in the shiny, Formica-topped kitchen.

Looking at his white punk-next-door face, I can't help feeling he is paying the price for stardom.

"I'm just a boy," he says defensively. "Hardly even a man yet. I just write songs. But some people seem to feel I'm a threat to their existance. Why they have to take me seriously I'll never know."

COMPLEX
They won't come back
You know it's always the same
and they're sure to forget
Saying 'Everyone lies'

So I'm down to this
I'm down to walking on air
and you're here by my side
with all your waving and smiles

Please keep them away
Don't let them touch me
Please don't let them lie
Don't let them see me

Reprinted by Kind Permission of Andrew Heath Music

Rock Star featuring Gary Numan. Packaged by Danacell Limited, 66 Uxbridge Road, London W7.

Printed in the UK. Distributed by COMAG, Tavistock Road, West Drayton, Middx.

GARY NUMAN: top-selling music video

Below left, the world's first commercially available long playing music video tape. Above right, the 1988 reissue by Palace Pictures.

WELL, you can't exactly blame us. Giving coverage to an expensive, to some even elitist, form of entertainment in these dark days of recession may seem odd.

GARY NUMAN
The Touring Principle '79

Recorded Live at Hammersmith Odeon, London
September 28, 1979

GARY NUMAN SOUND & VISION

GARY NUMAN makes his entry into the world of commercial video this month with the release of a 45 minute cassette filmed at Hammersmith Odeon on his last tour.

This will be the first time that a major pop act has put on the market a videocassette (though Blondie's "Eat To The Beat" has also been announced) and the first time that a recording will be available that can be played on all the various different video systems.

Beggar's Banquet are manufacturing VHS, Phillips, Betamax and Sonumatic versions of the film which features a promotional film of "Cars" plus the following live tracks; "Me I Disconnect From You", "M.E.", "We Are So Fragile", "Everyday I Die", "Conversations", "Remember I Was Vapour", "On Broadway", "Down In The Park", "My Shadow In Vain", "Are 'Friends' Electric?" and "Tracks".

Assuming that you're lucky enough to own or rent all the proper video equipment, you can purchase the cassette for either £19.99 for VHS and Betamax formats or £29.99 for Sonumatic and Phillips machines from Beggars' Banquet, 8, Hogarth Road, London W5.

GARY NUMAN

NUMAN'S FIRST

GARY NUMAN has pipped Blondie to the post . . . . by becoming the first top rock act to have a video cassette on general sale to the public.

The video contains 11 tracks filmed at Hammersmith Odeon last September, plus a "bonus" track of the 'Cars' promotional video.

And, unlike Blondie's 'Eat To The Beat' video — expected in May — the Numan film will be available in all video formats; VHS, Philips and both the Sony systems.

It will be available by mail order only at present, although there are plans for shop distribution at a later date, from Beggars Banquet, 8 Hogarth Road, London, SW5.

The video is priced at £19.99 for VHS and Betamax formats, and £29.99 for U-matic and Philips tapes.

BEGGAR'S BANQUET HOME VIDEO

GARY NUMAN
THE TOURING PRINCIPLE '79

RECORDED LIVE AT ODEON HAMMERSMITH
28th SEPTEMBER '79

THE **gary numan** SONGBOOK Vol. 1.

OFFICIAL

BEGGARS BANQUET MUSIC LTD

chappell

A Happy Rock 'n' Roll New Year

HAPPY NEW YEAR TO ALL
READERS OF
MUSIC LIFE
LOVE
Gary Numan
XXX

ゲイリー・ニューマン
GARY NUMAN

機械文明の発展が生みだした，まさに80年代ポップ・ミュージックの，ひとつのヒーロー像というものを，ボクらに見せつけてくれた，ゲイリー・ニューマン。その無機質な感性は、ボクらの精神に呼びかけているのだ。

Gary Numan

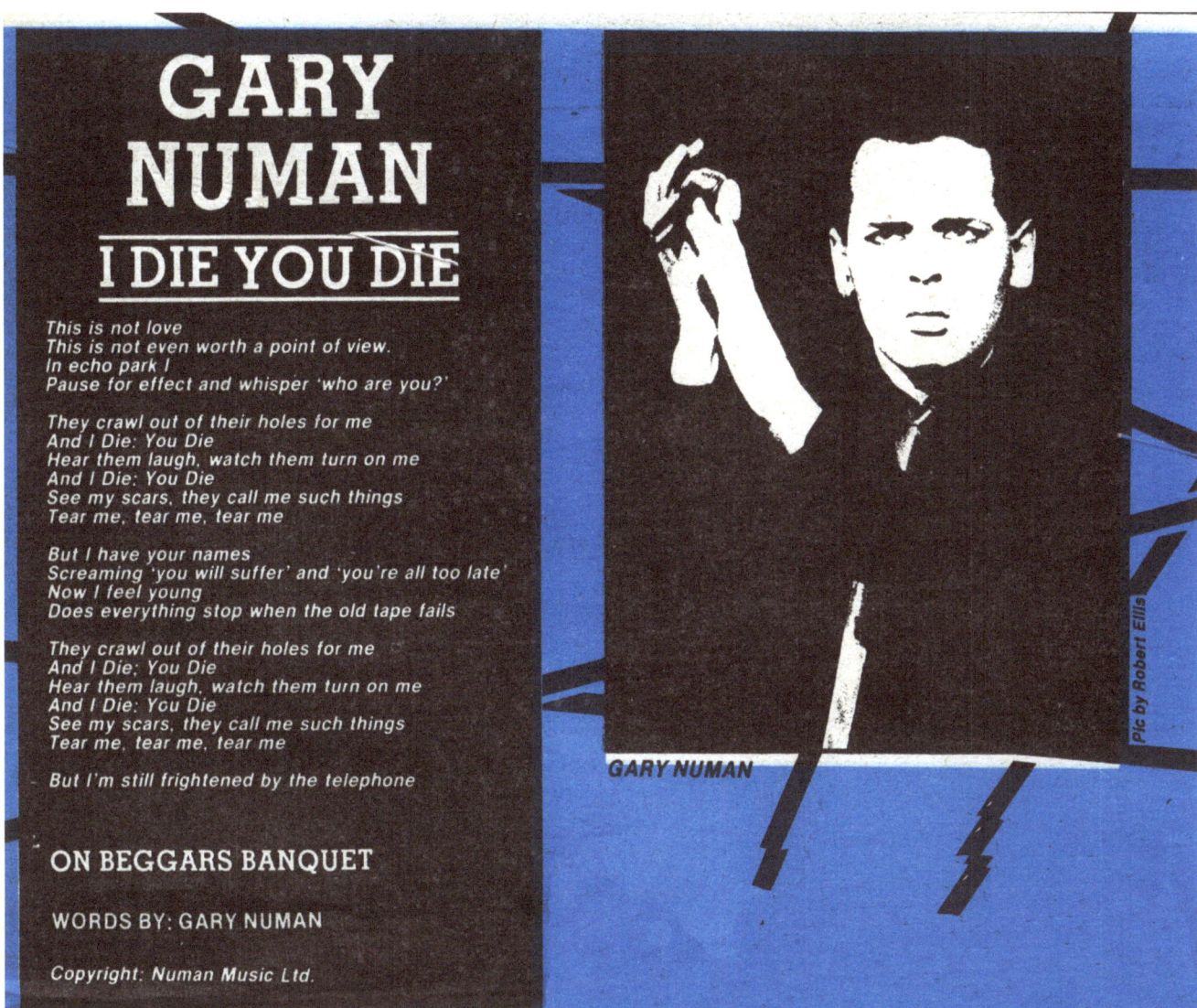

GARY NUMAN
I DIE YOU DIE

This is not love
This is not even worth a point of view.
In echo park I
Pause for effect and whisper 'who are you?'

They crawl out of their holes for me
And I Die: You Die
Hear them laugh, watch them turn on me
And I Die: You Die
See my scars, they call me such things
Tear me, tear me, tear me

But I have your names
Screaming 'you will suffer' and 'you're all too late'
Now I feel young
Does everything stop when the old tape fails

They crawl out of their holes for me
And I Die: You Die
Hear them laugh, watch them turn on me
And I Die: You Die
See my scars, they call me such things
Tear me, tear me, tear me

But I'm still frightened by the telephone

ON BEGGARS BANQUET

WORDS BY: GARY NUMAN

Copyright: Numan Music Ltd.

GARY NUMAN

Pic by Robert Ellis

The photograph on the left and those on the next five pages are from the world premiere performance of *I Die You Die* on *The Kenny Everett Television Show,* recorded in December 1979 for the New Year's Eve special. On the same show, a welcoming in of the new and a ringing out of the old, David Bowie, who had now ditched the retro Teddy Boy look, performed *John I'm Only Dancing* in a Numan-style black boiler suit, and thought that that would be good enough, an old song with a wink. It wasn't. He and the show's director, David Mallet (who had directed several Bowie videos) were absolutely not prepared for what Numan brought to the table. Gary Numan, whom Bowie and the press had slandered as a Bowie copyist, and who had that year already written, performed and produced two game-changing Number One singles and two Number One albums, and who had an additional top ten hit with *Complex*, the first electronic ballad ever to reach the charts, brought not an 'old' favourite but a brand new song, *I Die You Die*, a scorching attack on the music press, written in a new style that left behind the clean and clear melodies of *The Pleasure Principle,* and which took the electronic rock song genre into completely unchartered waters, aggressive melodies *without* guitars (guitars would be added in later versions). It was industrial dark wave before either term had been coined and it marked Gary Numan's third transformational style in *eight months*! Numan recalls: "They said that they wanted us to do the show in the first place because it would have been good to have a confrontation between David Bowie and me on the very last programme of the year, just to compare if nothing else. And I was all for that, because it would've cleared the air once and for all, and hopefully people would have realised, seeing us side by side, that we are really nothing alike at all. The way Bowie moves and sings and his music, is nothing like the way I move and sing my music." But, like The Who being bounced from The Stones' *Rock and Rock Circus* film, Numan's performance wasn't broadcast until the first show of the following series, on the 18th February 1980, because Bowie knew that he'd been beat. Numan's performance, confident where once there was nerves, is magnificent. It's a public statement that he is a bona fide superstar. Numan performed the song live for the first time at the Music Hall in Toronto on the very same day it was broadcast in Britain on the Kenny Everett show.

omething,
e."

is a family
ny, was a
driver at
ng Gary's
like a duck
een in the
He knows
— and be-
"

o goes on
he band's
utographs
s me. I'll
nan.
oner Inn
No, just
. He had
agh Deb-
to try a
success.
ntually
his auto-
wanted
with his
Gary.
re my
I had a
ay," he

I have
nt get-
ut for
that's
r him
s, the
yfair,
.
l par-
ising

ever
take
d. I
be
for
the
that

few
e. I
os-
I
n't

an
l-
o
ge
st

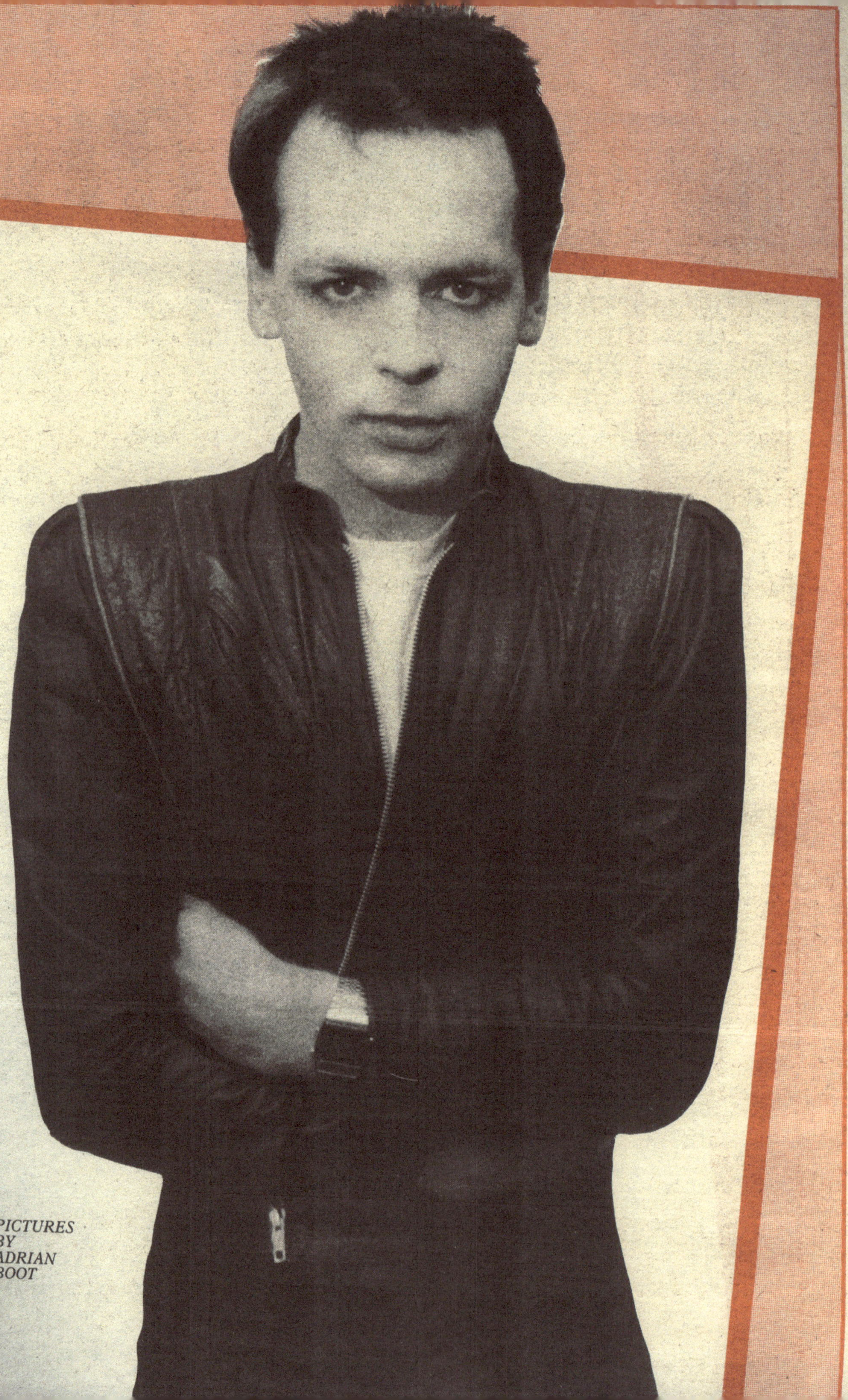

PICTURES BY ADRIAN BOOT

A wholly different version of the song, now with added guitars, and with the last line changed from 'We were walking in the silent bars' to 'I'm still frightened by the telephone', was released as single in August 1980. A third, though less markedly different version appeared at the same time in a 35mm short promo film, directed with style and atmophere by Derek Burbidge.

GARY NUMAN DICHIARA: "LASCIO LA MUSICA!"

ABBIAMO INCONTRATO A NEW YORK
GARY NUMAN PER UNA CHIACCHIERATA SULLA MUSICA.
DOPO SOLO QUALCHE TEMPO LA DICHIARAZIONE
È ESPLOSA: L'EFEBICO CANTANTE
ABBANDONA LA BATTAGLIA E LASCIA IL MUSIC BIZ!

GARY NUMAN: I Die: You Die (Beggars Banquet). Odd picture on the cover. He looks as if he's looking for a lost contact lens. Still, the record. Well, even an outsider like me, who really doesn't understand what all the fuss is about, can detect that this effort lacks the commercial clout of previous singles. Backing track reminds me of ELO. Song reminds me of being asleep.

DEAR OLD GAZZA, HE'S SUCH A LARF ETC
GARY NUMAN: I Die You Die (Beggars Banquet). How's about just *you* die, Gary? Still playing at Doomsies in sheltered corners while Heat Death and Clampdown become more and more obviously imminent, Gary Numan's latest instalment of sort-core computech sounds like a collision between Elton John and a Space Invaders machine. Cunningly released to coincide with the return of *Top Of The Pops*, this one will run and run.

Numan on *Saint Vincent Estate* (right). Teletour programme images (below).

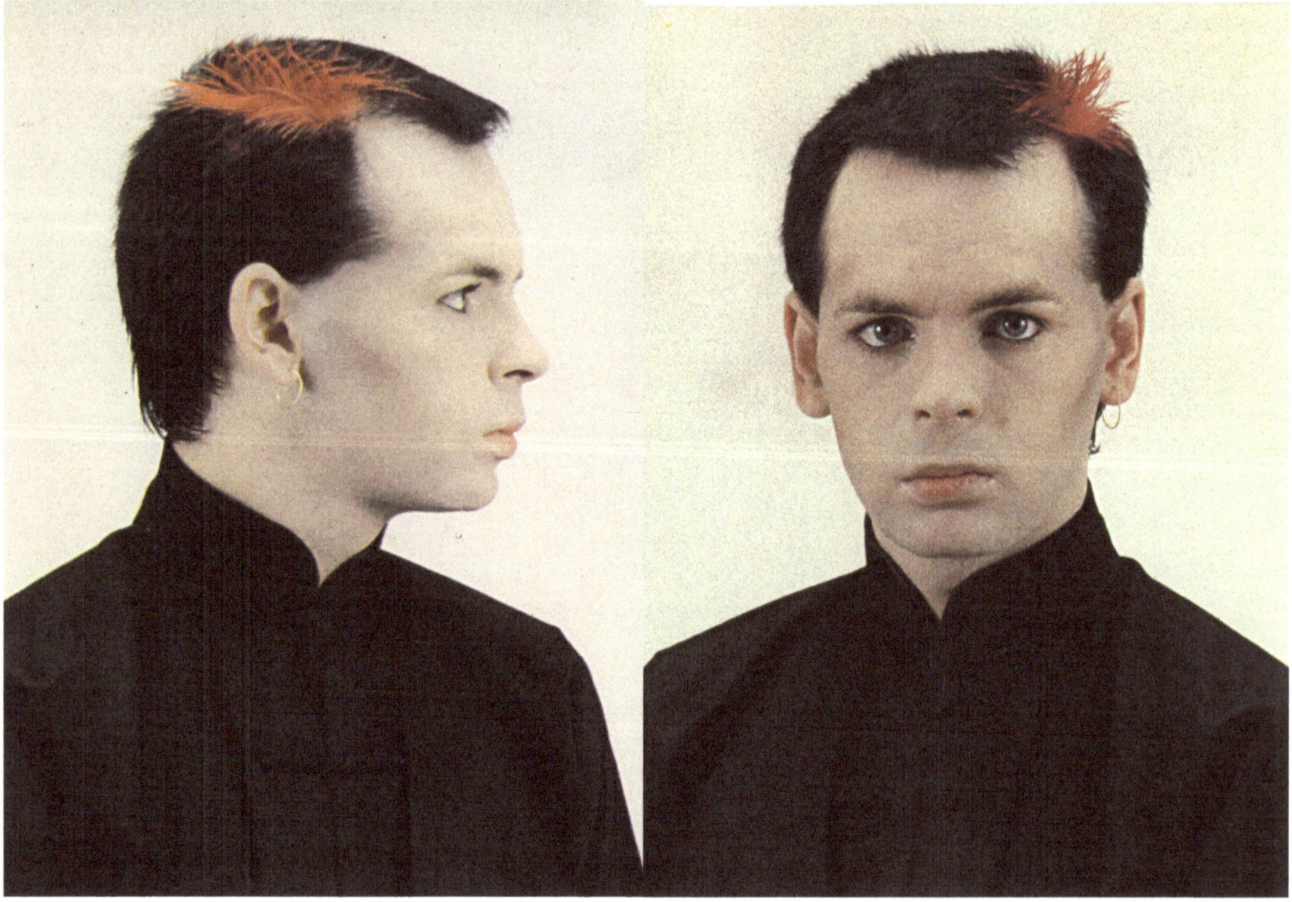

Gary Numan and his backing musicians have just come home for a well deserved rest after conquering the world with that distinctive Numan synthesiser sound. His major tour began with concerts in Britain late last year, and ended in mid-June with concerts in Australia, after shows all across America, throughout Europe, New Zealand and Japan. The result has been a phenomenal response everywhere he has played — which is even more remarkable when you remember that just over a year ago no-one had ever heard of him!

GARY'S ELECTRIC ARMY CONQUERS THE WORLD

Recently Gary has had top ten singles in all the major American charts, three albums in the New Zealand charts and a fanatical following in Japan. Yet he has not forgotten his British fans, even though we have not seen much of him for quite a long time. He has already completed most of the work on a new album, to be called **Telekon,** which will be released in September and will coincide with a major British tour.

The new show will feature a lot of material he has been trying out on the last lap of his world tour, and his record company, Beggars Banquet, say that it will be a spectacular show — in keeping with Gary's love of stunning visual effects. In fact he is already working on new types of visual presentations, with the intention of making **Telekon** available as a video disc. But it will not just feature Gary singing the songs, it will also have all kinds of clever and inventive special effects with lights and images, created by an amazing new camera, called a Squeeze Zoom. Gary's love of tinkering with electronic and computerised machines is reflected in this camera, because, by linking it up to a computer, all kinds of wierd and wonderful images can be conjured up.

He has already used it successfully, by completing a special video disc of his concert at the Hammersmith Odeon in London, and although it is not available in the shops, his record company have been supplying it through mail order.

Meanwhile, Gary has been writing new songs throughout his tour, and it is quite likely that he will want to go back into the studios to adapt songs on the **Telekon** album, or to substitute them with newer material. And, of course, he has recorded the big hit single **We Are Glass** — which incidentally, will not be on the album — and made a promotional film for the song.

He is also due to go back to Nassau in the Bahamas, where he spent some time before his concerts, working with a British singer who is a big success in America, Robert Palmer. Gary played keyboards on Robert's almost completed new album, and Robert is going to record two of Gary's songs on that LP.

So there seems to be no let up for Gary Numan, the man who last year said that he had always wanted to be in the rock music business, but, upon reaching the peak, discovered that he did not enjoy all the tinsel and glitter. His prediction that he will retire in just a few years has not changed, but if he does really carry out his threat to quit, he will have left an astonishing legacy.

Before his emergence, the German group *Kraftwerk* began to make synthesisers more acceptable to a wider audience, with a top twenty single called **Autobahn,** but they never developed and experimented with the sounds, and the full potential of electronic music was not realised.

Then came Gary, toying with rhythms and sounds, and his success has opened the doors for many of his electric friends.

Ultravox, the band who originally inspired Gary to his achievements, now have a following which they merited first time round, and former Ultravox leader *John Foxx*, with his **Metamic** album, has emerged as a star in his own right.

Another ex-Ultravox man, *Billy Currie*, who played a synthesiser in Gary's band, has now left to record his own album of electronic music in Germany.

Orchestral Manoeuvres In The Dark, two musicians who used to appear on stage with a tape recorder playing all their backing tracks, have enjoyed considerable success with their debut synthesiser album, and their single **Messages.**

Even groups like *New Musik*, with **Living By Numbers** and *The Buggles* with **Plastic Age** would not have found anything like the acclaim they have earned if it were not for the fact that Gary had made synthesiser sounds easily identifiable and readily acceptable.

So if Numan does retire early, he should certainly be remember long after he's pulled out the last plug on keyboards!

Colour pin-up: Robert Ellis

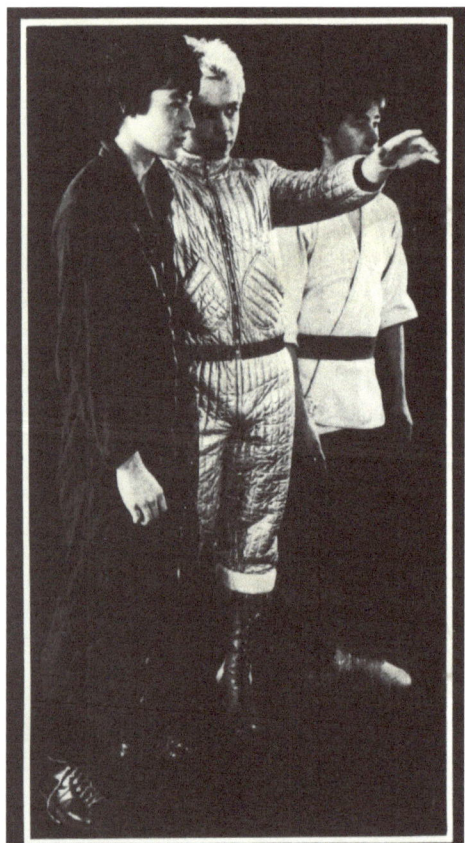

We Are Glass is a sort-of reworking of *We Are So Fragile* but sung now from experience. It's the song of man who has been crushed by fame. He has told the record company he is quitting the business. They are incredulous but he has done all that he set out to do. He is going to pursue a different dream, a different life, or is that train ride down to the sea a journey to end his life? A fall from Beachy Head? Is it him who ask's "Hey you, which way is down?" (i.e. where do you throw yourself off?). Is it the record company executives furious that he is killing their cash cow and his career? Or is it the mocking press praying for his career to fall? Probably all three.

For the picture sleeve, Numan wore the jacket first seen on the back of his debut single, *That's Too Bad.*

Telekon

This Wreckage

The Aircrash Bureau

Telekon

Remind Me To Smile

Sleep By Windows

I'm an Agent

Remember I was Vapour

Please Push No More

The Joy Circuit

GARY NUMAN

NEWSLETTER

Dear Member

As this is the first ever newsletter from the Gary Numan Fan Club I thought that I should write it personally.

As far as I know the next four months (January through to the end of April) will be as follows:

JANUARY
During January I hope to finish the rough demo recordings of the next album. This gives me time to sort out the best songs to use when the album is recorded properly later on in 1980. The songs I've written so far are called:-

TELEKON (possible album title)
REMEMBER, I WAS VAPOUR
I DIE, YOU DIE (possible single)
THE JOY CIRCUIT
SLEEP BY WINDOWS
PLEASE PUSH NO MORE
I'M A DRIVER
THE AIRCRASH BUREAU

I also hope to have finished the stage designs for the next British (and possible World) Tour.

FEBRUARY
The first half will be spent rehearsing for the American/European Tour (The Touring Principle '80). The dates for the American and European tours are as follows (although some of these are likely to be altered).

AMERICA
February 14 — Toronto
February 15 — Montreal
February 17 — Boston
February 18 — Providence
February 19 — New York
February 20 — Philadelphia
February 22 — Cleveland
February 23 — Chicago
February 24 — St. Paul
February 28 — Los Angeles
February 29 — San Francisco

EUROPE
15 March — Paris
16 March — Brussells
17 March — Amsterdam
18 March —
19 March — Oslo
20 March — Stockholm
21 March —
22 March —
23 March — Berlin
24 March — Hamburg
25 March — Dusseldorf
26 March — Frankfurt
27 March — Munich
28 March — Vienna
29 March —
30 March — Zurich

These pages from the Fan Club magazine give an insight into the making of *Telekon*. The first thing to strike one is that there must be demo versions of eight *Telekon* tracks, including an unheard song, *I'm a Driver* (which is probably *I'm an Agent* (the lyrics do start with driving). The demos haven't yet been released. Steve Malins scoured the archives during the making of the expanded CD but didn't find anything.

Hello, I hope the fan club is what you wanted and the early days aren't too inconvenient. Anyway, the next album "Telekon" is 99 per cent finished, and will definately be released during the first week of September. The final track listing is:

Side one:
Remind me to smile
I dream of wires
Telekon
I die: you die
Sleep by windows

Side two:
I'm an agent
The aircrash bureau
Remember I was vapour
Please push no more
The joy circuit

The album lasts for about 45 minutes, which makes it the longest so far. A single called "We are glass" was released on May 16 and its B side is an old classical piece that I've adapted for synthesizers. It was written by Eric Sartie in the 1880s, and in my opinion it's one of the loveliest pieces of music ever written.
About the recent tours, Canada and America were great successes. "The Pleasure Principle" has just gone gold in Canada, and is in the top twenty in America. "Cars" is also in the top twenty singles chart and is still rising. The gigs were sold out and the audiences were really great.
The European tour was also very good except that the Germans were a bit taken aback both by the clothes I wore and the visuals in general.
Next up is an album with Robert Palmer (his album — I will just be helping), so I will be spending a few days with him before going on to Japan to continue our tour. That's where I will be when you get this newsletter, then on to New Zealand and Australia.
We did the video for the single "We are glass" recently, and that promises to be very interesting. By the way, for anybody who bothered to read the Daily Star article, please ignore it. It was a mixture of lies, twisted truths, and false, malicious implications. I will be away when the single is released but I hope you like it. I also hope that you can get hold of a copy of the in-concert video. I had hoped that you could get this a bit cheaper through the fan club, but I'm told that it's being sold at very near cost price anyway, so the company can't really deduct anything. That's because it cost a fortune to make and nobody even knows how many people have got a video machine. If you know someone with one, perhaps a group of you could get together to buy the video as it's really good viewing.
Finally, I would say a special thankyou to all those of you who sent me cards and Easter eggs recently. They were greatly appreciated.
Bye for now,

Gary Numan

Hello,

I'm tired. Down to four hours sleep a night now. Busier than ever 'Telekon' is finished and cut. Track listing has changed again because I wrote a new song for it at the last minute, called 'This Wreckage'.

Telekon track listing (final for sure)
Side One This Wreckage
          The Aircrash Bureau
          Telekon
          Remind Me To Smile
          Sleep By Windows

Side Two I'm An Agent
          I Dream Of Wires
          Remember, I Was Vapour
          Please Push No More
          The Joy Circuit

The running time for the new album is about 50 minutes and a limited amount will have a free 'live' single inside. 'I Die: You Die' is the next single backed by a piano version of 'Down In The Park' which is of interest more than anything else.

The songs co-written on Robert Palmer's album are called 'Style Kills' and 'Fool For You'. He's also doing a version of 'I Dream Of Wires'. Also, I'm just finishing production of an album by a man known as James Freud. The album has ten tracks, two of them mine: 'Exhibition' and 'Stories'. He is NOT living in my house as a paper recently stated (I haven't even got a house) but lives in London with his band - a member of which, Roger Mason, has replaced Denis Haines in my band. Roger is now keyboard player for both James and myself. Denis didn't quite fit personally within the band.

A film is released at the end of the year called 'Time Out', 'Times Square' or 'Running Out', I forget now, but among the songs on it is the original 'Down In The Park'.

I'm not intending to do any filming after the next world tour as some papers have said. I intend to finish the next album and move heavily into the video phase of my career.

On the forthcoming tour I will be having another big stage production and will be playing to around 80,000 people. This limits where I can play and unfortunately I won't be returning to Sheffield, Liverpool and a couple of other places where you gave me so much support before. I'm trying to please most of the people most of the time and if the tour doesn't come near you, I'm sorry.

Rather than increase the ticket prices they will remain as before to allow everyone to benefit from fair prices. This means that I'll lose £80,000 but you will all get your seats at £1 below true cost. This seems to me a good way of giving you all something back for what you've given me.

Hope to see you soon.

Gary Numan

別れよう

The words in Japanese say 'I leave you'.

THIS WRECKAGE

By Gary Numan on Beggars Banquet Records

And what if God's dead?
We must have done something wrong
This dark facade ends
We're independent from someone

This wreckage I call me
Would like to frame your voice
This wreckage I call me
Would like to meet you, meet you
Soon

We write suggestions
Suggesting fading to silence
And that must please you
My mirrors tarnished with "no-help"

This wreckage I call me
Would like to frame your voice
This wreckage I call me
Would like to meet you, meet you
Soon

別れよう
(Mou wakareyo)
(Mou wakareyo)

Turn out, these eyes
Wipe off, my face
Erase me

Replay the end
It's all just show
Erase you

I need to, I need to, I need to

This wreckage I call me
Would like to frame your voice
This wreckage I call me
Would like to leave you, leave you
Leave you, leave you
Soon

別れよう
(Mou wakareyo)

Repeat to fade

Words and music by Gary Numan
Reproduced by permission Numan Music Ltd.

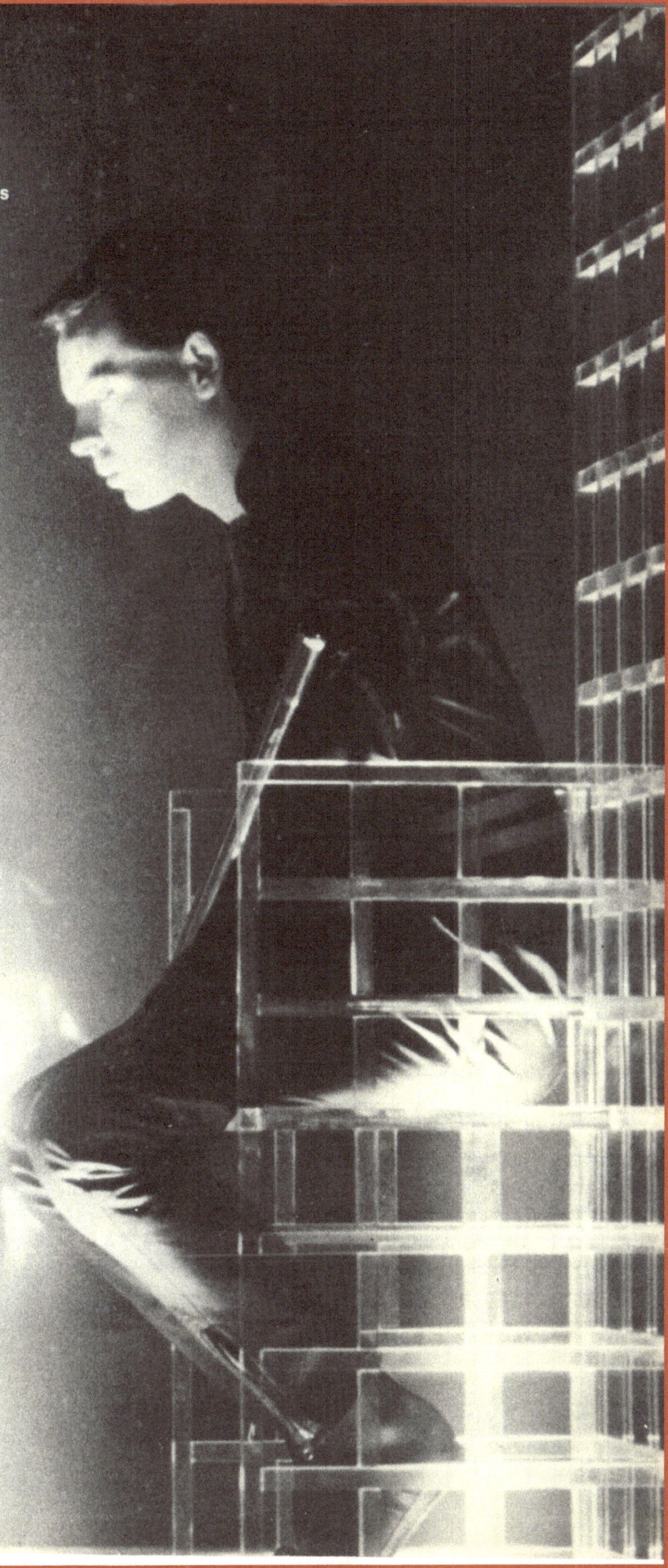

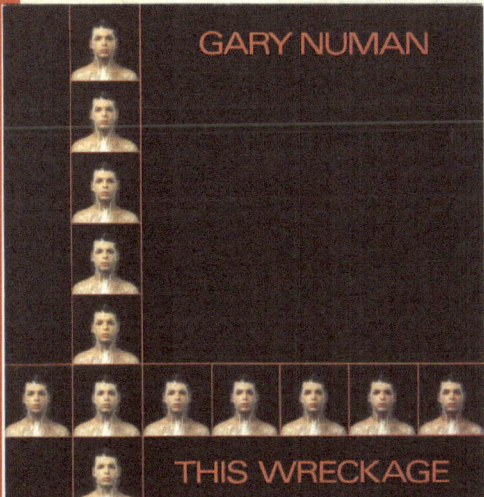

GARY NUMAN

THIS WRECKAGE

NEXT YEAR'S NUMAN

GARY NUMAN is close to finishing work on his new album, "Telekon". The track listing is as follows: "Telekon", "Remember I Was Vapour" (dedicated to his fans), "I Die, You Die" (dedicated to the music press), "Sleep By Windows", "The Joy Circuit" and "A Game Called Echo".

The bad news is that it's not due for release until next September under Gary's one-album-a-year contract with Beggars Banquet. We also hear that Gary is planning a series of ten four-minute videos and a film version of the "Replicas" album.

FEEL LIKE A NUMAN?

THE NEW Gary Numan album, "Telekon", which hits the shops on September 5th, includes the following tracks; "This Wreckage", "The Aircrash Bureau", "Telekon", "Remind Me To Smile", "Sleep By Windows", "I'm An Agent", "I Dream Of Wires", "Remember I Was Vapour", "Please Push No More" and "The Joy Circuit".

Neither side of the new single, "I Die: You Die" is included on the record, although they will both be featured as bonus tracks on the cassette version.

The first 100,000 copies of the album will contain a free 45 made up of live recordings from last year's show at Hammersmith Odeon. Talking of Hammersmith, both of Numan's shows at that venue in September have sold out and a third date has been added on the 17th.

Rare LP's, 45's, EP's, picture discs
SPEEDIES Let Me Take Your Foto/No Substitute $2.00
Victims **Real Wild Child** $5.98
XTC double-single, Towers of London/Scissor Man +2 live $3.98
XTC double-single Generals and Majors/Don't Lose Your Temper/Smokeless Zone/The Somnambulist $3.98
DAVID BOWIE Crystal Japan/Alabama Song $3.98
CLASH Clampdown/Guns of Brixton $3.98
PLASTICS Good/Pate $4.98
JOHN FOXX No-One Driving/Glimmer/Mr. No/This City (Aus.)* $3.98
KATE BUSH **Never Forever** $7.98
DEAD KENNEDYS **Fresh Fruit for Rotting Vegetables** $8.98
GARY NUMAN Telekon w/bonus live 45 $10.98
ROCK AGAINST RACISM's Greatest Hits (Costello, Clash, Members, others) $9.98

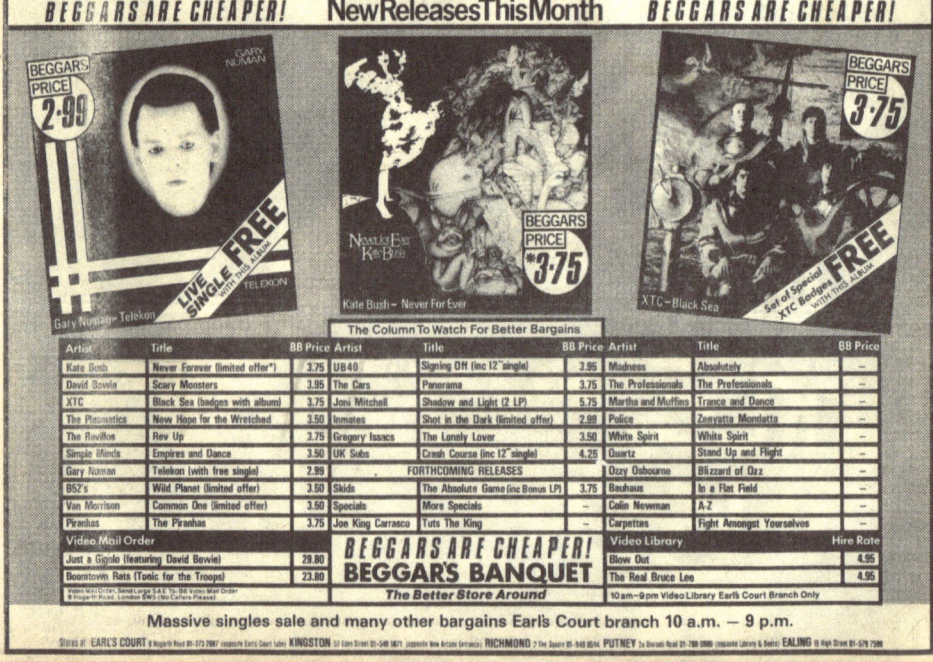

And Beggar's Banquet rose from being a record store to the publisher of an album that entered the charts at Number One.

PROGRAM: TELEKON, THE NEW ALBUM FROM GARY NUMAN.

PROGRAM: TELEKON, THE NEW ALBUM FROM GARY NUMAN.

GARY NUMAN

TELEKON
With the hit single
THIS WRECKAGE
Free poster with this album

wea

LP BEGA 19 Cassette BEGC 19

Cassette includes
Two Extra Tracks –
'I Die You Die' and 'We Are Glass'

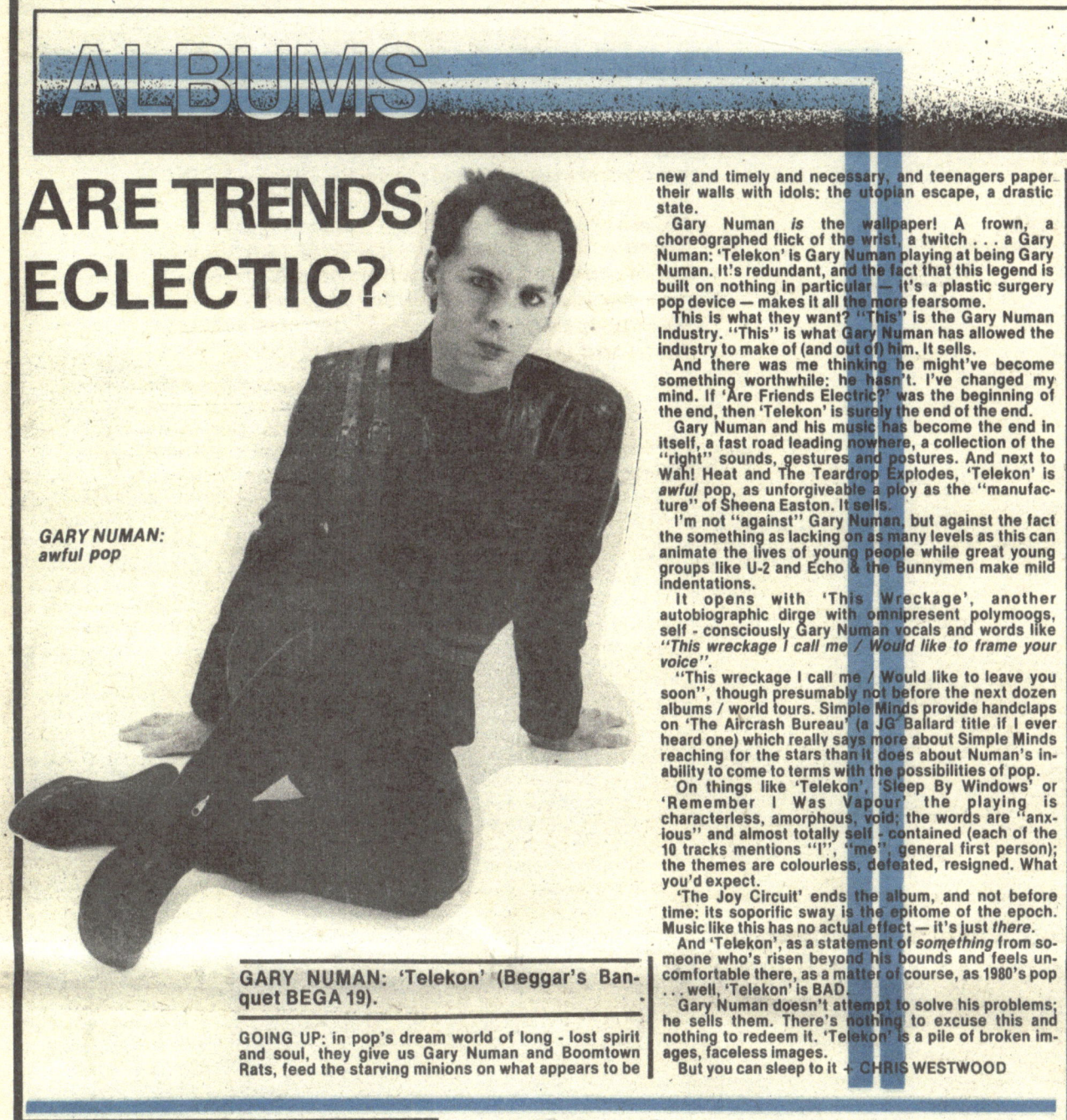

ALBUMS

ARE TRENDS ECLECTIC?

GARY NUMAN:
awful pop

GARY NUMAN: 'Telekon' (Beggar's Banquet BEGA 19).

GOING UP: in pop's dream world of long - lost spirit and soul, they give us Gary Numan and Boomtown Rats, feed the starving minions on what appears to be new and timely and necessary, and teenagers paper their walls with idols; the utopian escape, a drastic state.

Gary Numan *is* the wallpaper! A frown, a choreographed flick of the wrist, a twitch . . . a Gary Numan: 'Telekon' is Gary Numan playing at being Gary Numan. It's redundant, and the fact that this legend is built on nothing in particular — it's a plastic surgery pop device — makes it all the more fearsome.

This is what they want? "This" is the Gary Numan Industry. "This" is what Gary Numan has allowed the industry to make of (and out of) him. It sells.

And there was me thinking he might've become something worthwhile; he hasn't. I've changed my mind. If 'Are Friends Electric?' was the beginning of the end, then 'Telekon' is surely the end of the end.

Gary Numan and his music has become the end in itself, a fast road leading nowhere, a collection of the "right" sounds, gestures and postures. And next to Wah! Heat and The Teardrop Explodes, 'Telekon' is *awful* pop, as unforgiveable a ploy as the "manufacture" of Sheena Easton. It sells.

I'm not "against" Gary Numan, but against the fact the something as lacking on as many levels as this can animate the lives of young people while great young groups like U-2 and Echo & the Bunnymen make mild indentations.

It opens with 'This Wreckage', another autobiographic dirge with omnipresent polymoogs, self - consciously Gary Numan vocals and words like *"This wreckage I call me / Would like to frame your voice"*.

"This wreckage I call me / Would like to leave you soon", though presumably not before the next dozen albums / world tours. Simple Minds provide handclaps on 'The Aircrash Bureau' (a JG Ballard title if I ever heard one) which really says more about Simple Minds reaching for the stars than it does about Numan's inability to come to terms with the possibilities of pop.

On things like 'Telekon', 'Sleep By Windows' or 'Remember I Was Vapour' the playing is characterless, amorphous, void; the words are "anxious" and almost totally self - contained (each of the 10 tracks mentions "I", "me", general first person); the themes are colourless, defeated, resigned. What you'd expect.

'The Joy Circuit' ends the album, and not before time; its soporific sway is the epitome of the epoch. Music like this has no actual effect — it's just *there*.

And 'Telekon', as a statement of *something* from someone who's risen beyond his bounds and feels uncomfortable there, as a matter of course, as 1980's pop . . . well, 'Telekon' is BAD.

Gary Numan doesn't attempt to solve his problems; he sells them. There's nothing to excuse this and nothing to redeem it. 'Telekon' is a pile of broken images, faceless images.

But you can sleep to it — **CHRIS WESTWOOD**

Burning with jealousy over Numan's success, the critic has an adolescent tantrum so severe that he is unable to write in sentences. In place of a review he merely lists his own five favourite acts and says he wishes they were more successful than Numan. Then he shouts that *Telekon* is BAD pop, which is like shouting that Beethoven's string quartets are BAD opera. Gary Numan doesn't write pop. Westwood then kills his own credibility by giving the album one star out of five.

GARY NUMAN
Telekon (Beggars Banquet)

AH, THE shimmering dust-free corridors, the pleasure machines, the limitless possibilities opened up by microtechnology, the disturbing effects of cybernetic leisure upon the fragile human psyche . . . one can hardly wait for the future to arrive.

Of course, this particular future may not have much in common with what the majority of people can expect — a narrowing rather than a broadening of the range of possibilities, a retreat into austerity rather than an advance into hedonism — but fretting over the possible results of such a lifestyle is probably considerably more soothing than giving serious thought to the problems of life as is and will be.

Hence Gary Numan, and his success in the pop world. Martyn Ware of The Human League recently inveighed against what he termed 'phoney futurism', but Numan's work might better be described as 'reactionary futurism' or 'futurist kitsch'. Basically, reactionary futurism makes no attempt to come to terms with any real future that real people might have to face; it prefers to extrapolate from the vision of SF writers of the '30s to the accompaniment of large slabs of third or fourth-hand Kraftwerk (via Bowie, Eno and Ultravox).

'Telekon' is Gary Numan's fourth album. All non-musical considerations temporarily to one side, I'd say that it was a woefully dull and monotonous album, pompous in the extreme and exceptionally limited in its range of tempi and tonalities (how a man who owns so many different synthesisers can be satisfied with so few noises is utterly inexplicable). His mannered whine drives me completely up the wall, and titles like 'I Dream Of Wires' and 'Remember I Was Vapour' seem almost risible. Moreover, Numan's work seems almost entirely untained by anything even faintly resembling wit or passion.

Still, that's just me. Critics are frequently reminded by their correspondents that 'critical judgements' are simply self-validating opinions dignified only by their appearance in print, and I freely admit this to be the case. My quarrel with Gary Numan is based on the following opinions (a) his work bores me shitless (b) his posture as Most Tormented Shopwindow Dummy Of The 21st Century soars to heights of pomposity rivalled only by Yes and The Moody Blues (c) his brand of escapism — from an unattractive doom to an attractive one — is neither enlightened nor enlightening

(d) his vision of dehumanisation is already dehumanised in that it thinks of everything and everyone — including himself — as an object and encourages others to do likewise.

Actually, Numan's fans — the people who'll actually lay out the readies for this album — are probably in considerably better shape than Numan. They'll pick up on the noise and the pose as long as he continues to amuse them, but only the most committed will lock themselves into the spurious vision that informs the work. And since Numan's vision is reaching new heights of absurdity all the time, the possibility that a few of his punters are going to burst out laughing and spoil the whole thing is steadily increasing.

Any album that begins, *"And what if God's dead/we must have done something wrong"* and ends with *"but all I find is a reason to die"* has rather a lot to answer for. On 'I Dream Of Wires' we find Numan announcing *"I am the final silence, the last electrician alive"* and generally doing for David Bowie what The Cockney Rejects did for The Clash.

Give the devil his due: there's the odd nice riff or texture here and there and 'Sleep By Windows' is possibly the most effective Numan piece since 'Cars', but as an artist, Gary Numan is as hollow as the world he attempts to depict. In

song after song, he locks himself into his luxurious hi-tech cocoon and agonises complacently about how awful everything is there.

The album comes with a 'free' single (i.e. an extra sales-boosting incentive to the faithful to snap up the artefact) which features a live version of 'Remember We Are Vapour' and Numan's speciality version of the old Drifters hit 'On Broadway'. Framed in what even the most Numan resistant listener would have to admit is a moderately nifty arrangement, the Pudgy White Slug intones his way through the song: wildly out of tune and encouraged by his faithful to enter realms of sub-Bowie vocal posturing which Quality Control would never permit him to explore in the studio. The effect is shattering.

'The last electrician alive.' Few rock stars have deliberately saddled themselves with a more ludicrous soubriquet. It can be no coincidence that Numan has recently teamed himself up with Robert Palmer, a man who certainly knows a silly pose when he adopts it. Numan provides the illusion of spectacle, of wrestling with psychological terror, of coming to terms with the future, of producing a modern noise.

In fact, he does none of these things. In a world where we're getting screwed by the present, Gary Numan's solution is to make a career out of diddling with the future.

And the synths of the fathers shall be visited upon the sons.

Charles Shaar Murray

6/9/80 N.M.E.

A characteristic piece of brute nastiness by the man whose other claim to fame (and one he boasts about on his website) is that he upset Kate Bush so much with one of his 'reviews' that, like Numan, she more or less withdrew from the world.

YES! IT'S THE NUMAN BACKLASH!

CUDDLY ROBIN Smith, Record Mirror's **wonder kid**, reels under the great Gary Numan backlash this week. **Thousands of Numan acolytes have** crawled out of the woodwork, squeezed their zits and put pen to paper over his put down of the wimp's single. Read on.

WHAT SORT of morons employ Robin Smith? He's so stupid that I bet his brains are dripping out of his ears. How can he dare to take the piss out of gorgeous Gary Numan? Perhaps he doesn't appreciate the talent that goes into these Numanoid records. He certainly can't tell the difference between a "sandpaper voice" and a nasal voice.

By the way, if that is a futuristic vibrator in his belt on the cover of 'I Die You Die' tell Gary he can use it on me anytime.
Karen Green, Southampton

HOW DARE you insult the masterful Gary Numan. You lot of self centred tits, all you can think about is mods and heavy metal. Don't you know that electronic music is "the music for the eighties" and that Numan is the best new talent for ages. You make me puke, sitting in your comfy chairs giggling at your infantile statements. Robin Smith ought to be put down, I will never buy Record Mirror again.
A very angry group of Numanoids, Mid Glamorgan

GOD ALMIGHTY RM, who the hell does Robin Smith think he is. Did his hamster die that morning? He was obviously in such a depressed state when he wrote the review that something must have happened. I hope he isn't paid for dropping those boring futile irrelevant bits of sentences on to the paper. The only reason why I ploughed on and read the trash was

because I'm in hospital and there was nothing else to do. Half the time he didn't write about the bloody record. Please see that he gets the deserved punishment and don't let it happen again.
Jacqy, Shrewsbury

WHO THE HELL does Robin Smith think he is? Last week as he read through his diabolical column I noticed he reviewed Gary Numan's new single (well he got as far as reviewing the cover and Dr Who at least) and he admitted he didn't know what the hell it was all about. So for Robin Smith's information, it is about him and his colleagues who write him off. If he dies you will die because you will all be out of a job.
Many Gary Numan fans, Bury

I'VE JUST one thing to say. Apart from being a bummer, Robin Smith is an idiot. Next time he reviews the singles, I suggest he listens to them before taking off with his pen. Gary Numan's 'I Die You Die' is brilliant and Smith should listen 'cos the message is for people like him. Also is Smith seriously thinks that the metal tube through Gary's' belt is some sort of futuristic vibrator then all I can say is Smith must know from experience and should keep his stupid comments to himself. Someone who is as boring as Smith should not be let loose to write. So please find someone who can do this job and judge records on their true merits and not the fact that they like or dislike the person singing.
An Electric Friend, Birmingham

THE CASSETTE version of **Gary Numan's** fourth album 'Telekon' (Beggar's Banquet, September 5) will contain his last two singles — 'We Are Glass' and 'I Die: You Die' — which do not feature on the record version.

But buyers of the disc will receive some collectors-item compensation in that the first 100,000 copies of the album will also include a free single recorded live at Hammersmith Odeon last year, containing 'Remember I Was Vapour' and 'On Broadway'. The LP track lising is 'This Wreckage', 'The Aircrash Bureau', 'Telekon', 'Remind Me To Smile', 'Sleep By Windows', 'I'm An Agent', 'I Dream Of Wires', 'Remember I Was Vapour', 'Please Push No More' and 'The Joy Circuit'.

Numan's two shows at Hammersmith Odeon on September 15 and 16 have now sold out and a third has been added on September 17.

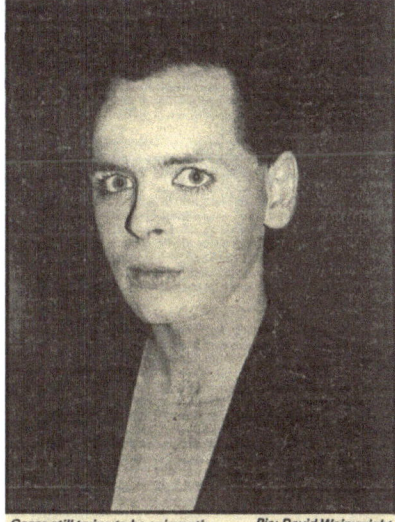

Gazza still trying to be enigmatic.   Pic: David Wainwright.

Sma**HITS**

35p October 2-15 1980

FREE FREE

HIT LYRICS including

I Told You So
My Old Piano
Another One Bites The Dust

GARY NUMAN
BAD MANNERS
ROCKPILE

PAUL WELLER
ROBERT PALMER
in colour

A KORG SYNTHESIZER
TO BE WON

THE HISTORY OF

ROCK

116

75p

OUR FRIENDS ELECTRIC

Aus $1.85 NZ $1.80 SA R1.85 US $1.85 IR 95p

They did a good job with the cover. Inside are sensible articles on The Human League, Kraftwerk and OMD, and a silly one on a solo artist that uses 'juvenile' as its first adjective and 'phoney' as its second. I haven't reproduced the article here because it is not worthy of preservation.

225

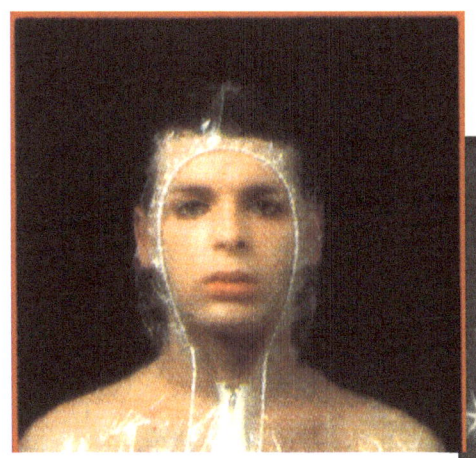

GARY NUMAN kicks-off his 27-dater September tour, coinciding with the release of a new album 'Telekon' at Birmingham Odeon, (Thursday/Friday), followed by more double-daters at Manchester Apollo, (Sunday/Monday), and Southampton Gaumont, (Wednesday and Thursday 11). The show has been changed for the better, it's rumoured, since his recent world trek.

Gary takes a trip

GARY NUMAN'S second major UK tour, finalised this week, occupies most of September and takes in 17 concerts nationwide.

Dates are Birmingham Odeon (September 4 and 5), Manchester Apollo (7 and 8), Southampton Gaumont (10 and 11), Bristol Hippodrome (12 and 13), London Hammersmith Odeon (15 and 16), Brighton Conference Centre (21), Coventry Theatre (22), Chester Deeside Leisure Centre (24), Preston Guildhall (25), Glasgow Apollo (26), Edinburgh Playhouse (27) and Newcastle City Hall (29).

It's likely that more dates will be added, including extra shows at venues already listed. Gigs are being billed as Gary Numan Teletour 80 — derived from the title of his new album 'Telekon', which is scheduled for release by Beggar's Banquet on September 5. The LP is preceded on August 15 by the single 'I Die You Die'.

Tickets for all concerts go on sale today (Thursday) priced £3.75, £3.25 and £3 — except Hammersmith £4.50, £4 and £3.50), Brighton (all £4) and Deeside (all £3.75).

Numan is currently planning and developing a new stage show which he reckons will be "even more spectacular" than the one with which he's just completed a world tour — and because of this, his schedule has been confined only to large venues capable of accommodating his production. This will probably be his last UK tour for some time, because — after following it up with visits to America and the Far East — he plans to concentrate mainly on filming and recording.

GARY NUMAN'S new album, "Telekon", which has been gathering dust for a number of months now, is set for release on September 5th and the man has announced the dates for his British tour in the same month.

Dates are as follows; Birmingham Odeon (September 4, 5), Manchester Apollo (7, 8), Southampton Gaumont (10, 11), Bristol Hippodrome (12, 13), Hammersmith Odeon (15, 16), Brighton Conference Centre (21), Coventry Theatre (22), Deeside Leisure Centre (24), Preston Guildhall (25), Glasgow Apollo (26), Edinburgh Playhouse (27) and Newcastle City Hall (29).

Tickets for the shows in Birmingham, Manchester, Southampton, Bristol, Coventry, Preston, Glasgow, Edinburgh and Newcastle are priced at £3.75, £3.25, £3.00; at Hammersmith they are £4.50, £4.00 and £3.50; at Brighton £4.00 and at Deeside Leisure Centre £3.75.

Numan is said to be devising a stage show even more spectacular than the one that he recently took round the world. The album is preceded by a single, "I Die, You Die" which will appear on August 15th

Numan plays on through inferno that destroyed Philadelphia's Tower Theatre. Pic: Lisa Haun.

On the Teletour (above). On Top of the Pops singing *This Wreckage* (below)

Gal's last stand

Gary Numan
Newcastle

SO THAT's it then. He's gone. Finito. Kaput. The end. But what I want to know is, who was that man in black? Roy Orbison? Johnny Cash? Zorro?

Gary Numan's nearest peer is Kate Bush. Both apparently burst out of their hiding places fully formed and spectacular. Both did their growing in private and made their mistakes anonymously. Both made their concert debuts with stage shows so lavish that troupers with ten times the experience wondered how they did it.

But where Bush seems able to handle the enormity of it all with a wisdom way beyond her years, Numan is floundering. Announcing retirement from

live work shortly before starting what is only your second tour is hardly the action of a man with a substantial grip on reality. But that's what Gary Numan has done. As far as Britian goes this is it, the last date on the last tour.

Numan is the nearest thing we've got these days to a teenybop idol. The atmosphere before he comes on is uncannily like the build-up to a David Essex gig.

The best bits are when he unwraps the cloak and lets the mask slip a bit and allows Numan the 'droid to become Numan the human. During 'Cars' he smiles (especially for Mick Middles) and, in direct contrast to the self-hugging and snakey strokes he otherwise pulls, ambles across the stage like it's Sunday morning down

in the park. He goes to the side of the stage (get this) laughing and picks up a can of liquid refreshment. Or maybe Havoline.

'Are Friends Electric' has a touch of the Lucy In The Sky's to it this time and also contains what is by far the most entertaining sequence of the night. Gaz is standing there, all moody and sombre when this baby robot very like Twikki from Buck Rogers trundles on. Numan approaches it, significance in every step. What's he going to do? Discuss logarhythmic aptitude with it? Check the micro chips? He is not. He's going to wheel round and with an almighty kick boot it into smithereens. Laugh? I thought I'd disconnected a transistor.

The strange thing about the show, though, is that Numan doesn't make any direct references to his retirement. 'Bye' and 'Thank You' are the total sum of the non-sung wordage. The actually farewells seem to be in the songs themselves.

Even allowing for The Man turning the spotlight on his audience like he's lining up targets before the crew haul out the anti-aircraft guns, 'Every Day I Die' has an enforced poignancy that it didn't have last time and doesn't have on the record. This is carried on in the next one, 'Nothing Every Lasts' when, unless my ears deceive me he re-routes the lyrics to include the couplet *'Remember Gary Numan/Remember I was just like you'*. And being so locked up in the Gary Numaness of himself that's as far as he can go.

IAN RAVENDALE

I pulled this review straight from Ravendale's own website (there's only so much money one can spend buying original back issues of extinct music papers). The review is of particular interest for the mention in the third column of the 'baby robot very like Twikki from Buck Rogers' that trundles on during *Are 'Friends' Electric?* and Numan, presumably inadvertently, kicks it to pieces, which at least explains what happened to it. At least we can be grateful that the audience didn't get the 'full satisfaction service show' of the man with the machine that the lyric hints at. I've heard of, but never seen, the fabled Big Al, the man-sized robot that made less than fleeting appearances at Numan's shows but which seemed to turn up in a *Blade Runner* shop window. Was this Geordie Little Al photographed? Ravendale's review is also interesting for noting that Numan may have altered the lyrics to *Remember I was Vapour*, and he makes the perceptive comment that the artist says 'farewell' not by talking to the audience by via his songs and music.

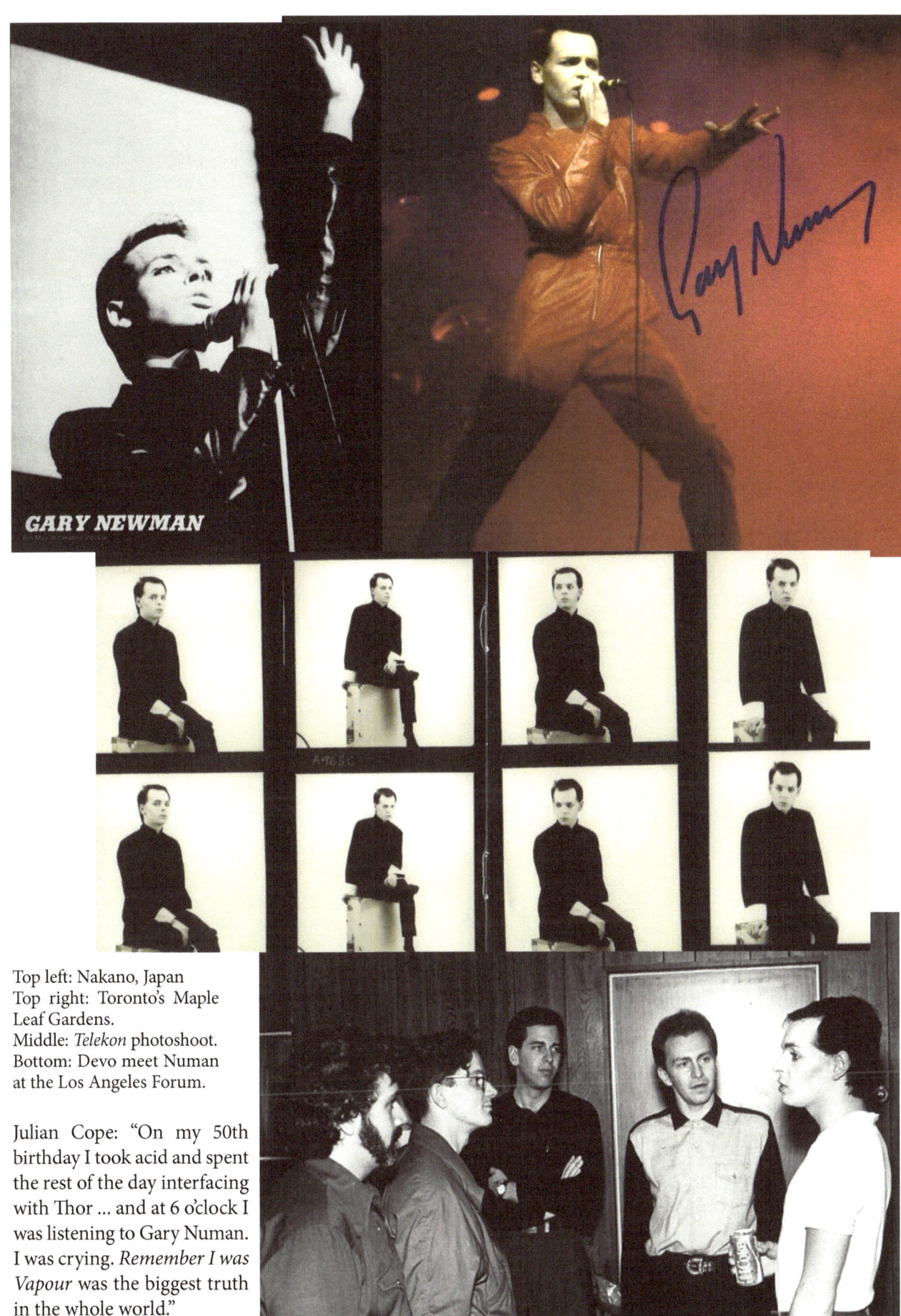

GARY NEWMAN

Top left: Nakano, Japan
Top right: Toronto's Maple Leaf Gardens.
Middle: *Telekon* photoshoot.
Bottom: Devo meet Numan at the Los Angeles Forum.

Julian Cope: "On my 50th birthday I took acid and spent the rest of the day interfacing with Thor ... and at 6 o'clock I was listening to Gary Numan. I was crying. *Remember I was Vapour* was the biggest truth in the whole world."
Bournemouth Gig, 20/10/11

I'm so hollow

Gary Numan
Manchester

WHY DOESN'T he smile? 18 months ago Gary Numan walked semi-consciously into a vaccum left free for use by the departing, ageing, hyper-fashionable Bowie generation. The jealous younger brothers of the Roxy age needed a figurehead of their own. No longer could they identify with the older superstar status of David Bowie.

With the excellent 'Are Friends Electric?', Gary Numan not only captured a sizeable market but also the frustrated teenybop generation who were always too soft for punk and had literally no strong idols since the demise of the long lost Bolan/Slade era. They grasped the Numan image so tightly that his tenth rate succession of singles following 'Electric' became enough to secure his future.

The rest of the rock media looked on with dismay, wishing it had been the Human League who had cornered the imagination of every youngster. But the roots of the Human League were always firmly planted in the joyfully absurd, whereas Numan clung to traditional means, thus remaining safe and dull and tedious and empty.

His phoney Mickey Mouse vision of the future has never been either convincing or trashy enough to be considered art. He has been but a grey stain on the pop music blanket.

In Manchester, the trendiest of the Numan clones wander about wearing micro chip circuits attached to their black and red boiler suits. Their eyes are black, their faces white and they always wear the same blank expression. I watched with interest as they filed quietly into the Apollo theatre, politely handing over their tickets and submissively forking out for programmes, t-shirts and silk scarves without the merest hint of rebellion.

I knew this had little to do with rock and roll, but I thought it could at least be plain old entertainment. A cosy night out and a chance to show off your latest hair colour, this could be rather enjoyable I thought.

But exactly what do you do once Gary Numan has walked on to the stage? First of all you absorb the impressive lightshow. Two huge rocket shaped stacks of flashing lights, both containing various nondescript musicians who thankfully give the occasional wave as if to prove they are indeed real human beings and not some kind of robotic product of Numan's imagination.

After being sent dizzy and bored silly by these hideous devices, you concentrate on the lonely figure centre stage. He makes a few expected poses whilst attempting to project his enigmatic (non) personality to the audience. He fails, perhaps because his personality is indeed as dull as his image.

And then of course there is the music, and this is the most sickening aspect of all. It's all so neatly and precisely in place, leaving nothing to chance. There is not a hint of emotion. There isn't even a whiff of atmospheric sci-fi coldness to horrify you. Nor is there an arrogant but enjoyable feeling of antagonism towards the audience like the stance of the very clever Public Image. You can't even dance to it (like Kraftwerk).

The music is altogether too thick, too clumsy to make you move a muscle. The only redeeming factor is the very occasional touch of melody which is quickly dispensed with by the atrocious heavy handed drumming. It is almost criminal that instruments like the synthesiser, instruments with such scope and such immense possibilities, should be repressed by the likes of Gary Numan and his gang of obedient sessionmen.

Gary Numan doesn't smile, not ever, and there is a reason. He hasn't any notable music, he doesn't know how to reproduce feeling, passion or commitment. He has no worthy observations to pass on. All Gary Numan has is his empty, useless image. That is something he must hang on to at all costs. That's why Gary Numan doesn't smile.

MICK MIDDLES

The writer acknowledges Numan's popularity, makes the standard single token pretence at balance by calling Are 'Friends' Electric? "excellent", before throwing as many insults as he can into the space allowed. When he describes Ced Sharpley's drumming as 'atrocious' and 'heavy handed' you know he isn't attempting to write serious criticism, he's playing silly buggers. The only interesting thing about Sounds' coverage of the Teletour concert in Manchester, is the contrast between the very low quality of the writing with the high quality of the accompanying photograph.

BUNNY CAN AND WILL: Numan Nuker David Bunny will surprise fans of electronic music with the news that he is currently in receipt of two death threats following his threatened nastiness to Our Gaz. His latest plant to thwart the purchase of Numanabilia is to convert the Hammersmith Odeon to gas so that Gal can't plug in his screeching synths. Nice one, Dave. Fans needn't bring their ovens on the night.

Response to his campaign stands at 70% for the cause and 30% against — the most explicit and lurid of the latter are pinned to his bedroom wall to be gloated on each night.

From the same edition of Sounds. I know that the public crucifixon of Numan was intended by the press to be a bit of fun and laughter, week after week, month after month of nastiness, but at what point does calculated nastiness stop being 'fun' and start being a criminal offence? When the writer uses the Nazi imagery of gas ovens and the suggestion of extermination.

GARY NUMAN: *plain old entertainment? No chance*

Three Reviews of Two Canadian Arena shows on the Teletour

Max Bell Arena - Calgary
November 12th 1980
James Muretich, *The Calgary Sun*

Electronic Perfection Space Man Seduction

With an awesome stage show, the king of electronic rock descended upon the Max Bell Arena last night.

The Gary Numan concert was unlike any Calgary has seen this year, weaving a compelling wall of synthesized music with a light show and stage construction that rivals anything ever done for a rock concert.

Moving about the stage like a space snake, Numan was constantly backed by musicians atop or within towers of pulsing light frames. As smoke hung about the stage, changing colors according to the shifting lights, the frames would move in geometrical precision horizontally and vertically.

The result was to merge the visual and musical aspects of Numan's sound perfectly.

As Numan stood there dressed in a black leather suit, with only two red leather stripes running across his waist and up his right side, the entire effect was like that of a German realism painting. The imagery is so strong it's intoxicating. It speaks to you directly yet is hard to convey verbally.

His music is the essence of the city with its pulsing rhythms matched perfectly on stage by the lights and the smoke wafting in the air. It is stunningly real in a strange way.

From the opening song, *The Wreckage I Call Me*, the music seldom changes with Numan supplying only different lyrics and occasionally one synthesizer player stopping or switching to a violin. Yet to label it simple and dismiss it is to miss the whole point. By his style, Numan creates a hypnotic state bordering on religious prayers. Soon, the body and mind are swept up in a soothing flow of his synthesized rock along with his droning, fragile voice. While Numan keeps up the face of the cold, alienated man on stage, the truth is different. I mean, he did smile when someone handed him a cloth reading - We Love Gary.

The spaceman has a heart.

The Diodes, from Toronto, opened things up with an interesting combination of new wave with rock reminiscent of the psychedelic era.

Roman Cooney, *The Calgary Herald*
Gary Numan Performs Like A Hypnotist...
reaching for a distant, emotive level.

Throughout Gary Numan's concert I kept expecting a droning metallic voice to break in and explain, "this is a recording... this is a recording..."

Even if it had happened, I'm not sure anyone would have noticed. Most were mesmerized by the stage set, a futuristic affair that perfectly suited Numan's mechanical, synthetic music.

Numan is either 20 years ahead of his time or so far out in left field that two decades from now they'll be laughing at how stupid his music was.

He poses with David Bowie-like aloofness, and even Numan's deadpan voice seems to have been run through the synthesizers that dominate his music. Numan's stark white features and jet black clothing paralleled the sterile precision of the stage and other-worldly atmosphere it created.

It's the stage set-up as much as the music that made Numan's presentation so interesting. On either side of the stage were two hexagonal pillars panelled with vertical rectangles of light. Inside were trapped two keyboard/synthesizer players, and in the background, raided about three metres off the stage were the bass, drum and guitar players (who also double on synthesizer). Stark, multi-colored light continually bathes the set, and the patterns are timed to coincide precisely with the music - not only as part of the beat, but to accentuate the cold, calculated mood. Ultimately, the lights became an integral part of the music. Everything Numan does is synthesizer oriented. In the long run the music is boring. Dull.

But to an extent the sound is captivating in its perverse intensity, the computer rhythms creating a feeling of dread, like some musical hell where the drums crash on and on into eternity while the drone of synthesizers echoes in the background.

Numan simply wanders about the stage, staring down at the audience, mugging occasionally, for all the world a programmed robot, more a technician than a musician. The music has no real beginning or end, always fading in or out and in a constant state of flux. Underneath Numan's music lies an incessant mechanical heartbeat, the synthesizers adding a fluid life and body, and Numan's vocals the precise, critical cerebral element. But no soul. No feeling.

Still, Numan must be approached and appreciated on his own grounds. The music is curious, even fascinating for its approach: Impersonal, yet reaching out for a distant emotive level that music seldom attempts to capture.

Numan is like a hypnotist, trying to draw out a deep perversion, something the conscious mind keeps closely guarded. And it only takes a glimpse, a mere fraction of a moment, to make it real.

Maple Leaf Gardens - Toronto
October 14th 1980
Paul McGrath, *The Toronto Globe And Mail*

Numan's Message Misses Despite Tricks
His Show Is A Parody
Gary Numan: his music may be a taste of things to come but that doesn't make it interesting.

I didn't quite grasp what Gary Numan was trying to put across at Maple Leaf Gardens last night. I think it had something to do with the anguished, dehumanized state of mankind in the technological world. Or maybe it had something to do with the puppy he lost when he was eight.

Whatever it was, the British electronic pop artist was doing his best to put something across, something complex and artistic, but it didn't work. It wasn't for lack of the proper materials; his lyrics and music succeed in portraying a stark world, not entirely stripped of intense human feeling, but a world that represses it in a way that makes any emotion at all sound like a cry, too late, from hell. It is left up to the composer to put this message across effectively on stage, something he failed to do.

It might seem appropriate that Numan is the uncharismatic, clumsy person he is on stage. But the heavier the message, the more dramatic is the technique required to transmit it, and Numan, even with all the visual tricks, could not conjure up the right mixture of movement and voice to pump this act up to something larger than parody. He was so serious and so convinced of the clarity in his work that he seemed at times entirely uninvolved in what he was doing. Again, that lack of concern might seem part and parcel of the sci-fi nature of his music, but it is difficult to comprehend anything from the rock stage that is not at least slightly over-stated. The vocal drone, rarely modulating, just wasn't enough.

Numan's music may be an accurate forecasting of pop music in the fascist world to come, but that doesn't make it interesting. Most of it was patently childish, harmonically crude, and rhythmically dull, with only the occasional intense background keyboards (from three separate sets) adding some body to the limp sound. For what it was worth, the keyboards were played with precision and, when hooked up with the formidable light show, provided a light, soothing environment.

You are getting sleepy. You are getting sleepier. You are now asleep. Now, repeat after me: "I have no name. I am a number."

© Pete Still

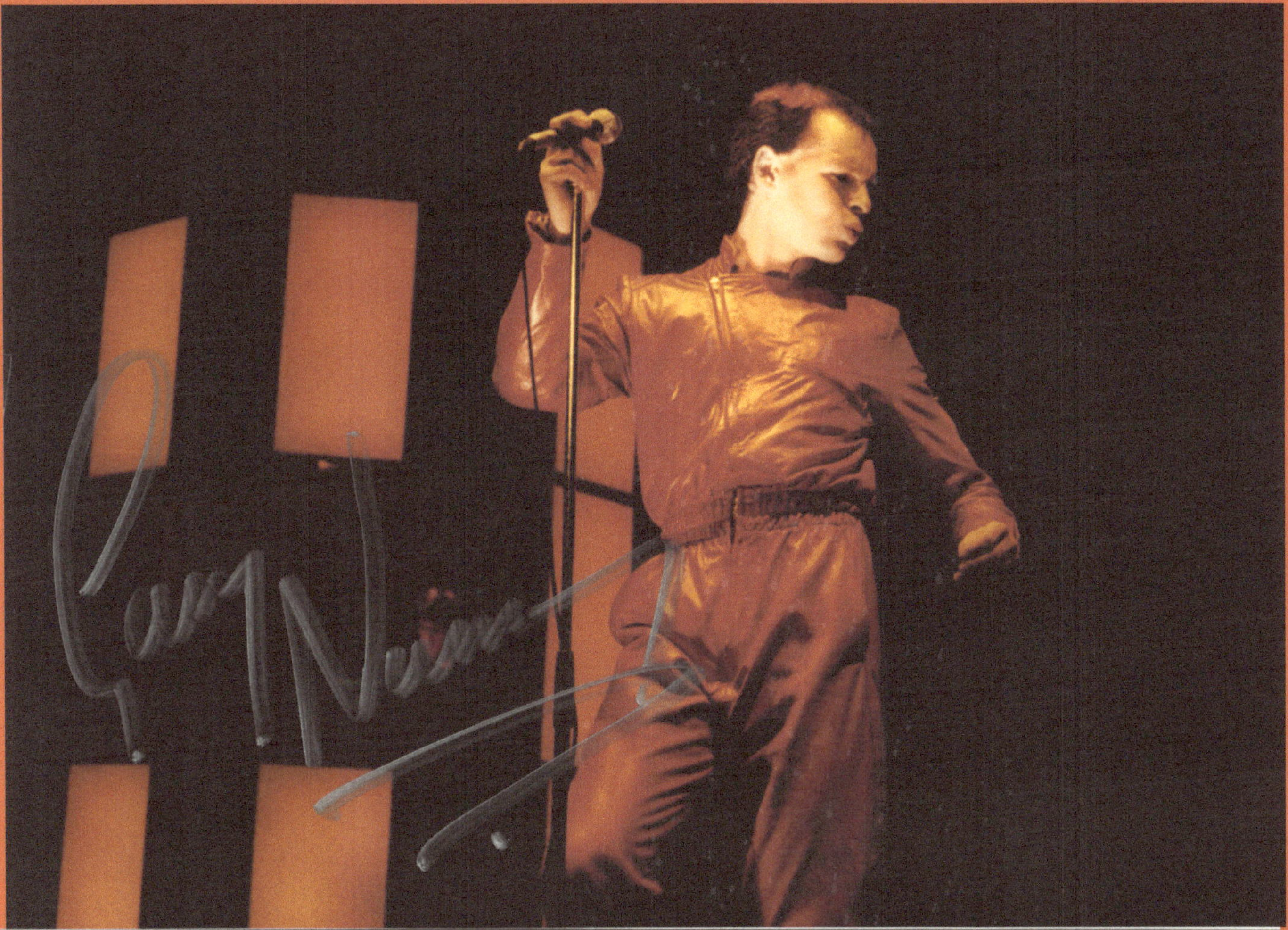

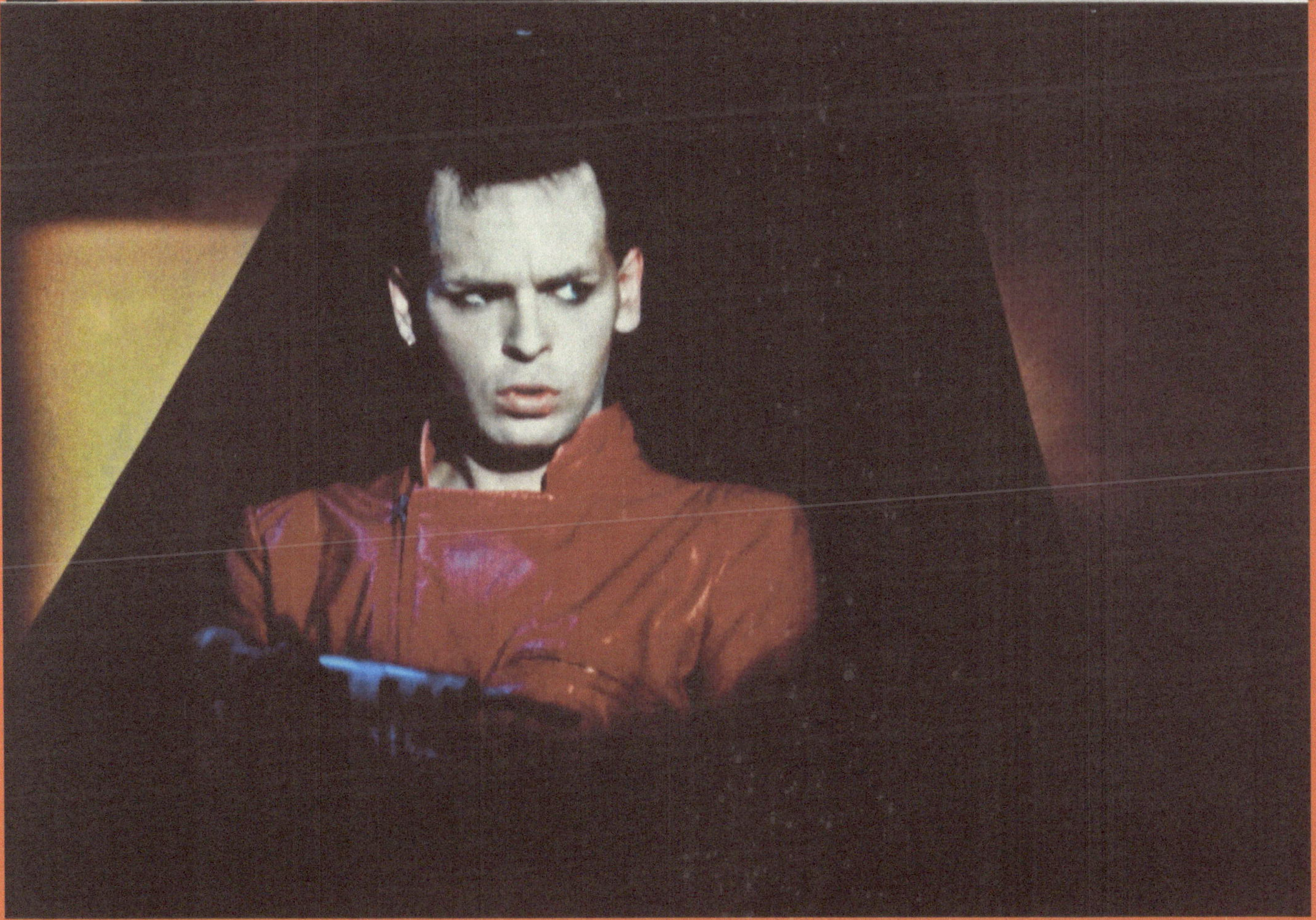

The Numan who fell to earth

by Ray Coleman

THAT morning, Gary Numan had a blazing row with his girl friend, Debbie. He stormed out of her home near Croydon, slammed the door, strapped himself into his £13,000 Stingray Corvette, and bombed up to Soho for our rendezvous.

He was visibly agitated. No amount of consolation or small talk, which was natural as this was our first meeting, was to divert his obsession for most of the day from that morning bust-up.

"What's happening to me?" he asked eventually. "One minute I reckon I've got complete control of everything, all around me. And the next I go to pieces with this violent temper and I can't handle myself, let alone a relationship.

"I'm really frightened of what I do, what I say, how I deal with people now. Is it the fame, the money, being a star? Sometimes, I feel my whole personality is out of control."

Melody Maker 18/10/80

TWO days earlier, Numan had made a riveting appearance on the BBC-TV children's Saturday programme, "Swap Shop." Palpably nervous, he fenced with innocent fans on the phone-in section of the show, and went all defensive when one young girl asked the most searing question ever put to him: why did he never smile?

He did, sometimes, he replied hesitantly. But his face hardly moved as he said it.

The programme had dealt also with Gary's threat to retire from concerts now that he had finished a British tour. After his current American visit and a trip to Japan, he was coming off the road for good, he declared. It was no fun. It was not satisfying. Too much aggravation. Anyway, he'd *done it.* Time to move on. He muttered something about getting into video.

Laughter and fun, it must be said, are words easily discarded when taking on Gary Numan. He's 22, a failure at school, but perhaps the most brilliantly successful manipulator the opportunistic, wonderful world of pop and rock have experienced. He's also a genuine star, a natural who will move on to more creativity if his tortuous, self-questioning character allows him to do so before he burns himself out with nervous energy.

His electronic music is uncomfortable, brooding, and morose — but hypnotic. At the dawn of the bleak Eighties, he was a perfect anchor for thousands of disillusioned young people wanting their fears articulated. He spoke for the New Depression.

Technically and musically, Numan releases simplistic records, but that has always been the case with the best pop music for the masses. He's a Buddy Holly for the Eighties; while Holly used a guitar and dainty love songs, Numan's all-black uniform matches the stark imagery of his message and perfectly catches the mood of today with the emphasis on synthesisers. His fans respond by dressing exactly like him.

If the Beatles spearheaded the optimism of the Sixties, and if Bowie and Bolan played a large part in the Seventies as mentors of the Glam-rock movement, Numan groomed himself to be heir to the throne at the start of the sombre Eighties.

The trouble is — he doesn't want the job.

SPENDING a day with Gary Numan was a daunting prospect. But having turned into his bizarre sounds three years ago through his haunting record "Cars," and being fascinated with the chance to penetrate that iron and doom-laden facade, it seemed a gamble worth taking.

He suggested a few hours of driving, ending up at Virginia Water where he has just bought a mansion. Numan's white car contrasted vividly that day with his black mood, but he quickly warmed to the problem of talking about himself.

"It's everything to me, this car," he said. "It symbolises everything I ever wanted. Really, it's like me recognising my own success, being able to drive it. I don't understand why people are so funny about having status symbols. This was my first and I love it and I'll be honest with you, I love showing it off.

"And yet," he said as we became ensnared in a Piccadilly Circus traffic jam and taxi drivers stared across at him, "people won't allow me to simply enjoy it. The car arouses people's jealousies. They shout nasty things. But I've developed a bit of a thick skin.

"I can take anything now. If my level of success meant that I'd not be able to drive my car around anywhere, and go where I choose, I'd stop that level of success. That's not the reason I'm giving up touring, but I want to pack it in before I'm a sort of captive.

"This is a powerful car. It would not be good for me to be in it if I lost my temper, and I find I lose my temper a lot in London. I hate London. Too much stopping at traffic lights, too many people, too busy and not enough trees.

"For the last couple of years I've been taking flying lessons and I've done 40 hours down at Blackbushe. It's a problem finding the time to finish off my training. The feeling of flying is marvellous. One day I'll have my own plane and people can call me even more flash. Oh well, at least up there they won't be able to shout rude things across at me."

Numan's driving was fast but safe. His judgment, particularly as he was driving a left-hand drive American motor, was excellent and his concentration was steely. Cars and planes and houses seemed to obsess him. What was he trying to prove with them?

"I'm out to prove to myself and those around me that I'm a success at what I set out to do," he answered frankly. "It's quite simple. I had a plan. I wanted to be rich and famous and be a star and sign autographs and have enough money to be free.

"Now I've done it, and it's time for the next chapter in my life, and that doesn't include touring. This last tour of this country cost me £100,000. That's a ridiculous amount of money.

"I might be prepared to carry on doing it in the future, even at a smaller loss, if I enjoyed it. But who's going to tell me it's fun? I don't need it, and I want other things. Buying the house and that tour have cleaned me out of cash."

And so, after America and Japan, he would probably plan a farewell appearance at his beloved Wembley Arena next April, and that would be the end. Nor would he change his mind. What could be more boring than declaring a retirement and then later making a comeback?

The fans, he said, deserved to know properly, and he was telling the truth. Wasn't he, then, seeking a kind of new power as a former star who could use his position in another way for two or three more years?

"No, I don't want that power even if it's there for me to take. Look, I can hardly handle myself, let alone be a leader. Right now, I'm trying to build a proper relationship with my girl friend so that we can get married and have children, and I'm so worried about my own personaltiy that *that's* the next job after the tour.

"Get myself straight — I can't seem to get to grips with whether it's all the rock star thing that's messed me up or whether I was going this way all along."

Time after time, through the day, Gary would return to this worry about himself; we pursued the theme because it seemed important. After all, if this worry and self-doubt was at the end of a rock 'n' roll rainbow for a meteorite who was cascading to earth at the age of 22, there was something wrong with the either him or the star system or both.

Numan didn't pretend to have the answers. But the staggering story of his method of reaching his current pinnacle must rank as the most brazenly successful piece of planning which the reeling record industry has experienced.

We went for a walk in the woods near his home, and the peaceful countryside relaxed him sufficiently to reflect and put himself in perspective.

Four years ago, as a Bowie and Bolan worshipper, Gary Numan watched the punk explosion and he mourned the passing of the superstar era.

"No matter how many new bands came up, I saw that every one had a singer or a guitarist the fans latched on to, but nobody behaved like a *star*.

They were all shouting about their attitudes and they were all saying how they didn't like this and that, but whatever band there was, the fans were *desperate for just one person to get hold of*. But nobody wanted to act the part.

"Well — I did. I saw the gap and went straight in and worked at it. I came on like a star, didn't say much so the fans could make up their own minds — unlike the punk bands who were all mouth — and it was so obvious to me that I was going to do it.

"I'm not saying this now to sound big-headed, and I'm sure that's how it might sound, but I just planned it. I had this band, Tubeway Army, and we went to the record company like hundreds of other young hopefuls and we got a contract through a bit of luck and the music was, in the early days, based on the guitar sound that was fashionable.

"That was just to get a contract — the record companies were signing anything that moved with a guitar.

"But when we signed, I decided to change the style to contrast with the other bands, and we concentrated on the synthesiser sound. By now, it was too late for the record company to drop us. They'd put so much money behind us, I knew they'd have to go along with my music. They didn't like it, but they put the record out." The record was "Cars."

*I*T WAS a grand plan, Numan agreed. "There was a desperate need for a solo star, and I also thought it was time for a change from the guitar. Bowie had done sex, Bolan had done the wizard and occult bit, and the rest of Seventies rock history was all good music based on guitar sounds and — what was it called, progressive rock. So I had to come up with something that wasn't necessarily based on the guitar and which also pushed me as an individual.

"I decided it was going to be machines. I thought: 'Right, the Eighties. Machines.' Synthesisers — and as it happens, I was no good on guitar and the synthesiser was dead easy to play. So I went and learned how to push synthesisers and it was simple.

"I also felt the kids would identify with me if I came on as a kind of sharp seer who said the right things and looked good.

"It was the whole rock star thing, plain and simple, working out a gap in the market and seeing it through. You call it manipulation? I call it a campaign . . . working out what people hadn't got and getting something right for the market. I got it right for a period of time.

"I wanted to be rich and famous and ever since I was 11 years old I dreamed of being a rock 'n' roll star. The only thing I misjudged was not important: I thought people needed someone who was a bit of a prophet, but as it turned out I got famous long before I needed to say anything."

He allowed himself a half smile of self-satisfaction.

So now, I teased him, having made the strategy work, and before the lifespan of a pop star meant that the public spat him out after chewing him up, he planned to ditch the public first.

Too harsh, said Numan. He had extremely strong views on a rock star's relationship with his audience. The fans had a basic right to say they made him, "but if I hadn't been up there on stage, or in the recording studios in the first place, they couldn't have made me.

"It's a funny way of looking at it, but I don't think they owe me anything and I don't feel I owe them anything. They took me because I decided to offer myself. It was a two-way agreement. I understand what it's like being a fan, because I was one myself.

"I grew up dancing and playing to my heroes as a kid, who were Dave Clark and Hank Marvin. But I don't recall thinking they owed me anything. I took them because they were there."

"You make shopping for a rock star sound like a visit to a supermarket," I said.

"I had my eye on the Eighties," he said crushingly. "I saw this opening in the market and the sound *had* to be machines."

*I*F ALL this makes Gary Numan sound like a robot who exploited a situation, that would be only partly true. He's much more vulnerable than his moody public exterior allows, and he says that although he's not sentimental, he fights back the tears sometimes.

Because people didn't feel like making the effort to understand his approach to rock, he had suffered jibes of abuse for music, his earring and face make-up, his mere *success*.

This had penetrated his iron mask. He didn't want a lot of praise, he said, just recognition for having achieved something, and for giving a good few thousands of fans a bit of pleasure.

Where was the tolerance, he wanted to know? Why were so many people down on him for making it? Even if they didn't like his music, why did they criticise him for what he was, in view of the fact that a lot of people liked him?

That hailstorm of jeering had taken the fun out of making it, for him. "Not long ago, a guy came up to me and said he assumed I would attack the likes of Genesis and Yes because I seemed to him to represent everything those bands weren't. I said no, I had no intention of criticising all those bands.

"I said I wasn't about to have a go at anything that had gone before me because they obviously had something going for them, and it wasn't up to me. It was up to the fans to judge.

"Genesis and Yes and Led Zeppelin *must* be doing something right if they have all those people going to their concerts and buying all those records. What gave me the right to slag them off just because I was in a different style?

"This guy persists. He says those older bands are ripping people off. They're charging too much for concert tickets, he says, and how come they can afford to live in these great mansions.

"Ah, now we *have* it. I now see what he's driving at. He's one of those idealists, and I can't stand idealists. You can't be into the rock 'n' roll thing, which is a lot to do with being free and feeling great and having a good time, and be an idealist. Rock 'n roll is a lot to do with live-and-let-live. That's where the punk thing was totally wrong. Well, not so much wrong as not sincere.

"Most of the musicians were saying one thing and doing another. I've nothing against the ones who set out to be famous and make a fortune, but why didn't they admit it? The bands that have survived have turned out to be the biggest capitalists the rock world's ever had.

"I looked at all these punk bands saying they didn't want to follow in the ways of those old bands like Genesis and Yes, didn't want to be rich, and I wondered who they thought they were kidding.

"Can anybody from that scene tell me they would rather drive a Mini than this Stingray Corvette? Who would't prefer my house to a little flat somewhere? There are lots of things wrong with fame, which I'm finding out pretty fast, but the benefits like cars and money aren't exactly a hindrance to my life.

"I enjoy hearing the fans scream my name. I enjoy signing autographs and having a good seat in a restaurant and all the pleasures that being well-known bring, and there are quite a lot.

"But now I've come to the end of that part of the story of my life and I know it's got to end because when a tour starts, I can't wait for it to end — even though I'm going to enjoy the concerts."

Still, in a couple of days' time, he was off to America, and flying Concorde. That was something, "another dream come true."

THE Numan operation is a family affair. His father, Tony, was a British Airways transport driver at Heathrow before becoming Gary's manager; "He's taking to it like a duck to water. It's as if he's been in the music business all his life. He knows exactly when to turn nasty – and believe me, it's a real jungle."

Gary's mother, Beryl, also goes on the road, and takes care of the band's wardrobe. "She has to sign autographs – she's almost as popular as me. I'll have to watch it," said Numan.

Lunch was taken at a Schooner Inn in Virginia Water. A drink? No, just Coke, of which he drank a lot. He had never drunk or smoked, although Debbie had tried to persuade him to try a little champagne – without success.

The waitress, who eventually plucked up courage to ask for his autograph, twice, asked whether he wanted French fries or a jacket potato with his steak. "Chips, please," said Gary. "McDonald's hamburgers are my favourite food, really, although I had a really nice Wimpey the other day," he confided.

"I don't like anything fancy. I have the chance to sit around all night getting stoned out of my head, but for what? I drink what I like, and that's Coke." A night on the town for him often means a visit to Legends, the showbiz restaurant/disco in Mayfair, which is where he met his lady.

The name of that haunt seemed particularly inappropriate to his surprising decision to surrender his status.

"A legend? I don't think I could ever be that. I never intended even to 'take the Eighties,' let alone be a legend. I remember always wanting to be famous, that's all. I had the talent for putting myself up for something at the right time, and I don't think that makes me a legend.

"I want a life, and even the past few years have made it frightening for me. I hadn't the talent to write the atmospheric songs needed on a guitar, so I went for the synthesiser which doesn't need so much.

"So my only talent musically is as an arranger of noises. And my second album went to number one! I learned to play piano by watching a man at college – it was as simple as that. In the last couple of years I've been learning more about keyboards, but they're just a means to an end for me." He cannot, of course, read music.

Numan was an educationist's nightmare. Born in Chiswick, West London but brought up mostly in Wraysbury, a few miles from Heathrow, Gary Webb was the joker in his class at Ashford Grammar School. He would sit in the back of the room and disrupt lessons by telling jokes and generally playing up, "making mischief."

"I'm intelligent, " he said modestly. "I was told I had an unusually high IQ when I went through a 'gifted children' survey, and although I haven't got any O-levels, I'm quick to pick things up. I was expelled from grammar school.

"I went to Stanwell Secondary School for a year and then to Brook-lands College in Weybridge but I didn't put in enough hours to qualify for a second term. I left there just before my 17th birthday.

"They said at grammar school that I was unstable, disturbed or something. I don't know about that, but I do know that I wouldn't recommend to any kid that they don't work at school like I didn't. I chucked away a natural ability to do well – and it's no good saying I made it to fame and fortune in the end.

"I'm just lucky. I was stupid not to take advantage of myself. Sometimes now, I miss not having worked hard at school." He was self-conscious, for example, about his poor ability to speak grammatically.

"The child psychologist called it 'star tensions' or something. I don't think it was that, just plain stupid behaviour. I only got the chance to learn properly at that period of my life and I blew it." He left college and drifted through jobs like air conditioning, driving, clerical work – writing as he went, and getting picked on by colleagues for having dyed hair.

It all came back, he ventured, to his failure to cope with situations. Right now, he wanted to plan some stability in his future – a big house, a wife, children and a determined move into making video films on subjects which inspired him from reading books. But the new, ratty, short-tempered side to his personality was frightening him.

He'd always been on a short fuse, but never this badly and it was affecting his relationship with Debbie. It infuriated him and yet he couldn't control his frayed edges properly. If he couldn't control himself, how could he enter the next serious phase of his life – and that worry had contributed to the decision to stop touring.

"Also, if I'm going to get married and have children, I don't want them to grow up as the son of a rock star. It's no way for children to live, with people all the time recognising who they are through their father. No child should have to suffer that. Mine certainly won't.

"I want to have leisure and enjoy myself. I never wanted to tour, but you have to do so to become a rock 'n' roll star. Having become one, I'm frightened about staying one.

"So I'm stopping."

His mother thought he was crazy. His father suspected so, too, but took the view that Gary had been right all along so far, so his judgement and timing should be respected.

"It's not the fun I thought it would be and the nasties have spoiled it for me," he said finally. "Put it this way: what I'm doing is like committing suicide before someone kills me."

WHILE Numan is plainly serious about retiring from the stage, he will continue to make albums. "The madness is at the moment that planning records and making them has to be fitted in between tours, as if the record-making is a hobby," he explained. "I want the records to be the thing, that and video."

Had it all happened too early in his life? "No, the fans had to be able to see a person of their age. If I'd left it until now, the right time would have passed, I think. By the time I'm 28, or 30, I want to be out of the limelight, anyway – I'm probably going to be one of those people everybody despises, who goes around in a flashy car and does nothing. I'd love that."

But he would, one suspects, be keeping an eye on his royalties. He confessed to "watching the markets" in America on the eve of his tour there, and was proud of the fact that in Canada they were playing 9,000-seater arenas.

And the age of the Numan audience was maturing. There were now people of *his age*, dammit, and that was encouraging – because he had begun by appealing mostly to the very young. It was good textbook stuff, we agreed, but growing old with his audience was something he was not equipped to do.

He was not sufficiently interested in advancing his music or adapting – like, say, Yes or Genesis. He did not like jazz, so influences from that area were out. Folk music was "too feminine."

Japanese and Indian music interested him and there might be scope in adapting some Eastern sounds into Western rhythms, but who knew? His mind was a whirlpool of problems and the future seemed a long way off.

"I'm not one of those writers or players who write songs that are simply excuses to solo. You can't say it's bad, because so many people like it, but I'm more interested in making a point with

"The new Yes album is great, by the way. They've changed from their last thing, and they obviously have something fresh in their minds, musically. I'm not that musical." For the record, he has about 60 albums, with the emphasis on Bowie/Bolan/Lou Reed and Bebop Deluxe; the newer artists are represented in his collection by Human League, Orchestral Manoeuvres in the Dark, Simple Minds and Ultravox.

The synthesiser, he insists, is just beginning as an instrument, and would make great strides, just as the guitar took a long time to become electrified. But he didn't particularly want to be a part of its evolution.

"I used it just like I used everything else," he said candidly. "Whatever you're doing in life, you should use the latest technology. I did that – I have no real love of the synthesiser as an instrument, but I like the noise it makes."

THE drive back to London was punctuated by more self-analysis and concern on how he was going to re-approach Debbie. Motoring through Wraysbury, Numan reflects on his family and old friends who were pleased to acknowledge his success now but had been sceptical, in his early days, of his dyed hair and whole star trip.

"A lot of people would say you can't do this and you'll never make that, but it was all much simpler to me, and I looked on the thing like a child looks at something. Children come out with the most original things because they have nothing else to judge it by . . . I was that child."

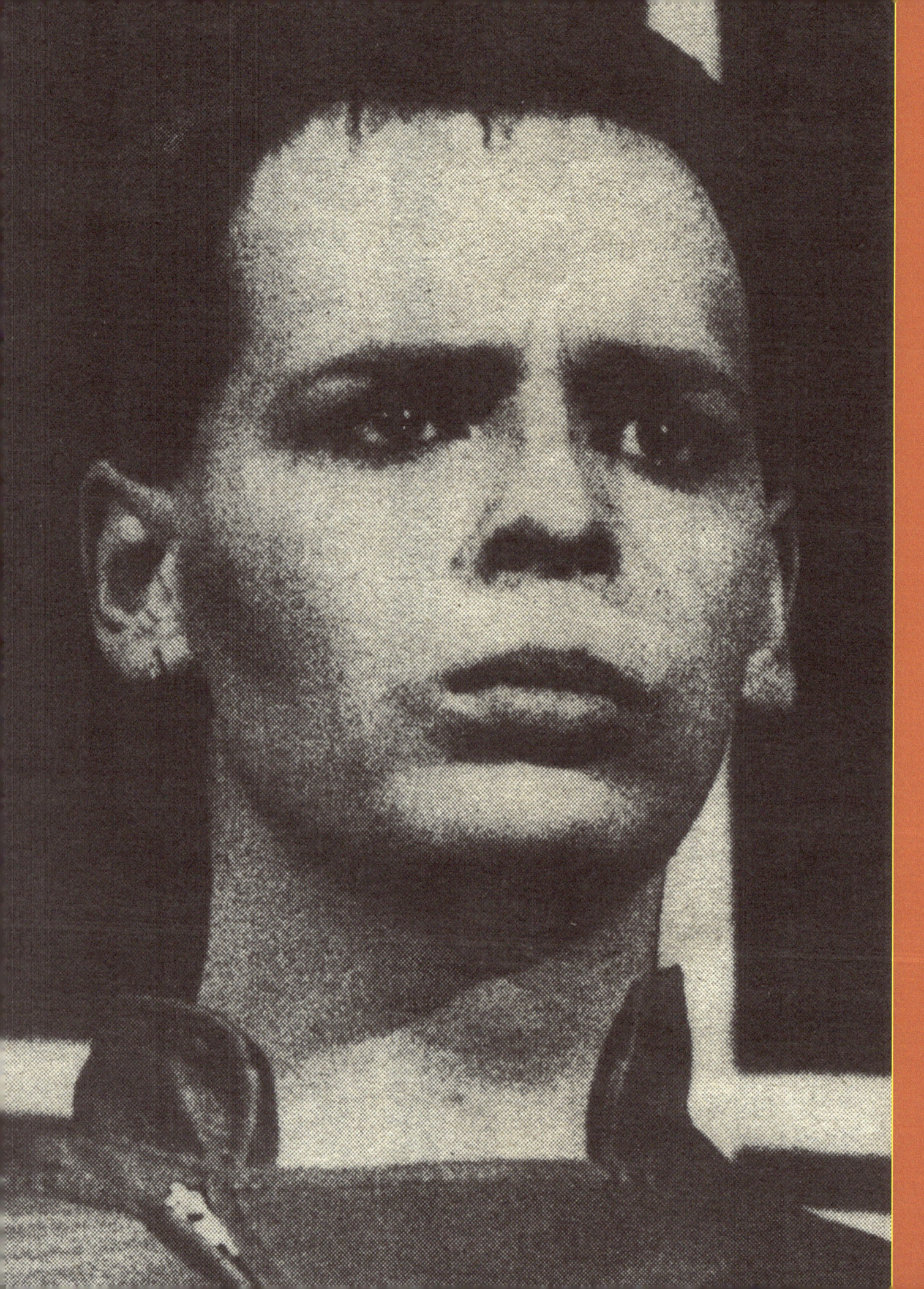

Had I been to see Frank Sinatra's recent London concerts, Numan suddenly asked as we drove into Knightsbridge. I said it was odd to reflect on a creature of the Eighties being even mildly interested in a 64-year-old ballad singer from such a different era.

"I'd like to have seen him because he seems to have a lot of style," Gary said simply.

But Sinatra sings chiefly songs about love and human encounters, totally removed from the cheerless, dark imagery of Gary Numan and his self-confessed machine music.

His music was designed to meet a national mood, he said. And this was where we came in.

Popular music at its most powerful always reflects the people, the society, the environment around which it is created. Numan got it right in one, at the dawn of 1980, with his elementary, sinister, ethereal synchronisation of daunting haunting keyboard-based songs that ingrained themselves into a nation's sub-consciousness. Uncomfortable sounds for a neurotic age, Numan's messages are, whether he aspires to notoriety, or not in the long term, anthems to mirror our world of computers and calculators and multi-storey car parks, advanced technology, self-service petrol and two million on the dole.

And then, he got his image right to sell it correctly. He was a loner who rarely smiled, and that was a help.

"FLOWERS!" he said quietly as we neared Soho again. "I'll send her some flowers. Always works."

Paradoxically, the machine proved human. For that, and his burning determination, for his candour and doggedness, and for a whole lot more which boils down to honesty, it was impossible not to warm to him. He's a speedy child of our time, the kid down the street who had a dream that came true. Before pop got too clever by half, Gary Numan was what it was all about, and for some of us, he still is.

REMIND ME TO SMILE

We'll take a taxi to the show
We could report by phone
We could remind ourselves that we must laugh.

Reconsider: 'fame'
I need new reasons
This is detention, it's not fun at all.

Remind me to smile, you know, the 'old friends' line
It gets so I feel like I'm in this cold, glass cage
I've got the horrors — check, over my shoulder
I punch the air and fight but no-one's there.

You, you — oh, no, old scars don't show
We fall, you see, crawl crawl, in love
I dive, so clean; young things, don't scream
Toys, toys, so far — boys, boys, you are .

Get off the car, get off the phone
Move from my window, leave me alone
Keep your revivals, keep your conventions
Keep all your fantasies, that's all we are.

Copyright Numan Music Ltd.

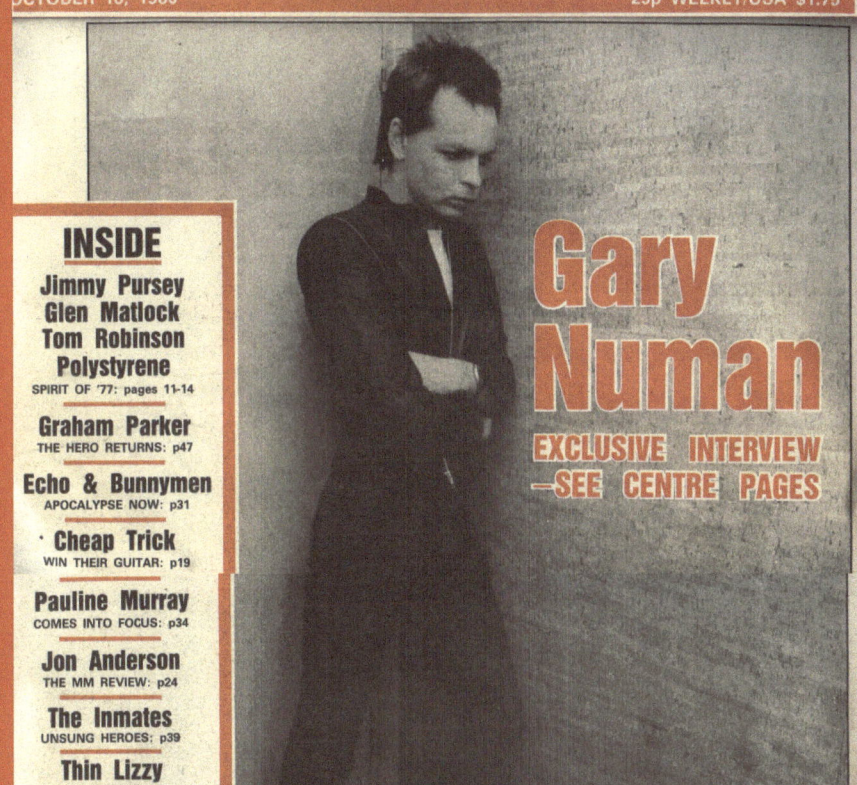

MELODY MAKER
OCTOBER 18, 1980   25p WEEKLY/USA $1.75

Gary Numan
EXCLUSIVE INTERVIEW —SEE CENTRE PAGES

PICTURE BY ADRIAN BOOT

The fine photographs are by Adrian Boot. The one on the opposite page seems to anticipate the moment in *Stand By Me* when Wil Wheaton sees the deer. (Numan looks like a fusion of Wheaton and the deer). It's a moment of awakening, the end of innocence and as such it is loaded with emotion. Perhaps it's the dawning moment that 'this must end'?

SUPERMAN OR VICTIM?

The Numan condition
by JOHN GILL

By being completely caught out by Numan's success and therefore bitten by his own condescension (see page 50), John Gill took this calculated revenge. With a careful pretence of balance (he concedes that Numan rendered the music press redundant), and some brilliant writing, he takes the boot to Gary Numan in the hope of doing even more damage to him. In the very second paragraph (after quoting from the Futurist manifesto), Gill writes that Numan is a "confessed plagiarist". In the same sentence he calls him an "inept copyist". In the fourth, and also in his final paragraph, he knifes Numan for the 'crime' of pulling the veils from, and popularising, what was "until then an obscure and elitist form of music". In the seventh paragraph he calls Numan a "confessed plagiarist". In the eighth, he uses the false evidence of others to say that Numan's wounded alienated persona is hollow and has no foundation in fact, and in doing so he proves to the modern reader he has no understanding whatsoever of Numan or of Aspergers Syndrome. In the tenth paragraph, he calls Numan a plagiarist. You get the picture.

"THIS MUSICAL EVOLUTION IS PARALLELED BY THE MULTIPLICATION OF MACHINES, which collaborate with man on every front. Not only in the roaring atmosphere of major cities, but in the country too, which until yesterday was normally silent, the machine today has created such a variety and rivalry of noises that pure sound . . . no longer arouses any feeling." (Luigi Russolo, 'The Art Of Noises' 1913, a manifesto of Futurist music.)

YOU CAN take the "machine" as being specific electronic instruments or even Gary Numan himself. Unintentionally, Numan has become a walking and (sometimes) talking update of Futurism. Although he replaces their healthy 'collaboration' with machines with helpless victimisation, Numan travels a wobbly parallel to the spirit of the Futurist.

I met him 18 months ago, while he was rehearsing Tubeway Army for an OGWT slot to mark the release of 'Are 'Friends' Electric?' and 'Replicas'. He was nervous, inarticulate and a confessed plagiarist. The backbone that kept the unstable (and sometimes inept) copyist on his feet was the private 'back-room' Numan; the aggressive, determined and, it seemed, spoilt kid I saw bullying his band into line for the rehearsal.

But there was something about the ingenuousness of Numan alone or — if he was capable of such subterfuge — the image of vulnerability he presented. With the single and album, he seemed to have tapped into a healthy vein of, well, call it the 'essence' of pop music.

He woke up one day and found he had the Midas Touch, which he promptly applied to electronics, up until then an obscure and elitist form of music. A touch of static and, in Numan-speak, his viewscreen flickered onto a strange channel where money, fame, personal aeroplanes and private tropical islands swam into his vision and grasp. Alice with a portable life-support system, he stepped through the screen.

Today Numan is a "22-year old millionaire", in the parlance of the tabloids. Shortly after the number one success of both 'Friends' and 'Replicas' he bust through the star speed-barrier. Cosseted, idolised and probably bunkered, he has short-circuited the star process. He has no need of the usual music biz processes including, unsurprisingly, the rock press.

"It (stardom) is the only thing I've wanted for such a long time," he told one journalist. "(But) I didn't plan on it this early."

The Gary Numan Story, as related by the protagonist to the world's media, is surprisingly consistent. The strange young schoolboy whose violent blackouts got him shunted from school to school, the nights spent singing standards in a local pub, the formative years in Mean Street, The Lasers and the pre-electronic Tubeway Army, the 'invaluable support' of good old Dad ("I owe it all to him."), mum standing in the shadows ready to darn his socks and run his fan clubs, those first — preparatory? — admissions of plagiarism leading on to the justifications of creative copying, the sold-out tours and hit albums, the loneliness, the angst, the Kurtzian horror of being the wrong boy on the wrong planet with the wrong bank account. Pain for sale, who will buy my pain for sale?

"Alienation is a viable theme for a rocker (or any artist) but there's nothing to indicate the root of (Numan's) alienation or what suffering or insight it has wrought." (Ira Mayer, *New York Post*, 25.2.80.)

Trust an American to point to Numan's washed-out roots. Even his para-mentor Bowie manages to find some human balance in *his* alienation. 'Scary Monsters' is probably Bowie's most depressing album to date, but at least he leaves some space for poor mankind to inhabit and find some semblance of comfort. From day one, Numan was content

merely to present the problem — a far-fetched problem, at that. The solution, presumably, would be revealed once Numan had achieved his admitted aim of earning enough money to buffer *him* from the problem.

BUT NUMAN's 'candour' has enabled him to partially disarm critics of his morality from the word go. He was open about his desire to become a star, his will to wealth and his plagiarism. As a merit-point for him, neither Bowie nor Foxx have ever criticised his mimicry. Foxx has even gone on record as saying he is a fan and friend of Numan's.

Numan began improvising on his rags-to-riches legend in August 1978, with the release of Tubeway Army's eponymous debut album. The initial 5,000 copy pressing sold out quickly, but it made little impact in the slipstream of the new wave. Frankly, it was a poor attempt at realising an incomplete vision. He sprayed semi-electronic stutter-rock with fearwords; lines as headlines speaking of submission, suspicion, death and — your starter for ten — paranoia/alienation. But the nascent Numan beat pulsed through the album and would, in a later souped-up version, give him free access to the highest regions of the charts.

'Replicas' arrived in March 1979, and bled the Burroughs-via-Bowie trip for all it was worth. Sexes blurred, dysfunctions became norms, people lost touch with each other in a world populated by robot escorts and "rape machines".

"It's basically what London — or any city really — will probably be like in about 10 or so years time. As you get more automatic cars, automatic car making machines, automatic buses, train, planes — so everyone that's employed with them has nothing to do, so they go back to basics, which revolves round sex, violence and sleeping." — was how Numan explained *his* Manifesto. Or should we call it his patent?

We already have automated factories and micro-chip industries, which are causing horrifying and, it would seem, irreversible unemployment. They might start off a chain of events leading towards Numan's sub-'Wild Boys' scenario but, holocaust notwithstanding, it's decades away.

245

But this was the strict, unchanging menu Numan offered his fans, one grim *plat du jour* that shows little sign of ever changing.

Interestingly, while his literary sources remained voyeuristically detached, Numan went to jelly and submitted to the horror. There are suggestions that this horror comes from personal experience, but rather than seek help or change, Numan wallowed in self-pity and dislocation. Decades previous, novelist E.M. Forster had taken up the communication-motto of "Only Connect". Reeling selfishly into the future, Gary could only snap "Me, I Disconnect From You."

Crucially, this coincided with the chart-topping success of 'Are 'Friends' Electric?' and 'Replicas', which rubbed off on 'Tubeway Army' and brought it up into the top twenty. Numan was put in the unenviable position of having his half-realised vision acclaimed as the final and quite literally apocalyptic musical statement of the Seventies. The public rushed into its local record shop and thrust this unsure and unstable young boy ("Not even a man yet," he told the *Evening News*) into the limelight. It's bound up with the shameful lie of 'paying one's dues', but Numan could have done with more time *out* of the limelight to sort out what he really wanted to say.

Instead his clumsy mish-mash of Fascism, Futurism and Freud went bleeping and flashing into rock history. Perhaps, grandiosely, he caught an undercurrent of the times; disbelief, despair and the almost cold-war paranoia making itself felt today. At a lower altitude, he probably happened upon a near-perfect balance between Bowie's consummate quick-change act and Foxx's understated games with (loss of) identity. Wherever Numan surfaced between the two, his jerry-built bubblegum future-shock found its way into the mass market, and the public loved it.

And like it or not, Numan's music *had* progressed. No matter how much the press railed against his debased synth syncopations, his gleaming machine music found and fed an untapped desire in the record-buying populace.

Whirring into a higher gear, the Numan organisation pushed 'The Pleasure Principle' out five months after 'Replicas'. Even in hindsight, 'Principle' sounds like more of the same but with a bigger production budget. So Gary had dropped guitars from his sound. Big deal. The lyrics? *More* pronouns a-go-go linking *more* images of loss of self, pain, fear, insecurity, death and well howdydo if it ain't our friend alienation back in town. If he'd booted his music upmarket between 'Tubeway Army' and 'Replicas', 'Principle' suggested that any further changes or improvements in his music would be purely cosmetic.

The clanking was almost audible as the "rape machines" came rushing up out of the past and, in the form of the media and music industry (becalmed and desperate for a symbol of Hope For The Future), pursued Numan, intent on screwing him witless. Money and ego were lavished on him. WEA bought him a powerful £5,000 sportscar (fittingly, the ultimate Futurist symbol) in the hope tht he wouldn't switch companies. Hacks from the tackiest teen rags ("Gary And The Ghosts! 'I seem to attract poltergeists.' " *My Guy*), the yellow tabloids ("GARY WE LOVE YOU! But Numan Is So Alone." *Daily Star*) and the most unlikely upmarket publications ("Numan — A Man For 1980" — *Now!* magazine) wanted a piece of the action.

As 'Pleasure Principle' went to number one in the album charts, 'Cars' to the same position in the singles charts and then 'Complex' to number six, Numan took his act on tour, triangular robots whirling as Gary waltzed his neurosis across the stage. As Phil Sutcliffe pointed out at the time, Numan was, and still is, indebted as much to Presley as Bowie for his stage persona; Elvis's starfish/swastika twitch, arms up high, knee bent and pivotting between toes and hips, fed through Bowie's tortured mime. The press laughed again. Gary made more money and got weirder.

Towards the end of the tour, Numan suffered a brief relapse of his teen blackouts — trashing a hotel room after two groupies had tried to very much "Connect" with him. The press was full of Numan's disturbed personality ("Gary Numan doesn't trust people much, and he won't let them get too close.") The whole caboodle was taking on Howard Hughes/Citizen Kane proportions. But, apart from maybe Jon Savage in the *MM*, no-one got deeper than the surface verfremdung'n'chips image of Numan. And if all the personality defects listed in the press were true, Numan should have been referred for institutional help.

Backstage, behind the five feet of agony jerking around out front, the other Numan was busy with the business. With his father's help, he formed his own publishing company, Numan Music (the radio performance rights collected by Numan Music will keep him in make-up until the 25th century) and his own merchandising company to, quite rightly, elbow the rip-off merchants outside his gigs. He may have lost £20,000 on staging the tour, but these two canny business moves set him up for life — or for as long as they kept playing his records.

The nightmare reached its sordid nadir with Numan making distasteful remarks about the sartorial elegance and appeal of the Nazis and the 'nastiness' of the colour black (as in dress, not race) to — of all papers — *The Sunday Times*.

WHEN SOMEONE, somewhere, decided that a change in marketing policy was in order, like Bowie and Foxx before him, Numan switched course before colliding head on with the logical conclusion of 'mechanitheism'; fascism. Privately, of course, we have no way of knowng if he is not still on course. Greater minds than his came a cropper after dabbling in such volatile subjects.

The New look Numan was photographed with — gosh! — a smile on his face. He played in aid of Save The Whales. Snippets of background info were fed to the press suggesting Gary was a homely kinda guy after all. His diet of burger and chips, his problem with spots, his trouble with girls all entered the public consciousness.

Gary was looking for someone to direct his film debut, Gary was going to write, Gary was giving up playing live, Gary was buying WW2 planes and 200 mph go-karts, Gary was thinking of buying a £150,000 island in the Pacific. Gary, from the outside, looked as though he was going on the biggest greedy nouveau riche blow-out of the decade.

Finishing the 'Pleasure Principle' world tour, he returned to start work on 'Telekon'. When it arrived a month back, it bore little resemblance to his promised concept album about "a man who can harness the power of telekinesis" and takes over the world. Repeated hearings/readings fail to reveal anything more than the usual Alphaville jive; more dislocation, more distancing himself from everyone and everything.

But! 'Telekon' sees Numan fleshing out his sound, perhaps a little belatedly. I completely agree with McCullough (well, he *is* bigger than me), but back in the mix unusual things are beginning to happen, new levels of interest, new layers of sound, both formal and free. His record company, Beggars Banquet, say this was intentional, that he wanted to make his music more "complicated". Certainly, it amounts to little difference in his overall sound, but he has now changed his photocopier from monochrome to colour.

He has just finished his British tour, the same Devo hop but this time set against a backdrop that mixes Celebrity Squares with Fritz Lang. Within the next two weeks he's off to America, Japan, The World. Bigger venues, bigger audiences, bigger Gary.

In the last 18 months, in Britain alone he has had two gold albums ('Telekon' promises to do similarly in the near future) and five of his singles have gone gold. Gold awards are also flooding in from America, Australia and other territories. Not bad for a spotty, balding and insecure 22-year-old, eh?

He told the *Sunday Times* early this year that "The music press are against me. They didn't make me — I did it by myself." His (not unfounded) resentment towards the press apart, his claim to have done it His Way seems largely true.

Britain's biggest radio network Radio 1, still hadn't playlisted 'Friends' when it hit number one last year — so much for the power of radio promotion. While giving him publicity the press also pooped on him from a great height, so he obviously managed to

bypass the press hype/attack syndrome. And not even the promotional talents of WEA could supply him with so consistent a string of hit albums and singles. You couldn't even get that through hyping.

No, Numan took a leap in the dark and landed on his fame. That fame is, of course, tempered by the fact that we haven't had a teenybop idol of his stature for years. He had the background, looks, pose and modicum of originality that the tabloid press thrives on and, as the tabloids roughly reflect mass culture, he also had the pre-requisites for superstardom. He was, he has said, as surprised as everyone else when the sort of music 'weird little bands' like The Normal and Human League were making became hugely profitable.

I RESENTFULLY commend the perfect poppiness of his music while feeling dismayed at the way he has degraded an exciting and innovative form of rock music. I tip my imaginary hat to his candour and business nous, but thank God I'm not inside his head. For one day he'll find his monetary idol has feet of clay. Perhaps it's already become apparent to him but he hasn't the native wit to appreciate it. But it's more likely that he will recognise it, and I wouldn't like to be around when his much-touted unstable personality tries to deal with it.

He has built the Numan edifice so high, and on so shaky a foundation, that he could become the most spectacular *victim* pop music has ever seen.

Smash Hits Gritty Documentaries Department present a day in the life of a Gary Numan tour.

THE JOY CIRCUIT

OUR lensman joins Gary on the afternoon of his Bristol Hippodrome show and stays with him through soundcheck, ablutions, autograph session and evening performance. Next morning we rejoin him as he conducts an interview over breakfast in the hotel restaurant and hitch a ride with the coach that conveys the concert party to London and the next string of shows. We bid farewell to the man outside his London home as he alights

to grab a couple of hours rest before heading for the next soundcheck and the next dressing room. And so the circuit continues.

Each picture has been matched up with a line from one of his songs by Gary himself, who is at pains to point out that life isn't quite as depressing as these captions might imply!

Words: **Gary Numan** Pictures: **David Sheinman** for Rocktography.

"Sing a chorus of 'On Broadway' and deny it all"

"Isn't it strange how times change?"

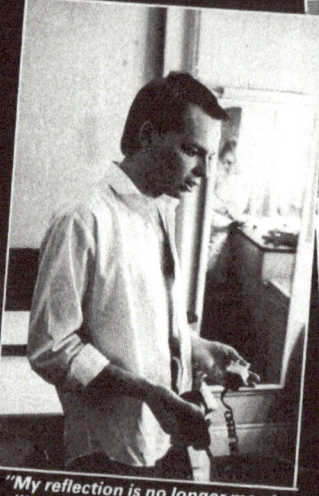

"My reflection is no longer me at all"

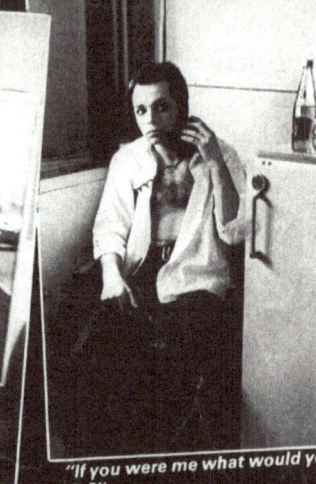

"If you were me what would you do?"

"My mirror's tarnished with 'no help'"

"No image in my mirror, bye, bye"

"Now that's what I call romance"

"You can be replaced you know"

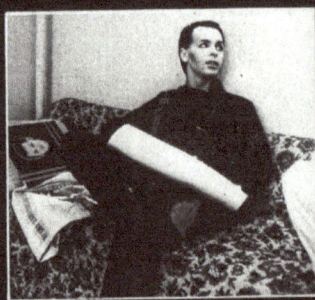

"Remember, I am human. Remember I feel just like you"

(Continues page 6)

"I feel the pressure like your eyes on me"

"The time to leave is always soon, I wonder if I'm lying"

"Oh it's so easy, when parts take over"

"We're so exposed anything can happen"

"We're in formation saying 'safe, safe, safe'"

"We could remind ourselves that we must laugh"

6

"Some people need the heroes, but I don't mind"

"And now dreams are real, and dreams are all you need"

With the need to cut costs now that he was winding down his career, Gary Numan reduced the design team to one, himself. He took pleasure in designing everything, including the merchandise. He was never very good at designing merchandise. Without wishing to offend either the artist or the fans, I'd go so far as to say that after the Machine Quartet and Living Ornaments, he didn't design an even nearly good album cover until *Splinter* (2013), though the imagery on the *Berserker* record covers was impressively cold, beautiful and strange.

THE NEW ENGLISH ART ROCK

Both XTC and Gary Numan express a sense of the new English isolation. Americans seem to like the car-crazy Numan, while the pure British pop of XTC is as yet unappreciated.

By Roy Trakin

Musician, Feb 1981

From *Sergeant Pepper* and *Rubber Soul* through *Ziggy Stardust* and *For Your Pleasure* right up to *The Wall*, England has always been a leader in that much-maligned genre of popular music known as progressive or art-rock. By adding either vocal phrasing, a synthesizer riff or a stray sitar run to the standard 4/4 guitar-bass-drums rock 'n' roll, the British have consistently managed to sell our own music back to us with a distinctive, stylistic flair. And, despite the inroads made by good ole uncomplicated rock 'n' roll lately, the studio continues to be an important breeding ground for experimentation and new sounds from the U.K.

As punk rock begins to fade, it has become apparent that there is a brand new generation of English art-rock bands ready to take the place of doddering dinosaurs like Yes, Genesis, Jethro Tull and ELP. Of course, these stalwarts can still fill Madison Square Garden and sell a great many records, as they always have, but their days of adventurous risk-taking and musical innovation are long gone — replaced by the smug satisfaction of commercial success. For true innovation, the discerning art-rock patron has been forced to turn to a new wave of British groups, most of whom have not quite broken through. These include more radical bands like Manchester's Joy Division, Cabaret Voltaire, Swell Maps, A Certain Ratio and Scritti Politti, who probably can't expect commercial success, as well as more accessible groups like Magazine, XTC, Ultravox and Human League, who probably can.

So, despite the proven sales potential of progressive rock, the American rock fan remains a conservative buyer slow to abandon an established entity for the novel. Which is why overly Anglophilic groups like XTC and the Jam have, so far, not caused a stir on this side of the Atlantic. How then can you explain the phenomenal success of one Gary Numan, who has already garnered a stateside Top 10 single ("Cars") and a pair of Top 40 albums (*Pleasure Principle* and the new *Telekon*)? The shy 22-year-old has created bubble-gum synth-rock for pre-pubescents, that's how, accompanied by a spectacular show that features innovative staging, lighting and props as well as time-tested

Gary Numan through clouds of dry ice and godless technological decadence.

winners like dry ice. The kid takes a vicious slagging from the press for his pretentions, but the bottom line is Numan, despite his dorkiness, can write catchy melodies. Did young Gary think the public would respond so favorably to a sound which was, if not entirely experimental, certainly futuristic?

"I had no idea," Numan tells me. "I didn't really care; I always thought I'd just continue making albums and, sooner or later, they would become acceptable. I wasn't sure when or how."

Of all the English progressive giants, perhaps none was as influential in the 70s as David Bowie, who ushered in pop music's high-tech future-shock with his series of chameleon-like changes of personality. It seems as if Gary Numan has seized on one aspect of Bowie —

the godless decadence of *Diamond Dogs* — and Xeroxed it.

"If I were only a second-rate Bowie," counters the man with the red streak in his coif, "I wouldn't sell as many records as he does. And I do. But he has no reason to be jealous. Bowie has done so much. I'm retiring now anyway, so, in six months, I won't be a threat at all. He's gonna be there when I'm long finished... Bowie will go on forever. No one can touch him. He's like the Elvis Presley of my generation. If he died, he would go on.

"It's like saying Beethoven and Bach were no different because they were living in the same time doing classical music. Same with me and Bowie."

You can see why the press has a field day with the lad.

Despite that suffocating pomposity, or

perhaps because of it, Numan's work achieves a comic grandeur, a pop portentousness of hilariously slapstick proportions. For the encore at his recent concert at the Palladium, Gary emerged from beneath the drum platform in a miniature sports car that whizzed around the stage flashing its head lights at the crowd while the band played "Down In The Park." What did it all mean?

"'Cars' is about my reason for being in cars rather than cars themselves. My reason for liking them and wanting to be in them. Taking it further than that, it's really the opposite — my reason for not wanting to walk anymore.

"I do enjoy performing, but I don't get that big buzz from it I think I'm supposed to. I don't live for that hour-and-a-half on-stage. It's simply something I do at

XTC, despite innovation and accessibility, have set few American hearts aflutter.

the end of the day before the party afterwards and that's all."

Did Gary feel responsible for delivering such bleak, despairing messages to his younger, more impressionable fans?

"I don't really know how many people actually take notice or understand what I'm singing about, " Numan admits. "Most of the people who come to see us are my age, though the first five rows are all 15-year-old girls. Further and further back, the audience gets older and older until you reach the 30-year-olds in the rear."

Will synthesizers one day replace guitars and drums?

"I hope not. The more sorts of music there are, the better. I don't want to see any music disappear...not classical, not rock. I hate jazz, but I hope that doesn't stop, either," the magnanimous popster declares.

"The problem with using synthesizers is, everyone expects you to have two thousand sounds in every song. It doesn't have to be like that. I used twenty-two different synthesizers on *Telekon*, each one has a distinct sound. What more do people expect?

"I'm getting a bit pissed off at what people want, to be honest. So I just say, screw it. The more you give, the more they seem to want, especially critics.

After thirty minutes of my show, they want more! Even though a half hour of my show has ten times as much as a two hour show by somebody else."

Final question, Mr. Numan. Were you aware of any experimental, electronic music in the 60s?

"I didn't really start listening to music as a fan until 1971," Gary confesses. "But I always liked the Monkees."

Goodbye, Gary.

While Gary Numan plans an early exit, Andy Partridge and Colin Moulding of XTC are still waiting to enter the hallowed halls of Stateside commercial success. Like Numan, XTC has released four albums; unlike him, only two of the LPs — last year's *Drums and Wires* and the new *Black Sea* — have come out over here. With Atlantic recently dropping the Virgin Records catalogue, *Black Sea* has been picked up for distribution by RSO, for whom the band contributed a song on the *Times Square* soundtrack, "Take This Town." After many disappointments, leader Andy Partridge hopes XTC's breakthrough is at hand.

"I don't know what to think about America," says the exasperated Partridge. "We can only play here and hope. We're not an American sounding group. We don't conform to any popular American fantasies — we don't have any strains in our music that Americans like because it's their culture or recent past history, such as that country music feel.

"If I sat down now, I could write the kind of song that Americans like to buy. Not to say they would, but every country loves its own reflection, it's that narcissistic thing. America likes that romantic, denim cowboy — expensive and cool — in their music. Our music is different. We don't live American life-styles. I want to be successful for what we are. To everyone in England, everybody in America is either John Wayne or Farrah Fawcett. For Americans, every Englishman is Terry Thomas and every woman is the Queen."

"You can either change your music to suit American tastes or hope what you

do will be acceptable without such a shift," adds Moulding. "Perhaps America should bend more than we should. For some bands, it's so important to be successful, they'll sacrifice their own musical satisfaction to that end. For us, it's not essential that we break here. We're not gonna worry about it. Musical satisfaction comes first. And, if financial rewards result from staying along our own course, all good and well. I'm glad we are what we are."

What XTC is is a band in the classic British pop mold, stretching back to the Beatles, Kinks and Small Faces. Between Andy Partridge and Colin Moulding, it has two distinct songwriters who excel in different areas.

"People say I write the melodic, softer, sweeter songs while Andy writes the more intellectual, phonetic songs," explains Colin. "But, if they care to look deeply enough into our material, they'll find I have written some intellectual songs and Andy has written some poppy tunes."

Indeed, on the Steve Lillywhite-produced *Black Sea*, Partridge's love of rhythm and Moulding's affinity for melody, rather than cleaving up the LP in two, as with *Drums and Wires*, now exist side-by-side. Songs like "Towers of London" and "Burning With Optimism's Flames" show the two approaches finally achieving a seamless synthesis.

"I'd like to be considered in the tradition of bands like the Kinks and Small Faces," says Andy, "when bands weren't quite naive, but they had a sort of group feeling about them and were gently experimental and psychedelic within pop song formats. It was like they had this little round soap bubble which was the pop single and they just sort of pushed it slightly out-of-shape with experimentation. Perhaps it was a little bit of studio phasing or double-tracking or some other new technique of the time."

Is XTC an heir to the English art-rock tradition of Genesis, Pink Floyd and Yes, or is it closer to New Wave bands like Magazine, the Jam and the Clash?

"We are from working class families, which is supposedly where English punks come from," answers Colin. "And only Andy ever went to art-school. Our families are quite poor, but we've all got the other sort of tendencies, too. We've always had the art-rock appeal rather than street credibility.

"We know what it's like to be on the street and we don't want to preach about it. We've been through it, *man*, and we don't like writing about it. I don't care to glamorize it because it's just not nice. I like to write about the other side, the romantic side of life.

"XTC let people make up their own minds. We merely make observations. I'd like to think we're the Vasco de Gamas of popular music, exploring new
continued on pg. 42

22

253

Art-Rock, cont. from pg. 22

grounds. This band has never really been fashionable at all."

Just as the English progressive outfits of the early 70s achieved commercial success, can't XTC eventually succeed with a steady diet of recording and touring?

"It's not quite cream floating to the top," suggest Andy P., "it's more like a being floated to the top, but it's transmuting all the time, so that when it does reach there, it's still gonna be brand new. I don't want to get to the top and be stale by the time we get there.

"I'd like to gently push XTC in the direction of more natural instruments — marimbas, saxophones, acoustic guitars. Music that is quieter, but aggressively so."

If there is a single strand running through the current British art-rock, from Numan's *Telekon* to Joy Division's *Closer* to XTC's *Black Sea*, it is the increasing isolation being felt by England from the seat of world influence. As Great Britain adjust to its role as a second-class power, its music reflects the once-proud Empire's impotence in world affairs, especially on a song like XTC's marvelous "Living Through Another Cuba:" *It's 1961 again and we are piggy in the middle...Russia and America are at each other's throats/but don't you cry/just on your knees and pray and while you're/down there, kiss your arse goodbye/We're the bulldog on the fence/while others play their tennis overhead.*

"Yeah, that's right, England's between the two big powers, like playing the ball-boy in a tennis match," suggests Partridge. "The English Empire is well gone and people there do feel helpless when big things start stirring in the world. What can you do? Just wait to see what they dish us out.

"I think America will be like that in a hundred years or so. Like a comet that reaches a huge peak of success only to burn out...Egypt, Babylon, China...any of those huge empires that rose, went nova and collapsed."

There could be an analogy there to the rock world, with new, upcoming bands replacing the lapsed ones.

"Bands don't really have renaissances because they get too old," explains Andy. "A band's idea can have a renaissance, like the Who now are getting big again because they're called the Jam. The actual people don't have a renaissance, but the music styles do. And it can be just as powerful as the original thing."

Or as Gary Numan puts it, "And what if God's dead...We're independent from someone." But the best still goes on as England's latest generation of progressive rockers escape from this socio-political isolation to the creative isolation of the recording studio. ◼

Reading this unimpressive and very schizophrenic article is like watching the retarded little kid at school building up the confidence to walk over to the bleeding boy, who has just been beaten by the bullies, and then kick him because he knows he can get away with it. The retarded kid hopes the bullies will be pleased with him. In the opening paragraphs, Roy Trakin, states his preference for "good ole uncomplicated rock 'n' roll" (presumably the kind where the singer dates and marries 14-year olds) and states, not incorrectly, that Britain's role in the American art form is, and has always been, to add a bit of "stylistic flair". He states that Britain "continues to be an important breeding ground for experimentation and new sounds". So far, so fair.

He acknowledges that the most successful new act, and new sounds and new style is Gary Numan, whom he concedes can write "catchy melodies", though he 'balances' this by throwing the insult 'dorkiness'. Then he puts on a pair of short trousers and cuts off his own bollocks to attain a working level of pre-pubescence (and insult he has already thrown at Numan and his fans). He knows that the British press have been bullying Numan mercilessly and with one voice: John Gill's false charge that Numan is "a second-rate Bowie". And although Trakin knows that the charge isn't true, as does anyone who has listened to Bowie and Numan, he slaps down a card, possibly of his own making, on which is written the rather good phrase that Numan "xeroxed the godless decadence" of Bowie's *Diamond Dogs*. It's a good phrase until you actually think about it. Bill, how do you then use that godless decadence to create a masterpiece like *Telekon*? Godless decadence is a theme or a thought, perhaps even a style, but every creative person knows that thoughts are ten a penny. The hard work comes in using those thoughts to *make* something. Imagine the scenario at music school: "Okay, children. Here's some godless decadence. Now let's see what you can do with it." And if there is one thing that *Telekon* isn't it is decadent. It's an almost sex-free album. It's an album about loss, not looselessness.

Thereafter Trakin does nothing but insult Numan in an unsuccessful attempt to provoke him. Contrast Trakin's creepiness with the honest generosity of Numan's thoughts and responses. Trakin tries to bully Numan because he knows the British press have bullied him. Joining in with that makes Trakin feel part of The Club. It proves that he is clueless but it makes him feel safe. Trakin is hoping the British press will like him. Perhaps the pinnacle of his dreams is being bought a pint in a Fleet Street pub?

I've included the rest of the article so you can read how differently Trakin treats XTC, a deservedly less successful band than Numan, and one who haven't been bullied mercilessly by the British press. To me, XTC seem to offer nothing but honest rock 'n' roll, certainly more literate than most, but often found lacking in rhythm and tunes. In the article, they say they want to be even more ordinary, which goes completely against the grain of the article the journalist was paid to write. That he asks them are they nearer to Genesis, Pink Floyd and Yes, or closer to The Jam and The Clash, shows that concept of originality is beyond him. To Trakin, everything has to be traced back to the banjo in the bayou, and anything that strays from that formula he thinks should be forced to squeal like a pig.

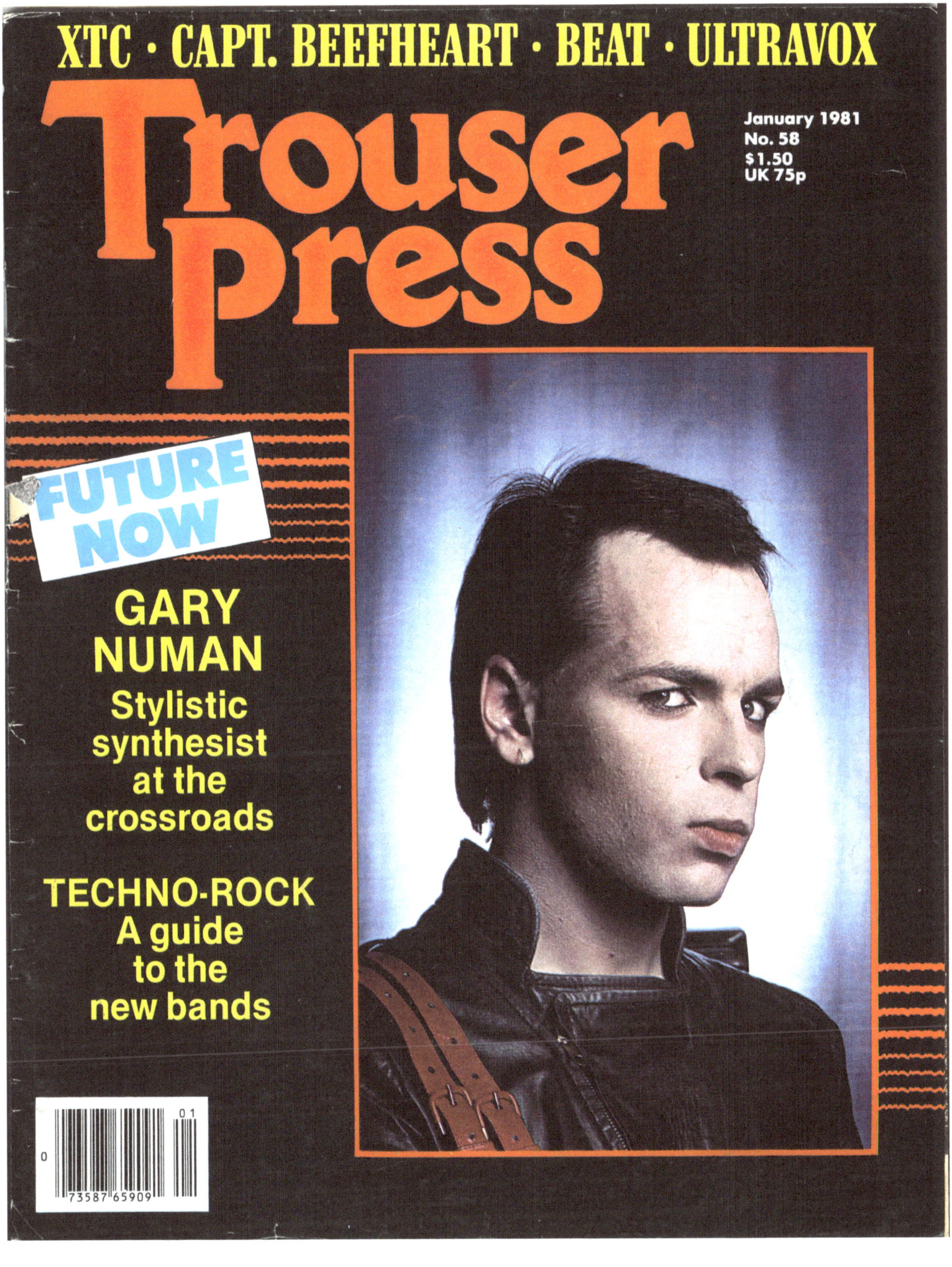

XTC · CAPT. BEEFHEART · BEAT · ULTRAVOX
Trouser Press
January 1981
No. 58
$1.50
UK 75p
FUTURE NOW
GARY NUMAN
Stylistic synthesist at the crossroads
TECHNO-ROCK
A guide to the new bands

Mitch Kearney

By Jim Green

touch

Gary Numan remains in contact

Contradictions, contradictions. (Sigh.) Gary Numan is not a simple proposition. Most people think he's simply wonderful—the electrono-pop tunesmith who's ever so cute—or he's simply awful—creator of synthesizer-laden Archies music who travesties the very influences he wears on his sleeve.

The closer the scrutiny, though, the clearer it becomes that while some criticisms are valid, others are gratuitous digs at an all-too-easy target whose commercial success is considered out of proportion to his artistic worth. It is thus unfair that Numan should achieve a level of fame denied presumably more talented artists—especially his inspirations.

The fault is hardly Numan's. Besides being in the right place at the right time, he had the ambition to seize the opportunity, if not actually create it. Young Gary Webb knew he had to be a rock star—even though he had no particular aptitude for playing an instrument. He sorted through his capabilities and interests, and figured out how to maximize their appeal to celebrity-hungry record buyers.

According to his plans, Numan will remove himself from the star-making/maintenance machinery come April, after two years in the limelight. That means no more touring, and a more leisurely recording pace.

Hard to swallow? Sounds like a strategem Elton John and David Bowie have used: just as—or *before*—people start taking you for granted, make an apocalyptic announcement about semi-retirement. It's second only to dying for stimulation of sales of back catalogue. The others have come back, but if Numan sticks to his word he could be the first pop star to curtail a career by personal fiat.

In New York, Numan, 22, is staying at the Empire Hotel, not a fashionable haven for visiting rockers. His blue-shaded casual dress is equally nondescript except for grey suede stack-heel boots, and his black hair sports a spiffy dab of red on one side. In other interviews Numan has been reported to speak in an unvarying whisper, but he now uses a more normal range of emotional color. He is still not what you'd call a loud individual.

"Image is to be copied. That's the essential reason I created mine." Numan's British audiences are peppered liberally with kids attempting to clone themselves into one of four versions of him (illustrated on his four UK album covers). " 'S all part of [stardom]," Numan laughs. "I used to do it." He then describes how, at age eight or nine, armed with an acoustic guitar and a wool cap knitted by his mother, he enacted Mike Nesmith in the Monkees Juniors. "We used

to go to people's houses and charge two shillings to mime to Monkees tunes for half an hour." Unaspirated h's betray Numan's West London origins.

He was apparently a moody kid, and "blew out" school due to sheer lack of interest. Although he'd told friends he wanted to be a star, it took a stiff challenge from one of them before he began to work in earnest toward that goal.

In 1977, after being thrown out of one band, Numan walked into a guitar audition for another (no one else showed up), became the front man and changed the band's name from the Lasers to Tubeway Army. Although Numan's songwriting had been blatantly Bowie-influenced in the past, Tubeway Army was a punk band intent on getting a contract. Beggar's Banquet, a small independent label begun as the recording arm of a London record store, took them on. After a couple of inchoate 45s ("That's Not It" and "Bombers") the company told them to make an album.

"They were expecting to get a nice little punk pop thing, but in the studio I'd stumbled across a synthesizer, and it got all these electronic noises," Numan recalls. (He'd picked the name Neuman—pronounced, he says, NOI-mon—out of the phone book but, wishing to avoid being laughed at as a fake German, removed the "e".) The company was taken aback—as was the band—by the electronic half of Tubeway Army's 16-track demo. The band also liked to play live, which Numan wanted to avoid. The others, then, with the exception of bassist Paul Gardiner, took a flyer and now perform as the Station Bombers. ("They're still a punk band, and I don't like the songs.")

Numan turned to his family for support. "If I owe anything to any one person, it's my father," he says. Tony Webb donated his savings and worked as a roadie towards helping out his son; he is now Numan's manager.

charts as well.

"I couldn't believe how much of an anti-climax it was when ["Are 'Friends' Electric?"] got to number one. When it got to number two it was such a dream come true that I wouldn't let myself believe it'd go to number one, so that I wouldn't be disappointed if it didn't." He was elated when notified by phone of his chart triumph, but "then I hung up, and I went back to watching television. It was the same house, same car in front; I'm sitting there with me mum and dad, and the dog. Nothing had changed.

"First off, WEA had taken over Beggar's Banquet, and taken me under their wing. The first single from **Replicas** was 'Down in the Park,' which they put out as a 12-inch in a picture bag. Then they put out 'Are "Friends" Electric?' as a picture disc, which was unusual for someone at our level because our work was unknown." The gimmick helped push the record into the "breaking" region of the chart—number 48, in Numan's case. After that, the momentum was self-sustaining.

"We'd gotten invited to go on [BBC TV

Ebet Roberts

Uncle Jess Lidyard, who had played drums on the first single, joined Numan and Gardiner to round out the band.

Beggar's Banquet wasn't won over so fast, and rejected Numan's next demo. Eventually a compromise was reached ("I said, 'If you don't put it out, you won't get an album'") and **Tubeway Army** came out in a limited edition of 5,000 (since re-released).

Album number two, **Replicas**, was whipped up in only a week, and reflected Numan's increasing expertise as a producer. More significantly, he suddenly became a star. In summer 1979, "Are 'Friends' Electric?," the second single from the album, went to number one in the British charts. **Replicas** soon copped the top spot in the LP

It's taken this long"—well over a year—"for it to sink in, and for me to get used to it."

By September, Numan's popularity was such that his "Cars" 45 reached number one the same week that **The Pleasure Principle** entered the album charts at that lofty position. "Cars" even breached the Top 10 in the US—no small event, considering the conservatism of the American record buying public.

Numan once said he'd known the British teenage market was aching for an idol ever since Bowie drifted too far afield. Asked more recently about the causes of Numan-mania, he sounds less cynically calculating.

pop show] *The Old Grey Whistle Test* on a Tuesday. It was part of their new policy; we were the token new wave band that week. When the charts came out on Wednesday, and the single was a 'breaker,' they asked us on *Top of the Pops* for the same week!"

On *Whistle Test* Numan was slotted between Bryan Ferry and David Bowie. "I'd never been on the telly and I hadn't gigged in over a year. I used to just stand there with my guitar, very nervous, not moving, and that was in front of like a hundred people. Now I had to go in front of millions on television. I started practicing in front of a mirror."

Ultimately, his mannerisms weren't as important as the lack of them, and the setting in which Numan put himself. "The *Whistle*

Test's lighting's all bilious green and amber, and the same for everybody. But I said, 'No colors, just white lights,' and they were pleased that somebody was taking an interest in the show's presentation.''

Numan waltzed right in with customized keyboard towers and a clear Perspex drum riser and set up—"just out of the blue. Two days later we did the same thing on *Top of the Pops*. We didn't smile, we didn't talk to the cameras, we didn't say a word." He credits this presentation with the creation of a striking overall atmosphere.

The preoccupation with visuals extended to his first post-hit live show, at the Glasgow Apollo. "I hadn't gigged for nearly a year and a half, and this was the first time I'd be going on without a guitar. I had no idea what I was going to move like, or how I was going to treat the audience"—3,500 strong. "I did like a collection of poses," he admits, with a heavy emphasis on his own idols Bowie and Bolan. Aided by a deluxe version of the stage gadgetry previewed on TV, the performance was a success.

Numan was equally concerned about how Atco wanted to present him in the States. At first he was reluctant to play the US, but then-Atco president Doug Morris wanted him and convinced Numan they'd be faithful to his image. A whale of a promotion job (documented in TP 55's article on American radio) sold "Cars" to d.j.'s, and it's difficult to imagine most of them viewing the record as anything more than a novel treatment of a topic close to the heart of the American Everyman.

One of Gary Numan's paradoxes is that, while he admits **Replicas** was a science-fiction concept LP about the future, and uses impressive technoflash in his stage shows, the "futurist" tag is beginning to annoy him.

"'Cars' is about being in cars, not cars themselves. My songs are mostly about *me*. I'm not a futurist; only about two songs on each of the last two albums are like that. **Telekon** [the latest album] is especially personal, about my problems at the time I wrote it." Yet his imagery is consistently fantastic; even when he insists "Remember I'm human," it's in a song titled "Remember I Was Vapour."

Another paradox is that, although Numan projects his grimmest fantasies of the future and innermost feelings of confusion and alienation to a mass audience, at heart he remains very much an English Joe Normal type. He's close to his family, loves his dog, house and car (his fancy for Corvettes is well documented in the press), likes fast-food hamburgers and French fries, and only *drinks* Coke. (No snorting for this lad—he doesn't even imbibe alcohol.) But there's a darker side as well.

"I hate being stared at like I'm some kind of freak. I never liked having to deal with people I didn't want to, even little things like having to talk to the electricians when they come to read the meter. What success is good for is that maybe I can hire people to do that for me! I had a job once delivering parcels. You have to talk to people; I lasted about two weeks.

Bob Leafe

"I've gotten my own style down over various tours and I now feel more at ease."

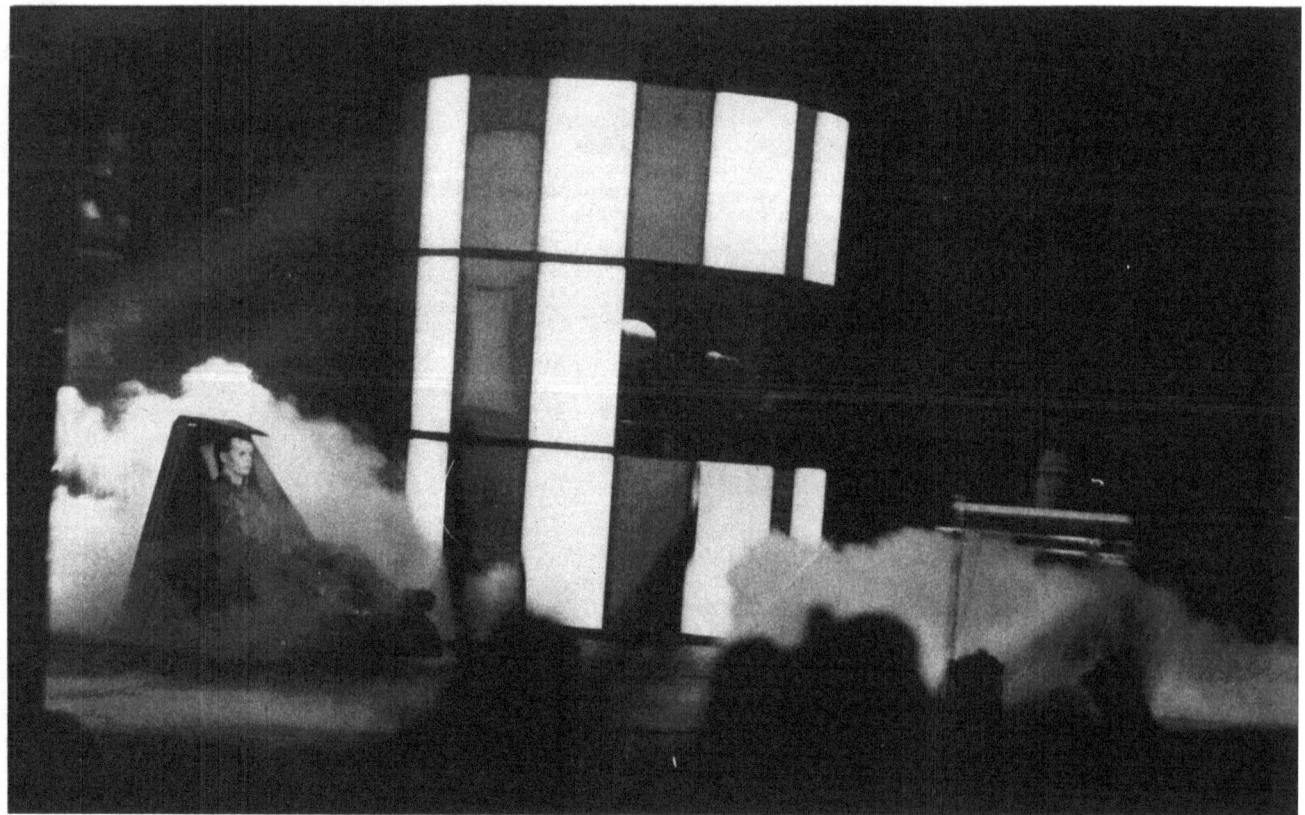

"But then there's another side of me that says I'm gonna dye my hair bright white [as on his android impersonation for the cover of **Replicas**], and there I am, terrified of people looking at me." He hates signing autographs, yet feels hurt if nobody asks.

"Over the various tours I've begun to get my own style down, and I feel more at ease." His recording technique has improved as well: Production is crisper, and it helps to have a bigger band. Lidyard left after **Replicas**, to be replaced by Cedric Sharpley; Chris Payne (viola/keyboards) signed on, too. Ultravox's Billy Currie, looking for work between editions of his band, enrolled as a guest member at the end of the **Pleasure Principle** sessions for touring and television appearances. He was replaced by Russell Bell on guitar, keyboards and violin, and Dennis Haines was also added on keyboards. The range of sounds on record indicate formidable potential.

But now Numan claims he's knocking it on the head: no more tours. "There are so many reasons to stop. I'll be able to write an album over most of a year, instead of a few weeks between tours, so there'll be different things mixed in—not just what I was feeling at the time." He enjoys the commercial com-

petition: "It's like playing Monopoly but with real money. What makes it a job is having to write songs at a certain time for a certain purpose for a certain release date."

So he's about to scale his career down to a hobby—one of several. "I've been trying to get my flying license for two bleeding years, and I just haven't put together enough time." There's also cars, of course, and video. "I'd like to do live collections of short plays, and how-to-play-synthesizer cassettes—it's much easier to learn if you see it demonstrated."

Numan's work with Robert Palmer is another milestone: his first session work. Palmer had been including a couple of Numan's songs in his live set. He brought Numan cassettes of material and played some of his own things on guitar, which Numan helped arrange for Palmer's **Clues** LP. In addition, Numan plays on the crooner's version of "I Dream of Wires" (from **Telekon**) and contributes a couple of other songs ("Found You Now" and "Style Kills," the flip of Palmer's "Johnny and Mary" single).

W hy stop so soon? The shows and music seem to be coming together better than ever, as Numan exudes a feeling of just hitting his stride. He still

hasn't won over the English press, but he's made inroads.

"They take it far more seriously than I do. I never claimed I was the first, or the best, or that I even wanted to be the best. I never claimed to be original." He would like credit for establishing the synthesizer style at the mass level. Even the alleged imitator is now being imitated: witness the American car commercial whose music is based on "Cars," or a stage set-up in the film *Breaking Glass*.

The US poses another problem. Unlike England, where "We Are Glass," "I Die, You Die" and **Telekon** have perpetuated his popularity, America hasn't fallen in line since Numan's initial breakthrough.

"I've got a very big fear of being a has-been. I'm getting out of it before I get too involved to get out of it. I have to avoid facing not being famous anymore. Besides, having said I'm going to stop, I'm obliged to stick by it. I'd lose too much face otherwise."

Gary Numan is a man of many faces (not all of them grim) but enough of a pessimist to opt out of the star game at 22. In conversation, he seemed so young, so childlike at times that I almost felt like asking what he'd like to do when he grows up. Then I'd remember—he's already done it. ■

Another disappointingly catty article, this time written for the American music paper, *Trouser Press* (quite the weakest title for a periodical). Like the Trakin article it also seems to be an audition piece for a British music paper. Again, the writer, Green, clearly doesn't understand the subject. His attempt at even-handedness fails by the second paragraph when he stands himself firmly in Camp Self-Delusion (just who are these more talented artists who have been denied fame? And what has that got to do with Numan? Numan, whose musical innovations have completely re-written the rule book on sound and rhythm and lyrics and style to the extent that even Minneapolis funk has been transformed and Chicago hip-hop will be born? Jimmy Green then has a go at Numan for not staying at a more fashionable hotel! One imagines that if Green had been given an unlimited word count he would have criticised the brand of cereal on offer at the hotel's breakfast counter and blamed it on Numan.

But the article is of interest because it shows how seriously Numan took his image. He was willing to forgo all attempts by WEA to market him and his music in the States, if WEA didn't bow completely to Numan's own presentation of his image. That's the kind of control-freakery that killed Numan's career in America and which separated Numan from his peers. And it is why he is An Artist and not A Stooge. Compare Numan's approach to that of, for example, Paul Weller and The Jam who happily acquiesced to their American handler's request for L.A. photo-shoots with 'London' double-decker buses and in 'English' pubs. And compare it to, for example, Elvis Costello's and Bowie's almost total kowtowing to American musical styles in their (admittedly very successful) love-me-love-me campaigns for American success. Mr. Joe Jealous makes the fair and partially accurate point that WEA were instrumental in the success of *Cars* by "getting the record to DJs", but that success is cancelled by WEA's failure to successfully market Numan's follow-up singles, possibly because Numan wouldn't play their game? (though in truth because the American mainstream wasn't ready to embrace the thrilling individualistic negativism of *I Die You Die* and *We Are Glass*). Reading the article one can see that the comparative failure in The States of *We Are Glass* and *I Die You Die* and *Telekon* contributed to Numan's decision to pull the plug on his career there (and everywhere outside Britain). His huge success and massive fame in the UK had almost crushed him. With America he decided to get out "before I get too involved to get out of it."

259

Numan, Roxy, Pretenders, in Stigwood movie

13.9.80 Sounds

AFTER EXPLOITING disco with 'Saturday Night Fever' and rock and roll with 'Grease', Robert Stigwood turns his attention (belatedly?) to the new wave for his next movie, 'Times Square'.

The film, which deals with 'the life and hard times of two juvenile runaways cast adrift in New York's jungleville' (it says here) will feature the music of **Gary Numan, Roxy Music, Pretenders, XTC, Lou Reed, Ramones, Talking Heads, Robin Gibb** (who?), **Patti Smith, The Cure, Joe Jackson, Ruts, David Johansen** and **Suzi Quatro.**

The film will be premiered in December but there'll be a soundtrack album (surprise!) in October and a slew of singles, starting with Suzi Quatro's Rock Hard', released on Dreamland Records on September 26.

Machine head

THE MUSIC MACHINE in Camden is hosting a series of one-off gigs this month. **Black Slate** promote the release of their first single 'Amigo' on Ensign Records with a gig there on September 13. **The Dark, The Wall** and **UK Decay** will take part in a Fresh Records night on the 15th and two new Manchester bands, the **Gammer**

In October 1980, Numan had songs on three albums in the American charts

Billboard TOP LPs &

FOR WEEK ENDING NOVEMBER 1, 1980

			Artist-TITLE-Label
☆	1	1	BARBRA STREISAND Guilty. Columbia PC 36750
	2	16	QUEEN The Game. Elektra 5E-513
☆	3	4	THE DOOBIE BROTHERS One Step Closer. Warner Bros. HS 3452
☆			BRUCE SPRINGSTEEN The River. Columbia PC 236854
	5	11	PAT BENATAR Crimes Of Passion. Chrysalis CHE 1275
☆	15	3	KENNY ROGERS Greatest Hits. Liberty LOO-1072
	7	4	21	DIANA ROSS Diana. Motown M8-936M1
☆	10	4	SUPERTRAMP Paris. A&M SP-6702
	9	11	AC/DC Back In Black. Atlantic SD 16018
	10	6	17	SOUNDTRACK Xanadu. MCA MCA-6100
	11	7	13	GEORGE BENSON

			Artist-TITLE-Label
☆	33	4	ELVIS COSTELLO Taking Liberties. Columbia JC 36839
	30	31	7	THE B-52's Wild Planet. Warner Bros. BSK 3471
	31	32	7	MOLLY HATCHET Beatin' The Odds. Epic FE 35672
	32	16	38	CHRISTOPHER CROSS Warner Bros. BSK 3383
☆	79	2	THE POLICE Zenyatta Mondatta. A&M SP 4831
☆	37	27	STEPHANIE MILLS Sweet Sensation 20th Century T-605 (RCA)
	35	10	MICHAEL HENDERSON Wide Receiver. Buddah BDS 6001 (Arista)
☆	51	5	ANNE MURRAY Anne Murray's Greatest Hits. Capitol SOO-12110
	37	25	22	SOUNDTRACK Fame. RSO RX-1-3080

			Artist-TITLE-Label
	56	58	3	BOB MARLEY & THE WAILERS Uprising. Island ILPS 9596 (Warner Bros.)
	57	57	14	DYNASTY Adventures In The Land Of Music. Solar BXL1-3576 (RCA)
	58	54	20	PETER GABRIEL Peter Gabriel. Mercury SRM1-3848
☆	67	4	ROBERT PALMER Clues. Island ILPS 9595 (Warner Bros.)
	60	63	55	PAT BENATAR In The Heat Of The Night. Chrysalis CHR 12
	61	61	13	DIONNE WARWICK No Night So Long. Arista AL 9526
	62	46	25	AIR SUPPLY Lost In Love. Arista AB 4268
☆	80	3	KOOL & THE GANG Celebrate. De-Lite DSR-9518 (Mercury)
☆	72	5	GARY NUMAN Telekon. Atco SD-32-103 (Atlantic)

STUTTGART – While many other record companies in West Germany are fighting to keep sales from nose-diving, Intercord of Stuttgart has enjoyed the most successful September in the company's 12-year history.

Marketing manager Ingo Kleinhammer reports a sales increase of 30% compared to September, 1979. "And there's every sign that October will be even more impressive," he says.

Spearheading the September sales boom have been two U.K. albums: Gary Numan's "Telekon," licensed through German independent company Aves, and "Signing Off" by UB40, licensed from Graduate. The Numan album reportedly sold 18,000 copies in the first three weeks of release.

			Times Square RSO RS-2 4203
0	89	18	BLACK SABBATH Heaven And Hell Warner Bros. BSK 3372
	101	21	EMMYLOU HARRIS Roses In The Snow Warner Bros. BSK 3422
2	87	19	BENNY MARDONES Never Run Never Hide Polydor PD 1 6263
	111	2	GARY NUMAN Telekon Atco SD-32-103 (Atlantic)
4	95	76	WAYLON JENNINGS Greatest Hits RCA AHL1 3378
	113	2	ANNE MURRAY Anne Murray's Greatest Hits Capitol SOO-12110
	NEW ENTRY		ROBERT PALMER Clues Island ILPS 9595 (Warner Bros.)

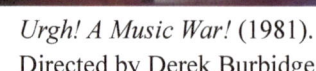

Urgh! A Music War! (1981). Directed by Derek Burbidge.

VARIOUS ARTISTS
'Machines'
(Virgin V2177) ****

'Cash Cows'
(Virgin Milk 1) **½

A NAUSEOUS K-Tel comic strip style cover does not bode well for a collection as crassly titled as 'Machines'. But heads down into the groove and we find an album's worth of tracks which, bar a few nasties, would put a smile the size of the Cheshire Cat on any self-respecting Futurist.

Side numero uno is, frankly, a joy, tinkerbells. Starting with one of the best 45s of the year, Orchestral Manoeuvres' 'Messages', spirits are subsequently uplifted by that wacky party ice-breaker, 'Memphis Tennessee' by Daniel Silicon and the Miller Teens; a brash, bright 'n' breezy throwaway trash-

electro-popper, gungily synthetic. Shaping up as a brill New Year Party disc, this 'un. The acceptable face of Gazza (ie early Tubeway Army) winds its pseudo-meaningful derivative way round the ears in 'Down In The Park', rescued from the jaws of doom by one of the catchiest but gently ethereal synth riffs Gal's ever played with his one finger.

The overwhelmingly rich-textured second version of 'Being Boiled' follows, and it's just as good as the League's original. Technically swisher, it's real cabaret, padded out with synthinastics at every juncture with a rousing ornate climax. Thomas Leer's 'Private Plane' is a welcome if unexpected inclusion. Obliquer than the rest, an understated one-man effort with outstanding idiosyncratic vocals. Ending as gently as OMD began, 'Dalek I Love You' sees Dalek I's delicate choirboy style and

simplistic synths add more credence to the New Romanticism.

Side Two makes mistakes. Not with John Foxx's perfectly-formed 'Underpass' or Henry Badowski's simply endearing 'Making Love With My Wife', but with Public Image's ghastly 'Pied Piper', a histrionic atonal miasma which jars after such lashings of melody. Mercifully, it's short. Compensation comes in the form of Fad 'Masochist' Gadget's 'Ricky's Hand', a modern electronic classic danced to in Futurist Discos across the land. A cornucopia of cross-firing rhythms.

The machine then slowly grinds to a halt. Karel Fialka's 'The Eyes Have It' is too poppily irritating, and Gal Numan's 'Aircrash Bureau' scans OK but is doggedly slow-moving. He doesn't deserve two tracks either. 'Somnambulist' is an inspired Andy Partridge quickie but

ROBERT PALMER
'Clues'
(Island ILPS 9595)****½

WHILE IT'S hip to be cynical about people who've been around as long as Palmer, and who manufacture sounds one could conveniently call MOR, it would be a mistake not to give serious scrutiny to anyone who rises above past form. In this instance, 'Clues' proves the point — surprisingly, it's one of the best albums of the year.

The record is an obvious attempt by Palmer to modernize his repertoire, mostly by getting wise to new wave — or, at least, Gary Numan's version of it. Numan actually wrote 'I Dream Of Wires' — here, Palmer's stab at Eurorock — guests on keyboards and proffers total spiritual commitment while Palmer perfects his dronezzzzz. It's the kind of number the Beatles used to do to please George,

the opener, six minutes of superbly sustained funk with Palmer working a Steve Miller double tracked vocal and drummer Dony Wynn striking some mean times. For 'Sulky Girl', Palmer takes us back to Vinegar Joe with dirty Stones-style guitars, pianos honkin' in the greatest tradition of Nicky Hopkins and guest bassist Andy Fraser weighing in with the lines that made Free famous. Palmer, as ever, struts his stuff with style, prompting us to ask whatever happened to his old chum Elkie. This is how he used to rock us in Hull ten years ago!

The single 'Johnny and Mary', already receiving radio exposure, deserves to be a hit. Palmer croons with class, while the staccato, up-tempo synthesised beat powers the song along, contriving a relentless, irresistible atmosphere. The guy's so laid back, it's beautiful! Next up, 'What Do You Care', another up-tempo funk excursion, ... remarkable ... this age ... find an

open-eyed veteran thinking big, embracing several styles with equal panache.

On the reverse, there are a couple of dull moments, but generally, Palmer, never a mug with a mike, continues his struggle with the Eighties, and wins hands down. High spot here is his interpretation of the worthy Beatles chestnut, 'Not a Second Time', Palmer opening up to give us his Paul Rodgers' vocal and Wynn again showing what drums are for. But even 'Found You Now', another weird one, a dirge, another (you guessed) Numan collaboration, 'Bites in Time'.

Indeed, an impressive work-out by Palmer, put together, it should be said, with some extremely tasteful studio science. The Man, currently a Bahamian resident, tours here in October and could be nearly famous by Christmas. Up till now, token touring has kept his UK impact pretty much low key, and one's inclined to ask whether he really cares what this does here. He should. He's good.

Sounds 13/9/80 **DES MOINES**

Perfect replica

A COUPLE of weeks ago, I bought a Gary Numan "best of . . ." album, 'Photograph', from Windows in Newcastle. My mate decided he wanted a copy too, but when we returned to the shop we were told it had been withdrawn. We've tried every other shop — without success.

Is anyone selling this? Why was it withdrawn? — **Alan, Newcastle-Upon-Tyne**

YOU HAVE a rarity on your hands. This German import on the Aves label was released without permission from either Gary Numan or Beggars Banquet and only a handful of copies managed to find their way into the hands of the record-buying public.

The story so far? While Beggars terminated an agreement with Aves, their one-time German licensee, in December last year, the label went blithely ahead with a somewhat premature compilation in January and attempted to stock the shops in both Germany and the UK illegally.

After a speedy injunction from Beggars banning sales, most of the 500 copies which managed to sneak into British record stores have been withdrawn and destroyed along with the rest of the pressing. In years to come, the few existing copies of 'Photograph', which includes Numan's 'Films'/'Are Friends Electric?'/'Replicas'/'I Die You Die'/'Down In The Park'/'This Wreckage'/'Cars'/'Metal'/'Remember I Was Vapour'/'Complex' could be "worth a fortune", according to Beggars Banquet director **Martin Mills**.

As far as Beggars are concerned it's too early to do a 'best of' Numan compilation: "We don't want to do it until we can put the best possible album together and have nothing planned until next year or the year after that."

People who have 'Photograph' aren't obliged to give it back for instant melting down though. Meanwhile, a new approved Numan live boxed set is due for UK release soon.

ROBERT PALMER
Clues (Island)

WHY 'CLUES'? I mean to say, Robert old chap, it's not as if there's some burning question to all this despite the wacky covershot of your hunky

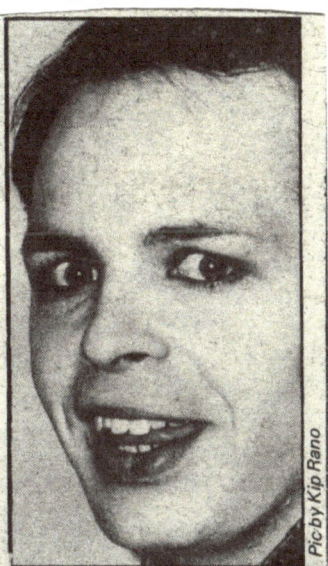

NUMAN proves he's human with a rare smile — see item left

Pic by Kip Rano

Wave numbers to pedal and was last heard performing Chrissie Hynde's 'Kid' amongst other tunes for what one presumed would be just another rich man's Linda Ronstadt affair.

Sharp-eared as ever, though, Palmer has now turned for inspiration to Talking Heads' 'Fear Of Music', Bowie's 'Heroes' and the like, going all out for the massed swarm of synthesizers, automaton funk rhythms and echoey discorporated vocal slant. In his search for a collaborator, Palmer — presumably finding David Bowie or Brian Eno unavailable — has plumped for (don't laugh) Gary Numan.

The splendour that is Gazza can be heard straining and soaring against the entire dark ages of aural piffle only on Side 2 of the record which allows the first side of 'Clues' to showcase the new sound of Palmer virtually on his tod.

Surprisingly, three out of his four cuts are very very good indeed. 'Looking For Clues' parries a natty variant on the one great funk bass riff punched

■ Continues over

261

ME, I DISCONNECT FROM YOU

Gary Numan now only talks to people he trusts. Frank Drake and Peter Gilbert give us an exclusive report on the latest in his controversial career.

WE PUSH the appropriate button on the wall outside Gary Numan's West London flat. After we announce our names through the grill of the outside security microphone, a buzz automatically opens the front door. Once inside, a lift whisks us quietly to the third floor. A knock on the door, an eye at the security peephole and we are inside Gary Numan's apartment.

Gary, dressed in a T shirt and jeans, is relaxed and chatty as he sits cross-legged on the floor. It's been exactly a year since we first chatted with Gary in a wine bar in the London suburb of Ealing. In that time he's become famous and the hero of hundreds of fans — is it frustrating for him now that he's reached his goal?

"Oh, you mean the 'now I need new reasons' bit? I wouldn't say it's frustrating, although I have noticed that I get very restless a lot of the time. I'm back to looking for something again, like I was before. Now I sit here for hours and hours, day after day, looking for something more.

"I still want to do something in films, but I'm not sure whether I'm confident enough, whether I've got enough talent to take it further than just one experiment, or that I could write enough short stories to take it any further than one collection of twelve.

"I don't even feel confident that I can go on writing songs sometimes. In fact, I feel very unconfident about the whole thing!"

Gary smiles at his last remark and we realise that he is a lot more relaxed these days. We asked him how he would describe himself?

"I feel like a very old man in a very young body."

Why old?

"I just feel old, I feel old and wise."

Is this because your success happened too quickly for you?

"I think I have experienced more at my age than maybe is wise for me. Maybe someone else of my age could take it all in, quite easily. As it is, for me personally, I find it a lot to take in. I wouldn't say I'm driven to insanity by it or anything like that, I just find it a lot to take in."

Gary pauses for a moment in order to explain himself better, and he thinks deeply before continuing.

"Maybe it's the same for eveyone at any age and I'm just going through that, but I think I would need to be few more years older before I could put up with all the knocking."

But doesn't the very fact that you have got where you are prove to those people that knock you, that they are not really important?

"Yes, it does, but I have never said that they are important to that extent. Not at this level they're not important, but it still doesn't alter the fact that everytime I pick up a paper I read some snide comment or other and that upsets me, and I get depressed about it naturally.

"I don't read papers anymore because each week they're tearing me down and that gets on my nerves after a while."

THE INSECURE, paranoid, weak-willed impression given by the media to describe Gary Numan in the late '70s certainly doesn't apply to the person now sitting before us in front of the television with the sound turned down.

We asked him if he still feels isolated from people generally? Gary still hasn't lost that sometimes naive honesty which is apparent in his answer to our question.

"Yeah, more than ever!"

But what about those at that write to you and go to your gigs, there's a lot of warmth there surely?

"Yes, maybe, but it's all very short lived isn't it? I'm not stupid enough to think that they are going to write letters to me saying they're going to love me for ever, say next year, because I know damn well that they probably won't.

"So all that you've mentioned isn't really any consolation at all because it's all sheer fantasy on their part and this makes me feel possibly lonelier than I would've felt if I had never got it in the first place."

We pointed out that, nevertheless, many people feel warm towards him for a number of reasons. Does Gary see and feel that warmth at all?

"I can see it and I can feel it but what I'm saying is, it's only real for today. It's not like loving somebody and loving that somebody for the next 50 years; it isn't that real.

"Most of it comes from young girls or sometimes young boys and it's sheer childhood fantasies and teenage crushes on the latest pop star. Y'know, they stick up a pretty picture and they fancy it and that's about as deep as the love they have for me goes and for very, very few of them it's anything more than that."

Has success changed you at all?

"Yes, it's made me much lonelier than I was before." That's very sad to hear you say that?

"Maybe it is, but it won't last forever. It won't always be that way. It's the price I'm paying now which I can take advantage of in the future; it's not such a big price to pay, really.

"Obviously we're talking about it on the dark side at the moment but there's lots of good things about it too. I suppose I tend to think more about the bad points," (Gary laughs) "that way I can write more songs."

IN HIS official fan club newsletter, it stated that he would be appearing on the Kenny Everett Video Show on New Years Eve, singing a version of "I Die, You Die." We wanted to know why he didn't appear on the show. What went wrong?

"Well, the reason we said we was going to do it was because we were asked by Thames Television to do it, and they said it would be for the New Years Eve show.

"We then went and filmed it and spent a whole day on it. I was dancing for about eight hours without a break filming this bloody thing, and there were promises all round that I could go and help with the editing.

"It was definitely going to be on the New Years Eve show because it was 'Looking into the 80's', and there was going to be people from the 70's like Bowie. And as it was New Years Eve, it was going to show what was happening in the 80's, that sort of thing. This was going to be us, that was our part in it.

"I went down to watch Bowie do his bit after we'd done ours

and I got thrown out. I was told by the director that Bowie didn't want me there, which was fair enough, I suppose."

Just you personally or everyone else as well?

"Well, me to start with and then apparently he was upset by it and then everyone had to go. Later on he stormed off and wouldn't do a sketch with Kenny Everett. The next thing we heard was, we were not being used at all.

"Then we were told that what we did and what Bowie did was not working well together. That was rubbish because I saw what Bowie did, because I was there, and they are nothing like each other at all. There is no way that they could not have gone together.

"They said they they wanted us to do the show in the first place because it would have been good to have a confrontation between David Bowie and me on the very last programme of the year, just to compare if nothing else.

"And I was all for that, because it would've cleared the air once and for all, and hopefully people would have realised, seeing us side by side, that we are really nothing alike at all. The way Bowie moves and sings and his music, is nothing like the way I move and sing and my music!

"Now the fact that he wore a black leather jumpsuit — and I wouldn't dare say he was copying me by wearing black — I wouldn't dare say that!

"Anyway, to go on from that, we found out later that the man who directs the Everett show also works with Bowie during the year on his own videos, so obviously there is a big cash involvement.

"And then we all came to the conclusion, which wasn't denied at the time by the producer of the show, that Bowie didn't want us on it and he had pulled this cash lever with the director to get us off it. And that seems to be what happened.

"The last thing we heard from Thames was that they had changed the format of the show and instead of looking into the 80's, it was now decided to look back at the 70's. But that was still not a good enough reason to take us off it because we were the last pop stars of the 70's, so we should've been on it for that reason, more than any other.

"So whatever reason they said, the fact is we were not on it and there was no reason for us not to have been on it, except that Bowie didn't want us on it and he used his influence with the director to get us off it. Now that may or may not be true."

IF WHAT Gary is saying is true, then surely he must be very disillusioned with Bowie?

"Completely! I look at him in a completely different light now, to how I saw him before. I've lost a lot of respect for him because,

if that's how he got where he is today, by doing that sort of thing to other people, then he's a shitbag!"

But doesn't Gary expect too much honesty from other people?

"No, I don't expect them to be taken off shows just because he's worried about opposition, especially as I'm considered by the press and most Bowie fans alike to be just a cheap Bowie rip-off anyway. If I am a cheap Bowie rip-off, why is he scared of having me on the same programme?

"Obviously I'm not a cheap Bowie rip-off and I must be the biggest competition he has had in about the last seven or eight years, and what's more, he's worried about it!"

If this is the case, that Bowie regards you as a threat, how does it make you feel?

"I'm pleased! I'm just disappointed that he should have to resort to such measures because I would like to have

spoken to him and met the man. I've idolised that bloke for seven years and the first chance I get to meet him, he decides to do that."

GARY NUMAN: still as outspoken, still as honest, still as interesting. Now he's speaking out more, against the press, the corruption in the bizz. A character that is easily underestimated by those who think they are so important!

As for Gary, he's doing okay and he's doing it the right way and doesn't that just get up his critics' noses? Don't it just!

Among the very first of Gary Numan's fans, Peter Gilbert and Francis Drake run a fanzine called "In The City". Issue 14 is now available containing more on Gary Numan, Adam & The Ants, Ultravox, Poison Girls and more, and costs 40p (including post) from: In The City, c/o Compendium Books, 234 Camden High Street, LONDON NW1.

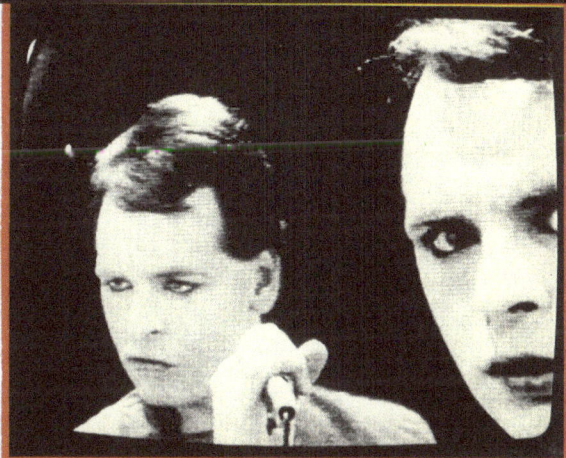

Gary Numan and Gary Numan in "We Are Glass".

Photo-Love 3/1/81

"I trust no-one..."

The loner of the rock world has declared at last:
"I'm ready to settle down . . ."

ON stage, he has all the appeal of a robot that someone forgot to turn on. Off-stage, the image remains the same. Unsmiling, serious and secretive, Gary's not giving anything away.

With his thinning hair and dramatically applied make-up, he is, perhaps, one of the most unlikely sex symbols of the last few years. He makes no effort to appeal to his female fans. He doesn't go out of his way to appeal to anyone! But appeal he's got with a capital 'A' – the kind of appeal that has girls and fellas alike, screaming for more at all his concerts.

Asked why he never smiles, he replies, straight-faced: "I do sometimes."

Gary, true to form, got where he is today on his own. From the dole queue to singing in pubs, then right on up to the top of the charts.

He did it by watching and waiting. Watching to see what the public wanted, and waiting until they wanted it.

His songs, all written by himself, are futuristically bleak. They'd be depressing if it wasn't for Gary's unique style and electric sound.

He admits that he trusts no-one but his parents. And you believe him when he says he gets bored easily. He wants to move on.

It's difficult to imagine him any other way, but, surprisingly, he does admit to a private life. And even more surprisingly, he agrees to talk about it. Yes, he's got a girlfriend. And yes, he's considering marriage . . .

"I'm trying to build a proper relationship . . ."

Could this be anything to do with his threat to come off the road and stop touring?

He's been heard to say that he enjoys hearing his fans scream and likes the fame and money that success brings. But he also knows that when a tour starts, he can't wait for it to end. The glamour of living from a suitcase and visiting one strange city after another soon wore off.

"I've come to the end of that part of my life. Right now, I'm trying to build a proper

relationship with my girl, so that we can get married and have children. And if I'm going to have children, I don't want them to grow up with a rock star for a father. It's no way for children to live, with people all the time recognising who they are through their father. Mine certainly aren't going to go through that."

Without knocking – or even mentioning – any other big names, Gary's confession sheds new light on his decision to retire. He's seen what's happened to other bands. The disillusionment and the tiredness. The invasion of private lives. And it's not going to happen to him.

Even so, he's going to use the business. The difference is, the business isn't going to use him.

"Most of all, I want stability"

"I want a big house (he's already got a mansion in Surrey) and I want to drive a big car (he's got a huge, expensive one already), but most of all I want stability."

When it comes to what fame can buy, he's getting out while he's got what he wants. Emotionally, he's getting out for his own good.

"Put it this way," he says, "what I'm doing is like committing suicide before someone kills me."

However, Gary's not planning to quit completely. He intends to continue making albums and get more heavily involved in video.

"I could go back to being an unknown again, but I couldn't go back to being poor. I couldn't do without the money," he ad-

mits. "But I've come to realise there are more important things in life than pop. Being a pop star came easily. It was a game. Now I want to play at something else."

And you know he means it! With the kind of success that Gary has enjoyed in such a short time, it would be tempting to sit back and revel in the security.

But, Gary's scared. He's frightened of failure.

"I always wanted to be a hero as a kid. Partly because I was unpopular at school. But maybe I got everything I wanted too quickly. I'm terrified of being a fallen hero – a has-been. I'm not waiting until my latest album doesn't sell. It hasn't happened to me — yet and I'm not going to let it!

"My only real talent musically is as an arranger of noises. I'll carry on doing that, but in the background.

"I never wanted to take the '80s. I just wanted to be famous. I want a life right now."

A life even more private than the one he's managed to keep so successfully from the public gaze over the last two years.

"I like the Clint Eastwood type"

You know that Gary, unlike other superstars, won't be attempting a comeback. He means what he says.

But, for someone who was once quoted as saying: "I'd like to be a film star – you know, the Clint Eastwood type" – take reassurance from the fact that he'll never disappear from our lives completely.

He may not want the '80s. But he'd got them before they even began!

16

HAS-BEEN...

"I always wanted to be a hero"

街を流れるジングル・ベル
年に1度のお楽しみ
サンタのおじさんやってくる
楽しい楽しい　クリスマス！
さあ、あなたの好きなミュージシュンは
どんなクリスマスを過ごしているのかな？
あなたにあったクリスマスをみつけて
一緒に祝おう
メリー・クリスマス！　イヤッホー！

Gary Numan

ゲイリー・ニューマン ─── 自画像撮影
　　　　　　　　　　　　　芸術のクリスマス

「ボクは、あくまでも芸術に生きる！」とばかりに、浮き足だつ巷にわき目もふらず、じっとカメラをかまえるはゲイリー・ニューマン。なんでもクリスマスの自画像撮影が、年中行事なんだそうな…。家族全員、またはなつかしいお友達が、一同に顔を揃えることもめったにないんだから、あなたも年に一度の記録撮影を、クリスマスに決めてみたら？
シャッターが切れる瞬間に……イェイ！　メリー・クリスマス！

九死に一生を得た男　ゲイリー・ニューマン特別手記

インドへは二度と行きたくない!!

もしあなたが乗っていた飛行機が突然エンジン・トラブルを起こし急降下をはじめたらどうしますか？　しかも、言葉すら通じない見知らぬ土地に不時着し、わけのわからぬまに捕えられてしまったら……？　ゲイリー・ニューマンは、そんな悪夢の中へ突きおとされたのです。

（1981年11月29日　於／東京・京王プラザホテル）
pic：Koh Hasebe／music life

267

コンサート予定が流れた
ので、ついトーキョーに足が
向いちゃってね

なぜか、ゲイリー・ニューマンがひょっこり再来日

インタビュアー●マーク・ボランスキー

クイーン武道館公演の客席にゲイリーの
姿を見つけた観客が大さわぎ。「え！な
んでゲイリーが日本にいるの？」「よく
似てるねネ。でも、まさか……」そうな
んデス。彼はジャパンと共に突然やって
来たのです。

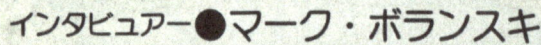

51

何故かゲイリー・ニューマンがボディガード（どんな風に守っているのか知らんが）一人連れて来日した。これは行かなければならない。イボシ人め、化けの皮をはいでやるぞと思って来た。ホテルの部屋で待っているとキチンと化粧したゲイリーが握手をするのだ。ヤバイ！病気が愛想よくやんわり包むように、ボクの手を両手でやんわり握りしめる。

——今回は、なんで来たの？

ゲイリー　まずはホリディなんだけど、色んな人と話したいと思って。

——突然思いたったの？

ゲイリー　コンサートの計画があったんだけど流れて。それでも気持ちは行きたかったから、ツアーじゃなくて色々話に行こうと。

——日本が好きなの？

ゲイリー　ウン。すごく新鮮で人々もフレンドリーだし、ここで思った日本と違うって感じがする。何かが変わったと思う。人とか気候とか文化とか何かが好きなの？

ゲイリー　人もすごくいい。あとカメラがすごい。いっぱい買ったんだヨ。ウーン、これが好きっていうのは言えないナァ。

——ボクは東京にずっと住んではその事は考えないヨ。だからレコードでいくけどネ。だからレコードでも、時々うんざりするけどネ。

——日本でもクイーンのコンサート2回も行ったんだって？

ゲイリー　3回だヨ。ジャパンも行ったし、トーキング・ヘッズも観たいけど、きっともう日本にいないから残念だナ。クイーンとは特に仲がいいんだ。ロジャーとフレディとは特に。

——アーティストとして見た場合アナタとクイーンは随分違うじゃない。どう思ってる？

ゲイリー　ウーン。クイーンはクレバーなグループだと思うし非常にプロフェッショナルだと思う。特にフレディの観客のひっぱり方はすごいと思うヨ。音楽的にも輝きがあってパワフルだ。だけどちょっとこの2～3年はアホっぽい歌が多いね。

——ステージの派手さは？

ゲイリー　ボクのステージもビジュアルが重要だということは同じだと思うんだ。

ウン、アナタがステージのビジュアルを大切にしているのは日本公演でわかったヨ。レコードではビジュアルなことはできないけど、その点どう思う？

ゲイリー　レコードでは全然できないネ。だからレコードでは

が好きなの？

ゲイリー　一人もすごくいい。あと

にパワフルに、観客とのコンタクトも含めてどんどん拡がっていくんだヨ。

——ボクは東京にずっと住んではその事は考えないヨ。だからレコードでは、時々うんざりするけどネ。それはロンドンもニューヨークも同じことだと思うし、その中では、ボクはトーキョーが一番カワイイと思うヨ。

ゲイリー　そうだね。今回はすごい興味があって脚本を書いたり、ビデオやりたいって言ってた事に関係あるのかな。

ゲイリー　ホント、有難う。フィルムの方は関心はあるけど、2時間物を創ろうとかいうんじゃなくてね。どんなとらえ方ができるかってことなんだ。

——ビデオに興味があるんだヨ。

ゲイリー・ニューマンのビデオってのは興味湧くよ。フィルムの方は関心はあるけど、2時間物を創ろうとか実験的なプロジェクトとして考えてるんだ。

じ位興味があるんだよ。

——飛行機の免許とったんだって？

ファン攻勢をさけジャパンとは別行動

てネ

ゲイリー　ウン。自分で好きなところにどこでも飛んでいけるから、これからは自分で飛んできたいネ。

——それは同感だナ。

ゲイリー　ミュージシャンとしてそう思うヨ。

——イギリスの人気投票で、色んな部門の一位をとったけど、自分のことキーボーダーだって思ってないでしょ？

ゲイリー　ボク、最近自分のことミュージシャンだとも思ってきたの？

——あのゲイリー・ニューマンスタイルはどんな風に出来あがってきたの？

ゲイリー　ビジュアルの面と音楽の面が並行してるんだけど、ビジュアルの面は、ストーリーなノイズが主人公になり切ることで自分が明確になってきた。音楽は……ちょっと待ってて、考え

少し高目の物静かな声で、ゲイリーは淡々と話す。早口でもなく乱暴でもなく、エラそうでもなく無口でもない。人の話を聞く時目は真直ぐ相手に注がれているけれど、自分で話している時は内気そうに伏目がちになる。

フッと笑った時に急にあどけない顔になる。アー、この人若いんだ、と思い出す。結局いつでもゲイリー・ニューマンって若いってことにすごく大きなポイントがあるような気がする。

楽器ってのは自分の好きしせまった音を出す為だけに必要な道具だと思うヨ。

ゲイリー　そう思うヨ。音に関わってると音楽に限界がきちゃうと思うんだ。歌を作るにしても歌作りのプロになるよりアウトサイダーでいた方が面白いものが作れると思うんだ。

んな部門の一位をとったけど、自分のことだけど、ボクはギターでもキーボードでも、シンプルなノイズを作ることが目的だと思ってるから。パフォーマーっていうのも、ちょっと恥ずかしいネ。

楽の面でも並行してるんだけど、する興味を失ってシンセサイザーに対する興味を失って——つまり自分の好きなノイズが作れるってことだけを失ってシンセサイザーに対する興味を失ってったんだと思う。

楽は……ギターに対する興味を失ってったんだと思う。つまり自分の好きだこと、徹底的にワン・パターンのサウンドばっかりなのには感動

ゲイリー　色んな音がいっぱいはいってるのが嫌いなんだ。多様化した感じっていうのかな。ボクは、気に入った音に徹底的にこだわっちゃう。アルバム一枚一つのユニットって感じに…

——『テレコン』はやさしさが出ちゃってる気がするけど。

ゲイリー　一番シニカルなアルバムのつもりだよ。成功しちゃった直後に書いたんだけど、やさしさっていうか、成功がバレたら、成功したって楽しくないって感じが出てるんだと思う。

——つまり、それまでにウジウジしてるみたいなこと。

ゲイリー　ああ、そうか。それはまったくその通りだよ。前二作はアウトサイダー的な立場とったんだけど『テレコン』では、もうインサイダーになったんだ。だから、折り返し地点みたいな感じで、ぐっと内にはいったんだ。

——そういうのって、すごく苦しくない。

ゲイリー　そうね。特に前はそうだった。今はそうでもないけど。すべてが起こったのが21歳の時で、若かったし、何もないところからの急激な変化だったし、どうしていいかわからなかった。特にボクはその前一年半位、閉じこもりっきりで外にも出ないみたいな生活してたからね。でも自分のやりたいことができて、閉じ込められる権利を得た今からみると、あの頃の自分って無意味だったんじゃないかナァと思うようになったんだ。

——ミックが手伝ってくれたのって、アナタのアルバム？今とりかかってるボクのアルバム。

ゲイリー　ウン。ただのパンクバンドのつもりだったんだ。何でバンドを始めたかっていうと自信がなかったんだ。まだ何にもなくて、どうなるかわからなくて、バンドという形を除すために、バンドという形が欲しかったんだ。今でもポールとは一緒にやってるけどね。

——ヘェ、でアナタはジャパンのアルバムは手伝わないの？

ゲイリー　ウン、頼まれればね。だけど、時間がとれないじゃないかナァ。

——時間があったらね。それはボクのでもジャパンのでもない実験的なアルバムにしたいって感じにしたいわけだ。

ゲイリー　ウン。そうだネ。ボクも今でやってきた自分のアルバム聴くのすごく嫌なんだ。ミックって言うんだろうナァ、ごい好きなんだ。ゆううつで暗くて陰湿なんだ。

——バーニング・ブリッジズとか「ザ・テナント」とかはアナタ好みなの？

ゲイリー　イエー（笑）グループで今でやってきた自分のアルバム聴くのすごく嫌なんだ。アメリカや日本でどっかに行くとゲイリーは救われたのかもしれない。

それでもゲイリーはアウトサイダーというボーズによってしか、自分を人前に出せなかったのだ。ここにも一人の落ちこぼれがいる。

そういう自閉症的な内向的な性格の人は社会に接する時に色んなポーズをとる。ポーズをとることで自分と社会とバランスがようやくとれるのだ。そのボーズが空いばりやひがみや無関心にならずに、音に向いただけゲイリーは救われたのかもしれない。

——子供の頃のこと教えて？

ゲイリー　ロンドンのハマースミスのそばで育って、5、6歳の頃までは……ちょっと問題児だった。14、5歳の頃になっても、ちっとも背が大きくならないで、その時から大人らしくならないし、その時からウチに閉じ込もるようになったんだ。

——あんまり友達もいなくて？

ゲイリー　あんまり話したくないくらい人嫌いなんだ。その頃の自分は。で閉じ込もって曲なんかを書き始めたんだ。

——チューブウェイ・アーミーを作った時に、こうなることは予想しなかったの。

ゲイリー　ウン。今とりかかってるボクのアルバム。ただのパンクバンドのつもりだったウイなんかに他にもデヴィッド・ボウイなんかにも出るかもしれないんだヨ。

ファンが群らがったりしてて異様な気持ちになるからね。

ゲイリーの面倒をみているレコード会社のTさん「たまんないヨヨ、静岡行こうか行くまいかって、前日の夜まで決めないんだヨ。予定だてるのが嫌いなんだヨ。で結局のとこ、一人で新京駅で待ってたら、一人で勝手に先に行っちゃうんだから」

ゲイリーは、ジャパンのステージを観に静岡まで行ったのだ。

——そうそう。ジャパンの曲の中で「バーニング・ブリッジズ」とか「ザ・テナント」とかはアナタ好みなの？

——ジャパンのミックとお友達だって？今回はジャパンにくっついてきたんじゃないの？

ゲイリー　3、4ヶ月の友達なんだ。ニュー・アルバムに6曲サクソフォンやベースをやってくれたんだヨ。一緒にきたけど、一緒に行動はしないんだヨ。だってジャパンと一緒にいると感じになるしね。すごく好きだ

——どうしてもボクは、ゲイリー・ニューマンと一人遊びの上手な鍵っ子のイメージが結びついてしまうのだ。一人遊びは、いつも危険だ。

ゲイリー　ボクは飛行機免許をとったから、今から冒険者なんだヨ。今年の夏頃、また自分の飛行機で遊びにこられるかもしれない。

でも、だから人をおとしめかといえば必ずしもそうじゃないし、時には明るい気分になったりするし、聴いて踊るっていうよりは何かを考えさせるって感じになるしね。すごく好きだ

The day high-flyer Gary nearly got his wings clipped

Basingstoke Gazette, 6/1/81

Chart topper, Gary Numan, at the controls: "I take my flying very seriously."

GARY'S UP ON CLOUD NINE!

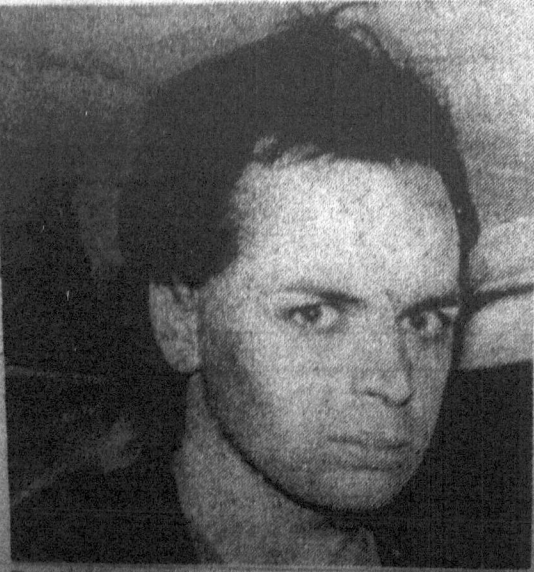

Top singing star Gary Numan, who's been riding high with a string of chart successes may be a very level-headed chap - but he hasn't always got his feet on the ground. See what we mean on page 3.

HIGH-FLYING pop star Gary Numan nearly came down to earth with a bump at Blackbushe airport.

Attempting a take-off in his own light 'plane, Gary (22), ran out of runway, skimmed across the busy A30 at a height of only ten feet and just squeezed through a gap in the trees on the far side of the road.

"We were so low, the trees on the other side of the road were above the 'plane," recalled Gary, a self-confessed flying addict, last week.

"I got a good telling-off from the controllers for that one," he laughed - although flying is something Gary takes very seriously.

Gary, who leapt to number one chart success with hit singles like *Are Friends Electric?* and *Cars*, has been a regular visitor to Blackbushe since he got his pilot's licence at the airfield a fortnight ago.

Celebrate

He bought himself £30,000 worth of Cessna light 'plane to celebrate that success and since then, he's notched up 15 hours' flying in it in just ten days.

But strangely enough, the man with the menacing stage presence has one big problem when it comes to using the 'plane's radio.

"I'm microphone shy," he admit-ted, as he talked to the *Gazette* at the controls of his 'plane.

"I get very nervous in case I say the wrong thing - I can never remember what to say to the controllers," he joked.

But now Gary's musical career is taking second place to his love of flying, despite the success of his new single, *This Wreckage*, now climbing the charts.

Interested

"I do it to get away from all that - this is a way to get into something completely different," he explained.

Gary reveals that he has been a flying addict ever since the age of four.

"I was given one of those stick-on steering wheels when I was about four, and I used to cut it in half and pretend I was flying a 'plane," he recalls.

His interest got another shot in the arm when he worked in a W. H. Smith's warehouse before chart success came his way.

"One of the blokes I knew there had a pilot's licence and he used to come up here to Blackbushe.

"When you see your mate driving a lorry around the place and then just get into an aircraft and take-off, it gets you interested," explained Gary.

So, two years ago, he started taking flying lessons at the Blackbushe-based Three Counties Aero Club under his real name of Gary Webb.

Since then, he's been a regular visitor to the airfield, just half-an-hour's car ride from his Surrey home.

And he's had a couple of hairy moments on his way to his pilot's licence.

"I nearly crashed here last week," he told the *Gazette*, with a grin.

"I had landed and I pulled the throttle back and I thought I had pulled it right back.

"Unfortunately I hadn't and I wasn't at a low enough speed to land so I bounced the 'plane five times."

There was also the time when he spun the 'plane in the mud on an airstrip on the Isle of Wight.

"It was so muddy, they weren't really expecting anyone to fly in that day," said Gary.

Spinning

To get out of that spot he needed a man holding each wing to stop the 'plane spinning round.

Although music has taken a back seat to flying in Gary's life, he's still in the studio between flights.

"I've been doing some songs for a new album and we'll be doing a farewell concert at Wembley in April," he told me.

But until then, all that local fans will see of Gary Numan is a tiny single engined Cessna buzzing round in the skies over Basingstoke.

Due apologies for the bad image quality of this page. It gives an idea of what researchers have to put up with when scrolling through rolls of microfiche. When you add to the image problems the fact I took them from the internet, and you factor in my limited photoshop clean-up abilities, you have what you have here.

I've included it for preservation because it does give a good account of Numan's days in the build-up to Wembley, and the first steps in his subsequent career as a pilot. From these humble beginnings he rose to become one of the country's top display pilots, and a Civil Aviation Authority examiner.

I include it too to remember that local newspapers did play a large part in news and information services, and local news reports are too often lost to the ether.

This article reminds me that when BBC Radio 1 stopped playing his records, Gary Numan made extensive use of local news and radio services for promoting the *Warriors*, *Berserker* and *The Fury* tours. Local radio stations, such as Signal Radio in Stoke, sponsored some of the concerts.

こぼればなし

●コンサート活動を一時休止していた彼だが、9月から再びツアーを開始する。しかも、日本からスタートするということだ。

●ニュー・アルバムはすでにレコーディング中ということで、今回の世界一周のあとで仕上げに入るそうだ。

●映画用のストーリーを書いているという彼。30年代の宇宙が舞台ということで、痛快な宇宙版〝必殺仕掛人〟といったところか。公開予定なし。

●で、映画「フレッシュ・ゴードン」(フラッシュ・ゴードンではない)の第2作目のサウンドトラックを手がけることが決まった。一作目ほどイヤらしくなく、もっとコメディ・タッチの作品になるそうで、公開はクリスマス頃とか? お楽しみ。

●最後に、今回の来日での彼の名言をひとつ。「ミュージシャンというのはお金を稼げる趣味であり、パイロットというのはお金が出ていく趣味だ」。若いのに立派なもんです。

For All readers of
MUSIC LIFE.

THANK-YOU FOR MAKING US
ALL SO WELCOME IN JAPAN. WE'VE
ENJOYED OUR VISIT VERY MUCH.
SEE YOU IN '81.
Love
Gary Numan
Xx.

九死に一生を得た男●
ゲイリー・ニューマン特別手記

ついにこのときがやって来た。自らの手で、ボクは世界の空を飛び回るのだ。感慨無量だ。

9月18日、世界一周飛行への第一歩はパリへ向けられた。とても神経質になっていた。

愛機 "セスナ210センチュリオン" の調子は、とても良好とはいえない。脳裏には、常に不安の陰が差し込んでいた。

そしてあの、いまいましい事件が待ち構えていた。9月25日、インド洋上空で突然のエンジン・トラブル！『サメ！』。瞬間、ボクの頭にひらめいた恐怖だ。飛行機の高度はどんどんと落ちていった。インドの空港上を旋回し、緊急着陸の指示を受けようと思ったが、他の飛行機が入ってくるという理由から拒否される。高度はどんどんと落ちていく。

そのうち、ガタガタという音とともにエンジンが止まった。死ぬだろう。それしか頭になかった。ボブ・トンプソン／副操縦士と必死で操縦桿を切った。力いっぱいに切った。

海の中なんてゴメンだ。近くの陸地に向かって飛行機は大きく弧を描いた。不時着は見事に成功した。そこは何もないところだった。ボクたちはまず、一刻も早くイギリスへ帰りたいところだった。そして近くの町まで歩き始めたのだ。不時着した飛行機を空港まで引き上げる手立てをとった。間もなくして現れたのは税関の役人たちだった。

"キミたちは着陸したことをまだ報告していない"。ボクたちは、ここヴィサカパトナムへ好きで来たわけじゃない。緊迫した状態の中で、税関への連絡なんてしてるんじゃない。ボクたちは空港へ引っぱられていった。そして機内に積んであったすべての機材をおろさせられたのだ。つまり、それらの機材が税関を通ってないということで…。何度でもいう。これは不時着なのだ。観光にきたわけじゃない。ボクたちは、その場で逮捕された。

映画 "ミッドナイト・エクスプレス" が実感となって甦っていた。言葉が思うように通じない恐怖。彼らは、お互いに英語を話しはするが、それはひどいものだった。別に生命への危機は感じなかった。4日間、ボクたちは拘束された。ホテルや空港への出入りはいただけない。あるときはスパイ扱い。またあるときは密輸容疑。彼らは結局、最後までボクたちの言ったことを信じなかった。インド側は最後の瞬間まで、ボクがだれであるか知らない、信じない、だった。大使館のあまりの冷たい措置にも驚かされた。イギリス政府は、まったく助けてくれなかったのだ。

ボクたちを助けてくれたのはイギリスの新聞社だった。新聞社の呼びかけが、ボクたちを救ってくれたのだ。本当に悪夢だった。しかし、いまとなっては楽しい想い出のひとつとして語ることができる。次の挑戦では失敗は許されない。すべてに完璧でなければならない、ということをボクは強く学んだような気がする。

210センチュリオンはいまだ修理中だし、航路に関しては、北極をまず先に通過しなければならなかったのだ。

今回の新たなスタートに際して、ボクは飛行機を "パイパー・ナバホ" にかえ、また航路を逆回りに変更した。これは前回の失敗を恐れてのことじゃない。ボクは、ジンクスなんてまったく信じない。

当然、問題のインド洋上空を通過することになるだろう。別に怖いことはないが、気分がいいとはお世辞にもやしない。

さて、大好きな国、日本へ自らの手によって上陸したときは何ともいえない感動がこみ上げてきたものだ。過酷な太平洋横断（40時間にも及ぶ）の最後を告げる国、それが日本だった。いままでの疲れが、一瞬のうちに消えさっていった。ボクは、ついに日本へ到着したのだ。

ボクはこの足で日本を踏みしめたとき、もう夢中で手をふった。ボクのこのときの笑顔は、生涯忘れることができないものだったはずだ。日本のファンのみなさんの温かい応援に、ボクは心から感動した。この感謝の気持ちは、9月、日本のステージで100パーセント爆発させるつもりだ。

Numan's vinyl score

GARY NUMAN releases a series of live albums next month to 'commemorate' his retirement from live work after his Wembley shows at the end of April. They will be deleted a month after release, thus causing maximum pandemonium and purchasing activity among his fans.

The albums come out on Beggars Banquet on April 17. 'Living Ornaments 79' is taken from the 'Touring Principle' tour, 'Living Ornaments 80' comes from the 'Teletour' last year and each album feaures a totally different song selection.

You can get the two albums boxed together, which has an additional free single with two more tracks. And the whole lot will also be available on cassette. The albums will be deleted on May 15, although they may be around in the shops a while after that.

Look sharp

GARY NUMAN collecters beware! Beggars Banquet have switched the release date of the limited series of live Numan albums to April 24 and you'll miss them if you're dozy because they'll subsequently be deleted from the WEA catalogue one month later on May 22. The three elpees, all culled from Gal's 1979 and 1980 UK tours, are respectively titled 'Living Ornaments '79', 'Living Ornaments '80' and (not forgetting the boxed set) 'Living Ornaments '79 and '80' and they're set to coincide with the farewell concerts at Wembley on April 26, 27 and 28.

OTHER THAN pygmies which Adam finds "very exciting", he expressed a fondness for **Gary Numan** ("Because he's got a lot of style"),

EAGLE-EYED M. Slevin of Stockport has been scanning **Gary Numan's** "Telekon" in vain for mention of a track entitled "A Game Called Echo", a song which we predicted back in January would be included on the finished album. I know this is going to be a bit hard for you folks to take, but fact is even we aren't perfect and there are people on this very paper who are suckers for a good rumour. The character who penned the fateful news item confesses that he doesn't recall where he got hold of this fictional piece of information and won't come out of the stationery cupboard until we promise not to hit him. Suffice to say that there never has been a **Gary Numan** track answering to the name of "A Game Called Echo" and The Editor promises he will not rest until this magazine is purged of such misleading, slipshod reporting. Gee, it's dark in here.

"Yeah . . . what *did* happen to that single??"

MATTHEW SLEVIN, an inhabitant of Stockport, is just one of many Smash Hits-reading **Gary Numan** fans who rushed out and bought the "Living Ornaments" Box Set when it appeared the other week. And he wasn't the only one disappointed to discover that it didn't contain the free single we'd said it would when we published details of the album back in March.

We checked with Beggars Banquet who explained the free 45 was just one of many ideas that were considered back in the planning stages. Unfortunately, an administrative error led to it being announced before it had been decided on. Apologies all round.

NUMAN LP

GARY NUMAN has confirmed that he intends to quit the live concert scene after his current world tour, which ends early next year.

Speaking on Radio One on Tuesday he repeated a statement issued to Record Mirror in July. "After this tour there will be no more live concerts. That's it. There will still be albums, as we have a few more songs to record yet."

And he said: "We're working on a possible live album, with a new studio album for next September. But outside that I think I will become more involved in video projects, perhaps like video stories or 'novels'.

"It's not that I'm trying to keep ahead of everybody else by doing something 'new' or 'futuristic', it's just that I feel that I have another 40 years left to live yet and a lot of different things to do." RM 6.9.80

"Heeeeerrree's Johnnie!"

Lead boots

GARY NUMAN
'Living Ornaments '79'
(Beggar's Banquet BEGA24)*

'Living Ornaments '80'
(Beggar's Banquet BEGA25)* ½

MORE THAN ever before, these two live albums illuminate the towering dreadfulness of the Numan phenomena. I say 'phenomena' because this isn't little fragile parvenue Gary Webb here but a tacky billboard trying to sell you plastic novelties from the twilight zone.

The fact that these albums were released separately, rather than as a double, shows you what They are after — bigger profits.

The pride and joy of Gary's bank manager, the leaden beat, is on show throughout all four sides, even though the Numanettes do take it at the wrong speed sometimes. The synthesiser is pure Janet and John electronics; the clumsy themes and upandown solo oscillators really do sound like they're produced by a Chinaman who's never seen a synth before. Perhaps Gary's trying to do for electronics what chimpanzees did for Shakespeare?

Surprisingly, all this isn't to say that Webb's music is totally worthless. He does trade fairly with his audience of under-achievers. But ultimately his bargain-basement horrorshow ditties are bereft of any quality.

His oafish futurism has long been known for the sham it is,. and the lame, two-dimensional performances on these albums (although '80 is a bit livelier) elevate the music to that same pedestal. If your perverse nature leads you anywhere near this deadly duo, the only things I can recommend are the points where his drooling fans go wild at the sound of a single oscillator being switched on.

JOHN GILL

'Honest' John Gill lets himself go and spews out green-bile, and a bit of characteristic racism, probably while spinning a little girl's head and forcing her to masturbate with a crucifix. What's impressive about this tantrum in print is that it does not contain a single word of truth, so it casts into full doubt everything Gill wrote in his career. I'd loved to have heard him hiss with shame when the double-album entered the charts at Number Four and, in doing so, exposed the deliberate lies of his opening sentences. Gill's reviews had been robbing the *Sounds* newspaper of its credibility, with the result that it started hemorrhaging readers. Numan's career outlived it by decades.

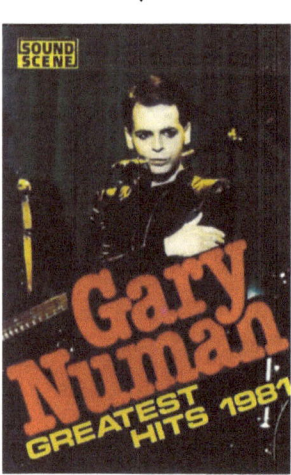

JOHN GILL will be shocked to learn that the lesbians, killjoys and cissies at Rock Against Sexism are putting on a concert with his new favourite band the Lemon Kittens (+ Table 12 and another band) on 26 September at Action Space in London.

He is not invited, however, to the gig at the same place the following night with the Androids of Mu, the Harpies and the Mistakes, as it is — horrors — a gig for women only. And not just for the lesbian separatists he is so appalled by, but for all women who get fed up with being pushed out of the way by the hunky men at ordinary gigs.

Gary Numan's live sets (Beggars Banquet) Gary Numan's (above left) farewell concerts are on at Wembley Arena from 26 April, and a variety of live albums are being released to mark the event. There will be two single albums – *Living Ornaments '79* and *Living Ornaments '80* – both taken from his concert tours, plus a boxed set that includes both. For some silly reason these albums will be released on 17 April, and then deleted on 15 May. I confess I won't be one of those rushing out to buy them.

GARY NUMAN - Living Ornaments '79 and '80.

We owe a lot to Gary Numan. His critics seem to forget that it was Gary who made synth-music popular. I'm not saying he's 'better' at the art than Kraftwerk or Eno or Ultravox, or that it wouldn't have happened without him sooner or later, simply that he was the <u>first</u> to open the general ear to the european synth-sound. ("good on him", says Gershwin). This attractively packaged boxed-set is to be admired as well. Many bands will take a mobile on tour with them, record every gig and select the best takes (as you would in a studio), leaving little to chance. Gary has recorded just two gigs, one in September 1979, the other in September 1980, both at the Hammersmith Odeon. Another thing; many so-called "live" albums cannot be relied on being live, as bands tend to do overdubs in the studio. i don't detect any fresh overdubs or extensive processing, so i admire Gary for releasing a true example of a gig. All the hits are here, all performed well but still refreshingly rough at the edges. Like uncut diamonds maybe? (BEGGARS BANQUET).

COMPETITION

HERE IS YOUR CHANCE TO WIN A GARY NUMAN BOX SET, REVIEWED ABOVE, AUTOGRAPHED PERSONALLY! SEND US A GARY NUMAN CARTOON OR DRAWING OR A JOKE. THE BEST FIVE WILL WIN A BOX SET. ALL ENTRIES TO BE SENT BY SEPTEMBER 30th 1981. ADDRESS ON PAGE THREE.

NOW I'M A GNOME I CAN FISH FOR MYSELF ...

In The City, No.17

GARY NUMAN plays a triple farewell this week, prior to concentrating exclusively on recording, film and video self-presentation, at London Wembley Arena (Sunday, Monday and Tuesday). Shock, recently signed to RCA, support on the brief goodbye.

Sounds, 13.9.80.

278

Come in, Space Cadet 16, your time is up

GARY NUMAN
Living Ornaments '79 (Beggars Banquet)
Living Ornaments '80 (Beggars Banquet)

SO FAREWELL then, Gary Numan. All good things must come to an end sometime, and ground control is evidently calling your number even as I write, in the same harsh, hollow cadence you yourself have utilised for your sound.

Last year there you were, coasting along in your little bubble, still notching up big commercial coups: 'Telekon', your last studio album, streaked up to No.1, whilst those two singles 'We Are Glass' and 'I Die You Die' shuttled into the Top Five. If only the aptly entitled 'This Wreckage' hadn't failed to even secure a place in the Top Thirty, you'd be exiting this humdrum mortal coil that is the music biz market place with the old log-book completely unblemished.

But then again, by the last days of 1980, there were the likes of Steve Strange, John Foxx, Spandau Ballet and Midge Ure's Ultravox corporate crowding out the same stratosphere you'd once held omnipotent control of. All these new faces, new haircuts, new uniforms — even though stripped of their kilts and fringes they were just a bunch of ungainly, pasty-faced dough-boys.

Worse still, the man you'd chosen to ape, one David Jones of Beckenham, had returned from his sojourns out in left-field to claim his throne, the very chair your bum had been keeping warm in his Nib's absence for — how long is it now? Two years, at least, eh? A good innings for a pretty uninspired bloke with only one good (i.e. commercially viable) idea like yourself, Gary. What else could you do under the circumstances?

On April 24th, the WEA corporate will release 'Living Ornaments '79' and ' '80' in three different packages. Your fans — for whom this inspired aural 'au revoir' has been especially released (it reads here, in this rather shoddy press-release I have before me) — can either buy the two records separately at £4 "or less", or they can buy the pair in a "special box-set" which includes an added two live tracks *plus* special free single which . . . Oh, hold on a tick, the girl from Beggars Banquet just phoned to say that the free single is *not* to be included. Instead your aficionados will be privileged to receive a "leaflet" (sic) with some fab photographs and special info. on the two tours immortalised herein. The boxed set retails at £8 "or less" with the crucial stipulation that all three artefacts will be made available from the WEA pressing plant to shops from April 24th until May 15th. Yes, for only one month will your many fans be able to share in this extravagant finale. Or so it would appear.

In fact, the latter ploy is the only truly inspired aspect to this whole spurious affair. Retailers have to order in bulk so as to fully accommodate the presumed flood of requests, thus rocketing the three records straight to the top of the album charts. Very canny, Gaz, very sharp. Even Big Brother Bowie hasn't come up with a piece of marketing strategy as wickedly on the ball as 'Living Ornaments 79/80'. The one-month stroke affords your followers the chance to bathe in the privilege of duping themselves into believing the whole ploy is a personal tribute to their fidelity while in reality the whole deal is simply arranged to ensure maximum sales returns.

Well, Nick, you really know how to hurt a guy . . .

Ah, if only the music were one fraction as inspired. Listen Gaz, I don't want to rehash all the old criticisms you've awkwardly cringed away from whilst scurrying off all the way to the bank. In fact, I imagine that you're a fairly genuine sort of bloke who genuinely considers your music to be complete evocation of a vision of a future devoid of passion, warmth and all-purpose humanity. Unfortunately, like your detractors, I view your music as being wretchedly one-dimensional, crass sci-fi drivel that would be merely a harmless ear-sore, were it not for the fact that a) your synth-obsessed bombast spotlights every negative aspect inherent in the very concept and practical appliance of contemporary technology in direct relationship to music, and b) your puerile sub-'Diamond Dogs' scenarios are — unwittingly — a highly pernicious influence on impressionable types who, if they take this pompous garbage as seriously as you

evidently do, are under certain highly dodgy delusions regarding their cultural bearings, simple human values and life 'as she is lived' in general. Listening to all four sides of your parting bouquet, all the old adjectives are summoned forth once more: the *eerie* synthesisers, the *dank, drab* metronome of a pulse-beat, your whining vocals, the empty gestures, the numbing bombast. It's unhealthy stuff, Gazza.

A snippet for Gazza fans: the live sound is slightly more fuzzily bombastic throughout both concerts (both recorded at the Hammersmith Odeon in the Septembers of the previous two years), with Numan's voice more strained and awkward than the studio would lead one to believe. ' '79' has Ultravox's Billy Currie in the backing group, though you can scarcely pinpoint his contributions on stiff, note-for-note reconstructions of 'Cars', 'Metal', 'Dream Police', 'Conversations', 'Films', and other ultra-precious pearls of half-baked pomp like 'We Are So Fragile'.

' '80' is a better buy for the poverty-stricken Gazzaphile, with the first side sounding slightly more solidly in synch with the "live" angle (although numbers like 'This Wreckage', 'I Die: You Die' and 'Every Day I Die' are so threadbare as to defy plausible renditions), and side two boasting some actual "punch", the corporation working overtime to provide tension, verve and a certain ominous extra dimension to 'Remind Me To Smile' (Numan's 'Joe The Lion' swipe), 'The Joy Circuit' (Gazza lifting Cat Stevens' ancient 'Matthew & Son' motif) and, to a lesser extent, 'We Are Glass'. Also 'Are Friends Electric?' is present and correct here, doled out with stern authority by his adept cronies.

And so it goes, around and around in ever-diminishing po-faced echoes. 'Living Ornaments' is your last twirl with the masses, Gaz. You kept Bowie's throne (luke)warm — in his divine absence — just like Steve Harley did way back in '74 and just like Steve Strange is doing now. You should be pleased — your success was longer-running and more widespread than Harley's was or Strange's will be. Last month's flavours and last year's favoured become this year's stale aromas. I don't like your music — never did — and find this final salvo as crass as it's loaded with empty gestures.

Nick Kent

279

The new age everyman

MM 25.4.81

Numan: *"Oh come on Adam . . . play the white man!"*

GARY NUMAN: "Living Ornaments '79", "Living Ornaments '80" (Beggars Banquet BEGA 24/BEGA 25).

To TIE in with his forthcoming London farewell concerts, Numancorp Inc swings smoothly into action with this brace of live albums by the Microchip Marvel.

"'79" was recorded at Hammersmith Odeon in September 1979, "'80" exactly a year later.

I imagine if you like him you'll enjoy this, but it's hard to tell what difference the live setting makes because the music seems identical to its studio-recorded counterpart. "'79"'s "Cars", for example, or "'80"'s "Are 'Friends Electric?" and "We Are Glass".

I've no idea why Gary Numan's sterile, symmetrical songs became so popular so fast. Perhaps it was because he offered bland nihilism, a bright laser-etched image of the very real sense of downhill futility which burdens people. He grasped some superficial mood, made it attractively simple and then sold it back to the teenagers who would shortly become its real victims.

Undoubtedly, Numan has assembled a fastidiously painstaking sales and marketing operation. It has refined a water-tight audio visual kit and sold it without compunction or ever looking back.

Numan's version of the "star" stands at the apex of a pyramid of technology, singing flatly of alienation while an anonymous band whirrs away on synthesizers. If Bowie realised that the only way to become a pop idol in the early Seventies was by inventing one of his own and then acting it out himself, Numan grasped that nobody needs pop stars at all — there have been too many already.

He thus became a sort of sterilised post-New Age Everyman, orating the feeble emotions still permitted by the post-digital brain. In short, he could wallow in technogloom — "This Wreckage", "I Die: You Die", "Everyday I Die", "Remind Me To Smile", "We Are So Fragile".

It ain't nothing like a house party!

The remarkable thing about Numan's stardom is (was) that he has no identity at all. His words and music, clear and flawless, are meaningless. He might as well sing about Nairn Cushionfloor or teabags for all the content he imparts to the listener.

Gary is ideal background music for the "Space Invaders" generation. You pay your money, rack up a boggling total of 60,000 and walk away. It means nothing but you'll be back. And if it isn't "Space Invaders", it's "Missile Command".

Just to make sure that his inevitable and built-in obsolescence doesn't leave him skint, thoughtful Gary has included an "Official Merchandise" brochure with each of these albums — sweat shirts £8, tee-shirts £4, button badge 40p and so on.

Please rush me one set of "Technobaffle" earplugs . . . — ADAM SWEETING.

Gary Numan's last stand

THIS weekend, Gary Numan plays two concerts at the Wembley Arena.

These, he has already promised, will be his final stage appearance; these performances are intended as a farewell, an elaborate swansong. Numan is retiring from the pressures of touring.

He's even brought into question his future involvement with music. There are other areas in which he's keen to work, that excite him more than recording and composing.

Genuine sentiments or a load of PR baloney?

Next week, we'll be confronting Numan in an exclusive interview and attempting to measure the depth of his sincerity.

Has he really become disillusioned with stardom?

Is he really prepared to turn his back on his enormous success, to wave goodbye to the adulation he has recently enjoyed?

Did the realisation of his fantasies of stardom mean so little to him after all?

Or will he merely emulate David Bowie, who made a similarly definite announcement only to return to the ring as soon as he'd prepared a new plan of attack?

You'll only find the answers in the MM.

And we'll also have a full-colour pictures of Numan — if one man can focus through the dry ice and tears.

The Syn-Rock Interview 1981

Numan was angry that the interview was subsequently sold to Melody Maker who published out of context extracts in two cover stories in June 1981. I include it here because it captures the twenty-three year old Numan's thoughts and mood at the very peak of his fame better than any other interview. It's a summing up of the era of The Machine Quartet. The interviewers are Derek Fischer, Michael Traszko and Lucy Hill.

Would you agree that the music press has been against you from the start?

It hasn't been helpful.

Then how come you've been able to become famous, because normally they have the power to make or break a group?

They've got the power to be a starting ground, that's all. They can't break anybody that gets to a certain level, and I was already big before they decided they'd like to break me.

Why do you think they're against you?

The situation between me and the music press is very hard for me to say because there are one or two that like me. You're talking about the ones that don't, which is the vast majority. They obviously don't like me. They seem to think that other electronic bands do it better and they resent the fact that they're not successful. They seem to dislike the fact that a lot of what I do is image. I'm concerned with what I look like as much as the music, which seems to be very much out of fashion at the moment. When I got famous, everyone was claiming that they didn't want to be stars and I think they were reluctant to give that up. Then along came me saying I liked being famous, I always wanted to be famous, I liked being rich; I liked the money! I liked everything about it, and I never claimed to be original. I've been accused of being pretentious. Now what that means, and I looked it up in the dictionary to get the exact definition, is making claims of great importance. I've never ever said that I was original. I've never claimed to have started anything. All I've ever claimed is to be the first to be successful at it, with electronics, and that's not a claim it's a fact. I was the first to be successful. I wasn't the first to do it, and I'm not saying I'm the best at it. I don't think I am actually. I just think, in terms of presenting it, I got it right at the right time.

What do you think Ultravox did wrong before?

They looked awful… sounded great but looked awful.

You think that if they'd have had an image they might have got somewhere?

If they would have presented it right, yeah. You see, a synthesizer is not a visual instrument. It doesn't move really unless you get one of those silly ones with a strap and run around with it, and it still looks pretty stupid. To present a synthesizer and its music, you have to put on a show rather than just stand there playing. You can stand there with a guitar and play it because there are certain things you can do with a guitar which make it good to look at, the axe-hero poses, that sort of routine, which, although it's cliches does look good. It's a very visual instrument which a synthesizer is not. I realised that before I even started playing the things. You can't put on a show with them unless you can put on a show that isn't centred around them. So I stuck them at the back in towers somewhere. We made the show the lights.

Midge Ure said that he didn't really agree with you doing such a big live show because he reckons it's up to the band to come across rather than the show.

Why? You go to see a show.

I can't say for sure, but the impression he gave me was that you went to see the group.

Then why is he now using a light show that is nearly as elaborate as mine?

I think that what he was trying to say was that when you go to see a Gary Numan show you go to see Gary Numan, and if Gary Numan is boring then the show is boring. He thinks it's centred around you too much.

Well it's up to him but I don't agree with that. The man's an arsehole. Do you think people come to see me or the stage show?

I don't know. It's a mixture I suppose. I would have seen you whether you had a stage show or not.

Exactly!

But then you get the people who go just for the stage show.

They wouldn't go just for the stage show because they wouldn't know what it was like, because they've never seen it before. Everyone who goes to that show goes for me. I think Midge Ure is possibly a bit envious. Let's see. Now they've made it, and all of a sudden they've got a bit of money coming in, let's see what they do. For a start, they won't do a large stage show like that because they know they're going to lose money that way, and very few people aren't reluctant to give up money. That lost show cost me £200,000 to do, and I got paid £100,000 to do it. So I lost £100,000 in four weeks to do the last tour. Now I doubt if Ultravox are gonna do that. There are only about four bands in the world that are losing that kind of money putting on a show. As far as I'm concerned you go to be entertained. If Midge Ure thinks that he has the charisma to entertain people for two hours, without any lights, then that to me is very pretentious. I'm admitting the fact that for me to be on the stage for two hours is rather boring, just strutting up and down without lights. So I give people something to look at. They can listen. They can look at me and listen. They can look at me or listen. They can look at the lights and listen, or the lights and me, or a mixture of all three. They can do whatever they want and they can change their attention. They can look at this or look at that. It depends where you draw the line. Midge Ure will have so many red lights and so many blue but who has the right to say you can only have so many blue lights? You can only have three, if you have four you're pretentious, if four people are looking at the lights and not you. The whole thing is crap. His whole argument is crap from start to finish.

You said that the only reason you played new wave music to start off with was to get a contract. When you got the contract did you want to change straight away to synthesizers?

Not straight away. We had to get the record company to put some money into us first or else they wouldn't have had anything to lose by dropping us. I had to get them to invest money in us so they had a financial interest. That's why we did the next single Bombers, to get them to put their interest in it, because when they signed us, the P.A. that we had was mine, the van was mine. They didn't actually put any money into it at all. So I couldn't then say I'm going to do this or that because they didn't give a shit one way or another, because they hadn't spent any money on me. I'd spent it all myself.

What did they think you wanted to change?

They weren't happy about it at all. The compromise was that the name stayed the same, as Tubeway Army, and the music was what I wanted.

Did you expect the early material to be successful, or was it just a means to an end?

It was a means to an end. I saw no reason why it should be, and I saw no reason why it shouldn't be. Really, I was doing it because I wanted to. It was a hobby that turned into a job. It became a job that I didn't enjoy.

Did you sit a long time and think about your first image?

Yeah. I've thought a long time about the next one as well.

Why did you choose the cold and distant one?

It was a character from a book I was writing. Before I wrote songs I used to write a lot of stories and, bit by bit, the stories were turned into songs because they were quicker to write, about ten minutes. And I just became the hero from all my stories. The hero was always very tall, taller than I am, very striking to look at, not in terms of being good or bad looking. He always wore black without ever demonstrating it. He would have that aura about him where, if you crossed him, then he could do things that you would never realise before. Do you ever meet people when you're going down the street and think that there's more to that person than meets the eye? And they have a certain feeling about them of power which you can't quite put your finger on.

Yes, but the air of mystery seems to be such a lot stronger.

That's cultivated. On stage it's amplified a thousand times because you're on stage.

Why did you go solo after the Replicas album?

I wanted to go solo before I started making albums and became Gary Numan and did electronic music. You see the band had split up before the first album. The deal with the record company was Beggars Banquet said, "We're not gonna put the album out", so I said, "Alright, you won't get any album at all. It's as simple as that. Unless I can do what I want there's no point in doing it because it's not me." So I said I'd just get a contract somewhere else. So we came to a compromise and that was I'd do the music, they'd keep the name. I had to call it *Tubeway Army*. Now, after *Are 'Friends' Electric?* then I could do anything I wanted and there was nothing they could do about it really, because I had everyone in the country offering my figures that long (stretches out his arms) to go and sign with them. So Beggars Banquet was nothing and so I said, okay, now I could do it, now I could be solo. It always was before. If you look at *The Pleasure Principle*, my first solo one, and *Replicas*, the one before it, there's actually more people on *The Pleasure Principle* than there was on the ones before it. So this (showing us *The Pleasure Principle*) is less solo than the ones before it were, but it's still solo. Before, I played the keyboards and guitar and did the singing, and wrote it, produced it and arranged it - the same as *The Pleasure Principle*. All I didn't do was play the bass and the drums. I did exactly the same on *The Pleasure Principle*, except some of the keyboards are played by someone else as well, and the violin is played by somebody else. But it's still more of a solo album than people like Ferry and Bowie. I still actually do more per album myself than either of those. I still don't play the drums because I can't, or the bass because the other people are better than me.

Why did you stop the image of the black clothes and white make-up?

Well it's not quite stopped yet. It will stop at Wembley. Wembley will be the last time you see it.

Yes, but on the album cover of The Pleasure Principle?

Oh! That one. I don't know. Well, there's a painting called The Pleasure Principle by Magritte, which is where the album cover came from, because I live Magritte, he's the king, and this is a parody of that painting. The colours are the same and the suit is the same. On the painting there is an oak table with a rock on it and there's light coming out of the head. All I did was to put my head in it and update it and make it a pyramid and a perspex table. It's meant as a perverted sort of tribute, I suppose, to Magritte. Nobody's actually noticed that, they were so busy slagging it they never noticed it was a Magritte painting, which I was surprised about. That shows the intelligence of the press I suppose.

If you could go back in time would you like to change anything?

No.

So everything went to plan?

I met one person which I wish I hadn't. I'd like to change that, that's all.

But nothing to do with the music?

It couldn't have been much better I suppose, but then again you can't knock what has been successful.

Do you think you set your targets too high?

No, because I achieved them. So they couldn't have been too high. I wanted to be famous. I wanted to be a millionaire. And I wanted to be recognised as being the front of something that was going on, which I have been.

Do you think it's been everything you expected it to be?

No, it's nothing like I expected to be.

But you still like to be successful?

Yes, could you imagine going back to driving Minis and driving a lorry for a job? I couldn't. I couldn't imagine not ever having the money any more. I could give up the fame tomorrow, the fame is more of a problem than it's worth. The money I couldn't give up. The fame I would. The fame I'd like to. The money I don't want to.

Do you think it was your image that got Are 'Friends' Electric? into the chart or the music itself?

The music obviously had something to do with it. An image brings the music to people's attention, that's all. It doesn't sell anything. It just brings the music home. That's why a good video is so important. It focuses attention on the act, and the act therefore goes on to play the music.

Do you think it's wrong that nowadays if you get a mediocre song with a good video it will probably go higher in the charts than a good song without a video?

I don't necessarily agree with that. I don't think that's true. I think the videos are important but I don't think you could say that a good video will sell a song. The *We Are Glass* video is much better than the *Cars* video but *Cars* got to number one and *We Are Glass* didn't. So that sort of knocks your argument on the head really.

Why do you think the recent singles haven't done so well as the first two hits?

I don't know. I really don't know. I've no idea.

Well, like This Wreckage. I expected that to do a lot better.

Yeah, I thought that might do better (than number 20). It was off the album and, remember, the album had gone gold. So, therefore, the majority of people who were going to buy the single already had it. So there's one thing against *This Wreckage* doing better. Maybe there's a lot more around in the chart now. It doesn't worry me really.

So you don't worry if the next record isn't a hit?

I don't care. If I wasn't famous this time next year or this time next month, I wouldn't care. There's other things I want to do anyway.

As long as you've got the money.

As long as I've got the money, and I've got the money. If you ever mention things about money when you're famous, people say you're only in it for the money. But then you say them, "I've just lost £100,000, more than you'll probably earn in a lifetime, on a show, just to give the fans something better to look at than anybody else is gonna give them." They ignore that and they all think you're a money-grabber, which I probably am, but I still am prepared to spend a fortune to give people something better to look at. Some of the fans' attitude is a little odd at times. It's like you give them an inch and they want a mile. You give them that light show, the Touring Principle show, and it gets slagged because they say it was good at first but then it got to be all the same, and you go to see somebody else who only has ten red lights and ten blue lights on either side, and they don't say that gets boring because they don't expect anything from it. Because you make a show which is a spectacle, then automatically they start slagging the show as well. How that Touring Principle lightshow could be boring and yet somebody else's lightshow at the Marquee isn't boring. I don't understand. I've never known why the English have such a thing against enjoying themselves. If you do a concert in Japan, Japan is the only country where the people seem intent on enjoying themselves no matter what. Even if the show is lousy they still enjoy themselves because they go out and enjoy themselves.

Is that because they don't get many concerts over there?

No, they get more concerts over there than we do here. People love playing in Japan. When I was there, The Police had just gone. Queen were there. Japan were there. Talking Heads were going as I left. The Rats were there. I should have been playing there but I had to cancel it. Everyone's going there. It's a great place.

How are the records doing over there? Do they get airplay?

Airplay? No, they get on the radio. It's all done at clubs and concerts. That's why the image is very important in Japan because it's all done by music papers/magazines. So if you look good then they like you. It's as simple as that. Nine times out of ten they'll be great fans, but they've never heard you, never listened to the music. They just know what you look like. And then, when you go over there, if they like the music, they stay your fans. If they don't like the music they will go and like someone else instead.

Do you like the way they like you without ever hearing the music?

Yeah, why not? Far too much importance is put upon the music. It doesn't matter. What does it matter whether they like the music or what you look like? or what you have for breakfast? Who gives a shit what they like as long as they like something? If they like something, they're getting enjoyment out of it, not matter what it is. It could be the way I walk for all I know. It doesn't matter what they like. The whole thing about entertainment i that somebody somewhere is getting enjoyment out of something. That's what's important. It doesn't matter if it's music, films, your way of talking of whatever. It doesn't matter at all. That's why I think people take the whole music business far too seriously, myself included sometimes because I get too involved in it and I don't think we should take it that seriously, and the vast majority of people take the music business as being the be all and end all of entertainment and it's not. It's a piss in the ocean.

Are you trying to widen the field of entertainment?

No, I'm not doing this for anybody. Anything I do I do for me. What I'm trying to do is do something else because I'm getting fed up with music, that's all. I'm not trying to widen it for anybody else. I'm very selfish.

What about the videos? Are you doing that just for yourself?

Yes. Who else am I doing it for?

The fans?

The fans is me. We're all one and the same really.

But if you get bored with the music then you're going to have to find some other way to keep your fame with you, and you've picked video. Is that right?

No, that's true. You see, the fans are fans of that (holds up a copy of *The Pleasure Principle*). Now, there's nothing to say that they're gonna be a fan of the next one or that they should be a fan of the one before that. They probably are but I'm saying they don't have to be. The fans will only be fans as long as they like what they're getting, and I'm only prepared to do what I want to do. And if they like it all well and good. But if they don't like it, too bad. I don't owe them anything because they're fans. And they don't owe me anything.

You've often been slagged off by the music press for saying that.

I know.

Don't you find that at all selfish?

No, not at all. What came first, the chicken or the egg? What came first, the popstar of the fan? Who wrote the record they bought that made them a fan? Now I'm not saying that I don't appreciate them, I'm saying I don't owe them anything. And I don't love them because I don't know them. You can't love something you've never seen, you've never spoken to. I appreciate the fact that they still come, that they're still fans despite all the press, probably more than any artist does for his fans, and I'm willing to lose £100,000 to give them a show. Now that show didn't sell the album because the album had already gone gold. That album (Telekon) didn't sell a fuck after the tour started. That was done solely for the fans to say 'Thank you' for the fact that they were still there, not to say 'Thank you, I owe you this.'

Would you feel hurt if, after the Wembley concerts, people started saying, 'He's not interested in us'.

They're already saying it.

What do you think of that?

It's a stupid, naive, boring attitude, and people that say that aren't worth caring about. That's what I think of that. They bought the record, paid five pounds for it and got a record that's worth five pounds. Now that doesn't give them the right to tell me what to do with my life.

No, obviously not, but that's what they think.

Yeah, well they're wrong. And they're gonna find out they're wrong. I hate all that. I can get really annoyed if you keep going on about that one... not you personally. If I want to do a tour next year, even though I said I wouldn't, then I will.

Is there a chance of that?

No, I don't think so.

Is one of the reasons why you're stopping because you're bored of having to do a tour every year?

No, it's because it takes too much time and I can't make a film, do a video album, if I'm touring, because it takes six months to do a film and nine months to do a tour, to rehearse it and to do it. So I can't do both. I've got to do one or the other. I've done about six or seven tours in the last two years already. I mean, I've had a pretty good go at it haven't it?

Have you considered not giving up totally but giving up for the moment. That way, if you do want to go back to touring, the press won't slag you off for it?

They'll slag me off anyway.

But if you don't say you're never going to do another concert after Wembley then you've got the choice of doing another one later.

I have anyway. I don't have to stick to my word. No one else seems to.

Do you want to talk about the fans any more?

I really want to clear that up, because I get a bit strong on what my opinions are and people often take it the wrong way. My opinion of the fans is one of great affection without love. Appreciation sounds really corny but that's all it is and I'm grateful that they're there. I think because they buy an album they shouldn't expect me to do another album which some of them are doing now. What they should say is, 'I bought your album. Thank you.' When it comes to the shows, they should say, 'I came to your last show and I came to this tour', and that's that. 'I paid my £3.50 to get in and it was great or it was bad'. They paid for what they got at the time and that's all they're entitled to, as far as that particular purchase goes. They buy a ticket, they buy a record, they buy a poster, they buy a T-shirt, they pay for what they get. By being a fan they get something out of it. It won't last forever because we die, if you take it to the extreme. It won't last forever because there are very few forty year old rock stars, except for Mick Jagger and a few others. They just don't last that long. They whole thing doesn't last that long.

Maybe they just want to carry on as long as possible.

Yeah. Until when? Until they get married, until they find someone else to be their favourite. Then they're going to drop me like a sack of hot potatoes and they wouldn't give an absolute shit about me. As soon as they find someone else they won't give two sods about me. They are going to

grow up and find a new favourite.

So what are you going to do after Wembley?

I've got the next album to finish off, which is called *Dance*. We're gonna do a video album, a whole series of videos for it, which is quite fun. I've never done that before. I've also got a new image to think about.

Can you explain the new image? Is it yourself?

Every image is an extension of your own character. Every character has a million facets. If you go to see Clint Eastwood in a film, you walk out of the picture house and all you want to be is Clint Eastwood. You go to see a Bruce Lee film and you come out doing karate kicks up and down the High Street. That's what films do, isn't it? And all those films are extensions of facets of personality, and all I do is pick up on one of those, take it to the extreme and make an image out of it. My latest hero is Howard Hughes. Now I think the way he looked was good. I like the way he dressed.

Would you draw a parallel between yourself and Howard Hughes?

Yes, I suppose so, but he was a lot richer. He was very shrewd. He could weigh up what was wanted and the timing that was involved. I can do that. But I don't think I can do it as well as he could. You can see that from what I've done so far, I suppose. The whole thing is manipulation and really critically thinking about what to do.

Do you think you could ever up being as paranoid as he became?

Yes!

Are you worried about that?

Yes!

You said that Replicas represented your ideas of the future?

It represented one idea that I thought was unlikely to happen but was quite interesting to write about. I think it could happen but I do think it's very unlikely. In terms of something to write about, it was really interesting to explore those ideas and to make an album out of it. I really enjoyed that one. I was really thinking in those days. It's all too personal now.

Did you think of that idea just for the album?

No, it was for a book, and the book was taking so long to write so I turned it into songs instead.

How different is the next album going to be?

We're using a lot of Latin-American rhythms and sticking some effects on it.

Is it more dance-able?

Yeah, some of it. The actual title track is called *Dance* but it isn't dance-able at all, which is a bit stupid I suppose. What I'm trying to do is make disco more atmospherics because, at the moment, it has no atmosphere, it's just an on beat bass drum which you can dance to. That's all disco is at the moment. Lyrically it's boring.

What type of disco are you talking about?

The straight club disco you get now.

Not the Spandau Ballet type music?

That's not disco, it's new romantic club music isn't it? New Romantics I find boring as well. Musically it's alright but I think it's two years too late. The funniest thing about New Romantics is that you go to a club of theirs, they have four inches of makeup on, clothes which are the most outrageous things you could see, and they look at somebody else and call them a poseur. Can you believe that! That's why I stopped going. Such blatant hypocrisy I used to laugh. And then they start having a go at me because I vaguely got an image for a while. I got banned from the club because I got to number two in the chart. I was too famous all of a sudden. I was no longer underground, no longer credible. And now those same people that banned me from the club are now little rockstars themselves and all of a sudden it's okay now. *Fade to Grey* was written by my keyboard player, Chris Payne. Did you know that? Then Midge Ure stuck the lyrics to it and claimed something else. Billy Currie did something else and claimed something else. I've got a cassette somewhere around of the Touring Principle when Chris played the song and it's virtually *Fade to Grey*. Musically it's ninety percent Chris.

Steve Strange told us the exact time and place when the idea came to him for the song.

Came to him?! He was only involved in the last second of it. It was recorded with lyrics and everything done up at some studio in Reading somewhere, before Steve Strange even knew it existed.

What happened to the four-track E.P. that was supposed to come out in March 1980?

It didn't. I thought that there are two live albums coming out and there's already been a free live single with the last album, and a couple of B-sides which are live. There's so much live stuff going around that to put out a live E.P. is a little bit too much really. I wanted to keep the best songs for the albums, so I'd only be putting the worst songs of the bunch on the E.P. which wouldn't be fair.

You said that Stories is going to be the B-side of the next but one single. Do you plan that far ahead in the future?

Yes. I know what I'm going to do when I'm thirty. I knew I'd be doing this sort of thing today, virtually, when I was about eighteen. The whole plan for pop stardom started when I was seventeen or eighteen. I worked out an image, what I would talk about, what the music would be like. It was based on what I wanted to do and what I thought was needed. I simply chose the two that corresponded.

There are ten things you want to do and ten things that people want, five of them are the same, so I can do those, get famous and, without ever selling out to myself or to anybody else, because it is what I wanted to do anyway, and the other five that I couldn't do at the time I'm doing now, because now I'm famous the fans would like virtually everything that I wanted to do, within reason. Eventually, by the time I am twenty five I will have done everything I ever wanted to do. It just depends on how you look at it, but I think it's a good way of doing it. Other people say that you should do what you want to do an stick to your principles, and they can still go round driving rusted Minis, and I can drive round in a Corvette. I'm still doing what I wanted to do.

What are you going to do once you're twenty five?

Start an aeroplane business. Actually that starts when I'm twenty-eight.

What will you do between twenty five and twenty eight?

Films.

Are you still going to do those cassettes on how to play synths?

I'd like to, yes. It'll be great. Yes, one day.

Don't you think Stories is good enough to be an A-side of a single?

Stories? I don't know. I could have put it on the live album, I suppose, but it will be out probably in September or August.

If you keep on writing about the future, rather than the present, do you think people might call you unemotional?

I've only done one album about the future and that was *Replicas*. *The Pleasure Principle* is not about the future. *Metal* is, and the song *M.E.* is, and *Engineers* is, it's like a dig at trade unions really. Then there's *I Dream of Wires* on *Telekon*. *The Pleasure Principle* was mainly about what I thought it would be like to be famous, songs like *Conversation*, *Cars* and *Tracks*.

Isn't Telekon about someone's mind taking over them?

That's the title. The whole album was going to be a theme album about a man that could harness the powers of telekinetics, and the government code-named him *Telekon*. As it went on, he was used and all that rubbish, the same old thing. So I didn't do that in the end. But I thought it was a good title so I kept it. *Sleep by Windows* is the only record that remains from that theme. It's about his girlfriend. When he was about my age he was beginning to realise exactly what he could do, and his girlfriend does a nasty on him so he's ripping trees out of the ground and scaring the shit out of his girlfriend.

Is that linked to your life at all?

Yeah, loosely. I didn't ever rip trees out of the ground. I ripped hair out of my head.

287

Is Remember I was Vapour a way of saying goodbye?

Yes, so is *This Wreckage*, so is *Please Push No More* and *The Joy Circuit*. The whole album's got that little hint of goodbye in it. In *This Wreckage*, the Japanese writing says 'I leave you'.

Do you think the fans, to quote Remember I was Vapour, are forgetting that you're only human and that you need oxygen?

Yes. You become a goldfish. If you can imagine a monkey at a zoo, or a goldfish in a bowl, where people come up to you and stare at you without any embarrassment. They do that. They walk right up to you about six feet away and stare at you like that. You get really nervous, and you think what are they gonna do? So you end up with things like this (indicates the Samurai sword, one of his many souvenirs which include a stuffed wolf). They totally forget you're another person, and you become something that it prodded and pulled and looked at and made to do things. You're told to smile, to sign this. Really rudely they get a bit of paper and say, 'Do that', and I say, 'Do what with it?', because I get annoyed. And they say, 'Sign it'. And I say, you mean 'Could I have an autograph please?' Then they get all embarrassed. Others get really ratty that you've actually reminded them that they should have manners. You feel like a monkey in a zoo. So I don't go to High Streets anymore. I very rarely go shopping anymore. There's one shop in London I go to, and one shop down here I go to because there's a little old lady and she doesn't know who the hell I am. For that reason, fame isn't what it's cracked up to be. It does have advantages, mind you. You can get into clubs for free. You become a product without a doubt. All you have to do is not let that effect you too much, and to take advantage of it, to use your status as a product to better yourself. Which is what I'm doing.

What do you think of David Bowie, considering what happened at The Kenny Everett Video Show? Has your opinion changed?

No. The man's a genius without a doubt. He's far more ruthless that I thought, but more than I intend to be.

Did you feel any anger towards him after what he did?

No. I did at the time.

Why have you changed your mind?

Because the whole music business is like a game of monopoly in real life, that's all. In that situation he got a double six and advanced to go, and I didn't. I will next time.

Why did he want you out of the studio?

Because he didn't want me to see what he was doing. I had a chat with Brian May when I was in Japan, who knows Bowie very well. We spoke for about three or four hours and he said that talking to me, if he shut his eyes, is like talking to Bowie. I don't know how true this is but two people have said that. Our outlook and attitude to the business is identical, and Bowie must know that I suppose, because he can see me as being him ten years ago.

Do you think he's a bit worried?

Possibly. He knows how quick I learn. He knows that potentially I can do whatever he can do, and I'm ten years younger, and I've got him to learn from and everybody else. There's more around now than there was when he started, so I can learn even quicker that he did.

Do you think he's learning from you?

Undoubtedly.

Like with the black jumpsuit on the Kenny Everett Video Show.

Yeah, you noticed that. You noticed also there was the whole thing about how he was giving up image and make-up. Then along came me and, on his next album, he's back into a clown suit, thick makeup and videos. Yeah, he's worried.

Do you believe that you took most of your ideas from Ultravox, because people are always slagging you off for it?

No. When I met Billy Currie, when he worked with me, I said I wrote *Listen to the Sirens* after I heard *Slow Motion* at a party. We were talking about the similarity thing that people had been saying, and Billy said that he couldn't actually understand it because we didn't sound at all like each other. Now that Ultravox are starting to get famous it's twisted slightly hasn't it? And I remember when every time I opened my mouth all I did was praise Ultravox. And now they're famous, which I think I can claim a lot of credit for.

Midge Ure told us that you helped a lot.

Well his sort thanks he can stick up his arse because the only thanks I got from him was when he did an interview and said that they don't owe me anything 'cos I stole it all off them in the first place.

Why do you mention death and dying in so many of your records?

It seems to suit. Die is like I. It's a nice word to sing. The same as 'suppose'. I like the word 'suppose', it's very flippant. You can use it to talk about something very serious.

(He showed us the lyrics to a new version of Metal he is recording with the words 'I suppose' in it. He also said that it will probably be the next single. After playing Moral to us, he explained how he's changed his style of singing).

That's my new way of singing. It's what I call gliding at random, because you go from one note to the other and you glide up and down. All my singing has been... well, you just stick to the notes. It's all been the same and very precise. I got really sick to death of that.

Haven't you changed a bit recently though? Like with We Are Glass?

288

It started to get better but the whole *Telekon* album is very much that old formula, but you can see that I'm struggling to get out of it somehow.

(He looks at the T.V. which has been on all through the interview with the sound turned off, and sees a gang of skinheads making Nazi signs. I remind him that it has been suggested that he was a fascist).

Yeah, I'm so political I've filled in my census form this time. The most political act I ever did was watching a party political broadcast. I'm totally not interested. Not interested at all. I don't even know what a fascist is. There you go. So I suppose I shouldn't deny it (laughs). I got accused of being a Nazi once. I said to the paper that I didn't agree with what they did but, you've got to admit it, they looked good, and they did. Didn't they? Those S.S. men looked really good. They were meant to be frightening and they looked the part, which is the perfect manipulation of image over their function. I was trying to explain that that was where the image was used to its full advantage, and why it's important for me to do the same thing,

Is that a bit like Crazies and U.Ds and all that?

Well that all went with the whole image thing of the *Replicas* album, like that hint of something more. I remember Machmen coming from an old Oz magazine. I kept the name but changed the meaning. Machmen in *Replicas* were humanoid machines. They would clone a human skin so it was a machine-man.

How long are going to carry on making records?

Till I get bored.

Have you a contract for a certain number of years?

Yes, but the contract isn't for a time, it's for a number of albums. I think it's seven. If I do two now I don't have to do any for fifty years. But when I'm seventy three, if I decide to do a comeback, I'll have to do the next five albums with WEA. I don't have to do them at a certain time, so I can quit whenever I like. The two live albums don't count. I probably will quit before I do seven albums.

Why did you change your mind and release This Wreckage instead of I Dream of Wires as the last single? Do you think I Dream of Wires wasn't commercial enough to get into the charts?

It probably would have done better than *This Wreckage*. It's more dance-able, there's a big build up and it's more exciting. I don't put out singles for what they're gonna do. Who would have said that *Are 'Friends' Electric?* at five minutes and thirty seconds would have got to number one? Nobody would have expected that in a million years.

What about Vienna? That's just as long.

Vienna to me is a very pretty conventional song. Electronic music is now considered established and no longer considered different. So releasing *Vienna* involved no risk whatsoever. I was going electronic music in the charts two years ago. There was no reason for it not to sell. They'd already had half a hit and so it was already well known. A lot of my fans would buy Ultravox records just because of their connection with me, and because of Billy Currie.

Can you explain the meaning of Remind Me To Smile?

You can't take your own car because it gets wrecked. You go up to London and it gets damaged, especially if people see that it's mine. The whole song is about me. *Remind Me To Smile* is very cynical. When I go out I really enjoy myself just standing in a corner watching things and I'm sick to death of forever being told or asked, 'What's the matter? Why are you miserable tonight?'. I say, 'I'm not miserable. What are you talking about?'. Apparently I don't have a happy expression when I'm out. I don't walk around with a grin on my face. People get the impression that I'm persistently fed up about something which I'm not at all. I just think a lot. It's very hard to stand around with a moronic grin on your face when you're thinking, isn't it?

Which are your favourite songs?

Down in the Park. We Are Glass. And this one that's playing. *(He is referring to a new song which is playing in the background).*

What about other people's songs?

Slow Motion. Ashes to Ashes. Can't Get Used to Losing You by Andy Williams. *Slow Water* by Eno... I could go on forever. *Antmusic*, I think that's brill. I really like that. The trouble with songs is that you like them and then you go off them. There are hundreds of songs that I really like and they always have little memories for me, and they always have.

Did The Beatles play any part in your life?

None whatsoever. Not even a minuscule.

So you felt nothing when John Lennon died?

As much as I feel when anybody dies. The fact that he's in the same business made it a little bit more real. The same as if an aeroplane crashes, I just feel a little more numb than I did before because I'm involved in it.

Someone said that technically and musically your songs are very simplistic. Do you agree with this?

It depends what they mean by simplistic. I use diminished fifths and augmented fourths, which are the same thing, all the time, which is not unique but very rare, although I had no knowledge of that, I was told by someone in the band who's got a music degree. On *Films*, It goes from one time to some really weird time signatures, which is all supposed to be very clever, though I can't claim credit for that because I didn't know that when I wrote it. It just sounds right. If it's simplistic then that (holds up two fingers) to people that can't do it because I can. And if it's that simple why isn't everyone else doing it?

When you started giggling, you said you didn't like it because of the uncertainty of the crowds. Is this still true now?

No, because we have the certainty of the crowds. Now we're big rock stars so we know exactly who's going to come and what they're going to do.

So you think that when you're on stage, the audience is going to like whatever you do?

It's a pretty safe bet, isn't it? It sounds a bit big headed but if you're realistic about it, it's true.

Why did you call Wembley your "Beloved Wembley Arena".

I didn't. Ray Coleman did. When he wrote that article he wasn't quoting me. But I do actually like it. It's got the best atmosphere of any gig in this country.
Most people think exactly the opposite.

Only because it's big, see. Preconceived, that's the trouble with people. If you tell them Berlin is heavy, they go to Berlin and say it's really heavy. Berlin is not heavy. There's no atmosphere in Berlin at all. Don't ever believe any of that shit because that's all it is, shit.

What about the people at the back? I don't know about the stage show this time but...

Oh, Christ, the thing is eighty five feet wide. If you imagine the last stage set it's twice as wide. That's how big it is. There's a bit in the air and there's a bit on the stage. It's huge. Of course they are going to see it. Anyway, they ain't going to stay there for long. They're gonna be up at the front as soon as the thing starts, I hope.

You've often said you feel nervous when the crowd rush up to the front. Do you still feel that? and do you still want them to do it?

Yes. Well, at Wembley there's an 8-feet barrier between the audience and the stage. If anybody is going to jump it they've got to be a kangaroo. That's no problem. I don't like it when they get up on the stage itself, then it's dangerous. For one thing it's dangerous for me and it could ruin it. I don't like having close contact with an audience in terms of having eye contact, when you can see their expressions. I don't like that. I never focus on the first quarter at all during the whole set. I actually did a show at Brighton where a girl got into the pit between me and the audience, took her clothes off, and was there for about three or four minutes before people got her out. I didn't see her once and nobody believes that I honestly didn't see her. The band all saw her but I didn't. It's happened a few times.

How did you go down in America? Was the reaction the same as in England?

Yes.

Did you get a lot of air play in America?

Cars did. When *Telekon* came out they had a little spate of playing album tracks, mainly F.M., not much A.M. play. In America you can break cities one at a time while, over here you break a country. If you break in America you can

break in Boston but not in New York. It's a strange place. I've been really big in the West Coast, fairly big in New York, huge in Canada. I've got platinum albums in Canada.

Because you went to Japan recently but didn't tour, did you go over just to say that you're still around?

I go for that, and because I love the place. I really like it. There's no other country like it. I love the people. I love the manners. You'd have to be there to see what it's like. They actually treat foreigners better than they treat themselves. Over here, a foreigners a foreigner. They bow all the time. They actually say thank you for going to their restaurant. Over here you're lucky if they let you in. If you don't dress right they won't let you in. If it's raining they like to leave you standing outside 'cos they think it's fun. Restaurants over here are diabolical.

Did you like the food?

No, I hate the food.

What did you have out there without any McDonalds?

They've got McDonalds over there. They didn't have McDonalds in the Philippines which bothered me a bit. I don't eat McDonalds that much actually, that's just a joke. I only eat them if I have to. I eat steak most of the time. My diet is very nonexistent really. I never look at menus. I just order sirloin steak, have done for years. I never vary it, just plain steak with french fries. And, when I'm at home, I have fish, chicken, sausages and chips.

What did you think of Australia when you toured over there?

It was good. We spent three nights in Sydney and Newcastle, Brisbane, Adelaide, Melbourne. My girlfriend's Australian, from Sydney. I love the people. Well, no that's not true. I really think a lot of her and her family. I met a lot of really nice Australians like James Freud and Roger (Mason), who did the last tour, he's the blond guy. And I've met a lot of them who aren't so nice. It's just the same as this country. There's very little difference.

After writing songs so long on your own, how did you get on with Robert Palmer? Because you've been quoted as saying that you found it impossible to work with other people.

We didn't actually write a song together. I was only there (in the Bahamas) for three days. The first day I spent looking at the sea. The second and third I was in the studio. That was it. I went in the studio and said, "I don't like the vocal line of that, try this one," and he said, "I don't like that one, try this'. It was like that really. There wasn't really a situation were we sat down for days on end and worked out the notes for a song. I did my bit of it it, the vocal line, and he did his bit. I did the arrangement and he did his part.

Why can't you work with other people?

Because I know exactly what I want.

So other people get in the way?

Yeah, so if anyone else is there putting in his ideas, there's a fair chance their's will be different. That has its problems because other people's ideas may be fresher and better than mine. However, I want to work with Richard Burgess who works with Landscape and Shock. Up until now I've seen no point in working with other people. Maybe I've been so busy trying to establish myself that I haven't wanted anybody else to be interfering with it. And now that I am fairly well established maybe I could take that risk. Maybe I'm strong enough now, or confident enough in my own ability to be able to work with someone else. It could be a number of things, but I'm not really sure why I've had such a thing against it.

What happened to your digital news printout machine?

It took them eighteen months to build it when it should have taken six weeks. We paid them £10,000 for it, and then they said they wanted £18,000.

Will you be having it at Wembley?

No. I haven't got it anymore.

What was it exactly?

You know those things that they wrap around buildings like the Swiss Watch Centre, with all these flashing lights? It was ten foot by ten feet and it would have had images and pictures put on it, like titles. For instance, if it was You Are in My Vision there would have been a big eye that moved across the screen looking at the audience. We were also going to split the screen into two 10x5" screens on either side of the 'T' so you would have had two pairs of eyes that would move across and eventually join up together. But it just didn't work like a lot of things that I was going to do. The intro to the next stage show at Wembley, which I can't tell you because it's a secret, is something that I've always wanted to do ever since I started touring. For some reason I couldn't do it because we didn't have the right stages, etc. but now we can. It's still been a lot of a problem but we've managed to do it now.

Why is it going to be so special?

It's just effective, nothing especially dramatic as far as an intro goes. It's better than just walking on stage from the side.

Do you still go to see gigs yourself?

Not a lot, no. I went to see Queen about five times in Tokyo. I went to see Japan a couple of times and I should have gone to Adam and the Ants last night but I didn't. I like them.

Do you ever get frightened of being recognised?

It's unavoidable being recognised, but I know what you mean. Yes I do but I'm normally looked after by security. I've got a team in case anything starts.

What do you think of old Ultravox in comparison with the new?

It's a more successful and less interesting.

What about John Foxx's solo stuff?

I think Ultravox without Foxx aren't as good and I think Foxx without Ultravox isn't as good. I think they were brilliant together but I don't think they are now. They were really good but they've lost that little bit of magic they had got together. They've lost that mystery, and gained money and fame.

Are you planning to explore the possibilities of using the fourth channel? Does that appeal to you?

T.V. appeals to me but the fourth channel is the same as the first three. Whatever happens on it will be up to someone else.

Yeah, but it might give you the opportunity to do something.

If it does I'll take advantage of it. If it's a music channel I'll write albums for it. If it's a channel that does plays I'll write plays. If it's one that does films, I'll make a film. It depends what it gives me to do. If it does all documentaries I'll probably have a documentary about me flying around the world in September in my little plane. I want to be an adventurer. Come the middle of September, I'll get in my little aeroplane in America and head across the Pacific and go to the Far East, Middle East, Africa, Iceland, Greenland and Alaska and back down to New York again. It should take about three weeks to a month.

Do you find flying a way of escaping from pressures?

You've got to be joking! Being in an aeroplane is not being free. It doesn't give you a sense of freedom, You're concentrating 110 percent on what you're doing, where you are, where the other planes are, etc. Navigation is very very difficult. Being in a plane is very hard work.

Do you find it relaxing?

No, not at all. I wouldn't do it if it was relaxing. I don't agree with relaxing. It doesn't agree with me. Flying isn't an escape, it's an alternative. It doesn't have critics but it has just as much pressures in its own way. But it's a different sort of pressure, the pressure in that is survival. The pressure in this is, well, I couldn't really say but it is certainly different from flying. It's a different sort of strain. I've a little bit of a problem when it comes to survival in living. That's just my Pisces tendencies. They've never been satisfied. I despair a lot, but being a Pisces, even though I'm not into star signs, I begin to think a little more that you're always searching for something. I know I am. I never ever have any idea what it is, and when you get something you never think that that's it. You could get a person or a thing and then that's not it. I thought flying was it but it wasn't.

Do you think you're looking for a line of freedom? For instance, you said once that you wouldn't mind buying an island.

I still do. I still will.

Is that to get away from people, or what?

No. On an island I can do what I want. I can have a gun. I can fly my plane at low level if I want, silly things like that that you might not realise mean something to me. I can do anything with an island. I could be on my own or with people. It would be like having my own country. It sounds all very very storybooky having an island, but they're not that much money. I don't think a million or a million and a half pounds for an island is a lot of money. If I could afford one and a half million pounds in four or five years time I will buy an island. I really will.

Are you going to lose a lot of money at Wembley?

Yes. It's been estimated at the moment at being between thirty or forty thousand.

Does that bother you?

Yeah, of course! (*laughs*) but not enough to not do it. I'd rather make forty thousand but I'm not going to.

Do you think you'll miss touring?

Probably, but then again I miss my dog but it's gone.

You can't bring the dog back but you could start touring again.

It'll never be the same. I could dig my dog up and stuff it and it would be back. IT wouldn't be alive. It's much the same thing. I could do concerts again but it would never be the same. That whole side of the career is over. It's gone. If I ever did it again it would have to be different. It could never be like this again. I don't know whether I'm going to miss the adulation or whether I'm going to miss that way of life, 'cos that way of life is fun. You have a lot of fun, but sometimes its sordid. However, it's a lot of fun. You're with the people that you like and it's like a party that just rolls around countries. I think I'm gonna miss that more than… you see, if you take notice of all the adulation and all the screaming, I think that it's likely that you're gonna get a bit of an ego problem and so, to not get that, which I try and avoid, you have to not take any notice of all the screaming and fantasies and you're the object for them. It's not lasting. I'm like a pregnant woman who has a craving for Mars bars. I'm the Mars bar to the fans, that's all, and it won't last. That's how I see it, and for that reason I don't take much notice of the adulation, so I don't get much out of it. You see?

You've often said that you hate crowds.

I hate being in them.

Is that since you became famous or before?

Before. I like it sometimes. I've been to concerts and the crowds have been great and there's been a great atmosphere and I've enjoyed it, but as a rule, I find being pressed together with a lot of people a little worrying, a little frightening. Not so much now as I used to. Just after I became famous I had a really very paranoid in-

secure period of about a year and a half which now I'm just starting to get out of somewhat. But my opinions on those things are changing now.

What about the lyrics for Cars?

What do you mean?

Well they say you feel safe on your own, locked up.

'Safest of all!' it says, quote, 'When I'm in a car I feel safest of all', which is true isn't it? I mean, if somebody starts attacking you with a knife would you rather be on the street or in a car? I mean, that's a silly example because it's very rarely that you get attacked by somebody with a knife. But, remember, I'm a writer and I'm allowed to have a poetic licence (*laughs*), I just take things to extremes when I write about them because if you don't it's not that interesting to write about. I mean, going down to the shops isn't very exciting unless you get attacked on the way. Then it becomes interesting. That's the thing about *Replicas*. It's very unlikely in that extreme sense, but it's interesting.

In an old interview it said that you had to be in a room that had two doors to feel safe, so that you could get out. Is that a lie?

Yeah, that's a lie. I mean, look at this room. It's only got one door. I like there to be a way out of something, that's true. There's a few silly things that I still worry about, like being bugged or spied upon, that's always been in me, but the music papers exaggerated it a hell of a lot. I exaggerated it myself and when this happened it bothered me quite a lot. I think now I'm getting slightly more used to it. I'm getting a more realistic view.

Do you feel that you've achieved your ambition, because you've just said that there was always something else to get?

What I said was, I never quite get what I'm looking for because when I get what I'm looking for it's no longer what I'm looking for. I wanted to be famous, got it. When I got it I realised that it wasn't what I wanted at all. That's what I mean. The only thing I'm worried about is that I really want to get married, and one of my biggest fears is that when I get married it isn't going to be what I wanted, or it isn't going to be what I thought it was gonna be. That worries me a lot. That, that constant reach for something is going to apply to my private life as well as my business.

It's been said that when it comes to record sales that you're successful but when it comes to yourself you're not. Do you agree?

I think in my personal life and my character I'm useless. I'm very bad at relationships. I tend to be cynical and totally distrusting of everything and everybody except my family. So, in terms of my social success I'm a complete failure. When it comes to business I'm very very successful. People often say to me when I get fed up at times, 'Why should you get fed up? You've got everything you could ever want, or you could get anything you want because of the money'. And I try to explain to them that I've got virtually nothing of what I want. It's very hard to try to explain to you really. I would like to be married with two kids, to love somebody, to trust somebody and that, to me, is very very important, much more important that this. If I could have one or the other, there's no hesitation about which I'd have, and it wouldn't be this.

Do you think more about what you're doing and about what you're going to be doing next?

I think about what I'm doing at lot. I don't know about more. It's more serious now in terms of if I make a wrong move then I've got more to lose. I worry about it now because there's am awful lot of people that rely upon it other than me, like my family - they don't depend on it totally, but it's certainly an advantage to them that I stay around. You see, in terms of fame I don't get much out of it, but I need it. It's like a paradox. I don't like being recognised when I'm out but I've got a white corvette. I don't want to die but I fly aeroplanes and I've got a powerboat that takes off at the slightest wave, and I've got a hovercraft that I crash all the time, and I drive fast. Everything I do has an equal and opposite feeling. There's more. I'm very very shy and yet I can go on stage. I'm emotionally unstable almost to the point of treatment and yet I can handle the whole business with precision that is almost mechanical.

Are you pressured by your label at all? And In what way?

Yeah, sometimes. Like this (He holds up a cassette of *Moral*). They want a brand new single. I want that. It's a new version of an old one.

Have you got the power to do what you want?

Yeah, they would never tell me what to put out because they know they wouldn't get anything. Now I'm in a position to say that but, before I was just being stubborn. Now I'm more important to them.

What did they think about you giving up touring?

Well, they know what the rest of the plan is so they're not worried now. They were very very worried. We had this big meeting were the directors and all the other sections of the company got together. I had to say to them exactly what I had in mind because they were worried. It all got very dodgy at one point. I just had to explain to them what was going on and why I was stopping. It's okay now.

Can you tell us a bit about the next album? The titles, for instance?

Yes. The title of the album is *Dance*. The tracks are so far: *Slow Car to China, Dance, A Subway Called You, She's Got Claws, We Take Mystery to Bed*, and there may be one called *1930's Rust*. I'm not sure about that one. *Exhibition* and *Stories* are two B-sides.

What happened to A Game Called Echo and I'm a Driver?

I never finished them. There was one called *We Have a Technical*. That was back in the days of *Replicas* about one of the Machmen that went off the rails. A Technical was a Machman that wasn't right, and a Random was Technical that went completely wrong. You see, a Machman was a machine and, when it went Technical they went out and got it. When a Machman went Random it took over itself and went off zapping people all over the place.

What do you think about the argument that when you use a drum machine you kill off your records?

I only use a drum machine on three records out of nearly seventy. *Remind Me To Smile* has got a drum machine, *I'm an Agent* has, *Remember I was Vapour* has got a drum machine on it. Nothing on *The Pleasure Principle* or *Replicas* has got drum machines. So that sorts that one out.

NUMAN BAILS OUT

GARY NUMAN is retiring from the concert platform, he tells us, to concentrate on recording and filming. He bids farewell to live audiences (just like Sinatra and Elton did at one stage) on Monday and Tuesday, when he plays Wembley Arena.

THE LONG GOODBYE

GARY NUMAN has confirmed details of his farewell concerts at London's Wembley Arena. There will be two shows, on April 27th and 28th. Tickets will be available from the Arena box office or via the usual agents from February 16th. Meanwhile, postal applications can be made to Wembley Box Office, Wembley, Middlesex HA9 0DW. Cheques and postal orders — tickets are £5 or £4 — should be made payable to "Wembley Stadium", with SAEs enclosed.

MALE SINGER OF THE YEAR

1. GARY NUMAN
2. STING
3. DAVID BOWIE
4. Paul Weller
5. Adam Ant
6. Cliff Richard
7. Suggs
8. John Lennon
9. Terry Hall
10. Jona Lewie

The only thing Gazza won last year was Twerp Of The Year so he'll no doubt be glad that this time his mountains of votes have been enough to capture a worthy category. Last year's winner, Sting, occupies second place purely because twenty or so fans didn't bother to mail off their form. (Stir, stir.)

Out of the running this year are Bob Geldof, Joe Jackson, John Lydon and Elvis Costello to be replaced by Adam, Suggs, Jona Lewie and the late John Lennon. Once again Cliff Richard makes it, proving that this isn't anything like as faddy a business as many people reckon.

Gary Numan

Numan's final gigs

GARY Numan has now finalised plans for his final live British concerts, recently predicted for Wembley in April.

The shows are now confirmed for Wembley Arena on April 27 and 28, and tickets are on sale from February 16 priced £5 and £4.

Tickets are available from the box office and usual agents, or by post from Wembley Arena Box Office, Wembley, Middlesex, with cheques or postal orders payable to Wembley Stadium.

These shows mark the official end of Numan's live touring — he last circulated the UK in September — in favour of his plans to work exclusively on various recording and film projects.

Gary, in the days when being a robot and carrying a toy panther was cool...

OFFICIAL GARY NUMAN TOUR POSTER
from Dick Wallis Photography

made available by mail order especially to Smash Hits readers

Full colour portrait poster measures 23" x 16" and costs only £1.00 plus 25p postage & package per order. A complete brochure with details of all photos available comes free with each order.

GARY NUMAN

WEMBLEY 1981

A DIFFERENT KIND OF LIFE
for Gary

GARY NUMAN believes there is more to life than being a pop superstar... As he has decided to become a pilot as well.

The gaunt singer with the pale complexion has sold nearly five million records over the last two years, and become so rich that he need never work again. But for Gary it is not enough.

He explains: "You don't get much respect from everyday people as a pop star.

"Even if you're stinking rich the average guy will respect you more if you tell him you're a pilot. And that's the kind of respect I want."

Final

Six months ago Gary announced he was giving up concert tours and last week gave his farewell show at Wembley. He still plans to make records, but hopes to explore other pursuits as well.

He insists that unlike David Bowie or Frank Sinatra his decision to give up concerts is final.

Gary says: "When I was 18 I sat down and worked out I was going to be famous. Now the first part

A NEW direction for rock idol Gary Numan.

by JAMES JOHNSON

of my plan is complete and I want to move on.

"Of course there will be times when I will miss going on stage. The last show was very emotional for me.

"Afterwards I had to go away and be alone for a few moments. I shed a few tears."

At the age of 22, he discusses fame and fortune like a gnarled veteran.

"I expected it to be much more glamourous really," he remarks. "Of course you can have that

kind of life if you want, but it's only fun for a brief period.

"I think becoming well-known is rather like sex. The first time you get there it is nothing like you expected. You have to learn what to get out of it and what to avoid."

Gary talks enthusiastically about marriage.

"Down to earth things like marriage and children mean an awful lot to me," he observes.

"I'd give up the whole fame and entertainment thing tomorrow if I

thought I couldn't have a family life one day.

"I'm still going to leave it for a few years yet though. At the moment I don't even have a steady girl-friend."

He has had no qualms about making the most of the huge sums of money that have come his way. As a result he now owns an airplane, several cars, a powerboat and even a hovercraft.

Trip

"My main ambition at the moment is to fly round the world. The trip is going to take three weeks and I plan to stop off and see friends on the way.

"I've always liked the idea of being an adventurer. Rock'n'roll is the closest I've been to adventure so far. Now I want to try something else as well."

Daily Mirror, May 1981

Below: Gary Numan, perhaps the first superstar of the synthesizer.

Please push no more

After the end — a new beginning. Exclusive GARY NUMAN interview by Ray Coleman. Pix: Tom Sheehan

Melody Maker, May 2, 1981

Written by Numan's first biographer, this article probably did more harm than most in creating a negative image of Numan in the press and among non-fans of his music. The main moment of 'Let Them Eat Cake' is when Numan is quoted as saying he won't be giving up music because he needs the money to buy and fly planes. Remember, this was a time when Thatcher was at war with the working class and the creative industries, and was tearing open the safety net that caught the honest poor. There were a lot of struggling workers and struggling musicians. It was unknown for a figurehead in any art to reduce his art to 'product' (Gene Simmons did and does and gets away with it because all he is selling is 'fun').

The article starts off on quite the wrong foot with Numan downplaying his achievements in music and taking pride on his abilities at marketing (always a suspect area at best), before saying that he owes his fans nothing and they can always fuck off and see Adam Ant. For the most part, they did. (He doesn't *say* 'fuck off' but that's the implication).

IN THE END, it was pure show business. This week, after three concerts at Wembley Arena which had sold out within hours of the tickets going on sale, Gary Numan retired from live performances after being inside the pop cage for just over two years. He won't change his mind because he's a man who sees things in black and white.

So showbiz it was, right down to the last grand "I quit!" flourish, the wonderful spectacle of his farewell concerts, the emotional self-examination of his decision as the irrevocable nature of his statements hit him and the great day dawned.

And to be sure, Numan will be in showbiz for the rest of his life as his route switches gear into films and video-making, books and records, flying aeroplanes and tapping the public's tastes in a variety of creative shapes.

"I always wanted to be a pop star," this quietly-spoken, painfully shy guy told me just before the Wembley concerts. "Some people said: OK, but remember you'll only last two years. So I've had my two years. Now I'm getting out of it before the public kicks me out. The public will get by without me on a concert stage. They'll still have Adam Ant and Ultravox."

Gary Numan is not a million mental miles from Frank Sinatra, not a thousand animated miles from Liberace or Gary Glitter, not a few hundred spiritual miles from David Bowie or the late, great Marc Bolan. One towering difference separates him from most of them in their love of the greasepaint and hunger for audience applause: Numan is overwhelmingly independent.

"What about your duty to the fans who have made you famous?" people have kept asking him in the last few months. His reply has been consistent: he owed the fans nothing and they owed him not a penny. He saw his relationship with them as a purely business arrangement.

He had provided them with something which they bought because they liked it at a certain moment. This did not give them any rights whatever to control his next move or his life. Similarly, he could demand nothing of the public. For concerts, at least, he had decided not to put himself on offer ever again.

If Numan sounds from all that like a clinical manipulator telling his fans, in the words of one of his best songs, "Please Push No More", he has only himself to blame. He plotted his entry into fame with a cold logic, and whatever those of us who respond sympathetically to his music may say, his stance has been a cheerless reflection of the bleak days in which we live.

Mechanised doom, synthesiser-laden songs bereft of love but with a haunting mirror up to the misery of the clapped-out society Numan envisioned when he hit upon his style, the titles encapsulate the whole scenario better than any of the word-spinning critics could ever hope to bounce from: "Me, I Disconnect From You", "This Wreckage", "The Aircrash Bureau", "Remind Me To Smile", "Remember I Was Vapour", "I Die You Die", "Are 'Friends' Electric", "I Dream Of Wires", "Cry, The Clock Said".

Two years ago, with Britain's unemployment graph inexorably rising towards its current total of two and half million, Numan hit the savage mood perfectly. Desperation, frustration, alienation, inflation — Numan sold sadness, which was not difficult as he's a doleful introvert by nature.

He's extremely modest about his achievements in

cont...

music, but not about his ability to *market* himself during a crucial time in the evolution of rock: that is to say, little was happening, and nobody was exploiting the obvious trend to synthesiser-based music.

"I wasn't first to see the synthesiser being so influential," he says quietly. "Not first by a long way. I was, though, the only one who saw that the public wanted a synthesiser *star*. So I worked on it."

His facial features freezing his vulnerability, his smile a very rare (and therefore special) crack, his wistful speaking voice often only a breath away from crying, he immediately touched a chord within the fluttering hearts of 14-year-old schoolgirls and 17-year-old male computer trainees. Once away with the beautiful, ethereal number one hit single "Are 'Friends' Electric", he played the trump card over and over.

Two years or more later and the space shuttle has returned to earth, bruised but not battered. The landing was bumpy, but a celebration, even so. The aircraft could fly again because technically everything is in order, but the pilot thinks it's time to ground it, adapt it, shoot off for a fresh star.

This analogy should not be taken too lightly. Numan, a qualified pilot, runs his own single-engined aeroplane based at Blackbushe, and plans in September to fly around the world, as a kind of Sheila Scott of rock 'n' roll.

Fiercely ambitious as a pilot — as the Wembley audiences

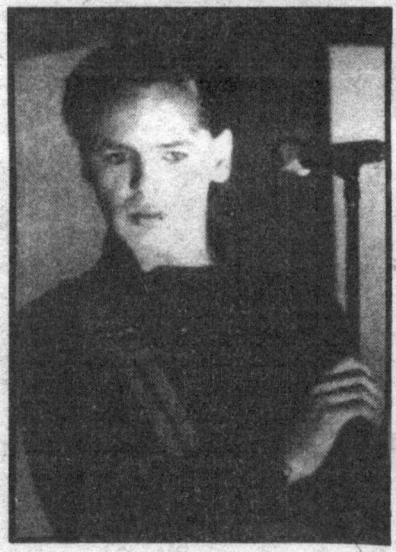

saw from the filmed backdrop of him flying gracefully around Hampshire — Numan also has plans to launch his own fleet of planes as a taxi service around Britain, based at either Herne or Blackbushe airport.

"There's no feeling in the world like flying your own plane," he said. "Oh, well, maybe a crowd yelling and screaming for you, and the realisation that you're famous and all that. I'm going to miss it, I'd be lying if I said otherwise. But I know I'm making the right decision."

Later that night, he was to expose deeper reasons for his decision to get off the stage. Numan is bitterly upset at the torrents of abuse, hatred, jealousy and misunderstanding that has surrounded his success. He's also angry with the expectations of the public now that he's a star.

He'd always hankered for fame, but was horrified at what people expected him to do in return for it. Demands for money, attempts to portray him as some kind of monster . . . Numan was furious about the whole charade.

WE MET at Shepperton Studios four days before the first Wembley concert. Rehearsal time, and a mighty painstaking, exhausting ritual it turned out to be. Two full run-throughs per day of the two-and-a half-hour show, plus dealing with the Greater London Council on safety matters and the logistical problems of putting on such an elaborate exhibition of lighting were giving Gary and his band a tiring time.

His father, Tony was there, of course. A sane, no-nonsense former van driver for British Airways, he brings to his role as Gary's manager an iron determination to stick to timekeeping schedules, and not let anything past his eagle-eyes that would offend his son, or not be in his business interests.

Beryl, his mother, was there too. Just as she travels everywhere around the world with Gary and Tony, she was at Shepperton, bustling about quietly and effectively,

dispensing big very British mugs of tea to the musicians and crew, concerning herself with Gary's wardrobe and getting cross about the special little fur jacket stolen from Gary at Sydney airport, and the irreplaceable hat he had apparently had pinched from his Range Rover.

"He's too trusting of people," says Beryl. "He just puts things down anywhere and honestly expects them to be there when he returns. People are amazing — they just take anything as souvenirs." Always ready to nourish the needs of the entourage with beans on toast or packeted soups, Beryl is the epitome of the proud Mum whose son realised her ambition.

She wears a permanent sunny smile of contentment. "I get ever so excited when rehearsals like this start and I see what's being worked on and all the trouble they're putting into it," she says. "Even here, in this dirty old hall . . ." Among many duties, she is Gary's hairdresser.

Numan did, indeed, work fastidiously on his farewell concerts. All the graphic ideas were his, implemented by a company called Gaslight, but creatively the brainchild of the school failure named Gary Webb who dreamed of this kind of lavishness when he flicked through the telephone directory in search of a more charismatic surname, chose Numan, and went gold.

The spectacular show, which even featured two lighting technicians being lowered from on high to the stage in capsules amid tons of dry ice and a mass of lighting effects, was a combination of three ideas: the "Pleasure Principle" tour, the "Telekon" tour, and now a bevy of new additions that would enable Gary to say goodbye to the concert platform in breathtaking style. He says he lost £150,000 on the concerts.

And if you think that the concert finale gave way to a rich idol flying off and lazing in the sun next day, counting his millions and laughing that he didn't have to work anymore, you would be underestimating the drive to work that Gary Numan (and most successful artists) have to retain.

The day after the final concert, Numan was in the studio, completing the last track of his new album. Called "Dance", it will be out in September, accompanied, of course, by a video.

All the sour cynics who insist on criticising what they can't understand, who cling to that curiously British custom of greeting success with envy or hatred and resentment, will have to get used to the fact that Numan will be around. He's just giving up touring, not his involvement with music and film-making.

Shrewdly he has realised that it's best to quit this part of his role "on a high", rather than let the concert-going public weary of him.

On the way to the BBC for a radio interview, Gary reflected on his recent trip to Japan, when he combined a holiday with some promotional work like radio and magazine interviews.

He'd also taken up sword fighting, and became very friendly with Queen who were playing a week of concerts at Tokyo's Budokan Theatre. As a result drummer Roger Taylor had guested on two tracks of Gary's next LP.

Visits to Japan make enormous impressions on rock stars, but Gary's reactions was typically reserved: "I love the Japanese but I found the whole thing about the place suspicious. Any people who are that polite have to have an ulterior motive. Nobody is that polite, not to complete strangers.

"I still think they are lovely people but I'm more cautious about the whole Japanese thing than I used to be. But I loved the place. If ever I had to go anywhere, I'd go to Japan." To live? "Yes, maybe, if I ever moved away from England. There or Los Angeles. I could stay there."

Did this mean he was slowly falling out of love with Britain? "No, I think England is very quickly falling out of love with me. I just don't feel right any more here."

Musically or personally? "Musically I don't think I fit in anywhere at the moment. I don't listen to anything any more. I don't try to find out what trends are coming and beat them to it now. I heard one or two comments about the New Romantics trend and someone said I was doing that kind of thing two years ago.

"It may or not be true, but I don't want to be thought of as

starting anything or finishing anything. I just want to have been somewhere and then not been somewhere. That's all I want — not to be a part of the fashion scene.

"See, I can go on now and do whatever I like as long as I don't join in or try to start a new direction. I've done all that. I want no tags to weigh me down. It puts me out on my own a little bit but I think it's for the best you know."

T HE CONCERTS, he affirmed, were positively the end of his touring career. "I have thought an awful lot about it, but I haven't changed my mind. I'll never say that I won't miss it because I will. But it is for the best.

"I can't make a film while I'm touring all the time. It drags you back from progressing your career. Maybe that's why David Bowie only tours every two years — it gives him a chance to catch up again. I didn't realise until now that that could be the reason.

"In any case, it will be good to get out of that routine. Two years doesn't sound like a long time but it seems like an awfully long time when you're actually doing it — touring, making records, flying here, there and everywhere.

"It was fun though, I did enjoy it. The Wembley crowds will get the best out of me that I've ever done before, and I hope to get the best goodbye from them that I could wish for."

His immediate project afterwards was to try to augment completion of his album with the making of an ambitious video cassette to link up with it. "I'd like to get back into creating stories and showing them as videos," he said.

"See, I can use these stage shows and break them down and turn them into buildings or sets or anything I want for videos and actually keep them uniform, without them being all the same. This, I think, was one of the problems with the Blondie video. It was a little bit samey — although it was good that they did it, but now we have all got to start to take video further.

"I also want to make a film, and for that I want to write it if you don't keep taking a chance and trying new things, there's no point in being around, really."

There was already a theme in his mind for the film. "It'll be set in the Thirties, not our Thirties, but somebody else's Thirties, and the film will be half looking backwards, half futurist. The main character will be taken from the main character I adopt on my new album. I'm already very excited about the new phase in my work in films and videos."

Eventually, anyway, he had to come a cropper. "I've done all right so far but one day I'm going to do something that doesn't work out well. I'm ready for it."

The end of touring and his change of direction in album-making also marked his split with the band Dramatis who had been with him for two years: Chris Payne (keyboards), Russell Bell (guitar and keyboards), Paul Gardiner (bass), Denis Haines (keyboards), and Cedric Sharpley (drums).

They have each been busy on other work and, says Numan, they have accepted the wind-up without rancour: "I think they're looking forward to the freedom. They are a few rungs up the ladder through our all being associated together, and they're in a much better position to go out on their own.

"They did an interview on the radio the other day and said they'd been a bit frustrated by being in my band, which surprised me because I've always encouraged them to go and do other sessions. They've never been restricted by me. Maybe they felt awkward.

"Anyway, now they have been behind me, in my shadow, they can go out and have a taste of it all themselves, perhaps. I wish them all a lot of luck — I like them all, and we've never had an argument in two years, which is amazing during all those tours. I really value that.

"They've stuck by me through an awful lot, because a lot of the mud that gets thrown at me they get themselves. Because they've been with me and I get a lot of criticism, they've caught it, too, and people have wrongly said they cannot play. Well, they are very good and now they will be able to prove it on their own. They can all do it."

Ah, the demon criticism. Gary was still recoiling from the barrage of abuse heaped by the negative critics who reviewed his new albums, "Living Ornaments 1979" and "1980". They had been analysed as a marketing plot to mark his exit from live shows by selling a lot of copies.

"I thought it was packaged so well. Of *course* I want to sell thousands of copies, and of *course* we all work at the record company to that goal. But I've always given people what they wanted at any time, and that's why I have sold myself well.

"Here, with the live LPs, I gave people two single albums at a maximum price of £4 so

they could afford them. And that's been misconstrued as solely an intention to sell more. Why don't people recognise the fact that now, more people can afford it?

"If giving people what they want is wrong, in the eyes of certain people, then to hell with the lot of them."

As the car neared the BBC, Gary contemplated the Wembley final thrusts, and said: "It seems one of the most exciting periods of my life is finishing. I must have the shows videoed so I can see who I was at a certain point in my life. I want everything I can possibly have to remember it. This is the end of my first-ever big dream . . ."

Difficult though it may be to comprehend, the Wembley concerts lost him about £150,000 but he expects the record sales generated by the shows to eventually bring back that cash.

Was he now very rich, to the point of not needing to work again? "No, I'm sure I will have to make more albums to keep the money coming in, although I don't see any real problems . . . I could probably retire on royalties to come from past glories, but that wouldn't be right for me. I don't want to stop making records.

"And anyway, I need the money for my aeroplane business. It costs £60,000 or £80,000 for a decent twin-engined aeroplane these days. £150 to £200 an hour to run, not including the pilot."

TO RADIO 1 and studio B15 for the recording of last Sunday's phone-in show of that title, hosted by the garrulous Adrian Love. The pre-show warm-up in the BBC bar, mingling cosily with the production team, is lost on Gary, who drinks only Coke.

An opinionated producer advances the theory to us all that marriage is a dangerous institution, and Numan retorts that marriage and having children definitely figures in his plan to ensure a full and balanced life. To the studio, by which time Gary is relaxed and happily dealing with the predictable barrage of questions from young fans phoning in from all parts of Britain.

"What did you feel like when you got your first number one, Gary?"

"Nothing changed. There was not a Rolls Royce suddenly outside my front door and there wasn't suddenly a lot of money. That came later. I was knocked out and jumped up and down for a few minutes then went back to doing nothing special. It was an anti-climax."

"Gary, do you think being famous has changed you and if so in what way?"

DISGUSTED

"I don't think I've changed. Other people's attitudes to me has changed and sometimes I've been disgusted by the way people's feeling towards me have come across. They think I'm not a person, or something, just because I'm a rock star."

"You seem a very hard person, or did when you began . . ."

"Oh, I'm told I'm harder now. I don't think I'm awkward but I suppose I can seem hard. I just know what I want and I set out to get it, and I know how to."

"Did you set out to wear the black gear to suit a moody image?"

"No, it just looked good."

"Why are you giving up touring?"

"Well, I started off wanting to be a rock star and now I am one and I want to be an ex-rock star."

Two fans in the studio asking questions with all the aplomb of professionals, Linda Eleman (15) from Morden, Surrey and Denise Hawkins (16) from Barton St David, Somerset, gave Gary a rose. Everyone admired his grey leather coat which he told them came from Reflections in Kensington, and cost between £150 and £200. The sincerity of his personality made him a lot of friends at the Beeb and among the fans.

But back in his Daimler, on the journey back to Shepperton for yet another rehearsal, he sank back slightly into that introspection that never seems far away.

He was, I said, surely aware that many people doubted his seriousness about retirement from concerts, and dismissed it as a publicity stunt. He'd be back, they said, as surely as Frank Sinatra and Gary Glitter couldn't resist the temptation to applause.

"No, I'll have to stick to it," he said after some thought. "The biggest of my desires in life so far is to stop and it's not going to be easy. I enjoy it when a crowd goes mad, I really do, but just because I'm giving up touring doesn't rule out TV, for example.

"I know some of the fans may think they've been used, or something – that's what gets to me most, not the decision to stop so much. Because that's my business, my decision. But when they start blaming me for wanting to plan my own life . . ."

DEMAND

He reiterated again his belief in the star-and-fan relationship. "We shouldn't demand so much of each other, the star or the fan," he said finally. "I should be grateful to them and they to me for offering them something they wanted to enjoy, and that's it.

"They don't own me, and just as they have a perfect right to reject what I sing, I have a perfect right not to sing it. Look, if I died they'd say I was a great martyr and accept that I could not do any more concerts. Do I have to die or can I make my own decision?"

On Tuesday night and into Wednesday morning, a party was held to mark Gary Numan's retirement from live performances. It was held at his favourite London restaurant in which he has spent many happy hours in the company of kindred spirits during these past two years.

The restaurant is called Legends.

THE real stars of this show were Nick Fisher and Alan Wild, who were responsible for the staging.

Seventy-two sheets of Perspex, 1,692 light bulbs, 300 theatre lights, and three tons of other suspended lighting going up and down over Gary Numan's head like the Venue disco set (only all the lights work!); electric hoists to raise and lower it, a ton of aluminium, three radio-controlled robots, a remote-controlled car from which Numan sang one of his many encores . . . the list is endless.

All this for what we are informed is to be his last public appearance after a professional life of a mere four years – two years, if you deduct the Tubeway Army period.

To be honest, he needs all that hardware. As a charismatic figure for the Eighties, he shares this era's general air of drabness made up of fag-ends of nostalgia, wrapped up in a boiler-suited superhero persona which is pure Marvel Comics.

The way he strolls around the stage has the studied casualness of a Frank Sinatra,

and hearing the massed sub-teen girls behind me squeal with delight brought back memories of an attitude to the artist-as-demigod which I thought had died with Beatlemania. I doubt if there was a dry pair of knickers in the house.

These are working class kids with their feet, I'd guess, fairly firmly on the ground – as distinct from the art school crowd that follow Roxy and the would-be drones who affect the new romanticism – and under the white pancake, blusher and eye-liner, the faces are individual people, dressing up to give the star a mirror image to gaze upon, but seemingly aware that it's all a game. I wish the Antpeople, for instance, shared this crowd's worldly wisdom.

Without it, this would be a frightening affair indeed, a true-life ritual straight out of "Privilege", a movie which in many ways anticipates the dragooned theatricality of much modern rock, making it potentially a modern-day equivalent to Nuremberg. But in the end, the crowd shows its enthusiasm, not hysteria.

He is the android, not they.

If Numan had a wider repertoire of gesture, a greater emotional range, if he communicated anything beyond his simple *presence*, if his songs addressed themselves to any of the problems affecting his audience, a sizeable section of whom might well have paid for their tickets with saved-up dole money, his power could be truly phenomenal.

As it is, if he holds to his avowed intention to quit the live stage – and that's a big "if" – he'll remain an interesting might-have-been, which is just as well.

– KARL DALLAS

Karl Dallas makes an interesting observation that Numan's audience is working class. It is something I have observed over the years, to the extent that it was a genuine surprise to hear a middle class voice in the crowd when he played London's Royal Festival Hall in 2015. I'm told by Jim Napier, an American fan who has travelled the world watching Numan concerts, that that is not true of Numan's audiences in the States, where Numan's fan-base is drawn more broadly from the working and the professional classes. Numan's failure to attract middle class fans in the UK (particularly in the mainstream media) was a contributing factor to his commercial decline after The Machine Quartet. A fascinating sociological study could be made into the probably uniquely working class composition of Numan's enduring UK fan-base, particularly when looked at in tandem with the dual social phenomena of the positive and progressive working class response to Numan and his machine music during the 1979-1981 period, and the violently negative middle class response to the man, his music and that phenomenal impact on the working classes. The title could be *Luddites Under The Looking Glass*.

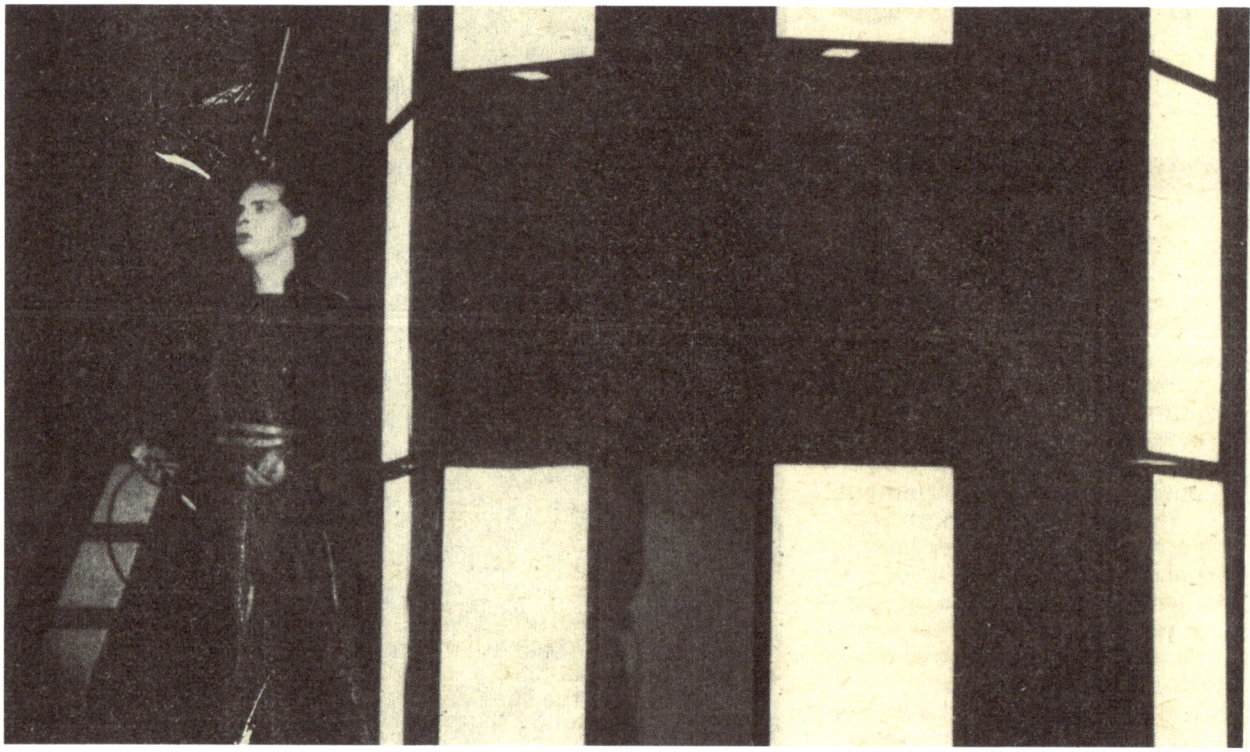

ARE ENDS PATHETIC?

GARY NUMAN
Wembley Arena

By Sunie

WELCOME TO the ultimate rock melodrama: the Farewell Gigs. The Star has been on your radio, on your wall, on your record player, in your heart, and now — he's going to leave you! Quick, rush out and buy those concert tickets, prepare for a huge emotional goodbye, tearful demands for fifth encores, etc, etc. Oh Gary!

Our hero appears amidst much dry ice and launches into 'This Wreckage'. Surrounded by a costly stage set of screens and podiums and some very impressive lighting, his complete lack of stage presence becomes embarrassingly apparent. He moves badly too, roaming around the stage because he knows he can't dance, mincing and pouting and finally looking so awkward and absurd that he wins you over not with charisma but with pathos.

His musicians comprise drummer, guitarist and bass player, all behind the Star, and two synth players in booths on opposite sides of the stage. They move efficiently through some standard Numan fodder, and only 'Me I Disconnect From You' with its guitary sound, stands out at all. When we come to 'Airplane' a welcome instrumental bursting with percussion and power chords, Gary slips off for a costume change, a screen is lowered and we're shown a home movie of Gary flying his plane. Laugh? I almost . . .

He re-emerges in white leather and does a number inside a cage of purple neon tubes, followed by a spectacular 'Every Day I Die' abetted by two masked and predictably robotic dancers and spotlights playing over the audience.

Whatever his failings, the boy is no cheapskate. The trappings become more and more fantastic. The entire lighting rig lowers then raises itself again during 'Films', the three Shock girls waft about in scanty Barbarella-style costumes during Erik Satie's 'Trois Gymnopaedies' and smoke bombs detonate at the beginning of 'Cars'. During 'I Dream Of Wires', your scribe begins to experience a feeling of being trapped inside a giant Space Invaders machine . . .

On to 'The Joy Circuit', with its frenzied violins, and halfway through, in the one truly inspired set-piece of the evening, Nash the Slash appears in all his awful bandaged glory and the fiddling gets quite hysterical. When he leaves the stage the audience's cheers are as much for him as for Numan. What a scene-stealer!

'I Die You Die' is the "closer", but Nash and the back-up boys are soon back for a lengthy new instrumental piece.

GARY NUMAN: *"that's me lot."*

Then Gary's off again, to return in what appears to be a Thunderbirds invalid carriage, from which he renders 'Down In The Park' as it spins him about the stage. The Numan torso is bared for 'My Shadow In Vain', an atypically rocky song whose syncopation is unnervingly reminiscent of 'My Sharona'. Then there's 'Please Push No More', 'Are Friends Electric' (screams) and 'We Are Glass'.

Credit where it's due. The shortcomings of Numan's music and of his appearance (he wants to be the sinister Count but always looks more like Igor) are compensated by the lavish trappings which surround him. He gives his audience their money's worth and more. It's as impossible to dislike him as it is to take his sub-Bowie posturing seriously.

Goodbye Gary. See you again soon.

Phew, you'd managed the snide and the sniggers, Sunie, but I thought for a moment you weren't going to say he's a pale imitation of Bowie. Instead of starting with that, like you've been shown (and probably been told) you saved it for the penultimate paragraph. You're so clever, Sunie. And you know you are writing nonsense, so you hide behind a pseudonym and, in doing so, you reach the trough of your ambition - you help to lay the foundation for what will become known as Trolling.

His last bow(ie).

A reference to Bowie in the cropped off caption? How clever. Alas, when Bowie tried to do this kind of big show, six-years-later, he called it *The Glass Spider Tour* and he fell on his arse. A glass spider going up against Numan's set inspired by the spaceship from *Close Encounters*? There was only ever going to be one winner. I saw the Bowie show in Boston. Peter Frampton was in the backing band to give Bowie much needed musical muscle and additional star power. Frampton was then the biggest selling live performer in America. In addition to the failings of the concept of the glass spider stage set, "Er, the leg's change colour", Bowie phoned his performance in, perhaps thinking that the stage set could do the work for him? The 'perm' in the tag-line is missing an 'anent'.

Gary Numan

Wembley Arena

DESPITE the eloquence of Nick Kent's write-off last week; one would be hard put to pretend that Gary Numan's farewell concerts at Wembley were anything but stunning.

Kent is right, of course. Gary is (or can we now say was?) just a funny little space cadet playing with ideas and images too big for his astro-booties. We can take it further: his derivation from Bowie is more than pale imitation, since his whole appeal is based on reducing the master to a pale, melancholy little boy, a child born into a soulless, inhuman present and hiding himself in a self-constructed toyland of the future which never comes under threat from the real adult world.

Gary Numan was authentic for anyone who hadn't advanced beyond this stage themselves. Nevertheless, even though it may fairly be said that he presented the acceptable face of futurism before futurism itself had come into being, he was an influence — witness the presence in a by no means capacity audience of grizzled Richard Burgess and natty Peter Murphy of Bauhaus. Many had come to wave a sincere farewell. Above all, Numan knew how to stage a great show, and not even the cheapness of his music could prevent him from getting away with it.

Thus his farewell from the stage is to be regretted. The show commenced with Shock, in whose tedious sexist antics Numan appears to have discerned some merit. Rampant, lavish females gyrate at the feet of muscular, domineering men; only Tic and Toc prevent the thing from becoming the choreography of a heavy metal album cover. But then Tic and Toc, standing with fluorescent light beams at the side of the stage on 'Angel Face', are just token eunuchs.

After a wait of only half an hour, the massive arena darkened and dry ice was pumped into the audience from behind the enormous screen which concealed the set. A terrific opening: two spacemen climbed aboard hydraulic lifts flashing with red lights and were raised to a position above the stage from which they could direct further lights. The stage glowed a sinister red. Finally, the screen was itself raised, and a vast circular relay of light was lowered in its place, forming a kind of crown over the stage. Out of the haze came 'This Wreckage'.

It was the largest, most spectacular stage set I've ever seen. No wonder the boy is retiring from live performance; this kind of extravaganza must eat up the best part of a month's income. But in the meantime, what's wrong with extravagance? As a kind of futurist expansion of Bowie's '78 set, it works on the principle of bars and boxes of light which are programmed with varying arrangements and colours. One never tires of watching it because each number brings a new arrangement of light, position, and colour.

Numan's songs are the barest outlines of tunes, but through the sheer quality of sound on stage he gets away with it. Every number is rendered note perfect, and every sound comes over with crystal clarity: the icy lacquer of the keyboards, the pulverising throb of the bass, Numan's ugly, grating voice. Much of it sounds identical, hence the importance of the stage's adaptability. 'Every Day I Die', for example, featured Mekon-like mutants on elevated platforms at the side of the stage (probably dear Tic and Toc again); at another point we were treated to a very nice film of Gary flying an aeroplane(?)

Superior moments came predictably with 'Conversations', 'Cars', 'Dream Police', and 'I Die, You Die', though the new single (title not announced) was pretty undistinguished. 'We Are Glass' brought an impromptu appearance from Nash the Slash (Gary's really getting in with the right people!), which was greeted with fervid delight. And at the end of it all, Gazza took the kind of bow commonly favoured by the likes of international pianists.

The show was really designed to promote the desired sense of Numan's isolation and fragility, and it's true that his snarling facial expressions and cute/ugly mug aren't those of an android. There *is* something fatally human about him, for he is every girl's little brother lost in space. And it was that which made him such a perfect teen idol.

Barney Hoskyns

Grudging admiration from young Barney Hoskyns who was clearly blown-away by the concert and is scared to fully admit it, because to do so would lose him/her the respect of The Colleagues With The Cosh. Hence the fawning and misplaced opening sentence, The Contextualisation ("Rule Two of CSE music reviewing: Context is more important that Content"). There is no context for Numan's landmark show because it completely rewrote the rules for arena/stadium concerts (including the sound quality, which Barney noticed and seemed to think was accidental!). So young Barney, out looking for Brownie points, contextualises the show in reference to the previous week's hatchet job! (see page 279) The final paragraph does contain a probably original analysis and thought, though the thought is from Nick Kent's point of view. That doesn't make it inaccurate though. But pulling the whole review down is Barney's need to mock the subject and attempt to belittle the artist and his fans, "anyone who hadn't advanced beyond this stage themselves". And who are you, Barney The Advanced, when you are not flashing your eyelids at Nick Kent?

GARY ... "Tired of feeling like an actor playing a part."

OUT

Gary wants a nu-image

ROCK STAR Gary Numan put on his final show last night after announcing that he never wants to appear in concerts again.

The singer staged his farewell performance in front of more than 8,000 fans at London's Wembley Arena.

"I'm tired of feeling like an actor playing a part," he said before going on. "Other things mean much more to me.

"I decided when I was 18 and planning how to become famous that I would give up going on stage at this point."

Gary, 22, still plans to make records, but he also wants to spend more time flying his own plane.

He is already a qualified pilot and later this year hopes to fly solo around the world.

"I've always wanted to be an adventurer," he said.

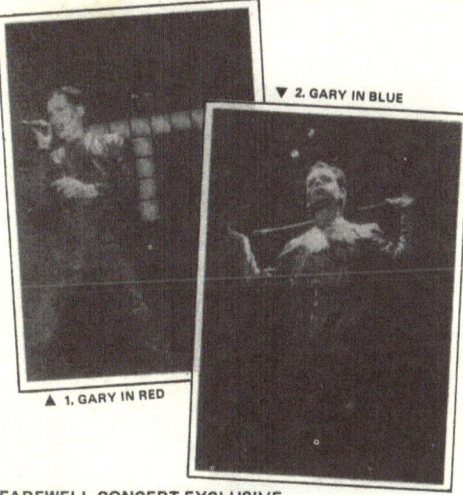

ゲイリー・ニューマン
これが最後のコンサートだ！

Gary Numan Farewell Concert

Gary Numan Farewell Concert

◀ この日のステージに、洗いざらい自分をぶちまけたゲイリーの表情は明るい。

81年4月28日。ゲイリー・ニューマンのステージ活動はこの日で終止符を打った。これがステージで見る彼の最後の姿かと思うと、観客も、そして彼自身も自然と熱くなってしまう。ステージ両端に置かれたピラミッドが、リモート・コントロールで動き出し、寒色のライトが輝き始めると、そこはもうゲイリーの支配する世界だった。

先月発売された2枚組ライブ・アルバム「幻想ライブ79＆80」は、この最後のコンサートを記念するとともに、これまでの活動に別れを告げるため、ゲイリーが私達にくれた素晴らしい贈り物だった。

これからの彼がどんな姿で生まれかわるのか、私達も新しい目でゲイリーを注目していたい。

◀ゲイリーの最後の叫びが宇宙の
彼方へとこだましていく。

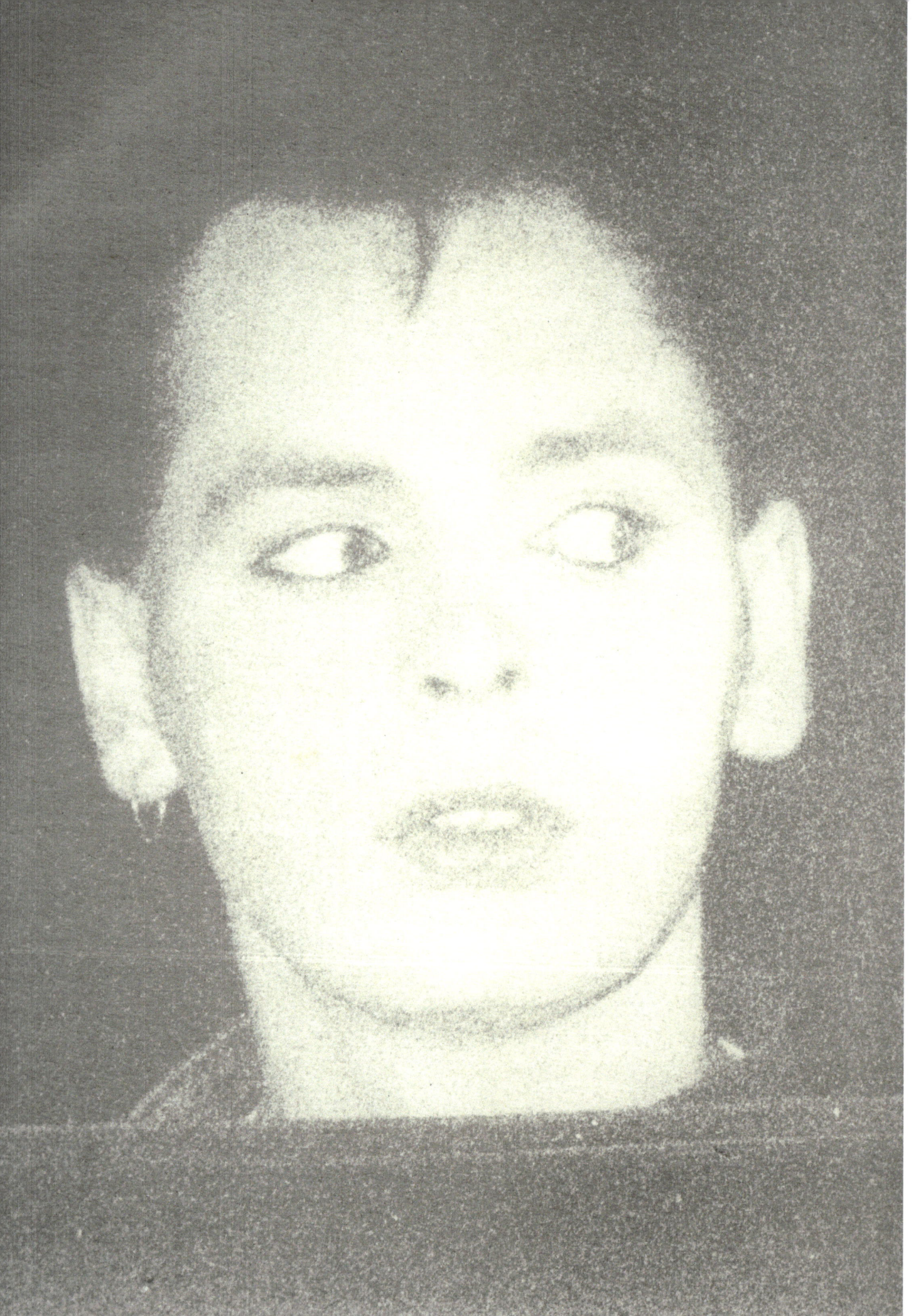

© Peter Gilbert

Palace were the most important film distribution company in Britain in the last quarter of the 20th century. They broke the strangehold of the majors and in doing so advanced the British understanding of 'cinema', which had always lagged behind the rest of the world on account of ruthless censorship and the middlebrow taste of the moguls and the critics. This was a rare moment when Numan stood shoulder to shoulder with pioneers in another art form.

© Stefan Jungklaus

Gary

ARE TRENDS electric? Gary Numan said yes three years ago when he first stepped onto the scene, straight into a superstar spot.

Equipped to his mascara-ed eyeballs with an astonishing arsenal of all things electronic, the pimply, pasty, painted popster charged up the charts.

The man most unlikely to succeed, DID. Our Gal was an overnight synthesised sensation.

Two number one singles, ten million albums and a few thousand fans later, the computer king has waved bye bye, announcing, at the ripe old age of 22, his decision to retire for ever from live work. The final farewell came in May with his last electrical extravaganza at Wembley. So, sigh . . . Gazza's gone. But he won't be forgotten. This month, FLEXIPOP goes behind the painted scowl to bring you the gurglings of gloomy Gal, the mutterings of Mr Micro hip himself.

Why is this man not smiling? FLEXIPOP finds out all you need to know about Numan and may now never have the chance to ask.

Over and out Gal . . .

ON SCHOOL:

I was really unpopular at school.

I'm intelligent. I was told I had an unusually high IQ at school. But I didn't get any 'O' levels. I would sit at the back of the room and disrupt lessons by telling jokes and making mischief.

They said at grammar school that I was unstable, disturbed or something.

I was expelled three times.

I do know that I wouldn't recommend to any kid that they don't work at school like I didn't. I chucked away a natural ability to do well. Sometimes now I miss not having worked hard at school. I only got the chance to work properly at that period in my life and I blew it. I really blew it.

ON FAME:

It's really quite simple. I had this plan. I wanted to be rich and famous and be a star and sign autographs and have enough money to be free.

I've wanted to be rich and famous ever since I was 11 years old when I dreamed of being a rock star. When I was 18, I sat down and worked out how to do it.

There are a lot of things wrong with fame, which I'm finding out pretty fast, but the benefits like cars and money aren't exactly a hindrance to my life. I could go back to being an unknown again but I couldn't go back to being poor. I couldn't do without the money.

ON RETIREMENT:

Of course there will be times when I will miss going onstage. The last show was very emotional for me. Afterwards I had to go away and be alone for a few moments. I shed a few tears. But I mean it when I say I'm never going to perform live again. This is not Frank Sinatra or Bowie talking. I really mean it.

ON HIS PARENTS:

My family are the only people in the world whom I trust. I want to repay them for everything they've ever done for me.

My parents are my closest friends. My dad's a genius and there's no pretence at all about him.

My mother has to sign autographs. She's almost as popular as me. I'll have to watch it.

ON HIS MUSIC:

I was no good on guitar and the synthesiser was dead easy to play.

The sound had to be machines.

Whatever you're doing in life you should use the latest technology. I did that.

I have no real love of the synthesiser but I like the noise it makes.

ON HIS FANS:

I can see and feel their warmth. But it's not like loving somebody for the next 50 years is it?

I'm not stupid enough to think that they are going to write letters to me saying they're going to love for me for ever, say even next year, because I know damn well they probably won't.

I don't feel I owe them anything. They took me because I decided to offer myself. It was a two way agreement. I understand what it's like being a fan. I was once one myself.

ON BOWIE:

We were supposed to appear on the same show at the end of last year. Then I was told we wouldn't be used. And we all came to the conclusion that it was because Bowie didn't want us.

I've idolised that bloke for seven years and the first chance I get to meet him he decides to do that. I've lost a lot of respect for him. If that's how he got where he is today then he's a sxxtbag. Obviously, I'm not just a cheap Bowie rip off. He must be scared of the competition.

N

ON LOVE:

I was in love once. We were engaged and everything. But it all went wrong. It really broke me up. If I feel I'm getting too close to someone, I attack them and get nasty.

At the same time I sit around in agony waiting for the phone to ring, and get jealous if my girl as much as stands next to another guy.

ON MARRIAGE:

Down to earth things like marriage and children mean an awful lot to me.

I'd give up the whole fame and entertainment thing tomorrow if I thought I couldn't have a family life one day.

If I'm going to get married and have children I don't want them to grow up as the son of a rock star. It's no way for kids to live.

No child should have to suffer that. Mine certainly won't.

ON SEX:

I love girls but if some bloke made a play for me and I liked it, I wouldn't be crippled with shock. Actually, I would prefer to be bi-sexual, because there's twice as many people you can sleep with. I get loads of offers from blokes all the time.

I'm sure that in future we'll all be bi-sexual. The trend already is to wear the same clothes and hairstyles, and perhaps we'll have the same organs one day. Sex in the future will be fascinating. We might well be doing it with machines soon.

ON FOOD:

McDonalds hamburgers are my favourite food. In fact I live on junk food.

I don't think it helps my bad skin. I also get a lot of stomach pains and go a bit giddy. But I can't stand fancy food.

ON DRINK:

Coke is the drink I like best. I've never touched alcohol. A girl once tried to get me to try champagne but I didn't.

ON DRUGS:

Never touch them.

ON HIMSELF

One minute I reckon I've got complete control of everything all round me. The next I go to pieces with this violent temper and I can't handle myself.

I can't seem to get to grips with whether it's this rock star thing that's messed me up or whether I was going this way all along.

Sometimes I feel my whole personality is out of control. I've always been worried about what people may say or do to me. I don't socialise much. I'm so nervous about going out I can hardly bear it. I don't even go shopping. I get someone else to do it.

I'm lonelier now than I've ever been. But it won't last for ever. I feel like a very old man in a very young body.

I'm very good at manipulating people. I have been ever since I was at school. I find it easy.

ON GROUPIES:

I don't mind taking advantage of them but the challenge has gone.

If they just want to talk I will talk. If they want to sleep with me I'll see what happens.

The one thing I can't abide is girls who mess you about. I haven't got time.

A while ago this beautiful 16 year old came backstage and obviously thought she was God's gift. I think she wanted me to want her so that she could turn me down. But I got rid of her straight away. I've no time for that.

ON HIS LOOKS:

I've always been very self conscious about my looks. I never think of myself as good looking. I'm too thin and I'm running out of hair fast.

I first started wearing make up to cover up my spots. My skin is terrible. I do take vitamin pills though.

ON SMILING:

I do smile sometimes. But not very often.

Numan

PAUL GARDINER

EMPIRE - Hot Seat/All These Things.

Two of Empire's members, Derwood on guitar and Mark Laff, drums, made up part of Generation X and as I didn't like Gen X at all it's not surprising that I dislike this band. Just a very straightforward rock song with all the normal cliches you'd expect. Plain boring. (DINOSAUR DISCS).

ARTERY - Cars In Motion/Life & Death.

Doomy sounding drum and guitar rhythm with the odd haunting noise in the background to embelish it. Personally, I prefer the Joy Division E.T.C. approach Not for those who like a "nice" tune.   (AARDVARK).

THE PAST SEVEN DAYS - Raindance So Many Others.

Two interesting songs with some nice touches, although tending to be a bit thin on production in parts. Still an interesting blueprint for what's to come. (4AD).

NEW ASIA - Central Position/ Here+There,Now+Then.

As much as I like bands that are into experimentation, this one sounds directionless, with instruments coming in and out at random. Sure, experiment but let's hear a worthwhile, end product. (SITUATION).

MY CAPTAINS - History, Nothing/ Fall, Converse.(ep)

Another 4AD band in the experimental mode with four very thoughtful and interesting songs, making some good use of the basic instruments, i.e. guitar, bass, drums, without over-producing and working within their own limits - Interesting!   (4AD).

RESISTANCE - Survival Kit/Big Flame.

One of those M.O.R. "pop" songs designed to capture your attention with that blatant "hook-line" chorus. Sorry boys, I know you say you don't like being categorised but why then go out of your way and fall into the same trap as other groups, who, blatantly and specifically design songs in order to get airplay they want (decided by a bunch of old women) and a possible place in the charts.   (FONTANA).

B.TROOP - Junior/Espionage A Go Go.

Another monotonous record trundles round the turntable to bore me even more - A miss! (HOTSPOT).

THE NIGHTINGALES - Idiot Strength /Seconds.

Monotony at its worst, why bother? Absolutely no production and nothing that makes it interesting - Crap!   (ROUGH TRADE).

THE FALL - Slates E.P.

Typical of The Fall, constantly changing and experimenting with their own brand of simple, repetitious rhythms. Mark Smith spitting out the words with a total disregard for any kind of fashion or trends. Typical examples in songs like, 'Leave The Capital', 'Slates', 'Slags' and 'Fit And Working Again'. A band that have always intrigued me live and on record - What comes next?
(ROUGH TRADE).

THE ONE TAKES - E.P.

Another band who have decided to release a record through their own outlet and although the four songs on this record don't appeal to me at all, they have at least done something about releasing their product without the involvement of the majors at low cost, while others sit on their arses and think about it. There is a difference!(NO CHOICE).

FREEZ - Flying High.

The follow-up to their successful (Southern Freez) and judging by the forceful production and Funkiness of this song, it will probably get them what they want Personally, I can't say I'm particularly into this song, preferring the funk, disco sound of Chic etc, but these records always attract me to that great funky bass sound - Man. (BEGGARS BANQUET)

BAUHAUS - Kick In The Eye/ Satori.

I thought their album was good and this single does them even more justice, very infectious indeed with its great production, haunting sound, funky bass-rhythm section and excellent vocals. The studio effects are great. Definitely a band with plenty of imagination and positive direction.
(BEGGARS BANQUET).

CUDDLY TOYS - Astral Joe/Slow Down.

This could be a potentially good song but the overall effect doesn not hit hard enough, the production tending to be very thin with no hints of "light-and-shade" throughout it. Instead, it comes out rather repetitive and predictable.   (FRESH).

DRAMATIS - Ex Luna Scientia / Lady D.J.

Ah, if I'm expected to give 'Me old touring partners' a rave review here, forgive me but I'm afraid this record just doesn't appeal to me. Not that it sounds unproffesional or anything,(these people know what they're doing). No, it's just that we appear to have our differences as regards to musical directions, which probably accounts for the reason I'm not involved with them.
(ROCKET RECORDS).

And there was Dance and planes and Warriors,
and an Assassin and back to the blue...

And the music kept going forward

Gary Numan, An Annotated Scrapbook 1977-1981

© Paul Sutton, 2016

Paul Sutton is identified as the author of this book.
The moral rights of the author have been asserted.

Published by Buffalo Books
Cambridge, UK
camerajournal@hotmail.com

ISBN: 978-0-9931770-7-1
(Hardback First Edition)
400 copies only

Also by Paul Sutton:

Talking about Ken Russell
The Moving Picture Boy Gallery
The Moving Picture Girl Gallery
Six English Filmmakers
Lindsay Anderson, The Diaries
if.... A British Film Guide
Becoming Ken Russell
The Lemon Popsicle Book
The Young and the Old
Charlie Ellis and the Daytrip to Mars
Understanding Gary Numan